THE BUSINESS OF GOLF— Why? How? What?

By
James J. Keegan,
Managing Principal
Golf Convergence

ISBNs: 978-0-9846268-6-1 (hardcover)
        978-0-9846268-8-5 (ePub)
        978-0-9846268-7-8 (ePDF)

Library of Congress Control Number: 2013953142

Printed in the United States of America.

Table of Contents

ACKNOWLEDGMENTS   vii

ATTRIBUTION   xiii

FOREWORD: FOCUS   xxv

INTRODUCTION   1

Section 1   Strategic Vision - Why?
Chapters 1 through 6

CHAPTER 1   **What Business Are You Truly In?**
Golf Is a Lifestyle—The Game Is Only a
Component   19

CHAPTER 2   **The Macroeconomics of the Golf**
Business   39

CHAPTER 3   **The Players: Associations and**
Equipment Manufacturers   59

CHAPTER 4   **Ownership and Governance**   87

CHAPTER 5   **Steps 1 and 2: The Geographic**
Local Market and Weather Playable Days   115

CHAPTER 6   The Conclusion of Why   **137**

Section 2   Tactical Planning - How?
Chapters 7 through 11

CHAPTER 7   Step 3: Technology   **151**

CHAPTER 8   Step 4: The Key Financial
Benchmarking   **175**

CHAPTER 9   Step 4: Financial Modeling   **199**

CHAPTER 10   Step 4: Yield Management   **221**

CHAPTER 11   Step 4: Golf Course Valuation   **239**

Section 3   Operational Execution - What?
Chapters 12 through 18

CHAPTER 12   Step 5: The Playing Field   **259**

CHAPTER 13   Step 6: Marketing, the Internet, and
Social Media   **285**

CHAPTER 14   Step 6: Game Time   **313**

CHAPTER 15   Step 7: Who Are Our Customers?   **329**

CHAPTER 16   Step 7: Creating Customer Loyalty   **361**

**CHAPTER 17   The Industry—What Path Is It On?
A Future Perspective on How to Grow the
Business of Golf   377**

**CHAPTER 18   The Courage to Change:
The Final Exam   407**

INDEX   425

Acknowledgments

*Gratitude makes sense of our past, brings peace for today,
and creates a vision for tomorrow.*

Melody Beattie

How does one get from there to here? No one is independent. No one person is self-made. All our lives we live in a community where we are dependent on each other.

Eugene O'Kelly was Chairman and CEO of KPMG when in May 2005, he was diagnosed with brain cancer and given three to six months to live. In his dying days, he wrote *Chasing Daylight—How My Death Transformed My Life*. In this book he constructed a circle of life which illustrates the order in which gratitude is due in one's life, as represented in the following[1]:

---

1 Eugene O'Kelly, *Chasing Daylight* (New York: McGraw-Hill, 2006), 105.

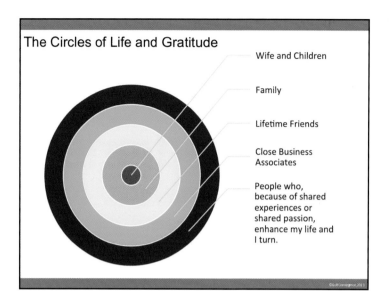

Personal Appreciation for Those Who Have Influenced My Life

To Debra, my wife, my friend, partner, confidante, and cheerleader; you make a house a home and your career finding others employment provides a balance. May we reach the end together.

To my father, George, who passed over a decade ago, his curiosity and desire to challenge the status quo lives on in me.

To my 95-year-old mother, Kathryn, your daily support continues to strengthen me, and your striving for perfection continues to influence my goals. I appreciate your thoughtful conservative perspective now more than ever.

To my brother Mark, though we have taken vastly different paths, we have reached the same plateau from which in silence, respect, and admiration are mutually conveyed.

Thanks to Martha and Michaela for the past that was memorable and for the potential joys and fellowship ahead. May we experience all there is in unity.

Father Patrick Dolan's philosophy regarding our role in humanity as components of a community at large continues to inspire me. His ecumenical views are unparalleled.

Professional Appreciation

Joe Beditz, Ph.D., President of the National Golf Foundation, and Greg Nathan provide the outstanding research which forms the platform upon which this book is grounded.

Stuart Hayden is incredible in his ability to cut the wheat from the chaff. Friends who take time to be your harshest critics and never give you the answer you want, but who confirm the answer you know is right, are invaluable.

Mike Jamison, Executive Director and Founder of International Network of Golf, provided the motivation to transfer my passion for the business of golf to paper.

Cindy Curtis, Deputy City Manager, Virginia Beach, and John Zobler, Deputy City Manager, recently retired, afforded me the opportunity with their golf courses to craft a solution that was far-reaching, and they became strong supporters of the concepts outlined in this book.

Serving in this industry for 25 years, I have been impacted by some amazing people whom I hold in deep admiration and respect and with whom I cross paths frequently: Eddie Ainsworth, Executive Director of the Colorado PGA Section; Hilda Allen, President, Hilda W. Allen Real Estate Inc.; Justin Apel, Executive Director, Golf Course Builders Association of America; Joe Assell, PGA, President of GolfTec; Ben Blake, Executive Vice President—Kemper Sports Management; Jeff Calderwood, Chief Executive Officer, NGCOA—Canada; Jack Crittenden, Editor, *Golf Inc.*; David Clark, Editor, *Golf Magazine*; Tim Eberlein, PGA Master Professional, Campus Director Golf Academy of America—Phoenix; Steve Ekovich, Vice President Investments, Marcus & Millichap Real Estate Investment Services; Jim Fedigan, President, Jonas Software; Niall Flanagan, Chairman, Club, Inc.; Jeff Foster, SVP New Media Group, Golf Channel; Steve Friedlander, Vice President—Golf, Pelican Hill and Oak Creek Golf Clubs; Ed Getherall, Senior Director of Operations, National Golf Foundation; Eric Greytok, Superintendent, Eagle Point Golf Club; Steve Grosz, General Manager, Hot Stix Golf; Jack Grum, Executive Vice President, Weather Trends International; Doug Hellman, Senior Vice President, Kemper Sports Inc.; Michael Holtzman, President, Profitable Food Facilities; Dr. Brian Horgan, Associate Professor, Turf Management, University of Minnesota; Chantel Jackson, General Manager, University of Michigan Golf Course; Brad Kirkman, PGA Master Professional, Golf Academy of America;

Brad Klein, Accomplished Writer, *Golfweek*; Michael Loustalot, President, Digital Caddies; Rick Lucas, PGA, Director PGA PGM Program at Clemson University; M.J. Mastalir, President, Real Estate Capital Corporation; Nick Mokelke, General Manager, Cog Hill Golf and Country Club; Kevin Norby, ASGCA, Herfort-Norby; Joe Passov, Travel Editor, *Golf Magazine*; Warren Pittman, PGA, Golf Academy of America; Del Ratcliffe, PGA, President, Ratcliffe Golf Services; Jon Rizzi, Editor, *Colorado Avid Golfer Magazine*; Rick and Tom Robshaw, Proprietors, Club Prophet Systems; James E. Roschek, PGA, President and CEO, Municipal Golf Association of San Antonio; Richard Singer, National Golf Foundation; David V. Smith, CEO, Golf Projects International; Tom Stine, Co-Founder and Partner, Golf Datatech; Armen Suny, Suny Zokol Golf Design; Michael Tinkey, Deputy Director, National Golf Course Owners Association; Michael Vogt, CGCS, McMahon Group; Allen Walters, Publisher, *Avid Golfer* magazine; and Rob Waldron, Investment Advisor, National Golf and Resort Properties Group.

Professional Appreciation for Assistance with This Endeavor

Sue Cummins, a fabulous editor whose attention to detail is amazing, has edited more than 500 pages, repeatedly correcting the same mistakes without commenting. I deeply appreciate her work.

Ed Travis provided his sage guidance as one of the golf industry's most experienced and gifted writers, ensuring that this book's message was positive. He contributed valuable insights, and his contribution was very much welcomed.

Sharon Anderson and Mike Topovski at Bookmasters are the heart and soul of publishing this book. These two employees are Hall of Fame.

Golf Convergence has been very fortunate to have many marvelous clients. This book was made possible by the inclusion of data that, while it is already in the public domain, was available from the following golf courses: City and County of Denver, City of Ann Arbor, City of Asbury, City of Atlanta, City of Becker, City of Bloomington, City of Brookings, City of Casper, City of Grand Rapids, City of Greenville, City of Midland, City of Minneapolis, City of Ocala, City of St. Paul, City of Virginia Beach, City of Winnipeg, Naperville Park District, Pacific Grove Golf Links, and University of Minnesota. Each of these golf courses granted permission to make available to readers of this book components of the strategic plans created on their behalf.

We are very fortunate that Bakker Crossing, Baywood Country, Bemidji Town and Country Club, Cog Hill Golf and Country Club, Colorado Golf Club, Four Mile Ranch, Island Hills Golf Club, Merrill Hills Country Club, Oitavos Dunes, Reignwood Pine Valley, Seneca Hills, and 3M's Tartan Park Golf Club afforded us the opportunity to work in partnership to enhance golfers' experiences on a foundation that improved the fiscal viability of their facilities.

Lastly, to the Alamo City Golf Trail, City of Bloomington, City of Brooklyn Park, City of Columbus, Crystal Mountain, Fernie Golf and Country Club, Irvine Companies, Oneida Nation, Pine Meadow, Ratcliffe Golf Services, and Western Illinois University, who participated in the Clemson University Pilot Study: Strategic Planning. The templates that are referred to in this book were thoroughly tested by them as part of Rick Lucas' doctoral dissertation. We are very grateful for your willingness to benefit the industry.

Concluding Thought

Gratitude is not only the greatest of virtues, but the parent of all the others.

Marcus Tullius Cicero

Attribution

Better is the enemy of good enough.

**Attributed to both Voltaire and Sergey Gorshkov,
Soviet Admiral of the Fleet**

"Good" is "excellent" compared to nothing.

Anonymous

This Is How You Will Benefit from Reading This Book

How does a writer measure success? Writing is a lonely sport. Hours are spent crafting words with alliterations and cadence to humor the writer and to ensure that the reader benefits from the research, insights, and perspectives offered. Long sentences are rewritten time and time again, with the hope of creating a single thought. When a client, reader, webinar participant, or caller sends an unsolicited comment, whether positive or negative, the circle of connection is complete, and each provides me valuable guidance.

Every day we strive to improve the profitability of our clients' golf courses. Our advice is delivered in many different ways; comprehensive strategic plans, targeted client engagements, teaching at Professional Golf Management programs, webinars, blogs, articles for leading golf industry magazines, social media, and by answering the frequently received telephone call asking our viewpoint. These efforts are perfected as we fly over 100,000 miles per year, often to as many as 10 countries and hundreds of cities and towns. I can often identify a golf course from 25,000 feet in the air, having flown some routes so frequently.

Are we making a difference? Change is very difficult. Excuses are easy to formulate. Perfection is not an attainable goal. Creating a consensus through inspired leadership is rare. It seems that our society has become one in which critics abound, critics who highlight the flaws of any idea rather than offering an alternative.

But we are motivated by those who take precious moments of their time to send us an **unsolicited comment or encouragement**. A smattering of those emails received during the past 2 years are presented below, not to fan my pride, but to share the insights provided by readers who are golfers alone, to students, to leaders in the golf industry.

Reader Feedback, *The Business of Golf— What Are You Thinking?*

I finished reading your book last week and have been meaning to send you a note of congratulations. What a great book for every golf professional or anyone running a golf property in our business! It should be *a required book for all PGA members and apprentices.* I would have enjoyed a piece like this years ago when I first entered the golf business in 1975. The fundamentals illustrated could be used in any business, but certainly apply to the golf business. I assure you I will use the book as a reference almost daily and certainly during my staff and mentoring meetings. Congratulations on a tremendous resource guide to the business of golf. **Steve Friedlander, General Manager and PGA Professional, Pelican Hills Golf Course**

Your book is a very fun, informative read. Thanks so much for taking the time to write such a thoughtful, informative and valuable resource for the golf industry. It's easy to see that your insights are right on-target, but actual application in the golf industry is sorely lacking. I'm planning on using a lot of your book for our strategic planning session for next year, and integrating some of the stuff you have into our own business model. Your book is a "must read" for anyone in the golf business. I can understand why Clemson wants to use it in the classroom. The knowledge the PGM students will gain from this exposure will be a HUGE benefit to them as they embark on a career in the golf industry. **Del Ratcliffe, PGA, President, Ratcliffe Golf Services, Inc.**

I just wanted to tell you how impressed I am with the book and all the time and effort you put towards the project. Obviously a labor of love and many years of dedicated service to the business. **John Cannon, President, Sunbelt Golf Corporation, Alabama's Robert Trent Jones Golf Trail**

Now that it is winter, I have finally had a chance to read your book. In two days I am on page 205 and I can't put it down. Even though it is not geared so much to private clubs, I can't begin to tell you how much I am getting out of reading it. I am one of the fifteen Master Club Managers worldwide through CMAA and I have over 5 pages of "take-away" ideas and I am only 2/3 through your book. *Bottom line—Everyone* in the industry should read this book, new managers in the industry, seasoned veterans, golf pro's, controllers, and superintendents! Even the board of directors could benefit. **Paul Kornfeind III MCM, CCE, General Manager/COO, Tippecanoe Lake Country Club**

I lent Frank Jemsek a copy of your book. He took it to Florida and called me the other day to tell me how much he was enjoying it! **Nick Mokelke, CCM, CCE, General Manager, Cog Hill Golf Club**

As a private club industry veteran, I have managed two golf courses (Nicklaus and Norman design) and served as project manager for the development of two others (one a Palmer design). I wish I had Keegan's book prior to those positions. Not only does he thoroughly explain the business of golf, but offers a proven methodology for operating a course efficiently and profitably. Using his long experience as a golf operations consultant, the author offers real life examples of how to identify the key issues in an under-performing golf course and how to maximize the financial return of the business. **Ed Rehkopf**

Have been studying your book. I think it is excellent! **Tony Bubenas, CGCS, Golf Supervisor, Pierce County Parks & Recreation Services Dept.**

A great book for sure! I am planning on using sections in the book for a class I teach at Kansas State University Professional Club Management. Very worth-while statistics for students to ponder over. Keep up the good work. **David W. Gourlay CGCS, CCM, Colbert Hills**

Your book is a valuable resource and will pay significant dividends—not only in money made but in less time I will need to spend educating board members on why I do what I do. Your research and experience will do that job for me. First thing was to deprogram the Exec. Dir., Board Members, and Golf Professional concerning key performance indicators. For 5 years, they had been hammered with, and finally convinced that, "Revenue per Round" was the only indicator to be considered. Additionally, I used the information mid-July to demonstrate that I believed price cutting had gone too far, as evidenced by a declining "RevPar/RevPatt." **Allen Parkes, Traditions at Chevy Chase, CGCS Supt/PGA Professional, General Manager**

I have been reading it as a textbook. I am half way through and plan on reading it a number of times. I will recommend this book to anyone in the business of golf. **Mike Miller, PGA Head Golf Professional, Indian Ridge Country Club**

I talked so much about your approach to the Golf Business. My book is in my office...dog eared, underlined, copied and quoted...so much the Regional VP asked to borrow it... I said "buy your own" and keep it with you and recommend to all the properties to read it! I'm a major fan.... You are my OPRAH! **Kate Minnock, Director of Sales/Marketing/Events, The Golf Club at Cypress Head**

This book comes at a time to me where I can benefit from everything and anything that can educate me about the game and its business. **Horacio De Leon, Jr., Asst. City Manager, City of Laredo, Texas**

I am a member of Olympic Hills Golf Club in Eden Prairie, MN. I was Vice President of the Board and Chairman of the Finance Committee for 3 years. Just prior to assuming the role of President I was asked by the owners to assist them evaluate the business opportunities. The need arose as a result of the ownership transferring to the next generation of family members. I found your book to be very helpful. I agree with many of your observations on the industry. **Peter L. Eaton**

Congratulations on the book! It is full of good information. **Cathy Jo Johnson, formerly Golf Courses at Incline Village Director of Golf, PGA/LPGA member**

I am reading this book along with Joe Fragala our new General Manager. I am learning a lot in this book so far. It is a "textbook" for depicting what successful golf operations are doing and what struggling ones *must* do. Jim's book says statistically that 90% of our business will come from a distance of 10 miles or less. I simply can't see how building golf villas would ever be justifiable for only 10% additional business. The math just doesn't work for me. **Bob Griffioen, Owner, Island Hills Golf Club**

The book looks at the business of golf and not just about managing the landscaping of the course. It is well written with several checklists to support the business side of a golf course. **Rocky Lippold, General Manager, Eagle Knoll Golf Course**

Thought the book was great. Mainly used it as a tool to solidify my long-standing beliefs on operational guidance. **Scott Hiles, Director of Operations, Stony Plain Golf Course, Alberta, Canada**

I know you are a leader in this forward thinking golf movement and appreciate your thoughts as well as the first of its kind textbook. **Trevor Tam, Coyote Hills Golf Course**

We found your book and bought one copy and are now buying another to let others in leadership positions read what the "the business of golf" really is about. I have read it and highly recommended we use it as our "text book" to guide the club's direction and policies. **Lindsay Harp, Greens Chairperson, Crossings Golf Club**

Industry, Trade & Research Groups, As Well As Vendors

You have toiled very hard and developed a valuable tool for golf owners and operators that will assist them to run more stable and profitable businesses. **Mike Tinkey, Deputy CEO, NGCOA**

Very excited about the content of your book. It covers a lot of aspects that we deal with on a daily basis. **Tibbe Bakker, European Golf Course Owners Association**

I found your book very enlightening. **Nancy Berkley, President, Berkley Golf Consulting, Inc.**

Just finished the book…it was pleasing to read someone who finally put the industry in its proper perspective. **Stewart Healey, President, International Golf League Federation and Handicomp**

Your book arrived today. I was stunned by it. It looks fabulous—totally fabulous. I think this book will bring great things to you Jim. Well done on bringing it to reality. **Colin Hegarty, Golf Research, Inc.**

I picked up your book at the GIS Show and I want you to know how much I am enjoying it. There are really great morsels in it and I am recommending it to all of my past, current and definitely future clients! I can only imagine what a laborious task it was to put it all together in your "spare" time. Kudos to you. **Heidi Voss, Bauer-Voss Consulting**

Jim, your book arrived yesterday. I was afraid to get too involved in reading because I knew it would be a "page turner." I will spend some time with it tonight. The golf industry is being destroyed by poorly trained personnel, absentee owners, lack of commitment to grow the game, bad management and many other reasons that I am sure you see on a regular basis. **Biggs Tabler, Golf Marketing By Biggs**

Congratulations about the new book. Seems like you have a home run. **Dennis Shirley, THE GOLF GUY**

Professional Golf Management Program

An excellent book, one of best I've ever seen on subject. I would love to use it… I've discussed it with my former boss at Methodist University, who also thinks it's a great book. Before this book, I always had to hunt and peck for what I could teach because there are NO golf text books! Love the book! **Ms. Kim Kincer, Director, Eastern Kentucky University, College of Business and Technology**

The book is fascinating reading. There is much for the UK golf industry to learn from this book. **Gary Jackson, Business Skills Development Manager, The PGA National Training Academy Ping House, The Belfry Sutton Coldfield, West Midlands B76 9PW**

Great job, enjoyed the webinar. Well done—smooth with great insight. You are an excellent teacher with a lot of passion and knowledge to share. I think your book provides timely information and the necessary customer and financial analysis required to manage a golf course as a "business entity" that adds true economic value. I'm going to show it to my class today as an example of why we are reviewing accounting, reading financial statements, and marketing in my course this semester. My students will achieve great insight and knowledge of golf facilities. By using your book and case study in the fall I hope to set them apart in applying for these management positions. **Rick Lucas, PGA, MBA, Doctoral Student, Director, PGA Golf Management Program, Clemson University**

I had opportunity this fall to take a senior level class using *The Business of Golf: What Are You Thinking?* as a textbook. It is interesting to read, incredibly informative, crisp, clear, concise and without the academic pabulum of most college textbooks. I highly recommend this book to any student who aspires to be a leader in the golf industry. **Garrett Chapman, PGM student at Clemson University**

I am so thankful for your knowledge, passion and professionalism that you shared last night. The student "buzz" has been amazing today and they are all so energized from last night! Your presentation was so organized, student-centered, informative and motivating. There was a ton of valuable content and I hope they soaked it ALL up and will apply it in the near future. Your survey numbers and interpretations were amazing and led us into some great discussions in class today! It is so beneficial for the students to experience professionalism, genuine care and knowledge like you possess. Your gift is much appreciated. **Molly Sutherland, Executive Director, University of Colorado—Colorado Springs, PGA PGM Program**

Thanks again for the inspiring talk. I cannot remember another time when the students gave a speaker a standing ovation! **Dr. Paul Miller, Professor of Accounting, Academic Advisor, PGM Program University of Colorado at Colorado Springs**

Students enjoyed the presentation. Great Stuff. **Timothy Eberlein, PGA Master Professional, Campus Director, Golf Academy of America—Phoenix**

I'm looking forward to including it in our curriculum. **Lew Gach, M.B.A., PGA, Academic Dean, Golf Academy of America, Myrtle Beach, SC**

I have previewed your book, J.J., and was quite pleased to see you do have many templates that are easily accessible through the PGA links as well as NGF for me to pull up. The students that I will be teaching next month will be our first graduates of the University and your book will be a great compass into the reality of the golf industry! Most are too concerned about their personal golf games and swings instead of an employer's bottom line, but can't we all remember our college days. **Donna H. White, LPGA, Keiser University—College of Golf**

Clients

Your insights and passion have made a huge difference in the profitability of our municipal golf courses. In these troubled times, you have provided the leadership and returned our courses to profitability. Your commitment to lifelong learning is admirable and something I deeply admire. We are a better organization and individual professionals after spending time with you. **Cindy Curtis, Assistant City Manager, Virginia Beach**

Wanted to give you an update on the VBGM lease performance. With 8 months into the contract VBGM has generated $1.83 million in gross revenue providing the city with $183,000 in rent. Based on or projections they should finish the year out around the $2.1-$2.2 million range. As you can imagine everyone is very pleased with the results. They have completed their improvements at the Kempsville Greens course and are beginning the Red Wing Lake clubhouse renovation tomorrow. You should be very proud of the job that Golf Convergence has done guiding the City of Virginia Beach into this public/private partnership. It has proved beneficial to all involved. **Kevin Bennington, Golf Operations Coordinator, Virginia Beach Parks & Recreation**

At the beginning of 2010 we had 172 full golf members and a dues line of approximately $1M. We currently have over 400 full golf members and a WAIT LIST! Our dues line has grown to almost $2.1M. Individual dues have dropped 27%, and we eliminated capital dues, assessments, and minimum spending requirements. Our biggest challenge has been the cultural shift to a full membership, but in these times those are good problems to have. Thanks again for your help in getting us back on the right path for the future. **Mark Bergman, PGA Head Golf Professional, Merrill Hills Country Club**

Bottom line is that Merrill Hills is back on solid ground and we're going to make it through this tough time. I think a lot of it can be attributed to your efforts on our behalf and getting us on track. I know we've said thank you before and really need to keep saying it. **Greg Ksicinski, former President of the Board, Merrill Hills Country Club**

Congratulations Jim! This is really quite an accomplishment. You crafted a strategic plan for the City of Ocala and correctly identified every relevant issue. While it took us five years to implement all of the recommendations, you were directly on point from the outset as to the challenges we faced. **John Zobler, former Assistant City Manager, City of Ocala, FL**

I recently joined the team at The Prairie Club in a marketing and sales position and am just starting to wrap my head around the golf industry. I have studied your strategic review (that you performed last October I believe) and attended a few Golf Convergence webinars—I like your approach and would like to learn more. I am reaching out to you because I believe you might be able to point me in the right direction. Your input/advice is truly appreciated. I'm very young in my career, but fully realize how much quality insight from an experienced and knowledgeable person means. **Kyle Schock, The Prairie Club**

Your insight during the last few years has been great for us. **Chad Hatch, The Prairie Club**

Today was great! Lots of positive feedback from my advisory committee; the Mayor was quoted as saying "some of the best money we have ever spent." It re-affirmed several of the thoughts we had previously and opened the group's eyes to several other issues we have yet to address. This entire experience has been informative, educational, and invaluable to me, and for that I cannot thank you enough. **Jeremy Hawkins, PGA, General Manager/Head Golf Professional, The Meadows Golf Club**

We are coming back strong. Imagine what is going to happen after we complete the course improvement and cart path projects that start in July. Number 9 green at Los Amigos turned out great. It's been open for several months. Lots of positive feedback on your design enhancements. I read your book. It is awesome. Just fantastic. Congratulations. I am very happy for you and the phenomenal accomplishment this book represents. You are the man. **Stuart Hayden, Co-Owner, Strato Partners**

Webinars

You were too humble in your involvement with CGC. It was a total team effort with you included. I appreciate everything you opened our eyes to at CGC with your assessments. Thanks for hosting the webinar today. I thought it was very well done. I already have the next one booked on my calendar!!! **Graham Cliff, Head Golf Professional, Colorado Golf Club, Host of the 2013 Solheim Cup, Parker, CO 80134**

Thank you for hosting your series of webinars expanding on the topics covered in *The Business of Golf*. I have enjoyed the first two sessions—although I must admit session two has me swimming in numbers. Nothing a little bit of studying won't cure! **Laura Provost, PGA, Weibring Golf Club at Illinois State University**

Thanks for doing the webinar. Very informative, but perhaps a little "tough love" toward someone (that would be me) who feels very strongly about keeping my staff as city employees while also providing a recreational sport that absolutely adds to the quality of life for our citizens and visitors to our city. I know what you are saying is logical and makes sense to consider, but our courses and the staff have become very personal for me, so sometimes it's difficult for me to be objective especially when I have to also deal with political leaders who aren't the least bit interested or supportive of golf because they don't play the game and they view it as an elitist sport. **Terri Leist, Assistant Director and Golf Administrator, City of Columbus, OH**

Linkedin

The following individuals were kind enough to endorse our professional skills on LinkedIn: Clayton Cole, PGA, Cherry Hills Country Club; John Strawn, President/CEO at Hills & Forrest; David Gourlay, CCM, GM/COO at Colbert Hills/Golf Generations Inc.; Jan Tellstrom, PGA, Head Golf Professional at The Pete Dye Course at French Lick Resort; Barry MacLeod President at Top Line Performance Consulting, Prince Edward Island, Canada; Bob Devitz, President and CEO at Legendary Golf Management; Mark Woodward, Principal at DaMarCo Golf, LLC; Bill Yates, Pace of Play & Continuous Performance Improvement Consultant; Peter Johncke, The Trick Shot Master; Pat Vanderstine, Director of Operations at ChipShot Interactive; Steve Patterson, PGA Certified Golf Professional at Fossil Trace Golf Club; Gene Diamond, Owner, Twin Lakes Golf Club; Hanford Choy, Entrepreneur & former President of EZLinks; Andrew Wood, Legendary Marketing; Andrew Birnbaum, Business and Funding Analyst at Private Capital Network; Gordon Bunker, Managing Director at Worcester Renewables Ltd.; Dick Willet, CEO, Willet Golf; Dr. Karl Fischer and Mike Stevens.

Given how little I use or even understand LinkedIn, it's sort of ironic that I received this notice from them.

Golfers

I am a novice golfer and I highly recommend the book. It is easy to read, funny, and provides insights about the business of golf that make me appreciate the game of golf far more. It even taught me how to ensure I was getting the best value from my entertainment dollars. **Debra Bryan, Denver, CO**

The book is lovely! Fantastic job; it is really good looking. I found the book to be very interesting, especially the back pages. I really enjoyed the story about the "Stone of Accord " and was greatly pleased and surprised to even see Shakespeare quoted in a golf book. Congratulations. **Cindy, Island Book Store, Mercer, WA**

Just a note to tell you that I received the three copies I ordered—one was given to the board of our golf club, another is going to the owner of a public course, and I retained the third. I have given it a read and it is outstanding! **Gordon W. LeRiche, BA, CFP, CLU, CH. F.C., TEP, EPC, Estate Planning Specialist, CIBC Wood Gundy Financial Services Inc.**

I am sitting here at beautiful Pegasus Golf Course in New Zealand reviewing literature from parts of your book again. If I ever wanted to write a book that delivered the issues so logically and on the money it would be like this one. Reads like silk. **Daniel Adriatico**

Concluding Thought

No one who achieves success does so without acknowledging the help of others.

Alfred North Whitehead

Foreword: Focus

An Industry Looking for Leadership AD 1457–2073? The Game of Golf—Will It Become Extinct?

Not every question deserves an answer.

Syrus

Where Will Tomorrow's Golfers Come From?

Think about it. There are only about 250,000 golfers alive today that will be living in 2073. Where will the 26 million golfers come from to sustain the industry?

With the turnover in those departing and new entrants to the game having been roughly equal over the past 5 years, with a contraction of facilities in excess of 10% required to balance demand with supply, what does the future of the game and the business of golf hold?

The game of golf takes a long time to play, is expensive, is impossible to master, and, frankly, if you aren't somewhat skilled, isn't a lot of fun. The business of golf requires a significant capital investment with an unpredictable return. The greatest asset of a golf course might simply be the value of its raw land.

But does it have to be that way? I hope not, for I believe the following:

- Golf is a great game and currently an okay business. Can both be great?
- The numerous initiatives recently launched to encourage new entrants to the game (such as Get Golf Ready and Tee It Forward) will have a positive

short-term impact in increasing participation in the sport but may not be sustaining in the long-term if attrition rates are consistent with industry norms. What can be done to ensure long-term growth?

- Why has female participation in the last 25 years decreased by 100,000 players? Are the barriers of entry to a fun, social, recreational experience that high? They need not be.

- Tomorrow's golfers will come from those seeking leisure who are welcomed and accorded respect by the industry's professionals. How can the historical culture of the pro shop and the attitudes of the golfers it attracts be changed?

- Success in the business of golf is directly correlated to the extent to which the experience provided equals or exceeds the price assessed. What are the appropriate benchmarks to measure value? Certainly not what the competitors are charging.

- A golf course requires a clear strategic vision, well developed tactical plans, and extremely precise and consistent execution. With every course being distinctive, how does one facility differentiate itself as to its unique value proposition?

- The financial potential of a golf course can be achieved by implementing the seven tenets contained in this book. While each golf course has a different personality, all golf courses operate based on a common business model. Can the historical business models that are based on the status quo be radically altered and implemented for the game to thrive?

This book answers those questions, framed within the creation of a simple strategic vision based on 7 tenets and 21 templates designed to ensure that each course reaches its potential.

Thus, this book represents a comprehensive study that identifies the key strategic, tactical, and operational benchmarks that differentiate successful from financially challenged golf courses.

WARNING: This book is edgy. It challenges the status quo and takes those to task who superficially talk about growing the game while protecting their established traditions, positions, and policies. This book is likely to offend the majority and laggards within the industry, who must protect the status quo of their turf.

The Challenge: Execution

The fundamental weakness in the golf industry is that many employees lack the business skills and acumen of those in other service and hospitality industries. Many got into the business for a love of the game but lacked the ability to make a living playing. Thus, by default, they became service level workers for their love of the game, not of the business. As a reader of this book, you are clearly not in that category as you are seeking knowledge rather than accepting the status quo.

As a writer for numerous golf magazines, I am frequently called by editors with story ideas. In October, 2012, I received the following email:

> "In developing new story ideas for our next edition - which is a high gloss, quarterly trade publication, delivered complimentary to every golf facility - we thought that a strong article on Building Customer Loyalty would be beneficial to our audience as they begin their planning for 2013.
>
> The goal is to help educate golf course owners and operators as to the benefits of improving their loyalty programs for the long-term growth of their businesses."

My reaction was immediate: Truth be told, I don't have a burning desire to write an article on "Building Customer Loyalty." That topic has been covered to excess, especially since 1993, when Pepper and Rogers brought "customer relationship management" to the forefront of every smart business owner's conscience.

Building customer loyalty in the golf business is simple. For a golf course to reach its financial potential, its owners must gather, analyze, and identify customer habits, preferences, and spending patterns while maintaining the course at a level consistent with the course's brand, promise, and price point. It is just that simple, and it is what the ski resorts do exceptionally well.

If the owners don't understand these basic facts more than two decades after the importance of customer relationship management has been brought to the forefront, perhaps, I thought for a brief moment, if the golf course owners are losing money, it is their own fault.

My opinion is that theories and meaningful facts to guide golf course owners are abundant. They are promulgated by trade associations, industry publications, and outliers like myself, but the information most often seems to fall on the deaf ears of those who believe only they have the answer to their woes.

Thus, my desire to write a sugar-coated article that 50% of those who obtained the publication would scan, 20% might read, and 1% might gain some benefit from was low. But the editor's question prompted an examination of my conscience about my reluctance. After some soul-searching, I believe I found the answer.

As Jack Nicholson stated in the movie *A Few Good Men,* "You want the truth, you can't handle the truth," but here it is:

> The heart of the golf industry's woes lies within the ***average* golf course owner's inability to consistently execute,** in not providing a customer experience that equals or exceeds the price, ensuring value.

Before you stop reading because you are offended, read closely the emphasized and operative word, *average.* As the famous New York catcher Yogi Berra correctly and so elegantly stated, "The average person is average." If we were to grade each golf course owner in the industry, one individual would head the list and one would be ranked at the bottom. Ranking, by its definition, causes separation. It would be naïve and incorrect to think that each golf course owner and each management team is superlative and that the team at one facility has the same skills as the team at a competitive course. That is just not the case.

A golf course experience represents the intersection of farmers, short-order cooks, teachers, and retail merchandisers, and golfers experience up to 14 potential customer touch points on the assembly line of golf. The services at these touch points are largely provided by low-paid, seasonal workers hired to fill a short-term need. Finding a team skilled in each of the seven disciplines (geographic local management analysis, playable days review, technology, financial modeling and benchmarking, the course [architecture, agronomy, operations], architecture, agronomy, operations [golf, restaurant, merchandising], customer service) is a huge challenge for those living a lifestyle that offers the potential to be elite and privileged.

A diversity of intellect, knowledge, and skills exists within the golf industry. Often assembled at a golf course are a few full-time and some seasonal workers who rarely have an understanding of the course owner's vision, receive scant training, and are seduced to serve by thinking the fringe benefit of free or discounted golf offsets the low wages and long hours. This is not a formula for consistent execution.

Thus, the business model on which the industry is based is flawed.

The Principal Four Reasons for Failure

There are four reasons a golf course owner can't execute: lack of knowledge, lack of time, lack of ability, and lack of money.

There is a plethora of information to guide an owner in the proper management of a golf course. However, the information that is available is so detailed and comprehensive that it is overwhelming. That is controllable and can be corrected, and my hope is that this book contains the solutions for you and your course.

If an individual wants to bemoan the lack of time, candidly, that is their own fault from the inability to prioritize; that person's ability is called into question. That factor, however, is controllable and can be corrected by implementing the straightforward concepts highlighted in this book.

If an individual lacks the ability to lead or manage a team, ultimately, that "leader" is likely to fail. Just as buying superior golf clubs doesn't guarantee success as a golfer, the acquisition of the tools necessary to run a golf course doesn't guarantee our success if we lack the fundamental ability, mental or physical, to use those tools correctly. That fault is largely uncontrollable, certainly in the short run. Thus, it is the harsh realization that the majority of golf courses are likely, based on the often-used quote from Theodore Roosevelt, "to take rank with those poor spirits who neither enjoy nor suffer much, because they live in the gray twilight that knows not victory..."[1] Good luck, poor spirits.

For the golf course owners who bemoan the lack of money, either they didn't capitalize properly as they started their businesses or they have managed their courses into the "death spiral" that comes from declining revenue and deferral of capital expenditures that erode the customer experience. Either alternative again points to the lack of knowledge at the outset and the lack of ability throughout. Hence, failure is likely for many.

1 Theodore Roosevelt, http://www.brainyquote.com/quotes/quotes/t/theodorero103499.html.

There is not a formula that will ensure success for everyone, for all are subject to the perils of capitalism; "capitalism creates, and capitalism destroys." Success can come only to those who acquire knowledge, for "knowledge itself is power."[2]

Source of Hope: Finding Consensus

In your hands you hold a book that offers a simple promise. By reading this book, you will be able to ascertain strategic potential for your golf course, determine the tactical resources required, and obtain the guidance for consistent operational execution. This process will ensure that sustained customer value is created to maximize your financial return. The question remains, "Will that potential be realized?"

Each golf course is unique in its brand promise, whether to the member at a private club or to a public golfer. Each course is also unique relative to the competing interests of the owners or to those responsible for governance, the employees, and the customers at the facility.

These conflicts are highlighted in the following figure.

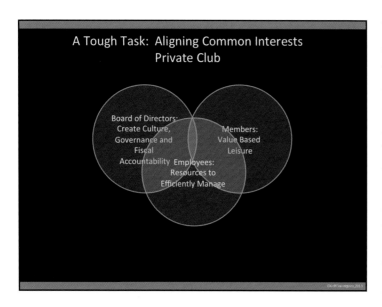

Whether it is the board of directors at a private club, the owner of a daily fee facility or a city council, they all want the facility be economically self-sustaining without the requirement for capital assessments, borrowing, or investing general fund assets to sustain the facility.

The employees at the facility, ranging from the general manager at a private club to the seasonal hourly workers, all seek adequate resources to achieve the defined service levels.

---

2 Francis Bacon, *The Oxford Essential Quotations Dictionary*, August 1998, pg. 234.

The members and golfers all seek to pay the lowest price to achieve the greatest value from their expenditure. In 25 years of serving the golf course industry, having attended a plethora of board, member, and golfer meetings, I await the first time when someone says, "For the value I am receiving, I should be paying a higher fee." It just hasn't happened. Contrary members and golfers are united in that they are currently paying too much, regardless of the experience they are receiving.

Thus, while this book will outline the tenets for success, it is fundamental that the conflicting interests be aligned and the interests of the facility as an enterprise serve as the overriding focus, as highlighted in the following figure.

How is that achieved? Through education. One of the weaknesses of the human spirit is that where there is no information forthcoming from ownership or management, the presumption is that something is being hidden that is contrary to the interests of employees and the public.

But sometimes, the self-interests of a small group can dominate the political agenda. To illustrate, on November 30, 2011, I appeared before a city council.

Its golf course for the fiscal year ending June 30, 2011, achieved gross revenues exceeding $2.6 million, with a resulting net loss of $446,000. It was one of the highest-grossing municipal golf courses in the United States, yet it was struggling to break even. They have reported net losses for four of their last seven years.

Simply, the municipal facility is one the finest links courses owned by a municipality in the United States. The economic potential of this facility is fabulous.

By applying the formulas contained in this book, we clearly demonstrated how that course could increase revenues by more than $250,000 and reduce expenses by more than $650,000.

Will it achieve those goals? I hope so, but I doubt it, because the politics of appeasement will dominate as the locals continue to insist on low rates and preferred times.

A forum dominated by a group is seeking unlimited-play season passes for $1,200. The Men's Club "demands" to reserve weekly the 8:00 a.m. tee time for 28 golfers for which they are willing to pay $20 per golfer. The cost to produce a round of golf at that facility last year was $45.09, prior to interest, depreciation, and amortization. I will never understand how selling your most valuable tee times at the lowest price to the golfers who create the most distractions and dominate the discussion is a good business practice. Though I have a BBA, an MBA, and was a CPA, I must have missed the finance class when that subject was covered.

The good news is some progress is being made, though not as quickly as would be possible if this was a private enterprise. For fiscal year 2013, revenues are projected to exceed expenses, even though there have been increases in water cost.

During the summer of 2011, we illustrated to a large seven-course municipality, after extensive research and fieldwork, how it could turn a $750,000 profit into a $2.0 million positive cash flow with judicious investment. It has done nothing, the profits foregone are in the millions, and the experience provided to the municipality's constituents remains substandard.

The promise of this book is that it will provide a clear path to define the potential of a country club or public facility, and it will facilitate creating the strategic vision, tactical plans, and operational procedures required for success. If success is not achieved, the fault is with the archer, not the bow.

I believe that this simple and easy-to-understand system will motivate and focus today's golf course owners and preclude them from being overwhelmed with the daily challenges they face. This book will provide a laser-like focus on how to execute.

For those willing to challenge the status quo, to seek creativity rather than accept conformity, the business of golf can be enjoyable and lucrative. I hope our paths cross on this journey.

Concluding Thought

The hardest thing to open is a closed mind.

Author Unknown

Introduction

People who do not break things first will never learn to create anything.

Philippine (Tagalog) Proverb

Change

This is a book about execution. This book is for seasoned golf industry professionals looking to positively and significantly impact their golf courses.

Can you recall a moment that changed your thinking? When something you saw, heard, or read alter your entire perspective?

On December 10, 2012, the Board of Directors of the Colorado PGA Section was having its annual business planning retreat. One goal was to form a non-profit called the "Colorado Alliance for Golf" to create a state-wide golf tee-time Internet reservation system from which revenue could be allocated into "grow the game" initiatives in Colorado. My role was to provide the results of a six-month study I facilitated with the members to guide the selection of a software vendor that could provide the technology platform, business model, and marketing expertise to achieve the Alliance's goal.

To start the meeting, Eddie Ainsworth, Executive Director, showed the following TED Talk by Simon Sinek: http://bit.ly/dcDsbx. In the video, Sinek asked an opening question, "How do you explain when things don't go as we assume, or even better, when others are able to achieve things that defy all of the assumptions?"[1]

Sinek explained a naturally occurring pattern, a way of thinking, acting and communicating that gives some leaders the ability to inspire those around them. He asked, "Why is Apple so innovative year after year after year? Why was Martin Luther King able to lead the civil rights movement when there were others who suffered in the pre–civil rights era and who were also great orators? Why were the Wright Brothers the first to achieve controlled and powered man flight when other teams were more qualified and better funded?"

He explained that our behavior is affected by our assumptions or our perceived truths. Not all decisions turn out to be the right ones. Regardless of the amount of data we collect, or how much we believe that information and data are key, we make decisions based on what we think we know.

Sinek postured that there are other factors that must be considered, factors that exist outside of our rational, analytical, information-hungry brains. This dance

---

1 http://www.ted.com/talks/simon_sinek_how_great_leaders_inspire_action.html

between gut and rational decision making is how we conduct our businesses and our lives.

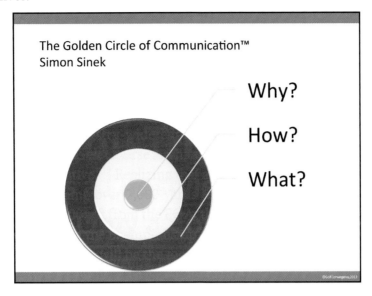

He described the "golden circle: WHY?—HOW?—WHAT?" All companies and organizations on the planet know WHAT they do. They are easily able to describe their products and services. Some companies are able to explain HOW they are different—their unique selling position. Few companies are able to clearly articulate WHY.

He concluded that the most successful companies communicate from the inside out. All other companies communicate from the outside in. People don't buy WHAT you do; they buy WHY you do it.

Why?

This video and Sinek's book *Start with Why* have redefined our approach to the business of golf.

We started with defining the WHY for Golf Convergence:

> "Our passion and purpose is to think differently, to change the status quo. Every day we strive to improve the profitability of our clients' golf courses."

It led to completely changing our Web site, our corporate logo, our wardrobe, and even our corporate photos. These superficial changes were made to convey our deep commitment to inspiring you to achieve your own individual potential and to achieve your potential as owners, managers, or players in this great business of golf.

We are observers. From traveling to 41 countries and having seen over 4,000 golf courses, we are keenly aware of why a golf course exists, how it creates value for golfers, and what it can do to offer a superior experience.

We are also keenly aware that few golf courses reach their full potential.

This book represents a discourse to stimulate debate, to encourage dialogue, to form a consensus, and to keep up with the constantly evolving optimum business model which golf courses can use.

The "Why" for each course is different but is grounded in the belief and passion of providing consumers with value-centered entertainment, leisure, and recreation. The fact that a course becomes fiscally self-sustaining is the result of the belief.

How?

We believe there are seven principles that define the potential of every golf course, regardless of whether it is government-owned (municipal and military), daily fee, resort, or private club. Embracing those doctrines, a golf course management team can create a strategic business blueprint that is easy to understand and simple to execute. When these principles are steadily and quickly fulfilled, the results, as we have witnessed with clients, are impressive. These are easy to learn, and they include those in the following figure.

Note: GLMA = geographic local market analysis.

While the course's location and the impact of weather are uncontrollable future factors, the integration of technology, benchmarking the financial performance of the course to industry metrics, the architectural and agronomy practices, operations—the assembly line of the golf experience, and the customers can all be managed to boost profitability.

What?

Extensive research, golf course and consumer surveys, and partnerships with clients form the genesis of the insights, perspectives, formulas, and methods that make up the intellectual property contained in this book.

This book represents nearly a decade of research conducted in partnership with golf courses worldwide. It features suggested actions that are simple to understand and easy to execute, actions involving architecture, agronomy, intellectual property, rate structures, social media, water utilization, yield management, and many more areas necessary to running a successful golf course. The insights presented are meant to be clear and simple, but the analysis undertaken was extensive.

Though they are not required for you to receive value, you may want to license the operational tools that are available on Golf Convergence's Web site (www.golfconvergence.com):

Step	Description	File Format	Level of Difficulty	Explanation
STRATEGIC TEMPLATES				
0	Strategic Planning	Web based survey	Introductory	This pre-test template asks 40 questions to ascertain the level of the respondent's knowledge of the business of golf. Your answers can be compared to a national survey.
1	A Geographic Local Market Analysis	Excel	Intermediate	Demographic profile (age, income, ethnicity & population density) contrasts your course with the golf courses within 30 miles of yours to determine strategic potential.

(Continued)

Step	Description	File Format	Level of Difficulty	Explanation
STRATEGIC TEMPLATES				
1	Vision—Private Golf Course	PowerPoint	Introductory	Promises versus performance. This templates helps a **private club** determine if its brand promise is at the platinum (5-star), gold (4-star), silver (3-star), bronze (2-star), or steel (1-star).
1	Vision—Public Golf Course	PowerPoint	Introductory	Promises versus performance. This template helps a **public course** (daily fee, municipal, or resort) determine if its brand promise is at the platinum (5-star), gold (4-star), silver (3-star), bronze (2-star), or steel (1-star).
2	Weather Playable Days Calculation	Excel	Intermediate	Is your facility under- or over-performing in relationship to the number of golf playable days? This template will help you measure that benchmark.
TACTICAL TEMPLATES				
3	Technology Integration Checkpoint	Excel	Intermediate	How are you leveraging technology to boost your revenue? This template grades your use of technology from 1st grade to the PhD level.
4	Cash Flow Forecast— 5 Years—Daily Fee/Municipal	Excel	Advanced	The operation of a daily fee or a municipal golf course can be forecast based on 60 controllable variables. This worksheet facilitates sensitivity analysis to quickly project revenues, income, and expenses for the next 5 years for daily fee and municipal golf courses.

Step	Description	File Format	Level of Difficulty	Explanation
\multicolumn{5}{TACTICAL TEMPLATES}

Step	Description	File Format	Level of Difficulty	Explanation
\multicolumn{5}{center}{**TACTICAL TEMPLATES**}				
4	Cash Flow Forecast—5 Years—Resort	Excel	Advanced	The operation of a resort can be forecast based on 75 controllable variables. This worksheet facilitates sensitivity analysis to quickly project revenues, income, and expenses for the next 5 years for resort golf courses.
4	Cash Flow Forecast—5 Years—Private Club	Excel	Advanced	The operation of a private club can be forecast based on 50 controllable variables. This worksheet facilitates sensitivity analysis to quickly project revenues, income, and expenses for the next 5 years for private club courses.
4	Green Fee Calculator—Complex: Quantitative	Excel	Advanced	There is a relationship between 18 weekend, weekday, 9 holes, morning, afternoon, senior, and junior green fee rates. This template confirms those interrelationships to ensure all of your prices are "in balance" for the fees posted.
4	Green Fee Yield—Revenue Modeling Exercise	Excel	Intermediate	The impact on future revenues from changes in rounds and associated yields from the top revenue categories are modeled to measure the impact of potential rate changes.
4	Season Pass—Fair Fee	Excel	Introductory	Utilizing weather playable days, anticipated rounds the season pass holder will play during the year, and an appropriate discount, determine the fair price to assess.
4	Sensitivity Pass Analysis	Excel	Intermediate	What is the impact of changing the season pass price on total revenues, considering the golfers who will choose to merely pay-as-they-go? This template facilitates calculating the revenue impact of price changes and the number of subscribers.
5	Budget/Business Plan Template	Excel	Advanced	Golf course maintenance is a considerable expense, often accounting for 40%–60% or more of gross income. The step-by-step budget process helps to build a business plan as well as an excellent, goal-based golf course maintenance operation budget.

(Continued)

Step	Description	File Format	Level of Difficulty	Explanation
—		**OPERATIONAL TEMPLATES**		
5	Deferred Capital Expenditures Template	Excel	Introductory	There are 14 depreciable capital components that comprise a golf course. This spreadsheet will help you determine the annual capital allocation that should be in reserve and the aggregate deferred component.
5	Equipment Template	Excel	Advanced	There are 44 different pieces of equipment required to properly maintain the course. This worksheet calculates the value of equipment on hand, capital reserves required, and components that should be acquired.
5	Annual Golf Maintenance Labor Scheduler	Excel	Advanced	A superintendent engages in 29 separate tasks that vary by day, week, season, or annually. This worksheet calculates the labor hours required annually to maintain a golf course and provides a comparison to actual labor expended.
5	Weekly Golf Maintenance Labor Scheduler	Excel	Advanced	By keeping track of the hours required per week, their cost, and who should be assigned the tasks at hand, this worksheet aids the superintendent in scheduling the week ahead.
6	Golf Course Checklist— Secret Shopper Service	Excel	Introductory	On the assembly line of golf, there are numerous customer touch points that contribute to the player's perception of value. This checklist provides guidance in measuring the experience provided at your golf course.
6	Customer Value Experience	Excel	Intermediate	What is the correct green fee price? The slope rating, the strategic elements, conditioning, grass texture, ambience; the amenities provided are the variables that should determine price.

Step	Description	File Format	Level of Difficulty	Explanation
7	Golfer Survey—Loyalty and Preference	Word	Introductory	There are 30 questions that a customer survey should include. Use of this document will help your golf course craft an effective survey to ensure insightful responses.

Throughout the book, if you see the image below, you have the option of going to www.golfconvergence.com to license the templates should you choose.

Download the pre-test survey and the national survey results on strategic planning from www.golfconvergence.com. This pre-test template asks 40 questions to ascertain the level of the respondent's knowledge of the business of golf. Your answers can be compared to a national survey.

Definitions

To ensure that you receive the greatest benefit from the time you invest in reading this book, we have segmented the material into three sections: •introductory, •intermediate, and •advanced as noted in the chart above as it identifies the depth of the subject matter.

INTRODUCTORY content is for readers who are new to the golf industry. This content typically includes the essential fundamental principles. After reading it, you will be able to understand basic theory.

INTERMEDIATE content is for staff and entry-level management at a golf course who are familiar with the subject but have only basic experience in executing strategies and tactics on the topic. This content typically covers the fundamentals and moves on to reveal more complex functions and examples. After reading it, you will feel comfortable leading projects on the subject matter covered.

ADVANCED content is for owners, general managers, and department supervisors who are, or want to be, experts on the subject. In it, we walk you through advanced features on the business of golf and develop a complete mastery of the subject. After reading it, you will feel ready not only to execute strategies and tactics, but also to teach others how to be successful.

Axioms

Throughout this material we use the following words to mean what is shown here in parentheses: "a few" (less than 10%), "some" (about 25%), "majority" (50%), "most" (75%), and "all" (100%).

It is not our intent to offend. Thus, if a statement reads "The procurement process of the majority of municipal governments is inefficient," we mean roughly half are inefficient, based on our experience and observations. There will be those who work for a municipal government and internalize that statement as though they are personally inefficient, and they may take offense.

This book was written with a focus on Don Miguel Ruiz, *The Four Agreements—A Toltec Wisdom Book*[2]:

- **Be impeccable with your words.** Speak with integrity. Say only what you mean.

- **Don't take anything personally.** Nothing others do is because of you. What others say and do is a projection of their own reality.

- **Don't make assumptions.** Find the courage to ask questions and to express what you really want. Communicate with others as clearly as you can to avoid misunderstandings, sadness, and drama. With just this one agreement, you can completely transform your life.

- **Always do your best.** Your best is going to change from moment to moment; it will be different when you are healthy as opposed to sick. Under any circumstance, simply do your best and you'll avoid self-judgment, self-abuse, and regret.

Who?

Is this book for you? Maybe not.

---

2 Don Miguel Ruiz, *The Four Agreements—A Toltec Wisdom Book*, 1997, Front Cover.

In 1991, Geoffrey Moore authored *Crossing the Chasm,* a book which accurately describes the adoption of new products or services, as shown in the chart[3]:

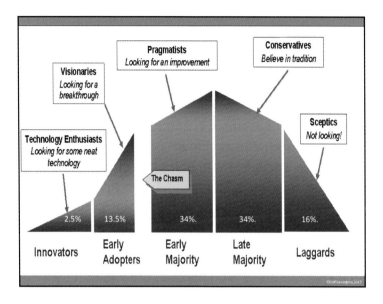

In applying Moore's model to the golf industry, I find that 60% of the industry is populated by cynics who cite "uncontrollable factors" as the cause for their woes. Thirty percent are skeptics who explain that their "unique" situation is more complicated. It is our opinion that only 10% of those in the golf industry are open to a discussion that can lead to them working together in creating a better way.

To illustrate that cynics and skeptics exist in the golf industry, I include here the response of a PGA PGM Golf Management Program college professor to the Sinek YouTube video:

> "It is my belief that we should be careful with biological (scientific only explanations for rational thought) and the reasons 'Why' people do things. We have approximately half of this university grounded in the fields of philosophy, sociology, humanities, and psychology that would refute Simon's premise for rational thought as chemical processes. Science cannot explain logic, intelligence, the abstract (mathematics) and the immaterial—we know they all exist, however. His

---

3 http://www.bing.com/images/search?q=Crossing+The+Chasm+Download+Diagram&FORM=
RESTAB#view=detail&id=AF90CDBC4ACEBA0CD194CC03A4609F2CE690D945&selected
Index=6

everything is material and the 'why' action reduced to a social construct of survival is in my mind, not correct and a logical fallacy.

Sorry for such a philosophical answer, but you have to understand my mind is well attuned to any leap of faith in developing constructs or processes. When speakers develop a construct to explain a human process for answering trust, truth, or thought, my mind will always run in overdrive to test the premise. I've been in academia long enough to detect worldview presuppositions. Simeon studied anthropology which has its roots in human evolution through natural selection. Anthropologists claim to bridge the gap between the social sciences and natural science.

The professor that assigns this video is an atheist. I don't share Simon's anthropological belief or the atheist's belief that biology (natural science can explain rational thought, and, or, truth). It cannot explain 'Why.'"[4]

Rather than finding a simple mantra that all can follow, resistance is created. No one can overstate the resistance to change that exists in the golf industry. Perhaps, we should conclude, as Damon Runyon did, that being successful in the business of golf is "six to five against."[5]

Thus, if you believe that together we can make a difference in the golf industry, if you are an innovator and you are willing to brainstorm what is possible, if you are an early adopter who likes to lead an industry by testing new paradigms, or if you are part of the early majority that seeks to benefit, confirm, and leverage the successful efforts of others to gain a competitive advantage, this book is for you.

Background

The Business of Golf—Why? How? What? is a sequel to the award-winning book, *The Business of Golf—What Are You Thinking?* that was published in 2010 and 2012.

The Business of Golf—What Are You Thinking? was written as a basic primer for avid golfers, college students in Professional Golf Management Programs,

---

4 Identity Restricted, Email Received from PGA Golf Management Program Instructor, January 9, 2013.

5 Robert I. Fitzhenry, Editor, *The Harper Book of Quotations*, Third Edition, 2005, pg. 16.

and golf industry professionals seeking to refresh their knowledge of the fundamentals of the golf industry and of the operation of a golf course. It covered the basics.

From the dearth of a central source providing strategic, tactical, and operational guidance, the book has gained widespread appeal. It has been purchased in 16 countries and is used by 15 universities and colleges in their Professional Golf Management curriculums. That book will be updated in 2014 and in even years thereafter.

In contrast to that basic primer, this book is written for the seasoned industry professional. The 2013 edition represents its first edition, and it will be updated in 2015 and in odd years thereafter.

It was our sincere intent in writing this treatise that, while we followed the outline of the original *The Business of Golf—What Are You Thinking?*, all of the content provided is completely new and reflective of the in-depth consulting engagements we have performed in partnership with many courses throughout Europe, across the United States, and in Asia.

Of the 123 illustrations integrated into *The Business of Golf—What Are You Thinking?*, only a few have been used herein to reflect vital new perspectives.

Applying: Who? How? What?

"Strategic," "tactical," and "operational" are three buzzwords in the business lexicon that make most people's eyes glaze over. Succinctly, they mean the following:

> **Strategic:** *culture*; vision, history, tradition, and governance.
>
> **Tactical:** *asset management*; comprising the facilities (golf course, clubhouse and other physical entities, finances, and human resources).
>
> **Operational:** *activities* (green fees, tournament, merchandise, food and beverage and range) and *management* (leadership, staffing and scheduling, marketing, and customer interaction).

In a well-managed operation, every operational decision can be traced up to the tactical plan and then up to the strategic vision. To illustrate, would you expect valet parking at a low-end municipal golf course? Not hardly. Would you expect bottled water, free range access, ball repair tools, and towels at a golf course charging in excess of $200? Very likely.

The vision statement is why the golf course exists. The mission statement is a definition of how that vision is to be achieved. If we apply the technical business jargon to a simple lay model, the WHY? HOW? and WHAT? perfectly align, as illustrated below:

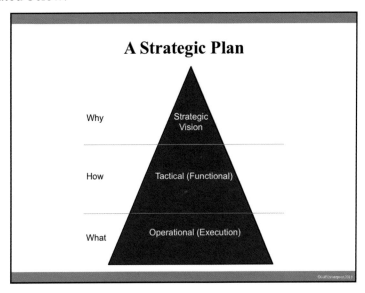

This book is intended to inspire you to create a strategic blueprint for your golf course facility—a blueprint that will be ever-changing but will keep you on the path to success as a professional leading your golf course to sustained profitability with continual reinvestment in the assets funded to ensure a valuable experience for the golfer.

This book is also intended as a compliment to the PGA of America's PGM programs as follows:

- Level 1: Customer Relations
  Business Planning
- Level 2: Golf Operations

With over 1,000 students currently enrolled in the PGA PGM Program, helping today's business of golf leaders embrace the fundamentals is enriching.

Path to Success

1) Watch the Simon Sinek YouTube video: http://www.ted.com/talks/
    simon_sinek_how_great_leaders_inspire_action.html

2) Create your personal "WHY?" statement.

3) Define the "WHY?" statement for your golf course. Each golf course
    is unique. Each course serves a different role. Each course attracts a
    different kind of golfer. Who is your customer? Clue—"everyone" is
    not the answer.

Concluding Thoughts

To get the right word in the right place is a rare achievement.

Mark Twain

There are no traffic jams along the extra mile.

Roger Staubach

SECTION 1

Strategic Vision - Why?
Chapters 1 through 6

To create a strategic plan, the vision of the experience to be created must first be identified. In Chapters 1 through 6, we progressively narrow the focus on uncontrollable factors that define the potential of a golf course and the elements required for it to be fiscally sustainable in the long-term.

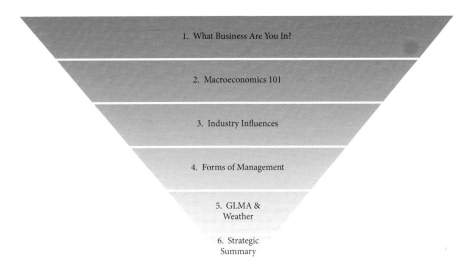

1. What Business Are You In?

2. Macroeconomics 101

3. Industry Influences

4. Forms of Management

5. GLMA & Weather

6. Strategic Summary

A comprehension of the barriers placed by friends and foes alike facilitates the ability to create a vision that defines the resources required to ensure consistent execution and, therefore, the desired investment return.

Hardcover catechisms are contradictions to our loose-leaf lives.
Gerhard Frost, *Loose-Leaf Lives*

Chapter 1

What Business Are You Truly In?
Golf Is a Lifestyle—The Game Is Only a Component

To attain knowledge, add things every day. To attain wisdom, remove things every day. Remove the things from your life that don't align with what's important to you for a happier, simpler life.

Lao Tzu

Chapter Highlights

The golf industry continues to cite "uncontrollable factors" as the principal cause for its financial underperformance.

This myopic focus dismisses the societal changes that are influencing a game which has been rooted in historical traditions. The perspective of those within the industry regarding what attracts individuals to the game is greatly askew when compared to the factors that actually motivate consumers. That gap is the chasm that is causing the industry's underperformance.

This chapter focuses on what the consumer seeks from the game of golf and why it is important to the financial stability of a course to ensure that the brand promise of each unique facility is consistent with the experience provided.

Nothing Has Changed

If you were to ask many in the golf industry what has changed within the industry during the last four years, the date the first edition of *The Business of Golf—What Are You Thinking?* was published, the likely answer would be "little has changed."

They would cite that the national economy has remained stagnant, that the market is thought to be oversupplied by 10%, and that it will take a decade for demand to once again equal supply. They would continue that the weather has been adverse (notwithstanding 2012), that third-party intermediaries are continuing to erode customer loyalty and increase downward price pressure on green fees, and that corporations are no longer sponsoring tournaments and corporate outings.

They would also cite that our society remains time-crunched and that the family structure has been fractured, with 50% of marriages ending in divorce. Gone are the days of the husband playing at the "club" on Saturday and Sunday to be joined by his wife for the dinner dance on Saturday night. One merely needs to note that private club membership has fallen from 62% in 1950 to 27% of U.S. golf courses in 2012.

David Smith, Chairman of Golf Projects International, founder of the World Club Championship, and golf's ultimate raconteur, spoke to us about the new private club membership structure evolving in America. He cited a prominent private club in Palm Springs as the prototypical example. The "campus" includes a $3 million steak house, Starbucks, 36 holes, and a $350,000 initiation fee. The typical member is a 50-year-old successful corporate executive who has a couple of kids in their 20s from his first marriage, and perhaps a couple of kids in their teens or under the age of 10 by his second or third marriage. This family is a picture of the disjointed structure we now call the American family. This couple is more likely to be watching their six-year-old play lacrosse game in Los Angeles than pounding the pellet on the driving range.

Clearly, the business of golf and what attracts and retains customers has changed along with of the fundamental changes in our society.

However, most of the excuses on the long list of woes proffered by many in the golf industry have one thing in common—they are uncontrollable factors that cause the financial performance of their facilities to suffer. They would cite this long list to exonerate themselves from their own self-inflicted wounds of poor management and lackadaisical execution.

Perhaps Eeyore should be the corporate mascot for the golf industry. ☺

In Case You Missed It—The Economy Has Improved

Clearly, the economy in 2013 and our confidence therein are not at the levels they were in 2000, as reflected in the following Conference Board Consumer Confidence Index.

The signals are mixed. In January, 2013 it was announced that the U.S. economy contracted at the annual rate of 0.01%, the first decline since the second quarter of 2009.

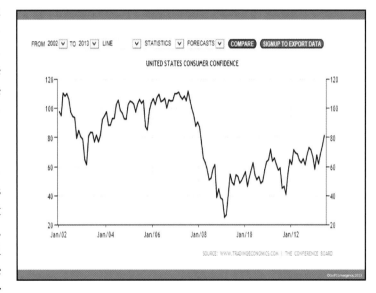

On the same day, it was announced that "Home sales rebounded to the strongest level in five years in 2012, as home building bounced back to levels not seen since early in the recession. Near record low mortgage rates, rising home prices, and a drop in foreclosures have combined to bring buyers back to the market."[1]

The headlines the next day were "Personal incomes post biggest gain in eight years."[2]

---

1 http://money.cnn.com/2013/01/27/news/economy/housing-economic-growth/index.html

2 http://www.foxbusiness.com/news/2013/01/31/personal-income-posts-biggest-gain-in-eight-years/

We get absorbed by the daily details that flood our consciousness, and we lose sight of the major trends. One merely need to reflect on the tremendous changes that have occurred in the U.S. during the last four years, as evidenced in the following table, to realize a lot has changed[3]:

Category	2009	2012
Annual Consumer Price Index	−0.10%	1.70%
Consumer Spending	−1.60%	1.60%
Economic Growth – GDP	−5.30%	3.10%
Foreclosures	66,777	53,054
Gas Prices	$1.62	$3.29
Government Spending (Billions)	$3,517	$3,540
Housing Prices	$175,500	$189,000
Interest Rates (10-Yr Treasury Rate)	2.46%	1.86%
Job Growth - Monthly Payroll	−818,000	114,000
Manufacturing (Industrial Production Index)	87.4	98.1
National Debt % of GNP	54.10%	72.80%
Standard & Poor Stock Index	931.8	1472.6
Unemployment	7.80%	7.80%

Clearly, the economy in 2013 is performing at a level comparable to the year the recession began. Merely sit on an airplane or wait in a Red Carpet room and the fact that the economy is a lot better is apparent.

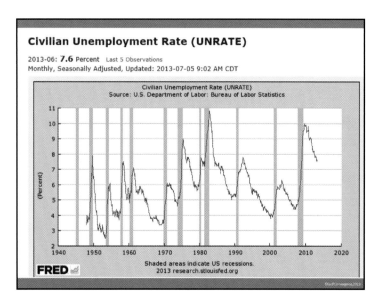

Sure the nattering nabobs of negativism will cite that the civilian unemployment rate remains at historically low levels, as illustrated by the figure to the left.[4]

They will cite, correctly, that unfortunately the recovery has largely escaped some segments of the nation. While one can watch Bill O'Reilly of the *O'Reilly Factor* on Fox News describe

3 http://money.cnn.com/galleries/2012/news/economy/1206/gallery.Obama-economy/13.html

4 http://research.stlouisfed.org/fred2/graph/?id=UNRATE

the economic condition of America with a self-brewed cauldron of doom and gloom, the harsh reality is that those who remain unemployed or under-employed represented a small segment of the golf industry in the past, are slim prospects to play currently, and, unless their financial fortunes dramatically change, are unlikely to be casual, core, or avid golfers in the future.

If they do play, municipal and low-end daily fee golf courses are the venue of choice for the vast majority. The money you have largely influences where you play.

A benchmark that may be relevant is corporate profits, the growth of which is staggering, as shown in the figure to the right.[5]

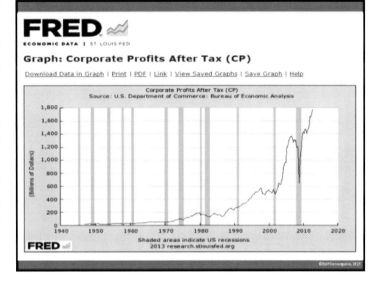

Those who say "nothing has changed" are on the sidelines in the game of life. From any baseline, change is a constant, for "there is nothing permanent except change."[6]

As reported by Golf Datatech, green-grass sales were up in all major categories in 2012 over 2011: gloves 63%, shoes 19.4%, woods 12.2%, irons 11.6%, and putters 8.2%.[7]

Despite these gains, many challenges persist. Michael Hughes, NGCOA CEO, believes that "Pricing, for one remains a particularly devilish issue at courses around the country. Be that as it may, I've heard during my travels and from conversation with a number of our members that the time is (finally) right for some course owners to raise rates."[8]

We agree, for golf is a sport of the well-to-do.

---

5 http://research.stlouisfed.org/fred2/series/CP

6 Heraclitus, *The Harper Book of Quotations*, 2005, pg. 86.

7 *Golf Business*, "Leading Indicators," April 2013, pg. 14.

8 Ibid., pg. 4.

A Pricey Sport

Golf was labeled in a CNBC story as one of the nine pricey sports of the wealthy, as evidenced in the following image.

Golf was included in the list with dressage, yachting, croquet, figure skating, polo, pheasant hunting, snowboarding, and horse racing.[9]

I am confident that every golf industry trade association shuddered at this classification of the game, for they will maintain that growth of the game is vital.

But why? The motivation from associations is largely rooted in self-interest, not in a philanthropic motivation for the "good of the game." Association bureaucracy is hurting, not helping. More golfers are simply needed to ensure that PGA Pros and members of the CMAA, GCSAA, and NRPA remain employed. More golfers are needed to ensure golf course owners receive a return on their investment. More golfers are needed to buy equipment to sustain that segment of the industry.

That raises the question, "Should the focus for golf be on the business or on the consumers?" We believe the sole focus should be on the consumers. They drive the economic engine. Thus, identifying what attracts an individual to play golf is vital.

Golf's Appeal Is Far Different Than What the Insiders in the Industry Perceive

Despite the well-intended efforts to broaden the base of golfers by First Tee since its founding in 1997[10] (financially underwritten by the USGA, the Masters

---

9 http://money.msn.com/investing/9-pricey-sports-of-the-wealthy

10 http://www.thefirsttee.org/club/scripts/library/view_document.asp?NS=WWD&DN=STATISTICS

Tournament, LPGA, PGA, and PGA Tour), touching 6.5 million individuals right, wrong, good, or bad—golf is a game of the leisure class.

It attracts those who like to spend to spend time outdoors, enjoy light exercise, and remove their minds from day-to-day cares. It provides a method to build social and business contacts, affords the opportunity to spend time with loved ones, entices some with the love the challenge, and attracts those simply seeking fun. The mental game, the competition, the values of the game, and its history and traditions are also factors that attract individuals to play this fabulous game.

In 2012, the National Golf Foundation (NGF) reported that those who make up what is called "the latent demand" (those who have never played and have an interest or those who played in the past but now are not actively engaged) are primarily attracted to the sport to "spend time outdoors" and "for exercise and fitness."[11]

In 2013, NGF expanded its research to current golfers, asking them why they play the game. The responses were very insightful and consistent with those who have an interest but do play golf currently, as highlighted in the following figure.

So despite all the commercials you see about longer, straighter, fewer strokes, they only matter to a small segment of those who play golf. And despite the PGA Tour, the Golf Channel, and the plethora of talk shows focused on championship golf, all segments of golfers are attracted to the sport by the opportunity to spend time outdoors, the social aspects of the game, and exercise. History and traditions, the competition, and ball striking don't make the top three categories.

Why We Play	Not and Fringe	Casual	Hooked and Nuts	Average
Time outdoors	43	54	63	53
Social aspect	33	46	53	44
The exercise	32	44	48	41
Ball striking	23	40	59	41
The challenge	18	36	66	40
The courses	20	28	52	33
Stress relief	19	36	43	33
Mental game	10	23	39	24
Values of the Game	9	23	39	24
The competition	6	13	34	18
Keeping score	6	10	35	17
History & Traditions	6	9	27	14
Practicing	5	9	26	13

---

11 National Golf Foundation, "Attrition and Attraction," April 2012, Slide 19.

There is disconnect between the brand image of the game in the minds of the public at large (reinforced by the industry through its advertising) and what is actually sought by golfers; a lesson to be learned.

Despite the Best Efforts to Broaden Golf's Appeal—It Is What It Is

Those three themes—spending time outdoors, the social aspects of the game, and exercise—should be hallmarks for the industry and the mantra of every golf course to attract and retain players to a game that still, at its core, is a game of the wealthy. The average household income of a golfer is $85,700[12] contrasted to an average household income of $53,214 in the United States.[13] That's quite a contrast to the average income of golfers. Surveys across the country consistently show similar results. In 2012, a sample from surveys conducted of **golfers** measured median household incomes as follows:

City	Age	Median Household Income
Asbury, Iowa	50.4	$118,913
Atlanta, Georgia	45.8	137,135
Becker, Minnesota	48.4	99,563
Brookings, Oregon	57.1	75,691
Casper, Wyoming	47.8	107,509
Fort McMurray, Alberta, Canada	39.9	143,672
Grand Rapids, Michigan	44.7	67,366
Greenville, North Carolina (Public Golfers)	47.8	88,285
Greenville, North Carolina (Private Club Members)	52.4	138,411
Northcliffe, Texas	51.6	78,555
Pacific Grove, California	53.8	118,179
Sioux Falls, South Dakota	48.5	93,283

The consistency of the demographics across the United States really paints a picture of the sport and its current customer base. Even realizing that some survey respondents may have inflated their median household incomes, you

12 National Golf Foundation, "2012 Golf Participation in the United States," pg. 6.

13 Tactician, "Income and Disposable Income Report," January 2013, pg. 3.

could discount the survey results by 25% and still find that golfers' incomes are above the national median average.

So how much does the national economy directly impact the business of golf? Only to the extent that the financial resources and psyche of the wealthy are negatively impacted.

The Central Problem of Our Age

There is a current malaise in the golf industry: lots of theories, lots of wishes, lots of spinning about, and lots of inaction.

The formula for success in attracting and retaining customers is simple. To the extent that the experience received exceeds or equals the price paid, customer loyalty is created. To the extent the experience received is less than the price paid, customer attrition occurs.

Consumers will not spend money unless they are having fun. Golf is in the entertainment business; pure and simple. Thus, the formula for financial success at a golf course is rooted fundamentally in matching a consumer's need

to his pocketbook. Maslow's Hierarchy of Needs,[14] as shown in the figure, is an appropriate model to define the niche each golfer seeks.

A RIDDLE TO SOLVE: Do the golfers determine the policies of a course or do the policies of a course determine which individuals are attracted to that course? The proverbial

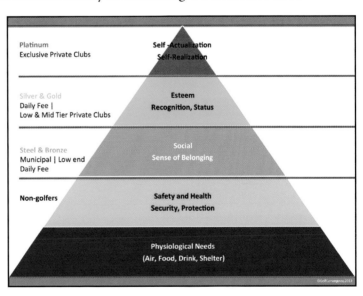

---

14 http://www.bing.com/images/search?q=maslow's+hierarchy+of+needs+diagram&qpvt=maslow %27s+hierarchy+of+needs+diagram&FORM=IGRE

catch-22. The chart shown here would suggest the vision of the course determines the golfers attracted to it.

Environment and Culture Determine the Customer

Every golf course can be categorized by the environment and by the culture that emanates from that facility. Each golf course is unique. Each experience offered is different. Play the Black and the Red courses at Bethpage State Park, play #1 and #4 at Cog Hill Golf and Country Club, play Olympic Club and TPC Harding Park—the experiences are as different as the different fees charged.

While the unique differentiations between courses are endless, in presenting a simplified and streamlined version of golf management, we have reduced the delineations between facilities to 25 variables for a private club and 18 variables for a municipal or daily fee golf course. To illustrate the concept, the following figure highlights the process of determining in which niche a club should be slotted.

What Is Your Strategic Vision – Private Club?
Determines Financial Resources Allocated

	Platinum	Gold	Silver	Bronze	Steel
Vision	Rolls Royce	BMW	Volvo	Chevrolet	Hyundai
Examples	Pine Valley Seminole Whispering Pines	Cherry Hills, Los Angeles Rivera	TPC Clubs	Lakewood	Brookhaven Pinery
Cost (green fee + cart)	Over $250 per round	$175 to $500 per round	$75 to $200 per round	$50 to $100 per round	$50 or less
Access	By Invitation	Waiting List	Available	Seeking	Open Access
Style	Formal	Professional	Relaxed	Very Casual	Loose
Social Status	Generational Wealth	Upper Class	Upper Middle Class	Middle Class	Anyone

©GolfConvergence 2013

For a private club, the criteria for differentiation may include national rankings, the architect, championships hosted, slope rating, course conditioning, type of carts (electric, gas, GPS), number of amenities (tees, towels, water, fruit, etc.), customer touch points from arrival to departure, cell phone policy, clubhouse dress code, jeans, collared shirts, ladies pants, smoking areas, supplemental activities, business allowed in clubhouse, computers, tipping policy, gifts to employees from members.

For a public facility, the criteria for differentiation would be similar but far more relaxed regarding cell phones, dress codes, and conducting business in the clubhouse, etc.

How does an individual determine which golf course to frequent regularly? Proximity to home or work is certainly a primary factor. Course conditions and price are always important also. But price becomes an immediate differentiator as to who plays what course.

The "standard" golf course has 18 tees, 18 fairways, and 18 greens. How can you justify the difference between a $35 green fee to play a municipal course and a six-figure non-refundable deposit at a private club nearby?

The answer is simple. The experience received establishes the price. Pounding the pellet with yellow floating golf balls into a slime-covered filthy pond off rubber mats is a different experience than hitting Titleist practice balls on the range next to John Elway or Mario Lemieux at their private clubs that have hosted numerous major championships.

Golf is a lifestyle. We seek to affiliate with people with whom with are comfortable. Family, educational backgrounds, our professions and life experiences define who we are. Though the proper goal is to be of one people, Montague Francis Ashley-Montagu (born Israel Ehrenberg on June 28, 1905, and grew to be an anthropologist, humanist, and college lecturer) stated, "Equality is an ethical and not a biological principle."

If we look at major cities, we usually find neighborhoods that represent pockets of ethnicity or religious orientation. While we idealistically, philosophically, and properly desire to be one with everyone, that journey of life finds us socializing with those with whom we have common interests.

Golf, at its base element, is a social venue for entertainment, and it attracts to a facility people of like life experiences.

Go

If you licensed the supplemental template that accompanies this Field book, it is highly recommended (to gain the full benefit of your investment in this material) that you complete the following exercise:

Step 1: Vision—Private Golf Course

Step 1: Vision—Public Golf Course

Why does completing the exercise matter? First, the goal of this textbook is to help guide you to create a strategic plan that is easy to execute.

Public Club – Financial Base

	Platinum Top 10%	Gold Top 25%	Silver Median	Bronze 3rd Quintile	Steel - Bottom 25%
Rounds Played	30,000	35,000	40,000	45,000	Over 50,000
Full Time Employees	> 40	>20	> 10	> 5	< 5
Total Revenues	> $3.5 million	> $2 million	>$1.5 million	> $1 million	< $1 million
Green Fes, Guest, Cart, Trail	> $1.8 million	> $1.0 million	$750,000	>$500,000	< $500,000
Merchandise	> $300,000	$200,000	$100,000	> $75,000	< $75,000
Maintenance	> $800,000	> $700,000	> $500,000	> $400,000	< $400,000
Annual Renovation	> $800,000	> $700,000	> $85,000	> $50,000	< $50,000
EBITDA	> 1,200,000	> $600,000	> $400,000	> $200,000	< $200,000

Source: PGA PerformanceTrak – Annual Operating Survey

©GolfConvergence,2013

Note: Each data element (i.e., Top 10% rounds played) represents the operating results of that individual category and does not represent the consolidated financial performance of any single entity.

Second, this exercise will help you define your niche, the capital required to create the experience, and your potential return on investment. The figure to the left is a summary of the financial performance of public golf courses.

The comparison of the vision to a course's financial base establishes if the brand promise matches the experience. A facility's ability to create and sustain the experience is limited to its earnings plus any capital (debt or equity) invested.

Naturally when the brand promise exceeds the experience delivered, the financial performance will fall short. Thus, it is essential to identify and understand your customers and to know what experience they seek.

What Does Today's Golfer Really Seek from the Experience? Fun and Entertainment

Fun and entertainment start with matching the golfer's ability with the course layout. Only the masochistic segment of the golfing population, speculated at less than 1%, likes to get beat up. When a golfer plays a round near his or her average score, he or she instantly tells you that score. Rarely is the score of a badly played round revealed.

Golf courses come in all flavors. The chart below shows the diversity of venues available.

In 2012, we conducted numerous consumer studies for clients. This process of understanding their customers' hopes, desires, and needs is an evolutionary process and usually includes up to 40 questions per survey. For the first time, when asking the respondents "What is the average score for 18 holes?" we added an additional answer choice: "Don't keep score. I merely play for fun and recreation." The following figure shows those results.

We were surprised that 13.4% of players representing over 62 million rounds don't even keep score. Note that the USGA reports that the average men's score is 92[15] and the women's is 110.[16]

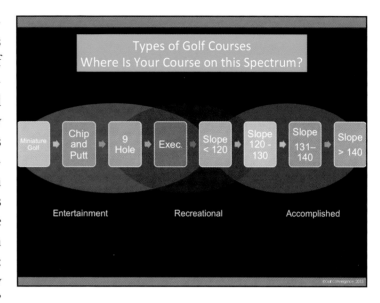

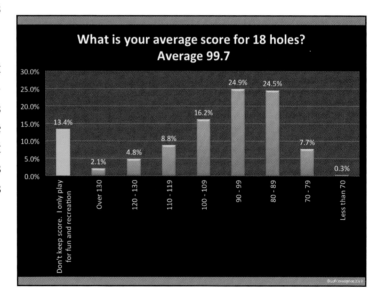

15 http://www.usga.org/handicapping/articles_resources/Men-s-USGA-Handicap-Indexes/

16 Ibid.

How to Provide the Experience the Golfer Seeks: A Shorter Course

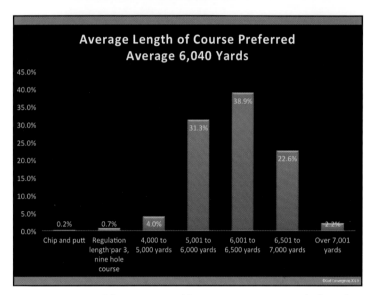

The insight regarding how many golfers keep score led to a further question, "What is the average length course you prefer?" Again, as an avid golfer who plays frequently around the world and having moved from the tips to 1 up only within the last five years, I was surprised by the results in the chart on the left.

This study was of men who are public course golfers. Women responded with a preferred length of 4,920 yards.

Arthur Little, who is a strong supporter of women's golf (http://www.golfwith women.com), believes that the right length of a golf course for a woman who has an average club head speed of 65 mph is 4,200 yards. He also believes that to attract women to the game, the golf course has the responsibility to create a course of the right length, encourage a more flexible format that eliminates stroke and distance penalties, and de-emphasize scoring while still highlighting the importance of maintaining a course that can be enjoyed by both men and women. It is about having fun in a courteous and respectful environment.

With the objective of helping golfers have more fun on the course, the PGA, in combination with the USGA, launched a campaign titled "Tee It Forward." The objective was to encourage golfers to play a course that is aligned with their driving distance. The research we performed across the United States in 2012 clearly supports the national initiative.

The TEE IT FORWARD initiative was introduced at the GOLF 20/20 Forum through the efforts of Barney Adams, the PGA of America, and the United States Golf Association. The results are impressive[17]:

---

17 *Divot Magazine*, "Expo Issue 2013—Tee It Forward PGA Colorado Section," pg. 12.

- 85% of golfers found playing more enjoyable with TEE IT FORWARD.

- 56% felt they played faster.

- 93% are likely to use it again.

- 56% stated they were likely to play golf more often knowing they could TEE IT FORWARD.

One of the golf industry's leading innovators is Del Ratcliffe, President of Ratcliffe Golf Services, Inc. He oversees the operation of the city's four golf courses in Charlotte, North Carolina. Ratcliffe was appointed in 2013 to the PGA Committee along with Suzy Whaley, PGA Professional at TPC River Highlands, and Kyle Heyen, PGA at Hiwan Golf Club, to focus on growing the game initiatives. Intuitively sensing the golfers' desire for courses that were fun to play and consistent with the "Tee It Forward" initiative, Ratcliffe implemented a tee marker system using symbols consistent with the ski industry, as illustrated in the following figure.

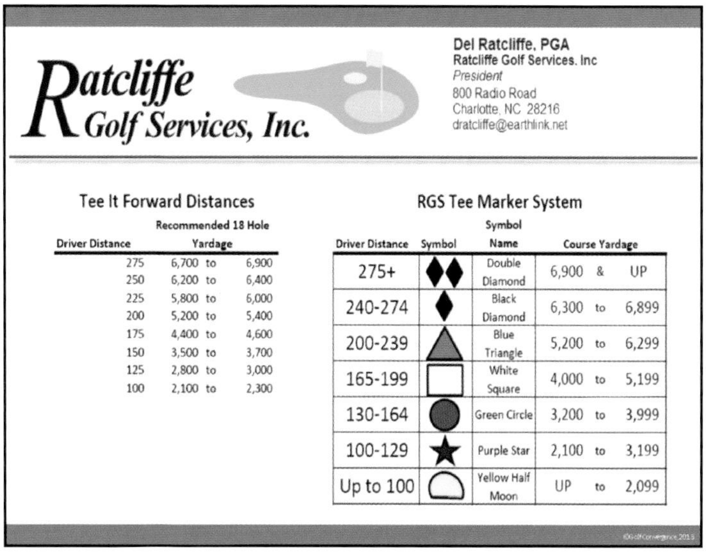

When golfers approach the starter at Del's managed course, the starter asks the customer, "How far do you drive the ball?" Based on that answer, the customer is gently guided to the appropriate tee.

To ensure the customer derives fun, the importance of the tees used cannot be underestimated. When the Robert Trent Jones Trail opened in 1997, the tee markers were a diverse array of colors: purple, lime, fuchsia, rose, lemon, etc. Within a week, the markers were changed. Golfers without the necessary historical frame of reference were playing too long a course, and rounds were taking in excess of 5 hours. The traditional markers of red, yellow, white, blue, and black were quickly reintroduced.

Ratcliffe Golf Services, Inc.

Del Ratcliffe, PGA
Ratcliffe Golf Services. Inc
President
800 Radio Road
Charlotte, NC 28216
dratcliffe@earthlink.net

Tee It Forward Distances

Driver Distance	Recommended 18 Hole Yardage	
275	6,700 to	6,900
250	6,200 to	6,400
225	5,800 to	6,000
200	5,200 to	5,400
175	4,400 to	4,600
150	3,500 to	3,700
125	2,800 to	3,000
100	2,100 to	2,300

RGS Tee Marker System

Driver Distance	Symbol	Symbol Name	Course Yardage		
275+	♦♦	Double Diamond	6,900	&	UP
240-274	♦	Black Diamond	6,300	to	6,899
200-239	▲	Blue Triangle	5,200	to	6,299
165-199	☐	White Square	4,000	to	5,199
130-164	●	Green Circle	3,200	to	3,999
100-129	★	Purple Star	2,100	to	3,199
Up to 100	◠	Yellow Half Moon	UP	to	2,099

This concept of ensuring that the golfer has fun is evidenced at the Sand Barrens Golf Club in New Jersey. The markers near the tees have the following designations:

Tee Marker	Designation
Back Tee	Pro: 0–6 handicap
1 Up	Championship: 7–12 handicap
2 Up	Amateur: 13–24 handicap
3 Up	Rookie: 25–35 handicap
4 Up	Beginner: 36+ handicap

What Has Changed?

Those who say "nothing has changed" in the golf industry in the last four years are simply out of touch. While more courses have now closed than opened for the past seven years, rounds in 2012 were up 5.7%, as shown below.

The National Golf Foundation annually updates its comprehensive database of U.S. golf facility listings. Additionally, in 2013, NGF refined the methodology for estimating the number of golfing households, golfers, and rounds demanded in the U.S. or for any market or custom geographic. NGF's "Golf Demand Model" also provides several key metrics around demand, supply, and the interaction between the two. These metrics are more accurate than ever, as the new model puts much more weight on facility-reported rounds than in the past due to the increased sophistication and accuracy of collection methods (e.g., improved POS systems, Golf Coalition).[18]

To help grow the game, in 2012, the PGA of America launched Golf 2.0 as a targeted, focused, long-range strategic plan for the golf industry.

Hoping to join an industry-wide effort to reverse sagging participation, the American Society of Golf Course Architects paired with the PGA to launch the "Bunny Slopes initiative."[19] Realizing that allowing new entrants to the game to play courses stretching over 7,000 yards serves nobody's interest, and under-written with a $50,000 gift from the PGA, their goal is to create a venue between the driving range and the championship course. The emphasis on short-game practice and par-3 holes will be the focus of this program, and it is designed to lessen the intimidation new players often feel.

Positive changes are brewing. Those facilities that will be successful will match the experience they offer to the customers they serve.

Golf Is a Lifestyle

The changes in golf during the past four years have been many, but the biggest may be the awakened realization that consumers are seeking fun and entertainment and that, therefore, the principal product of the business of golf needs to be fun and entertainment.

Sport is an important part of the culture of the United States. Many view golf, incorrectly we believe, as principally an athletic competition.

While the number of fans who choose to view the major golf championships dwarfs the number of participants in the sport, golf's place in the sporting consciousness of the U.S. is very low. You need only look at golf's placement on the ESPN Web site to realize that only after eight keystrokes and three clicks can an inquiring fan get to the PGA Tour information, as shown in the figure on the following page.

---

18 National Golf Foundation, "Golf Industry Overview," September 10, 2013, pg 1.

19 http://golfweek.com/news/2012/dec/05/first-links-blueprint-golf-bunny-slopes/

Golf is not on the fore-front of Americans' minds. Its brand is narrow and isolated.

That begs the following question in the short term: Should the industry seek customers that are not active players to grow the game, or should the industry better identify, communicate and serve its existing customers?

The short-term answer is that the golf industry, as the ski industry has successfully done, should focus on its current core customers, engaging them in a manner that will grow the game as they introduce their family, friends, and associates to golf for fun, for entertainment, and for the lifestyle that this great game offers.

Path to Success

1) Complete Step 1 exercise—Vision—Private Golf Course or Step 1—Vision—Public Golf Course.

2) Identify your niche and ascertain that the brand promise equals the experience being provided.

3) Implement the "Tee It Forward" program with tee markers comparable to ski resorts.

4) Begin outlining the questions for a customer survey.

5) Review all advertising and collateral marketing materials. Focus on what motivates your customers: being outdoors, exercising, and the social aspects of the game.

6) Determine *what* programs you can offer to women, juniors, and all golfers, emphasizing 18-hole rounds in less than 4 hours along with alternate formats.

7) Evaluate the efficacy of your customer relationship management program and your adoption of social media with bi-weekly communication.

Concluding Thoughts

The central problem of our age is how to act decisively in the absence of certainty.

Bertrand Russell

He who desires, but acts not, breeds pestilence.

William Blake, "The Marriage of Heaven and Hell"

Chapter 2

The Macroeconomics of the Golf Business

There can be no economy where there is no efficiency.
Benjamin Disraeli

Chapter Highlights

Because daily business is so focused on the details, it is important to frame the industry within which your business operates. While you may believe your facility is unique, there are parallels between golf courses and their associated customer bases.

This chapter focuses on golf around the world. As you read, ask yourself, "What is each course doing that is different from our current focus?" and "What can we learn from their successes and failures, and how can we apply that knowledge?"

No One Knows

How many golf courses are on planet earth? The Royal and Ancient Golf Club, along with other industry groups, retained the National Golf Foundation in 2010 to answer that question. Definitive research indicates that 33,331 golf courses in 200 countries may exist. Of those courses, 85% are located in 20 countries as shown below.

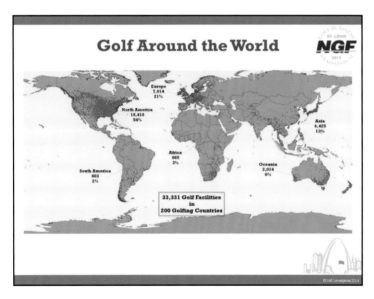

Four countries, the United Kingdom (2,761), Canada (2,401), Japan (2,387), and Australia (1,550), follow the U.S. in the number of golf courses operating. As reported in NGF research, growth is occurring in China, Egypt, India, Mexico, Morocco, and Vietnam: Even countries like Albania, Azerbaijan, Belarus, Cape Verde, Georgia, Lebanon, and Mongolia have built golf courses.[1]

The United States still dominates, and its courses can be segmented as shown in the figure to the left.[2]

The United States Golf Market

Type of Course	Courses	Percentage	Holes	Median Age	Average Age	Median Fee	Average Fee
United States							
Daily Fee	9,199	58.79%	150,948	1972	1971	37	45.19
Municipal	2,445	15.63%	41,022	1964	1961	38	39.79
Private Equity	2,415	15.43%	42,255	1949	1946	72	74.60
Private Non-Equity	1,561	9.98%	30,024	1974	1968	75	79.76
Private Resort	27	0.17%	432	1973	1981	38	47.00
Total Private	4,003	25.58%	72,711	1961	1955	73	76.44
Total	15,647		264,681	1969	1965	41.00	52.35

---

1 National Golf Foundation, "Golf Around the World—International Database Project," April 2013, Slides 13 and 16.

2 National Golf Foundation, "NGF Golf Supply Support," 2012.

Same Sport—Different Trends?

What is more important than the actual number of golf courses that exist is whether the business practices of those "international courses" vary significantly from those at U.S. courses and what trends will shape the future of golf both internationally and domestically.

Andrew Satori, KPMG—Hungary, has done some simply fabulous research (www.golfbenchmark.com) in analyzing the financial performance of golf courses worldwide, as highlighted in the following tables.[3]

Country	Courses	Playable Days	Golfers	Rounds	Gross Revenue
Africa - North	43	*	8,900	20,400	$1,256,850
Africa - South	450	346	150,000	33,575	$1,317,273
Caribbean	142	354	*	18,450	$1,720,000
China	300	*	~1,000,000	*	*
Europe - Central	908	235	673,868	19,964	$1,478,960
Europe - Eastern	135	249	45,000	9,637	$536,019
Europe - North	900	234	931,000	19,472	$919,161
Europe - Western	1,128	340	774,864	26,600	$1,725,010
Holland	192	361	361,000	37,500	$2,128,000
India	186	336	100,000	30,303	$190,000
Japan	2,350	320	9,000,000	39,999	$5,100,000
Middle East	20	359	16,900	40,237	$6,700,000
United Kingdom	3,084	357	287,000	30,500	$1,377,880
South America	561	330	117,600	13,500	$1,200,000
International Benchmarks	10,399	318	12,466,132	26,645	$2,032,692

---

3 KPMG—Hungary, "Golf Benchmarking Survey," 2006–2010.

Country	Initiation Fee	Annual Dues	Green Fee	Staff – Full Time	Staff – Seasonal
Africa - North	$325	$847	$77	45	14
Africa - South	$447	$596	$32	42	6
Caribbean	$7,880	$2,839	$129	*	*
China	$50,000	$2,750	$161	258	0
Europe - Central	$4,619	$1,598	$74	9	5
Europe - Eastern	$2,435	$919	$49	27	5
Europe - North	$867	$572	$56	6	5
Europe - Western	$8,599	$2,136	$75	22	2
Holland	$931	$1,197	$73	*	*
India	$1,865	$112	$18	48	10
Japan	$15,000	$3,600	$73	40	23
Middle East	$1,460	$3,741	$134	188	0
United Kingdom	$3,108	$1,091	$66	14	7
South America	$2,108	$1,349	$52	32	4
International Benchmarks	$7,640	$1,731	$76	62	6

* Data not available.

Note: It should be noted that for each country an individual analysis was performed by KPMG. For the purposes of this book, we extracted the data from each report, with full attribution to KPMG. Our goal was to highlight the financial performance of 18-hole golf courses. Readers should refer to www.golf benchmarking.com to review the source data for these charts.

There are some striking parallels and some vast differences with respect to the financial performance of international and U.S. golf courses. While the average number of rounds played, gross revenues, initiation fees, annual dues, and rounds played per member are comparable to U.S. facilities, there are some striking variances:

1. Is the facility operated for profit? Of the courses in Central Europe, 44% are not.

2. What is the participation in the sport among the general population? In most of the countries listed earlier, the participation rate is far less than 1%. Even in the United Kingdom, the participation rate is only 2.1%, which is about three times higher than that in the rest of Europe. In contrast, the United States boasts a relatively high 8.6% participation rate.

3. In which countries is golf truly limited to the elite? China and India.

4. Which country ranks second after the United States in demand and fourth after the United Kingdom in supply? Japan.

5. What is the balance between male, female, juniors, and corporate employees using the facility? Many countries that were not part of the original British Empire, such as Sweden, Norway, and Denmark, have far higher female participation than does the United States. Western Europe's female participation rate of 18% is comparable to the United States' female participation rate of 20%.

6. Is management outsourced? Far less so in international locations than in the United States.

7. What percentage of total rounds is member-based? In nearly all countries outside the United States, members play the majority of rounds. For example, in North Africa, outside play comprises only 11% of play. The United States concept of "daily fee" or "municipal" is rarely in evidence internationally, except in India, where 43% of the courses are owned by the military.

8. What one cost in the Middle East would bankrupt nearly all other golf courses internationally? Water. Each golf course in the Middle East spends approximately $500,000 annually to pump about 750,000 gallons of water daily.

9. How can a course that only generates $190,000 in annual revenue (yes, that number is correct) make a small profit? The cost of living and materials is exceedingly low in India.

10. The number of rounds played per playable day rarely exceeds 150 anywhere in the world. In most countries, an 80-rounds-per-day statistic is considered busy.

With golf becoming an Olympic sport in 2016, the game is entering the world stage. The Golf 20/20 Vision report by HSBC highlights those trends internationally as follows:

1. "Golf is a large business which continues to grow globally despite the financial crisis.

2. Golf is moving east. In China it is becoming the game of choice for the wealthier, as Chinese men and women become rich enough to enjoy their leisure, and there are also signs that in India golf is gaining momentum.

3. In many markets, golf is getting younger.

4. Golf participation is becoming less male as women increasingly take it up. At a social level, we expect the sport to become more unisex, with mixed games more common.

5. Golf is adapting to urbanization and to technology, moving beyond the 18-hole format and introducing new shorter forms of the game.

6. The golf tourism market has bounced back from the recession, and golf continues to form an important part of tourism development strategies, especially in emerging markets."[4]

An HSGC report concludes that "There are risks here for a sport which is associated with affluence. In a world in which inequality is moving up the political agenda and resources such as land [are] becoming more contested, golf will need to learn the language of inclusion and sustainability."[5]

There are some great warnings here for the future of golf operations in the United States and its economic impact.

U.S. Economic Impact Study

Golf's Economic Impact

Size of the U.S. Golf Economy by Industry Segment in 2000, 2005 and 2011 ($ millions)			
Core Industries	**2000**	**2005**	**2011**
Golf Facility Operations	$20,496	$28,052	$29,852
Golf Course Capital Investment	$7,812	$3,578	$2,073
Golfer Supplies	$5,982	$6,151	$5,639
Endorsements, Tournaments & Associations	$1,293	$1,682	$2,045
Charities	$3,200	$3,501	$3,900
Total Core Industries	**$38,783**	**$42,964**	**$43,509**
Enabled Industries			
Real Estate	$9,904	$14,973	$4,745
Hospitality/Tourism	$13,480	$18,001	$20,555
Total Enabled Industries	**$23,384**	**$32,974**	**$25,300**
TOTAL GOLF ECONOMY	**$62,167**	**$75,939**	**$68,809**

Note: Columns sum based on rounding of individual estimates. Numbers also have not been adjusted for inflation but are expressed as nominal dollars.

©GolfConvergence 2013

The general economic downturn experienced in the United States from 2007 to 2011, as would be expected, also shrank the golf industry, as reported by Golf 20/20 as illustrated in the figure to the left.[6]

Despite the recession, golf facility operations continued to grow from 2005 through 2011. Only because of the collapse of new golf course constructions and real estate associated with golf course facilities did golf's economic impact shrink. But … there is a silver lining in that dark cloud.

4 The Futures Company for HSBC, "Golf's 20/20 Vision: The HSBC Report," 2012, pg. 9.

5 Ibid., pg. 9.

6 http://golf2020.com/media/31526/2011_golf_econ_exec_sum_sri_final_12.17.12.pdf, pg. 5.

The Multiplier Effect of Golf's Economic Impact

As most economists appreciate, golf has direct as well as indirect and multiplier effects on the overall U.S. economy. For example, for every dollar spent by a golf facility for goods and services, other businesses derive economic benefit. The wages paid to golf course employees are spent by them for living expenses.

In 2011, the $68.8 billion impact generated by the golf industry translated into a total economic impact, calculated by SRI International, an independent non-profit research institute, as follows[7]:

- $176.8 billion for the U.S. economy, including the indirect and induced economic impacts stimulated by golf sector activity;

- 1.98 million jobs; and

- $55.6 billion of total wage income.

As a comparison, in Canada, "The game of golf accounts for an estimated **$11.3 billion** of Canada's Gross Domestic Product (GDP), which includes:

- 29.6 billion for the Canadian economy, including the indirect and induced economic impacts stimulated by golf sector activity;

- 341,794 jobs;

- $7.6 billion in household income;

- $1.2 billion in property and other indirect taxes;

- $1.9 billion in income taxes."[8]

Interestingly, in Canada, "the revenues generated directly by golf courses and their facilities and stand-alone driving and practice ranges (**$4.7 billion**) rivals the revenues generated by **all other** participation sports and recreation facilities combined (**$4.8 billion**) in Canada."[9]

---

7 http://golf2020.com/media/31526/2011_golf_econ_exec_sum_sri_final_12.17.12. pdf, pg. 7.

8 http://golf2020.com/media/12784/economicimpact_golfcanada_2009_execsummary_en_ issuedaug17_09_25.pdf, pg. 1.

9 Ibid., pg. 2.

Golf's Place as a Participant in Recreational Sports

The role of golf in competing for the consumers' entertainment capital is high-lighted by the following table presented in the World Golf Foundation Golf 20/20 report.[10]

Description	Amount
TV Broadcasting, cable and other subscription broadcasting	92.4
Motion pictures and videos	83.1
Golf (core industries)	43.5
Spectator sports (baseball, basketball, football, hockey, etc.)	33.1
Other amusement (skiing, fitness and recreational centers, bowling, etc.)	32.3
Performing Arts	15.1
Note: in billions	

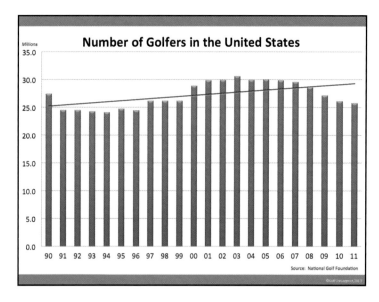

Golf currently attracts 25.7 million participants, according to the National Golf Foundation, as shown here. That represents that each participant would spend over $1,150 annually on the sport. One of the challenges with the sport is its cost, which narrows the potential market to those of financial means.

In examining the chart to the left, one would note a 3.3% decrease in the number of golfers. That downward trend has also been experienced internationally, as rounds are down 16% in Australia, 9% in Canada, 17% in Sweden, and 15% in the United Kingdom, as illustrated in the next figure.[11]

10 http://golf2020.com/media/31526/2011_golf_econ_exec_sum_sri_final_12.17.12 pdf, pg. 6.

11 National Golf Foundation, "Big Questions on Golf's Participation," April 2013, Slide 5.

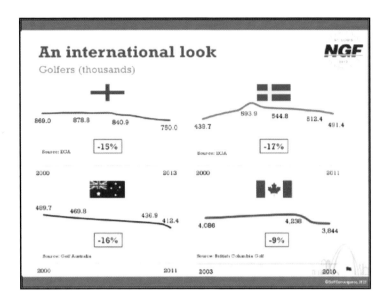

The National Sporting Goods Association undertakes research measuring data on the annual number of participants in each sport, the frequency of participation, total days of participation, and the mean (average) and median (midpoint) number of days of participation. This study is based on an online survey of more than 55,000 U.S. households, and it reflected the following participation in sports in the United States.[12]

Rank	Sports	Participants	Growth
1	Walking—Exercise	97.1	1.30%
2	Exercising with Equipment	55.5	0.30%
3	Swimming	46.0	−11.4%
4	Camping—Overnight	42.8	−4.3%
5	Aerobic Exercising	42.0	8.90%
6	Hiking	39.1	3.80%
7	Bicycle	39.1	−1.6%
8	Running/Jogging	38.7	8.90%
9	Bowling	34.9	−10.6%
10	Workout at Club	34.5	−4.8%
11	Weightlifting	29.1	−7.4%
12	Fishing—Fresh Water	28.0	−6.4%
13	Basketball	26.1	−2.9%
14	Yoga	21.6	6.90%

(Continued)

Rank	Sports	Participants	Growth
15	Golf	20.9	−4.3%
16	Billiards/Pool	20.0	−16.9%
17	Target Shooting	19.6	−1.2%
18	Boating—Motor/Power	16.7	−17.0%
19	Hunting with Firearms	16.4	0.60%
20	Soccer	13.9	3.00%
21	Tennis	13.1	7.00%
22	Baseball	12.3	−1.9%
23	Backpacking/Wilderness	11.6	3.70%
24	Table Tennis	10.9	−15.2%
25	Softball	10.4	−4.2%

Nearly all participant sports listed above golf have several things in common: They can be done individually, the cost of participation is low, the time required to participate is usually about 1 hour, and the activity bolsters the participants' personal physical fitness.

Is the Data Accurate?

It is interesting to note that the NSGA has identified 20.9 million as participants in golf compared to the National Golf Foundation benchmark of 25.7 million. Why the difference? There are several reasons, including the ages of those surveyed and the frequency of their participation.

But the variance identifies a larger problem that has some unintended consequences for the future of golf research. The National Golf Foundation (NGF), under the continued strong leadership of Dr. Joseph Beditz and Greg Nathan, takes its responsibility very seriously.

The NGF defines its role as

> "the most trusted source of information and insights on the business of golf. As the only trade association serving 4,000 members from all segments of the golf industry, NGF is a non-profit, objective and independent resource dedicated to supporting all the people, companies, facilities and associations that earn their living in golf."[13]

---

13 http://www.ngf.org/

Part-time pundits license the National Golf Foundation data, add their own mystical brews to the formulas, and then attack the NGF's work as inaccurate, inflated, and lacking independence. The only thing transparently clear about their musings is that they are the harbingers of doom, taking glee in their role as the nattering nabobs of negativism. Rather than providing clarity, they offer distortion through their contorted messages and constant attacks.

Such attacks are having a negative impact on golf research.

Over the past five years, we have observed that the National Golf Foundation has grown more conservative in the types of data that it publishes to the masses, at least partially due to withering, but often unfounded, criticism from some researchers who consider themselves direct competitors in NGF's space. As a result, I believe that NGF is narrowing, rather than expanding, the research information that is available to the broader industry. To illustrate, in 2012, the National Golf Foundation updated its national Golf Demand Model.

The task of assembling empirical data is really difficult. Respondents often inflate their responses on consumer surveys. Rather than indicating how much they actually played or spent, their responses are reflective of how they had intended to play or wished they had played. For instance, the NGF reported, based on consumer-reported data, that in 2011, 463 million rounds were played in the United States. But according to course-reported data, only 424 million rounds were played in the United States in 2011. Who is right? We can only assume that the numbers that are golf-course-reported are more accurate than are the consumer-reported data used.

Gathering data from golf courses became easier with the advent of golf management information reporting systems during the past decade. But though the accuracy of data is improved, its precision remains sorely lacking.

Thus, the NGF and other organizations reporting operating data and metrics are challenged because the underlying accuracy of the data they are collecting is, in some cases, highly suspect.

What is the solution? In an industry that lacks vital benchmarks, it would be far preferable if research studies identified the degree of confidence indices and margins of error. It would be far preferable, for example, to publish consumer spending if it was labeled 80% confidence with a 20% margin of error, rather than have no data at all. Wouldn't it be better to know that consumer spending was between $700 and $900 or $1,400 and $1,800 than to not have any benchmark at all? We believe so.

Busting a Myth

The industry at large believes that the source of golf's woes in the United States is attributable to the economy and to the fact that the supply of golf courses exceeds the demand. Viewed from a macroeconomic perspective for the country as a whole, that conclusion is correct, but within that "average," there are many deviations.

The chart below highlights golfers per 18 holes available and indicates when the industry may have undersupplied and oversupplied.

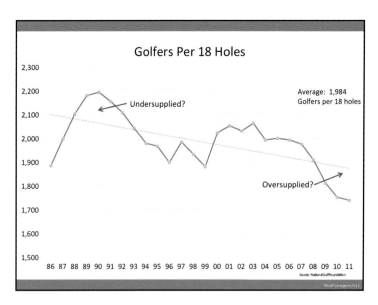

We are confident that a golf course operator sincerely believes that it is impossible for the golf industry to have ever been undersupplied. It is easy to side with that argument, since golf courses as a whole have historically operated at less than 60% of capacity. Hotels and airlines have utilization benchmarks at 80%, and the utilization of golf courses pales in comparison.

Examining the details of determining demand, the following are some industry benchmarks:

1. There are 1.4 golfers per household. The 18,334,168 golfing households in the United States form the basis for calculating that there are 25,667,835 golfers currently playing.

2. In the United States, 8.31% of the population plays golf. Interestingly, with the growth in the African American (1.3 million golfers), Asian American

(1.0 million golfers), and Hispanic American (3.1 million golfers) communities in the United States at a rate faster than the Caucasian segment (20.3 million golfers), golf participation in the United States is likely to continue to decrease for the foreseeable future.

3. Avid golfers represent 26.8% of all golfers. Thus, if there are 1,746 golfers per 18 holes, there are 468 avid golfers per 18 holes, 645 avid golfers per public facility, and 1,705 avid golfers per private facility in the United States.

Based on these statistics, many pundits feel that the golf market is oversupplied by more than 10%. The seriousness of the oversupply of golf courses in the United States is suggested by the following:

	Category	Number
Facilities	Golf Facilities	15,647
Rounds	Rounds Played—NGF Demand Model	424,447,967
	Rounds Played/Facility	27,126
Utilization Benchmarks	Current Utilization	48.00%
	Leisure Industry Benchmark	80.00%
	Excess Capacity	32.00%
Target Round	Target Rounds/Facility	35,807
Courses Required for Supply/Demand to Be Balanced	Number of Facilities Required	11,854
Excess Courses	Potential Excess Number of Facilities	3,793
Percent of Excess	Percent Exceed Number of Facilities Oversupplied	24.24%

While some may question whether it is operationally realistic for a course to achieve 80% of capacity every playable day, clearly, to some extent, there are simply too many golf courses in the United States for all of them to be financially vibrant.

But here is the rub—not every golf market is oversupplied by the same measure. The extent to which the golf market in a major metropolitan market is possibly oversupplied would be far different than that measure in a rural part of the United States. To presume an equal distribution of golfers in relationship to the supply in each market would be fallacious.

In actuality, if examining the number of golfers within the major metropolitan markets compared to the number of golf courses, you might conclude that the Top 100 core-based statistical areas in the United States are vastly under-supplied, as illustrated below:

	Nation	Top 100 Core Based Statistical Areas (CBSA)	% in Top 100 CBSA	Remaining USA	% in Non–Top 100 CBSA
Households	18,334,168	12,017,942	65.55%	6,316,226	34.24%
Rounds	424,452,832	251,382,304	59.23%	173,070,528	41.85%
Rounds per Household	23.15	20.92		27.40	
Courses	15,647	7,202	46.10%	8,475	53.90%
Rounds/Course	27,075	34,912		20,415	
Golfers > Courses			19.45%		−19.45%

It is hard to believe that although 65.55% of all golfing households live within the Top 100 core-based statistical areas in the United States, only 46.10% of the nation's golf courses are located in those areas. The Top 100 core-based statistical areas are shown in the following figure.

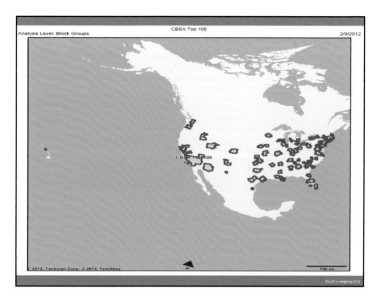

This is where a trap lies for the researcher and author. An irresponsible journalist will take one statistic out of context, blow it out of proportion, and challenge all of the findings, when merely one statistic is paradoxical.

The quote that would be taken out of context would be "Golf in the Top 100 core-based statistical areas is undersupplied by 19.45%." No one in the industry would present that fact as truth for many reasons, including self-denial and also because they may realize to some extent that their course's economic underperformance is attributable to management and not to uncontrollable factors. The journalist would become culpable by implying that the author was calling for more new course construction.

Such is not the case here. What it does mean is that golf courses located within the Top 100 CBSA might have more price flexibility than has been historically perceived. If a golf course were to raise its rates, golfers in a densely populated market would have fewer courses to choose from; thus, course revenues are likely to rise.

What about the reverse, when those non–Top 100 CBSA would be considered to be oversupplied by 19.45%?

One management company executive, when presented with this fact, wrote, "I'm not sure on the value an operator would put on it. A smart one would put the product to good use and create more value. The average knucklehead won't use it and will perceive the data point regarding oversupply as having low value."

My perspective is different. In a market that is overcrowded, it becomes increasingly hard to differentiate, as price often becomes a dominant factor that seduces the owners into believing that volume of rounds, not yield per round, is more important. Such markets fall prey to third-party providers which builds their success, in my opinion, on a recession, and on desperate inferior providers seeking some revenue stream to stay afloat.

Thus, the golf operators who emphasize volume over yield per round have a flawed concept.

In buying or selling a golf course, a premium might be associated with a course in a densely populated area beyond the normal revenue multiple, and a high discount will probably be accorded a course in a less populated area; its ability to produce a superior experience becomes challenged by a small potential revenue base.

Reading the Tea Leaves

If we analyze each state (50), core-based statistical area (942), and counties (3,144) in the United States, some interesting insights are revealed.

States Where Demand for Golf Is Strong Compared to Supply

State	Golfing Households	Total Golfers	Avid Golfers	Rounds Played	Total Facilities	Facilities Suggested at 468 Avid Golfers/Facility	Under Supplied (?)
California	1,674,214	2,343,900	628,165	23,180,548	918	1,342	424
Texas	1,235,578	1,729,809	463,589	26,805,772	796	991	195
New Jersey	459,641	643,497	172,457	6,927,721	290	368	78
New York	1,095,389	1,533,545	410,990	19,470,492	820	878	58
Illinois	882,734	1,235,828	331,202	16,626,776	658	708	50
Virginia	457,665	640,731	171,716	8,819,089	327	367	40
Colorado	334,659	468,523	125,564	8,269,781	240	268	28
Washington	378,910	530,474	142,167	8,004,083	278	304	26
Nevada	149,656	209,518	56,151	3,484,903	95	120	25
Utah	175,317	245,444	65,779	4,116,975	118	141	23

Source: National Golf Foundation
©Golf Convergence 2013

This analysis suggests that the demand for golf is very healthy, in relationship to the supply of golf courses, in the figure to the left.

The top five markets where demand is strong have some of the largest population centers in the United States. It is intuitive that landlocked locations like Los Angeles, San Francisco, the New York metropolitan area, Chicago, and Washington D.C., where urban construction of golf courses is highly unlikely due to the value of real estate, would reflect strength. The sheer masses, though they may play less frequently than avid golfers, should bolster the average number of rounds per year.

Golf course owners in California, Texas, New Jersey, New York, Illinois, Virginia, and Colorado have a competitive edge over their peers nationally. Because of the number of golfers available per facility, they have a "margin on error" in operating their facilities. They have the advantage of greater price flexibility, and they probably can get away with offering a less attractive experience than those in other areas of the country because demand is higher.

States Where Demand for Golf Is Weak Compared to Supply

State	Golfing Households	Total Golfers	Avid Golfers	Rounds Played	Total Facilities	Facilities Suggested at 468 Avid Golfers/Facility	Over Supplied (?)
Iowa	268,038	375,253	100,568	8,132,700	398	215	-183
Michigan	816,484	1,143,078	306,345	21,562,540	811	655	-156
Kansas	181,930	254,702	68,260	5,103,218	250	146	-104
Nebraska	155,509	217,713	58,347	4,536,421	219	125	-94
Arkansas	129,607	181,450	48,629	4,414,403	189	104	-85
Minnesota	479,799	671,719	180,021	11,481,272	469	385	-84
South Carolina	337,226	472,116	126,527	10,532,085	352	270	-82
Maine	77,590	108,626	29,112	2,038,437	143	62	-81
Pennsylvania	745,509	1,043,713	279,715	15,822,417	674	598	-76
North Dakota	49,998	69,997	18,759	2,100,350	115	40	-75
South Dakota	57,236	80,130	21,475	2,302,903	118	46	-72
Wisconsin	538,138	753,393	201,909	12,268,295	498	431	-67
Kentucky	258,292	361,609	96,911	7,033,151	268	207	-61
North Carolina	595,894	834,252	223,579	15,820,100	534	478	-56
Oklahoma	184,840	258,776	69,352	4,826,718	203	148	-55

Source: National Golf Foundation
©Golf Convergence 2013

But what about where demand for golf is weak compared to supply? As shown in the figure to the left, the following states would appear to present challenges to even the skilled golf course operator.

Iowa leads the nation in 9-hole facilities. Michigan

(819 courses), considering its limited playing season of less than 200 playable days, has long been branded as a summer tourist destination and regarded as an anomaly, with the fourth most golf courses in the country, after Florida (1,049), California (918), and New York (820).

Then why would so many courses have been built in Michigan? Interestingly, golf in the summer is viewed as alternative to ice hockey in the winter.

These numbers serve as interesting fodder for thought and beg the question of whether the analysis can be extended to individual core-based statistical areas or counties.

In examining the demand for golf by core statistical area, the numbers do appear highly consistent, as reflected in the table to the right.

The rounds per facility far exceed the national average of 27,126.

Where demand for golf is weak is reflected in the second table to the right.

Five of the first six markets (Naples, Cape Coral, Myrtle Beach, Hilton Head Island, and Port St. Lucie) have one thing in common—they are popular tourist destinations in the United States.

While the National Golf Foundation demand models consider seasonal household and seasonal rounds played, tourist data need to be integrated to obtain a more accurate reflection of

Statistical Areas Where Demand for Golf Is Strong

Geography Name	Total Golfers	Rounds Played	Rounds Per Golfer	Total facilities	Rounds Per Facility	Demand based on 468 Avid Golfers per facility	Under Supplied (?)
New York-Northern New Jersey-Long Island	1,362,206	15,324,936	11.25	409	37,469	780.07	371.07
Los Angeles-Long Beach-Santa Ana	739,262	6,831,875	9.24	161	42,434	423.34	262.34
Chicago-Joliet-Naperville	929,890	12,291,695	13.22	346	35,525	532.5	186.50
Dallas-Fort Worth-Arlington	486,569	6,913,036	14.21	155	44,600	278.63	123.63
Houston-Sugar Land-Baytown	429,320	6,318,651	14.72	124	50,957	245.85	121.85
San Francisco-Oakland-Fremont	325,846	3,102,641	9.52	79	39,274	186.6	107.60
Detroit-Warren-Livonia	504,571	8,772,319	17.39	192	45,689	288.94	96.94
Washington-Arlington-Alexandria	425,383	5,346,947	12.57	147	36,374	243.6	96.60
Philadelphia-Camden-Wilmington	486,347	6,437,981	13.24	192	33,531	278.51	86.51
Seattle-Tacoma-Bellevue	291,522	4,041,705	13.86	88	45,928	166.94	78.94

Source: National Golf Foundation
©Golf Convergence 2013

Statistical Areas Where Demand for Golf Is Weak

Geography Name	Total Golfers	Rounds Played	Rounds Per Golfer	Total facilities	Rounds Per Facility	Demand based on 468 Avid Golfers per facility	Over Supplied (?)
Naples-Marco Island	40,573	1,420,216	35	72	19,725	23	-48.77
Cape Coral-Fort Myers	71,165	2,334,617	33	79	29,552	41	-38.25
Myrtle Beach-North Myrtle Beach-Conway	32,775	1,206,500	37	55	21,936	19	-36.23
Riverside-San Bernardino-Ontario	242,182	2,591,363	11	174	14,893	139	-35.31
Hilton Head Island-Beaufort	28,679	916,509	32	51	17,971	16	-34.58
Port St. Lucie	44,929	1,310,723	29	57	22,995	26	-31.27
Pittsburgh	209,016	3,233,094	15	149	21,699	120	-29.31
Syracuse	67,234	895,480	13	66	13,568	39	-27.50
Rochester	98,790	1,296,550	13	82	15,812	57	-25.43
Utica-Rome	29,359	462,543	16	40	11,564	17	-23.19

Source: National Golf Foundation
©Golf Convergence 2013

each market's economic potential for golf. The impact of tourists on a market is based on occupancy rates times room nights times estimated golf participation.

Differentiating between import markets (e.g., Myrtle Beach) vs. export markets (e.g., northern US which exports a lot of rounds to warm weather clients during the winter) is important to truly measure demand.

However, if I were managing a course in Pittsburgh, Syracuse, Rochester, or Utica-Rome, I would have serious concerns regarding the economic viability of the facility. The potential in these markets to operate a successful high-end daily fee course at rates above national averages would be slim. A detailed geographic local market analysis (Chapter 5) would be appropriate to determine each course's unique niche and the brand position that might be successful.

For those in states where few golfers per facility reside or where rounds are dominant, the alternatives become a series of non-capital intensive programs:

- Heavy player development programs
- Heavy lesson programs
- First Tee programs
- Aggressive practice facility programs
- Aggressive F&B programs
- Aggressive loyalty programs
- 9-hole leagues
- Leveraging social media through a well-executed customer relationship management system.

But in the end, give me location. And if you can't make money in the Top 100 core-based statistical areas, the reason isn't likely the economy or the weather, but the course's management team and its inability to consistently execute and provide a value-based experience to the golfers.

The Future of Golf: When Will Demand Equal Supply

One of the statistics that constantly amazes is the annual turnover in individuals who participate in golf. Presented on the next page is a chart reflecting that 3.9 million golfers (14.9%) departed the sport between 2010 and 2011.[14]

14 NGF, "State of the Industry," April 2012, Slide 3.

This chart, presented annually at the National Golf Foundation Symposium, always surprises, as it reflects the high number of individuals coming into and departing the game.

During the 2012 Symposium, Dr. Beditz, President and Chief Executive Officer of the NGF, said that there are 21 million people who have played golf at some time during their lives but

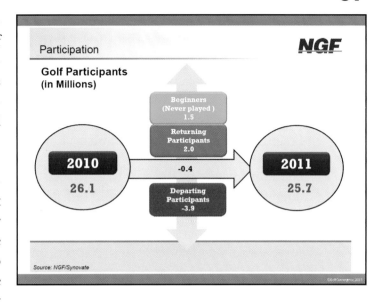

have not in the last two years. Of those, Dr. Beditz stated, "About two-thirds were never really committed to the game. Most never played 10 rounds of golf (ever). They were not golfers. About 1/3rd were committed golfers, but most were NOT in the Hooked or Golf Nut category. We don't lose those (hooked or golf nuts) people very often."[15]

In 2010, the NGF forecast that the game was likely to grow to 30 million golfers by 2020 and that they are likely to come principally from population growth. It was also forecast that "most of the growth would result from high income/high participation rate clusters and that rounds would increase by 73 million due to the increase the number of golfers and the aging of the population."[16]

For this to occur, emphasis must be placed on the core golfer's social network as a foundation to grow the game.

For the Game to Thrive

Trends in the sport that foretell more women, younger players, and the acceptance of shorter rounds as the norm should be healthy indications for a successful future. The game of golf must appeal to women, younger players, and offer a faster alternative to the 5-hour rounds that have become the standard. Time is such a precious commodity in our electronically connected world.

---

15 NGF, "Attraction and Attraction," May 2012, Slide 4.

16 NGF, "State of the Golf Industry," May 2012, Slide 35.

Architecturally, shorter is better than longer, easier is preferred over hard, brown must become the new green, and firm must be the new fast. The luscious mannered courses featured weekly on the TV should become the exception—not the rule. Why can't the golf courses in the United States be maintained consistent with the scruffy and ragged standards experienced in the United Kingdom? Why does a golf course in the United States need to spend in excess of $1.0 million on maintenance? Why can't a golfer take 3½ hours to play 18 holes?

The lessons taught by the industry's international peers must be incorporated into our domestic mantra if the golf industry is going to thrive.

Who has the primary responsibility to introduce these changes? While golf course owners and industry associations understand and endorse the need for these changes, how will the change come about? Through educating the consumers. The editorial staff of golf's leading consumer magazines (i.e., *Golf Magazine*, *Golf Digest*, *Golfweek*, and *Links*) must collectively unite and redefine the game in the public golfer's mind.

Further, those magazines and the luscious photos of perfectly maintained golf courses define the game of golf in the minds of U.S. consumers. Changing the message and providing the justification will begin the modifications needed for the game to grow.

Path to Success

1) Determine, based on your facility's location, whether your market is over- or undersupplied within 10-, 20-, and 30-minute drive times to your golf course. The National Golf Foundation and Golf Convergence can help you complete this step.

2) Measure the turnover of your customers through analysis of reports with your POS system.

3) If you are located in a top 100 core-based statistical area, evaluate if you have the leverage to increase your rates.

4) For those golf courses located in less populated areas, understanding the value provided to the consumer in relationship to the price charged will be fundamental to the facility's profitability.

Concluding Thought

It is impossible to begin to learn that which one thinks one already knows.

Epictetus

Chapter 3

The Players
Associations and Equipment Manufacturers

If you cannot find the truth right where you are,
where else do you expect to find it?

Dogen Zenji

There are no absolute truths in this world.

Eddie Ainsworth, Executive Director,
Colorado PGA Section

Chapter Highlights

The golf industry is segmented into three sectors: the game of golf, the business of golf, and the media, principally television entertainment. The distinctions, while very clear, often become confused as the plethora of associations, golf courses, and companies jockey for space within the arena of golf. Many have morphed from the purpose for which they were formed to become diverse organizations operating within at least two sectors.

Thus, some take umbrage when pronouncements from associations (such as defining the game of golf) have the potential to be detrimental to other areas of the game (such as the business of golf).

The purpose of this chapter is to review how associations and equipment manufacturers help or sometimes hinder, however unintended, the business of golf.

The chapter concludes with a holistic view of how the business of golf might be better served by associations and equipment manufacturers being faithful to their primary mission while adopting a more collegial approach to the accomplishment of their objectives.

Can You Separate the Game of Golf from the Business of Golf?

What purpose would it serve if there were rules to define a game and no one played? What would happen if golf courses were built and no one came because engaging in the activity wasn't fun? Would anyone choose to participate if the tools of the game, the equipment, didn't enhance their ability to play the game?

Do we take for granted that people will always want to play golf? Perhaps so.

What is more important? Should we protect the history of game founded over 450 years ago as perceived by today's historically sensitive golfers? Or should we allow the game to evolve based on a changing society's desire for recreation? And, as in every other major sport, should there be a set of guidelines for the professionals and a different set of guidelines for amateurs. There is no clear agreement on this matter, but the enjoyment of many and the financial fortunes of some are dependent on the results of the debate.

At its core, if people are engaged in an activity that doesn't serve their self-interest, whether it is a competitive activity that serves as a barometer of their ability or a way to foster social connections with family, friends, and associates, they will not continue to do it for long.

The actual origins of golf can be traced

> "to a region in eastern Scotland known as the Kingdom of Fife in the early 1400s. The ball was a pebble, and players used existing dunes and rugged terrain as their courses.
>
> Handcrafted clubs and balls followed, and by the middle of the 15th century, golf was so popular in Scotland, King James II had to outlaw the sport to get the men of Scotland ready for an impending battle with England.
>
> In the 16th century, golf's popularity spread in England thanks to the support of King Charles I. Mary Queen of Scots helped spread the popularity in France during her studies there. In Belgium, where a similar game had been played for centuries, golf also exploded in popularity.
>
> Golf would soon become a more organized activity. In 1744, the Gentlemen Golfers of Leith, an area in the northern section

of Edinburgh, formed the first golf club to promote an annual competition.

St. Andrews, often incorrectly credited as being the birthplace of golf, became in many ways a symbolic home for golf. After Leith's rules, the Society of St. Andrews Golfers was formed, with its own rules and a tournament to crown it champion."[1]

This society morphed over time to become The Royal and Ancient Golf Club of St. Andrews.

From those meager beginnings, golf is now enjoyed by over 60 million people worldwide. As the game evolved, associations were formed to foster and aid the growth of the game.

Some associations were formed to define the rules of the game; these included The Royal and Ancient (1754) and the United States Golf Association (1895). Like the clubs formed at Leith and St. Andrews, state and golf associations in countries around the world were formed to crown champions. Some were "open competitions," and others narrowed the competition by gender, age, or ability; hence, the need for the formulation of a handicap system.

The game of golf comprises "hitting a ball that weighs no more than 1.620 ounces (45.93 grams) with a diameter not less than 1.680 inches (42.67 mm), performing within specified velocity, distance, and symmetry limits into a series of 18-holes, 4¼ inches wide over varying terrain with obstacles created by nature and by humans."[2]

And then there is the business of golf. The business of golf would be defined as the sale of "anything" related to the game of golf, such as memberships, green fees, cart rental, equipment, merchandise, food and beverage, etc.

To serve the business of golf, numerous associations have emerged in the United States. They are a $2 billion sector of the $68 billion golf industry.

Currently, most of the associations that serve the business of golf have one thing in common: Education of their members to ensure that their segment of the industry, whether designing and engineering, maintenance, operations, or management, is well served. The chart that follows might symbolize the organizational chart for the golf industry.

---

1 http://www.golflink.com/facts_5034_was-golf-invented.html

2 http://en.wikipedia.org/wiki/Golf_ball

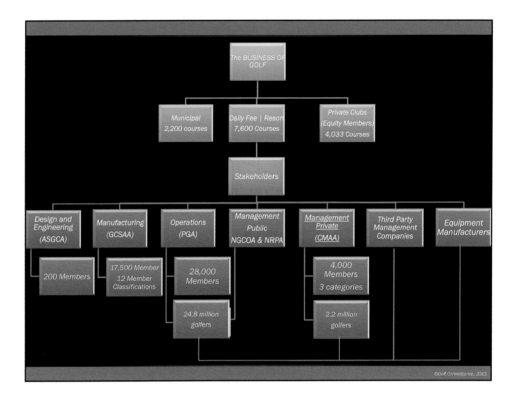

The game of golf and the business of golf have one thing in common—active participants: 25.7 million in the United States.

But there is a third equally influential component that generates over $2 billion for the golf industry—watching the game of golf. Entertainment is big business, as illustrated in the golf industry cocktail in the following figure.

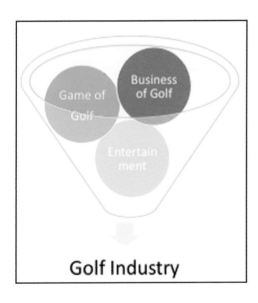

Golf Industry

It is estimated that as many people watch golf on television as play the game. For the individuals who watch, golf serves simply as entertainment. The PGA Tour, the LPGA Tour, and the USGA are the principal associations focused on filling this niche.

Industries are formed and evolve to serve consumers. There isn't an industry (manufacturing, travel, information services) that is led with a uniform vision. All industries exist through the invisible hand of capitalism, where the ebb and flow of individual self-interests compete against the welfare of the community in the aggregate.

Such is also the case within the golf industry—the lack of a unified vision. Creating a consensus as to what serves the mutual welfare between the game of golf, the business of golf, and golf as an entertainment product would be difficult to achieve.

Every major professional sport from the National Football League to Major League Baseball to the National Basketball Association all have one thing in common—a commissioner who balances the interests of the owners, the players, and the fans. Rules are changed annually based on reviews by the competition or the rules committees to ensure player safety, equity, and fan enjoyment.

This provides a topic for debate as to how the game of golf and the business of golf can complement each other's interests. Should there be a Commissioner for Amateur Golf? While shattering many historical traditions and vexing in its implementation, it raises the point of how the professional game that serves principally as an entertainment vehicle should control an amateur game that is largely social.

Until that riddle is solved, the business of golf will suffer.

Interestingly, the growing importance of entertainment caused a schism within the PGA. It was reported that

> "With an increase of revenue in the late 1960s due to expanded television coverage, a dispute arose between the touring professionals and the PGA of America on how to distribute the windfall. The tour players wanted larger purses, while the PGA desired the money to go to the general fund to help grow the game at the local level. Following the final major in July 1968, the PGA Championship, several leading tour pros voiced their dissatisfaction with the venue and the abundance of club pros in the field. The increased friction resulted in a new entity in August, what would eventually become the PGA Tour. Tournament players formed their own organization, American Professional Golfers, Inc. (APG), independent of the PGA of America.
>
> After several months, a compromise was reached in December: the tour players agreed to abolish the APG and form the PGA 'Tournament Players Division,' a fully autonomous division under the supervision of a new 10-member Tournament Policy Board. The board consisted of four tour players, three PGA of America executives, and three outside members, initially business executives.

Joseph Dey, the recently retired USGA executive director, was selected by the board as the tour's first commissioner in January 1969, and he agreed to a five-year contract. He was succeeded by tour player Deane Beman in early 1974, who served for 20 years. The name officially changed to the 'PGA Tour' in 1975."[3]

The Professional Golfers Association of America (PGA) and the PGA Tour are two separate organizations.

The PGA with 22,654 male and 847 female members continues to evolve. For example, the PGA has continued to discuss with Turner Broadcasting, a national tee time reservation system.

The Ladies Professional Golf Association (LPGA), with 1,400 members, also has evolved from its roots in 1950 as a playing tour for the finest women professionals "into a non-profit organization involved in every facet of golf. The LPGA Tour and the LPGA Teaching & Club Professionals (T&CP) comprise the backbone of what has become the premier women's professional sports organization in the world today. The LPGA maintains a strong focus on charity through its tournaments; its grassroots junior and women's programs; its affiliation with Susan G. Komen for the Cure; and the formation of The LPGA Foundation."[4]

The USGA, "golf's governing body"[5] has evolved also. From its promise to "preserve its past, foster its future, and champion its best interests for everyone who enjoys the game,"[6] the USGA conducts amateur and open championships that generate substantial revenue and provide great entertainment. It offers a handicapping system that affiliated golf course owners and PGA pros administer. It also provides guidance to golf course owners through its green section, spending $5.7 million, and it tests equipment to ensure compliance with the rules.

Associations have evolved based on self-interest. But they have evolved citing a common mantra, "for the good of the game." That begs the questions, "Good for whom?" and "How do golf course owners protect their investment in this industry from the associations that exist within it?"

---

3 http://en.wikipedia.org/wiki/PGA_Tour

4 http://www.lpga.com/corporate/ladies-golf/about-the-lpga.aspx

5 http://www.usga.org/about_usga/mission/Mission/

6 Ibid.

Who Are the Real Players?

If there is any lesson to be learned by the golf course owner, though we all preach the values of the recreational aspects of the game, truthfully, within the golf industry, money = power and power = influence.

The following table presents the industry's principal trade associations, their roles, and a financial snapshot of their operations.

Association	Role	Date	Assets	Fund Balance	Revenue	Expenses
PGA Tour	Entertain	December 31, 2010	$1,558,426,506	$663,561,519	$897,204,399	$870,721,883
PGA of America	Educate, Entertain	June 30, 2011	304,306,444	274,487,301	93,458,805	78,643,768
United States Golf Association	Define the game, Entertain	November 30, 2011	300,810,069	237,215,705	155,074,841	121,780,178
World Golf Foundation	Support industry initiatives	December 31, 2010	46,764,472	−884,172	31,683,418	30,958,506
Ladies Professional Golf Association	Entertain	December 31, 2010	39,453,603	7,332,367	73,688,161	72,367,546
Royal Canadian Golf Association	Define the game, Entertain	October 31, 2011	34,588,584	29,380,433	31,383,010	32,976,943
Golf Course Superintendents Association of America	Manufacture, Educate Agronomists	December 31, 2011	18,587,499	11,011,744	12,267,555	12,518,034
National Recreation and Park Association	Educate	June 30, 2011	11,397,871	5,092,051	11,620,730	12,961,677
National Golf Foundation	Research	December 31, 2010	4,498,501	4,056,962	1,698,917	1,430,965
Scottish Golf Union	Entertain, Educate	September 30, 2012	4,069,752	2,294,978	4,069,752	4,169,269
National Golf Course Owners Association	Educate Owners	May 31, 2010	3,436,189	2,008,510	1,578,296	1,796,740
Club Managers Association of America	Educate Private Club Managers	October 31, 2011	3,340,508	-1,316,889	8,338,207	8,370,827

Source: The financial data for all associations were obtained from http://www.guidestar.org, except for the Royal Canadian Golf Association, which were sourced at http://www.rcga.org.

Note that many of the associations, such as the PGA and the USGA, post their financial statements on their respective Web sites. Those financial statements show a far greater financial strength than other sources, because investments and other non-operating income are included in those statements. To illustrate, the PGA of America, for the year ending June 30, 2011, shows total income of $155,973,000, contrasted to the $93,458,805 posted on GuideStar.

The financial performance of the PGA Tour, the PGA of America, the USGA, the LPGA, and even the Royal Canadian Golf Association (due to its sale of Glen Abbey Golf Club) are impressive. However, from the financial statements available for download on the Guidestar web site, it appears that the World Golf Foundation and the Club Managers Association of America are financially challenged, with negative fund balances of $884,172 and $1.3 million, respectively. That possible financial predicament is of note.

All of these numbers are inconsequential compared to the financial performance of some equipment manufacturers. TaylorMade-Adidas Golf reported net sales of $1.38 billion,[7] while Fila Korea (Titleist) reported revenue of $1.24 billion, of which 50% was from outside the United States.[8]

How Do We Simultaneously Protect the Game and Grow the Business?

The hypothesis of this chapter is that the business of golf is directly influenced by associations, particularly the R&A and the USGA. The rules that define the game and the equipment that is allowed directly impact all other sectors of the industry.

What support is there for the truth of this hypothesis?

On January 25, 2013, at the PGA Merchandise Show, a panel of industry leaders debated what will be required for the game of golf to grow. The panel included PGA of America President Ted Bishop, PGA TOUR Commissioner Tim Finchem, TaylorMade-Adidas Golf President and CEO Mark King, *Golf Digest* Chairman and Editor-in-Chief Jerry Tarde, National Golf Foundation President

7 http://adidas-group.corporate-publications.com/2011/gb/en/group-management-report-our-group/other-businesses-strategy/taylormade-adidas-golf-strategy.html

8 http://www.reuters.com/article/2011/05/20/us-fila-fortunebrands-idUSTRE74J2O520110520

and CEO Joe Beditz, LPGA Tour Commissioner Michael Whan, Dottie Pepper, newly appointed member of The PGA of America Board of Directors, European Ryder Cup Director Richard Hills, and Golf Channel President Mike McCarley.

Their discussion was dominated by the following topics: the experience of golf is not fun for a non-core golfer, the industry's focus on history rather than natural progression, the accelerating cost of water and why green must become brown and conditioning must become shaggy, latent demand, and bifurcation of the rules.

In frustration, Mark King indicated that the group should decide now what is in the best interest of the industry at large and implement those changes. King clearly and correctly has his sights on what makes business economically successful—satisfied customers.

Obviously there is a national concern for growth of the game.

As Michael Hughes, Executive Director of the National Golf Course Owners Association, wrote in the January 2013 edition of *Golf Business*,

> "Few in the industry would argue [against the fact] that one of the primary roles of the USGA is to protect and preserve the game. However, quite a few—namely those whose livelihoods depend on golfers enjoying their playing experiences—would contend that the USGA has become so focused on this particular aspect of its charge that the organization might be missing the bigger picture. If nothing else, it begs the question: Who are you protecting the game for—the golfer of yesterday, today, or tomorrow? It certainly seems that growing the game and keeping it relevant for more people substantially increases the chances that golf will thrive in the future rather than becoming an anachronism. Isn't that preservation in its most basic form?

> Think about it. The golf consumer has changed dramatically in recent years, and all indications are that this evolution will continue and even accelerate. Golfers gave gotten younger, and they're looking for more family-oriented offerings from their clubs. Women and minorities have also emerged as prominent and influential customer segments, and what they look for in a golf experience is vastly different than what the 'traditional' golfer seeks. Most course operators can see this clearly because they experience it every day when they open their doors. Do golf's governing bodies fail to recognize this?

Shortly after the USGA and the R&A announced their proposed ruling against anchored putters, the PGA of America publicly asked the groups to reconsider. I applaud them for the effort. As an organization, the PGA has made growing the game its highest priority because they're well aware that, as an industry, we can ill afford to run people out of the game.

The fact of the matter is people have an almost infinite number of leisure activities to choose from for themselves and their families. There's ample data to prove that the vast majority of people—especially those in the generations following the baby boomers and also women—play golf simply to have fun, not to compete.

Regardless of the ultimate impact of the ruling, it should serve as something of a wakeup call for the industry. Perhaps it's time we seriously consider a separate set of rules (or an addendum, if you will) for the tiny slice of golfers who play for money and high-level competition and the rest of us. In other words, maybe it's time to get real."[9]

These sentiments were echoed by Ted Bishop at the PGA Business seminar. And *Golfweek* writer, Alex Miceli reported the following:

"When PGA Tour commissioner Tim Finchem brought up bifurcation in a news conference two weeks ago at the Farmers Insurance Open in San Diego, it was because a **majority of the Player Advisory Council showed interest in controlling the professional game** [emphasis added].

On January 25, The PGA of America surveyed its members for their opinions on the possibility of two sets of rules in the game: one for professionals and elite amateurs and another for the rest of us. A slim majority of the club professionals oppose bifurcation, according to the results. Of 3,155 respondents sampled, 53 percent support one set of rules for all golfers.

The survey results contrast with the association's survey on the proposed ban on the anchoring stroke. That initiative was conducted in November, before the U.S. Golf Association and the R&A

---

9 NGCOA, "Golf Business," January 2013, pg. 4.

made public their recommendation to ban the stroke commonly associated with long and belly putters. In that survey, nearly **two-thirds of the 4,228 PGA professionals who responded opposed a change in the Rules of Golf that would ban anchoring** [emphasis added]."[10]

It Is Not About Bifurcation

Everyone may be missing the point. Golf already has bifurcation in nearly every aspect of the game, except for equipment, and even that line has gotten blurry, with different rules for professionals and amateurs with respect to grooves on wedges and the timetable for the forthcoming ban on anchored putters.

On Golf Channel's annual "State of the Game" presented on February 22, 2012, at the Accenture Match Play Championship, moderated by Dan Hicks, a panel comprised of Nick Faldo, Johnny Miller, Brandel Chamblee and Frank Nobilo, all former Players on the PGA TOUR and now analysts on the Golf Channel, discussed bifurcation. An article by Martin Kaufman of *Golfweek* summarized the discussion as follows:

> "Most of the panel sided with the U.S. Golf Association's one-set-of-rules stance. Miller compared bifurcation to 'changing the Constitution for one state like Texas.'
>
> Nobilo trotted out a familiar bogeyman. 'This used to be a manufacturer-supported game,' he said. 'It's now a manufacturer-driven game. So when you talk about the spirit of the game, we have deviated. The talk of bifurcation is so dangerous to the game.'
>
> Leave it to Chamblee, the iconoclast, to make an expansive case for bifurcation.
>
> 'People say that the best thing about golf is that it's governed by one set of rules. That's an opinion, it's not a fact,' Chamblee said. 'The fact is that golf is flat, growth is flat; the fact is that golf is too expensive, takes too long, it's too elitist and it's too complicated.' (Camera cuts to Faldo frowning.)

---

10 http://golfweek.com/news/2013/feb/06/pga-survey-most-club-pros-oppose-two-sets-rules/

'In one fell swoop, if you had bifurcation at the professional level, you could roll golf equipment back, you could roll the COR back, the co-efficient of restitution back, you could disallow the anchored putter. You could allow all of those things at the amateur level, you could shrink golf courses back to two decades ago, you make golf cheaper, you make it faster. And I promise you, nobody quits golf because two different sets of rules govern it. But lots of people will come to the game because they're allowed to play with equipment that makes it more fun.'"[11]

In a Google consumer survey, 73% of golfers admit to not following USGA rules, and 63% of golfers consider playing with non-conforming equipment. Of the 26 million golfers, less than 5 million maintain a USGA handicap.[12]

Of the nearly 467 million rounds of golf played in 2011, perhaps over 90% of those are not played in accordance with the precise rules of golf. Local rules, mulligans, putts given, incorrect drops taken, playing the desert as a lateral hazard taking a one-stroke and distance penalty rather than the one-stroke and distance penalties, etc.; the list of daily transgressions that occur on a golf course is long.

And who has been hurt by these transgressions? No one. While tradition is a nice accoutrement of the golf experience, balancing tradition with commercial common sense seems appropriate.

What seems well established is that the USGA is focused exclusively on the game and cares little for the business of golf and the livelihood of the industry at large. That may be its charter, but does it serve the $68 billion industry well?

Perhaps not. The recently appointed Sheila Johnson, the 63-year-old co-founder of Black Entertainment Television who became the first African American woman elected to the 15-member USGA executive committee, stated,

"We have so many groups, women and people of color who love golf, but aren't feeling included inside this bubble," Johnson said. "We

11 http://golfweek.com/news/2013/feb/23/chamblee-nobilo-spark-state-game-panel/

12 NGCOA, Golf Business, January 2013, pg. 50.

need to start a whole p.r. marketing campaign to let people know that we want to be inclusive rather than exclusive.

It's got to be talked about through the media, through the USGA, the PGA Tour and The PGA of America that we need more people of color on television other than Tiger. We need to see more people of color in the anchoring booth. We need to see more people of color in the galleries."[13]

She continued:

"Golf is now in a real transitional situation in the sense that rounds have gone down, and this is now the time to rethink the game in terms of how we are going to bring the recreational golfer back to resorts."[14]

With only 85 African American PGA members out of a 26,000 membership base including apprentices, it is time that those who proclaim the role of "golf's governing body" redefine the game to be more reflective of the population.

Is it time for change? Should non-profit associations be governing a for-profit industry? The real question is, "What recreational experience should the golf industry create that will be compelling for today's golfers, and more importantly, for tomorrow's golfers, who we can hope will be of more varying genders, ages, and ethnicities than those who play today?"

In a survey conducted in the Spring of 2013, golf industry leaders were polled. Joe Beditz, President & CEO, National Golf Foundation; Brandel Chamblee, Golf Channel Commentator; Tom Doak, Golf Course Architect; Pete Dye, Golf Course Architect; Sir Nick Faldo, Hall of Fame Golfer and CBS Golf Analyst; Tim Finchem, Commissioner, PGA Tour; Mark King, President and CEO, TaylorMade-Adidas Golf; Greg Norman, Hall of Fame Golfer; and Gary Player, Hall of Fame Golfer; all of these experts in their fields were supportive of one set of guidelines for professionals (equipment, balls, rules) and another set for amateurs.[15]

---

13 http://espn.go.com/golf/story/_/id/8965988/sheila-johnson-poised-play-key-role-golf-member-usga-executive-committee

14 Ibid.

15 LinksMagazine.com, "Bifurcation: Yes, No, and Maybe," Spring 2013, pg. 74.

The golf industry, via the leadership within the associations, is introducing new concepts regarding the business of golf at a glacier pace. Incremental or revolutionary changes that would shake up the status quo are met with great resistance by current leaders within the industry who believe they have the only solutions. The game of golf has many exclusive clubs; so does the business of golf. Golf, which should respect tradition, nonetheless needs to re-invent the game to appeal to today's society.

There Are Great Changes Blowing in the Wind, Led by ...

While it is easy to rail negatively to highlight the challenges that currently exist, it is more important to hail those who may, for the first time, be breaking the mold and bringing about the change necessary to sustain the business of golf. Perhaps a benefit of the recession is that the industry is realizing that the time for action is now.

In 2012, Ted Bishop was elected President of The PGA of America, Peter Bevacqua was hired as the Chief Executive Officer, and Daryl Crall was designated the Chief Operating Officer.

Collectively, I am thinking that they aren't going to be taking any prisoners, as the expression goes. The organization maybe about to undergo a 180-degree change in direction. To illustrate, the PGA has spoken against the USGA's position of banning anchored putters. Wisely, PGA members were polled. Changes at the Executive level are already occurring.

For the first time, some of the directors of the 41 sections feel the channel of communication within the PGA is now up rather than down. PGA members are beginning to feel they are being listened to rather than dictated to.

These changes have been reflected during the past two years in numerous PGA growth-of-the-game initiatives; Golf 2.0, Get Golf Ready, Tee It Forward, PGA PerformanceTrak, and other programs. The PGA may allow its Get Golf Ready program to be taught by non-PGA professionals.

Golf 2.0 is a 2012 strategic plan of the PGA of America. It is a targeted, long-range strategic plan for the golf industry to substantially increase the number of golfers, the rounds of golf played, and the revenue generated from golf over the next decade by retaining and strengthening the core golfer, engaging the lapsed golfer, and attracting new players based on the changing demographics noted in the following figure.[16]

The lofty goal is to increase the number of golfers from 26 million to 40 million by 2020. Rather than the one-and-done programs of the past, the PGA has created a separate department for this initiative and retained 24 full-time employees and nine consultants to ensure its successful execution.

The Boston Consulting Group, retained by the PGA during the formation of 2.0,

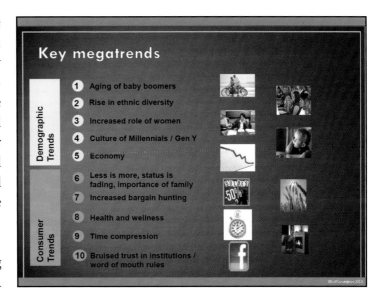

felt that to achieve these goals, the Association would need to make sure it is "tailoring messages and delivering customized programs to each of nine consumer groups identified: core golfers making at least $150,000 annually; occasional men and women golfers with no children; lapsed or former golfers, including men, women, retirees and parents; children; and Latinos familiar with the game."[17]

At www.golf20.net (the login page for PGA professionals), numerous resources are provided to PGA professionals to facilitate their implementation of this program.

---

16 PGA, "Golf 2.0 Industry Commitment to Creating Golfers, Rounds, and Revenue," 2010, Slide 14.

17 http://golfweek.com/news/2012/feb/20/pga-america-touts-golf-20-means-grow-golf/

In addition, the PGA of America has created a 42-page Player Development Playbook that can be downloaded.

While Golf 2.0 may be the watershed for the resurgence within the industry, work remains to adequately disseminate the message to the masses. In a survey conducted by Golf Convergence in May, 2012, the program was still largely unknown to many within the industry, as reflected in the following figure.

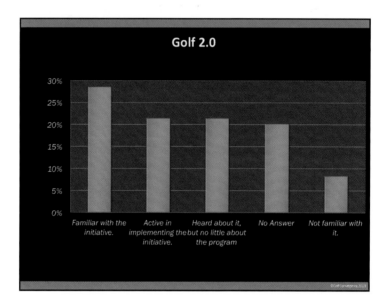

Get Golf Ready: Just Fabulous!

The concept of Get Golf Ready provides a welcoming environment for those seeking to learn and play golf, and it is so simple. Through a series of five lessons, an individual can be introduced to the game and have the opportunity to learn to play.

The first lesson is "putting"; everyone can putt; no excuses for drops at this level. Lesson 2 is "chipping." Lesson 3 is for "short irons." Lesson 4 is about "hybrids." And the last 1-hour lesson covers "the driver." During every lesson the students are taken on the course, and there they learn both the etiquette and the fundamental rules of the game, all for only $99. What a deal!

Every golf facility should offer this program. Yes, selflessly, for the benefit of the industry at large. But also, of course, selfishly, because any golf facility will make a lot money by implementing this program successfully.

The program is meeting with great success:

> "A record number of 75,900 students participated in Get Golf Ready in 2012, a 47-percent increase over 2011. Not only has Get Golf Ready had an exceptional impact on consumer participation, it has also had a favorable impact on the overall industry as well. More than 170,000 students have participated in Get Golf Ready programs since its inception in 2009, generating more than $200 million in revenue, including a record amount of $52.6 million in 2012.
>
> A total of 3,065 facilities were certified to host Get Golf Ready in 2012, a 62 percent increase from 2011, which is the largest annual increase to date."[18]

GGR participants consist primarily of women (61%), and 20% of the participants are minorities. Forty-two percent have never played the game. In August, 2013, the PGA expanded this initiative to corporate America in a professional development offering to companies, large and small.[19]

What is fabulous about Get Golf Ready is the retention rate (83% continue to play or practice their first year) and the incremental spending by the new players—they play an average of 10.8 rounds their first year, as illustrated below.

New Golfers are Consumers!

What GGR New Golfers Spent in the First Year	Average Spend
Range Fees	$91
Green Fees	$330
Food & Beverage	$125
Additional Lessons	$64
Equipment	$248
Apparel	$126
Total Spent for Each New Golfer (not including $99 GGR Fee)	$984

These new participants purchase new equipment, apparel, lessons, green fees, and more, all of which helps to grow the overall golf industry.

---

18 PGA of America Press Release, "2013_Jan24_PGAShow_GetGolfReady_FINAL", January 24, 2013.

19 https://www.golfbusinesscommunity.com/article/get_golf_ready_adds_business_program

New Golfers Are Great for Business!

# of Get Golf Ready: Average 40.9 per facility	50
Per Student Revenue	$99
GGR Program Revenue	$4,950
GGR Graduates who Continue Playing Golf (78%)	39
Average Spend for Each Retained Golfer (Not including $99 GGR Program Fee)	$984
New Golfer Spending (Not including $99 GGR Program Fee)	$38,376
Total Spend From New Golfers	$43,326

Potential - 250 students: $216,630

Get Golf Ready offers each course the potential of $216,630 in incremental income. Truly a no-brainer, you would think. Yet a survey conducted by Golf Convergence in May 2012, indicated that 43% of golf courses have yet to implement the program. With all the golf course operators we are in contact with, it is always disappointing when they whine about their economic challenges yet fail to implement programs that are proven winners, like Get Golf Ready.

GO GCSAA

Which is the most important of all the trade associations? In my opinion, the Golf Course Superintendents Association of America. Its members create the "product" that we all enjoy. Their members have scientific training from some of the finest universities.

The educational programs offered by the GCSAA are vastly superior in depth and breadth to the information presented by any other organization. Proposals by educators and lecturers are vetted in advance to ensure they meet the association's quality standards.

How their members haven't made it from the maintenance buildings to the board room escapes me. Well, actually, it may be because they prefer working with things rather than people, and that has defined their career path. However, they hold the key to the future success of the golf industry in "manufacturing" a product that produces consumer satisfaction.

David Kohler is the Chief Operating Officer of Kohler Enterprises, which owns four fabulous golf courses and an amazing hotel—The American

Club, in Wisconsin. In a meeting with Sandy Queen, the 2012 President of the GCSAA, Kohler made a statement that Queen commented represented one of the Top 10 things he learned as president. Kohler said, "You can't change what consumers desire and want. Consumers say they support water conservation, we develop incredibly efficient shower headers and faucets, and the consumer reaction is they don't like the reduced water pressure."

The lesson? While the industry says green must become brown, and firm must become fast, it is unrealistic to think consumers will change their desire for luscious turf and the finest in playing conditions. That trend will start when TV broadcasts of golf tournaments reflect golf courses with more economically sustainable playing conditions.

Queen, a 32-year veteran of managing the Overland Park, Kansas, golf courses, lamented that most joint allied trade association meetings are "meet, greet, and do nothing." Events like the 2012 USGA Water Summit, while a good concept, lacked any meaningful and actionable take-aways.

Only by joint cooperative participation with unified goals will the industry thrive.

Here is the probable solution. Look to the GCSAA and the USGA to jointly engage leading universities in meaningful research to develop grasses that are green and require far less water; keeping grass green remains the Achilles' heel of the golf industry. These programs might be funded by the USGA's financial resources through investment in universities' research programs like those being conducted by Dr. Brian Horgan at the University of Minnesota, by Dr. Fred Yelverton at North Carolina State, and by many other very qualified research professionals.

There has to be a solution if we aggressively research the problem.

Equipment Manufacturers

I recently read the equipment reviews in *Golf Magazine*, *Golf Digest*, and *Links Magazine*. Upon finishing the articles, I was totally confused as to which of the latest equipment designs would be suited for me. How could any consumer know, from those articles, what to buy? Where there is confusion and doubt, there is delay. And when equipment purchases are delayed, the growth of the industry is slowed. The process of selecting the right equipment is daunting.

As part of the research conducted for this book, guidance was sought from Steve Grosz, PGA, General Manager of Hot Stix Golf. Hot Stix is completely independent and passionate about fitting clubs optimally to each player. Thus, a customer, after a fitting, may end up with four or five different manufacturers' clubs.

To help golfers understand the process, Grosz explained for us the concepts that are reviewed with students of club fitting:

> **"1. Ball Flight.** Every player has an optimum launch angle and spin rate. It is the fitter's job to determine those numbers based on the player's swing. Factors that affect the optimum launch and spin include attack angle (the angle at which the club approaches the ball), and club head speed. These factors are unique to each player.
>
> A player with a steep angle of attack (hitting down on the ball) will benefit by launching the ball lower than a player who has a positive angle of attack and hits up on the ball. As a result of this, the player who launches the ball lower will need more spin to keep the ball in the air. The player with a positive angle of attack, who launches the ball higher, needs less spin to keep the ball from ballooning.
>
> For example, a player with average swing speed, who has a negative three degree (−3 degrees) angle of attack will get maximum distance with a launch angle of approximately 10 degrees and 3000 rpm of backspin. A player with a positive three degree (+3 degrees) angle of attack will get maximum distance with a launch angle of 13 to 14 degrees and 2000–2500 rpm of backspin.
>
> The second factor in determining the proper launch and spin for a player is club head speed. The slower the club head speed, the higher the player needs to launch the ball, and the more spin he needs to keep the ball in the air. Players with faster club head speed will benefit from a lower launch angle than the slower swinging player. A good analogy is what happens with a garden hose. If you have the water pressure as high as it can go, you don't have to tip the hose up very

high to make the water shoot as far as it can go. But as you turn the water pressure down, you need to start tipping that hose higher, to get the water to shoot as far as it can go.

If the launch angle and spin rate are optimized, the result will be the proper descent angle. This is the angle at which the ball comes into the ground. A descent angle of 30 to 35 degrees with a driver will provide the perfect combination of carry and roll to maximize distance.

2. Ball Speed. Ball speed is related to two things; solid contact and club head speed. The USGA limits how fast the ball can come off the face of the club on drivers. The USGA doesn't limit how fast the ball can come off all the other clubs. There is a measurement called the Power Transfer Index (PTI), or 'smash factor,' that measures the ratio of club head speed to ball speed. If your club head speed is 100 mph, and your ball speed is 150 mph, your PTI would be 1.5. That is the legal limit as defined by the USGA.

As fitters, we try to maximize ball speed by doing two things. The first is to give the player the best chance to make solid contact. There is a trend toward longer, lighter drivers, which definitely yields more speed on a hitting robot. But we are not robots; we strive to find the longest club that the player can consistently hit solidly. Secondly, we need to find the shaft weight and flex that responds best to each player's tempo. The correct flex gives the player the best chance to square the clubface at impact, which aids solid contact, not to mention accuracy.

3. Launch Angle. When asked if most players need higher or lower launch, the most common answer is 'higher launch.' I would submit that it depends on two factors; the conditions the player usually plays in and the way they swing the club. If a player plays in wet soggy conditions, he will usually benefit from higher launch/more carry, because there will be very little roll no matter how the ball launches. That player needs to maximize carry distance. On hard, fast conditions, lower launch and more roll will benefit the player.

When fitting a player for a driver, my #1 concern isn't necessarily distance. I want to get them the most distance I can while keeping the ball in play. My job is to help the player shoot lower scores, and that means keeping the ball in play off the tee. Optimizing launch angle, spin rate and selecting a shaft that squares the clubface up at impact will do that.

When talking about fairway woods/hybrids/irons, we want 'playable loft.' This means shots with a trajectory that allows the ball to stop on the green if it lands on it. If a player struggles to get the ball in the air, fairway woods tend to go higher, so they may be a better fit than hybrids. For the same player, hybrids would be a better choice than long irons. The opposite is usually true for a stronger player.

4. Spin. Backspin is what provides lift and keeps the ball in the air. Too much spin will cause the ball to balloon, and reduce distance. Too much backspin also translates to too much sidespin, so it is imperative to keep spin within the player's optimal range.

Some players also struggle with too little spin. With too little spin, the ball will act like a knuckleball when struck, and just fall out of the sky. Carry distance will be lower than it should be, and if the ball lands on the green it will be hard to make it stop.

5. Distance. The most important factor in creating distance is hitting the ball solidly. If a player swings a club three to four miles per hour faster, but misses the sweet spot by ¼", he will hit it a shorter distance than if he hit it solidly at his normal swing speed. Finding club specifications that give the player the best chance to hit the ball solidly is the #1 goal in maximizing distance. As proof of this, look no further than the PGA Tour. These are the best players in the world, who hit the ball solidly almost every time. Very few Tour players use over-length clubs, because they know that even they need to insure solid contact. They also understand that even if they make a perfect swing, and gain 5 yards with a longer club, the trade-off of less consistency and loss of accuracy isn't worth it.

The proper club specifications will give the player the best chance for solid contact, the proper launch angle, and the correct amount of backspin. That is the key to maximizing distance."[20]

Other points to be considered are the greater the flex, the greater the speed, but the greater the chance of mishits.

---

20 Steve Grosz, PGA, HotStix Golf, "Club Fitting, 101," March 2013.

With respect to shafts, high kick points will keep the ball low, and conversely, low kick points will increase the loft of the club. The difference between a low kick point shaft and a high kick point shat might only be a difference of 1 degree in launch angle. The loft of the club is the most important factor.

With every shaft having a different bend profile, the club fitter's focus is to find the shaft with the overall bend profile that helps the player square the shaft at impact. This mainly involves torque, or how stiff the shaft is at the tip end. There are some generalities; players who load the club really hard (think Sergio Garcia) usually prefer low torque shafts. Players with slower tempos (think Freddie Couples) typically prefer more torque. To this point, Couples made a comment in his Hall of Fame Induction speech on May 6, 2013, about finding a women's driver at Tom Watson's house. He took it and used it as a 3 wood and won the Masters with it.

Another aspect is shaft weight. A heavier shaft will result in a lower club head speed.

Thus, in implementing these concepts, Hot Stix developed the following chart.

Driver Fitting Chart

Swing Speed (MPH's)	65			70			75			80		
Attack Angle (Degrees)	-3	0	+3	-3	0	+3	-3	0	+3	-3	0	+3
Ball Speed (MPH's)	90.7	91.3	91.9	98.6	99.2	99.8	106.5	107.1	107.7	114.4	115	115.6
Launch (Degrees)	17.8	19.2	20.6	16.4	17.8	19.2	15.3	16.7	18.1	14.2	15.7	17.1
Spin (RPM's)	3403	3148	2893	3389	3134	2879	3375	3120	2865	3361	3106	2851
Carry (Yards)	114	120	126	131	137	143	148	154	160	165	171	177
Total (Yards)	143	149	155	159	165	171	174	180	186	190	196	202

Swing Speed (MPH's)	85			90			95			100		
Attack Angle (Degrees)	-3	0	+3	-3	0	+3	-3	0	+3	-3	0	+3
Ball Speed (MPH's)	122.2	122.8	123.4	129.9	130.5	131.1	137.9	138.5	139.9	145.9	146.5	147.1
Launch (Degrees)	13.3	14.8	16.2	12.1	13.7	15.3	11.4	13	14.6	10.8	21.4	13.9
Spin (RPM's)	3347	3092	2837	3375	3090	2805	3361	3076	2791	3347	3062	2777
Carry (Yards)	181	187	193	196	203	209	213	219	226	230	236	242
Total (Yards)	205	211	217	233	239	245	249	255	261	265	271	277

Swing Speed (MPH's)	105			110			115			120		
Attack Angle (Degrees)	-3	0	+3	-3	0	+3	-3	0	+3	-3	0	+3
Ball Speed (MPH's)	152.7	153.3	153.9	160.8	161.4	161.9	168.8	169.4	170	177	177.6	178.2
Launch (Degrees)	9.9	11.5	13.2	9.4	11	12.7	8.9	10.6	12.3	7.4	9.3	11.2
Spin (RPM's)	3355	3040	2725	3341	3026	2711	3327	3012	2697	3220	2890	2560
Carry (Yards)	244	251	258	260	266	273	275	282	289	288	295	302
Total (Yards)	283	289	295	298	304	310	313	319	325	327	333	339

©GolfConvergence,2013

Interestingly, for every 5 mph of swing speed, total distance is increased about 16 yards, except between 85 and 90 mph, the typical golfer's average club speed; there the distance increases by 28 yards.

The process of adjusting one's driver featuring multiple adjustment possibilities might be reduced to a simple chart shown below.

The ABCs of Club Fitting: Manufacturers Should Promote

Path Angle	Club Head Speed	Club Fitting Adjustment
Steep	Fast	Several degrees decrease in loft
Steep	Slow	None
Even	Fast	Small decrease in loft
Even	Slow	Small increase in loft
Up	Fast	None
Up	Slow	Several degrees increase in loft

©GolfConvergence 2012

Note: A steep path angle would suggest a decreased loft. A slow club head speed would suggest an increased loft.

Manufacturers create confusion with technical jargon rather than clarity. Until we make it simpler, growth of the game and, in turn, the business, will remain challenged.

What Are the Implications for Golf Course Owners?

Associations and Equipment Manufacturers have mainly their own interests at heart.

For instance, third-party tee time vendors have drawn the ire of many. That subject is extensively debated later in this book, and the NGCOA has issued numerous position papers on "best practices."

To help grow the game of golf, it is the goal of the Colorado PGA Section to introduce the sport to the masses through targeted advertising and instruction. To fund such initiatives, the Colorado PGA is attempting to create a statewide reservation system. The organization has negotiated with a software vendor to provide all golf courses in Colorado with an impressive array of software that would achieve the goal.

The Colorado PGA Section was also able to negotiate a new revenue model for third-party software vendors featuring the following benefits for the golf course owner:

1. The golf course was provided the option of paying the annual license fee in cash or barter. Historically, barter was the only payment accepted.

2. The course has sole control of the tee times sold and the prices offered. Currently third-party vendors can sell the tee times at whatever price they deem appropriate, potentially devaluing the a golf course's brand.

3. The fees to be paid for the software are to be capped at $10,000 annually. It is thought that third-party vendors make up to $40,000 annually in liquidated trade in some markets.

In Colorado, it is forecast that in 2013 third-party vendors will earn $1,952,500 from liquidating the tee times of golf courses, as illustrated in the following table.

2013 Colorado Third-Party Tee Time Model			
	Daily Fee	**Municipal**	**Total**
Colorado Courses on Line	50	21	71
Bartered Tee Times Sold: Revenue per Course	27,500	27,500	27,500
2013 Revenue Earned by Third-Party Tee Time Vendor	$1,375,000	577,500	1,952,500
PGA Proposed Model—Fee Cap: $10,000			
Savings to Golf Course Owners (64%)	875,000	367,500	1,242,500
Funds Allocated to Growth of the Game (24%)	325,000	136,500	461,500
Funds Allocated for Operational Tools—Yield Management, Web Site, Email Marketing (12%). Note technology is boosting owners' profits by 14% in Arizona.	175,000	73,500	248,500
PGA Proposed Model—Fee Cap	$1,375,000	577,500	1,952,500

The Colorado PGA model might have saved golf course owners $1,242,500, provided them software for $3,600, and generated $461,500 for marketing initiatives in the state presuming the Colorado golf courses currently engaged in barter adopted the proposed solution.

The NGCOA reaction? Though the Colorado PGA took the initiative and invested one year to formulate the project to the point of implementation, the NGCOA initially wanted to control the state-wide reservation system through the creation of a state chapter, this in spite of the fact that the NGCOA's Colorado chapter failed several years ago. The NGCOA did indicate they would allocate some money to grow-the-game initiatives, suggesting that the Colorado PGA hold fund-raising tournaments to supplement its capital needs.

In my opinion, this example of self-interest is illustrative of why the industry is so challenged.

Therefore, the responsibility for profitability rests upon you, the golf course owner. Associations can create programs to grow the game, educate their membership to assist you, and sponsor governmental and research initiatives. But in the end, you control your own destiny as a golf course owner or as an integral part of the management team at a course, you create the entertainment value of your course, and you alone should define the golf experience you choose to offer.

Path to Success

1) Associations create noise. Don't get caught up in the speculation and debate of what might be some day.

2) Cherry-pick your investments with associations, selecting educational programs and attending classes that have direct relevance to identified needs.

3) As a private club, cautiously consider having your management participate in the Club Managers Association Business Management School classes unless you are looking for them to earn the designation of "Certified Club Manager" for which these classes are required. We felt that the education value was light and the main value is the networking opportunities.

4) Refrain from hosting any amateur tournaments at your course sponsored by golf associations unless you receive the full value in green fees for the tee times used. Don't get sucked in by "it's good for the game." They are using your asset to benefit themselves, not you.

5) Finally, remember that associations are business enterprises unto themselves. While they tell you, as any vendor would, that they care about you and have your interests at heart, their principal interest is in assuring their association's financial stability and keeping their jobs.

6) Recall that the purpose of this book is to illustrate how to maximize your investment return, not to be merely a constant source of inventory for charity. While we wish that they were not mutually exclusive, often they are.

Concluding Thoughts

He is often in error, but never in doubt.

Unknown

An editor is like your mother.
She makes you change things you don't want to that you know you should.

Unknown

Chapter 4

Ownership and Governance

One can present people with opportunities.
One cannot make them equal to them.

Rosamond Lehmann in *The Ballad and the Source*

Chapter Highlights

Should municipalities be in the golf business? There is no subject that draws the ire and the diatribe of daily fee owners more than the perceived economic advantages municipalities have in operating what is a private enterprise. "How dare municipalities escape paying property taxes, receive financial support from the general fund to cover operating deficits, and be provided investment capital" is the cry often heard. The common refrain is that they have a "safety net" protecting them from their inefficiency and incompetency, and this doesn't seem right in a capitalist country.

As this chapter illustrates and as Shakespeare said, "all that glitters is not gold." Actually, private clubs and daily fee golf courses have significant competitive advantages over their municipal brethren, despite some of the financial handicaps dictated by their form of governance.

88

Should Municipalities Be Involved in the Golf Business?

When Van Cortlandt Golf Course opened in New York City in 1895, it became the first public golf course in America that was built for the masses.[1] The need to create golf courses for the masses became clear because the sport was dominated by private clubs during its early years, as illustrated in the following figure.[2]

Course Name	City	State	Total Holes	Year Open	Type
Rockaway Hunting Club	Lawrence	NY	18	1878	Private
Indian Oaks Golf Club	Peru	IN	9	1880	Daily Fee
Pittsburgh Field Club	Pittsburgh	PA	18	1882	Private
Forest Lake Club	Hawley	PA	9	1882	Private
The Country Club Brookline	Chestnut Hill	MA	27	1882	Private
Edgewood Club of Tivoli	Tivoli	NY	9	1884	Private
Megunticook Golf Club	Rockport	ME	9	1884	Private
Westport Country Club	Westport	NY	18	1885	Private
The Tuxedo Club	Tuxedo Park	NY	18	1886	Private
Dorset Field Club	Dorset	VT	18	1886	Private
Foxburg Country Club	Foxburg	PA	9	1887	Daily Fee
Essex County Country Club	West Orange	NJ	18	1887	Private
Onteora Golf Club	Tannersville	NY	9	1887	Private
Quogue Field Club	Quogue	NY	9	1887	Private
Sioux Golf & Country Club	Alton	IA	9	1888	Daily Fee
Kebo Valley Golf Club	Bar Harbor	ME	18	1888	Daily Fee
Town and Country Club	Saint Paul	MN	18	1888	Private
Richmond County Country Club	Staten Island	NY	18	1888	Private
Ausable Club	Keene Valley	NY	9	1888	Private
Sharon Country Club	Sharon	MA	9	1888	Private
Saint Andrew's Golf Club	Hastings On Hudson	NY	18	1888	Private
Middlesboro Country Club	Middlesboro	KY	9	1889	Daily Fee
Exeter Country Club	Exeter	NH	9	1889	Daily Fee
The Country Club	Pepper Pike	OH	18	1889	Private
Binghamton Country Club	Endwell	NY	18	1889	Private

The opportunities to play golf, early on (and some would maintain even today) were limited to the well-to-do.

What is often lost in the debate on the viability of municipal golf courses is that golf is classified as a discretionary program. The allocation of resources for parks and recreation departments is determined by a matrix of core, important, and discretionary areas of importance by national standards, as highlighted in the chart below.

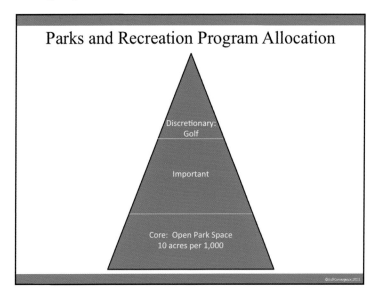

Parks and Recreation Program Allocation

Discretionary: Golf

Important

Core: Open Park Space 10 acres per 1,000

1 http://golf.about.com/cs/historyofgolf/a/hist_oldestuspu.htm
2 National Golf Foundation, "Facility List," 2012.

A priority of the Parks and Recreation Department is to ensure that the entire community has open park space at a minimum of 10 acres per 1,000 in population.

During the past few years, with the economic downturn, and specifically since 9/11, the decision for the allocation of municipal funds has been to provide police and fire with the highest priority, with other municipal services competing for the remaining resources.

A substantial number of municipal golfers believe a profit focus for golf is inappropriate, since other activities like libraries, parks, trails, and swimming pools, are supported by the taxpayers. Golfers feel that the real estate taxes they pay and their expenditure of disposable income in the community, creates employment for all residents and justifies the financial support of a golf course by a municipality. To view and hear the philosophy of entitlement on full display, attend any city council meeting where golf course rate increases are being discussed. The golfers are often present in droves demanding that to which they believe they are entitled.

Recently, I witnessed two members of a Golf Advisory Council (who played over 100 rounds in 2012, paid $400 for an unlimited play pass, and obtained preferential times from the golf manager, who had a lucrative concession contract) maintain that the rate should not be raised; this in spite of the fact that the golf course had deferred capital expenditures exceeding $3.0 million. Golfers all too often adopt such unreasonable and inflexible positions.

It is often falsely perceived that the role of government is to provide all things to all sectors. That is just not the case. There is a clear mandate that the community's needs outweigh those of a smaller sector. Thus, there is not a mandate for government to provide a golf experience for every level of ability, nor is there a mandate, for example, for government to subsidize a special interest group such as seniors or junior golfers.

Where the golfers' position breaks down, in my opinion, is when you consider that other leisure and recreational activities provided by a municipality are not offered by the private sector. How can you justify the fact that 92% of the taxpayers support a recreational activity played by participants who have a median household income that far exceeds the national average? A conservative position would reflect that golf is clearly discretionary, as private enterprise adequately provides this recreational amenity to the community-at-large.

Adopting a far more liberal, ecumenical, or philanthropic viewpoint consistent with the beliefs of Abraham Lincoln that the "legitimate object of government is to do for a community of people, whatever they need to have done, but cannot do at all, or cannot so well do for themselves,"[3] one might conclude that the role of government is to provide golf to the extent that the desire ("need" would be an inappropriate description) is not filled by the private sector.

The evolution of golf in the United States might suggest that the need for municipalities to provide golf began to subside in 1970, as illustrated in the following figure.

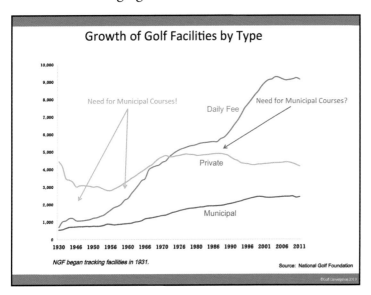

The extent to which the number of daily fee courses exceeds the number of private clubs might be one benchmark that would ascertain the need for a municipal golf course within a defined market.

But if we acknowledge that there is a valid need for a golf course operated by a municipality, what niche of the golf market should it serve? Should it be an entry door to the game, like most "city park" golf courses, or should it be more like the lavish Bolingbrook Golf Course that serves as a community center for many functions but has averaged a loss of $1.3 million a year since its opening in 2002, according to a *Chicago Times* report?[4]

Qualitatively, it is fairly easy to justify a municipal golf course as a place for kids to learn, for First Tee chapters to be operated, for senior citizens living on social security to enjoy outdoor recreation, and for new entrants to the game to play with friends and family without the pressures of social decorum and etiquette that are so tightly observed at high-end daily fee courses and private clubs.

What is the answer? Should municipalities be in the golf business? The answer is clearly based on each person's value system, but the hope of most would be that the municipal golf course would be self-sustaining after reserves are established for the ongoing capital investment required.

But are municipal courses achieving that benchmark?

---

3 Robert I. Fitzhenry, Editor, *The Harper Book of Quotations—Third Edition*, 2005, pg. 187.

4 http://www.golfdigest.com/golf-courses/blogs/golf-real-estate/2009/08

The Financial Profile of a Municipal Course

Both municipal and daily fee courses were asked to participate in the 2011 PGA Performance Trak annual operating survey. Results published in 2012 reflected the completed surveys of 407 of the 2,415 municipal golf courses queried (16.85%) and 861 of the 9,199 daily fee golf courses (9.4%) surveyed. As illustrated by the figure to the right, that study reflects the fact that daily fee golf courses financially outperform municipal golf courses.

Financial Performance Municipal Golf Courses vs. Daily Fee				
	Platinum Top 10%	Gold Top 25%	Silver Median	Steel - Bottom 25%
MUNICIPALITIES				
Rounds Played	50,000	40,000	30,000	22,865
Full Time Employees	> 20	>11	> 6	> 5
Total Revenues	$1,860,000	$1,450,000	$822,000	512,500
EBITDA	$1,000,000	$572,541	$142,406	$58,000
ALL GOLF COURSES				
Rounds Played	40,000	30,400	22,000	15,000
Full Time Employees	58	30	14	6
Total Revenues	$4,500,000	$2,500,000	$1,375,000	$800,000
EBITDA	$1,295,777	$613,419	$205,435	$73,000

©Golf Convergence 2013

Median earnings before interest, taxes, depreciation, and amortization of $142,406 for municipal golf courses contrasted to median earnings of $205,435 for daily fee courses. While this isn't necessarily alarming on the face of it, the National Golf Foundation reported that only 70% of municipal golf courses are covering operating expenses, 40% are covering debt service, 45% are investing less than $5,000 in marketing, 73% are deferring capital improvements, and 39% are lowering their maintenance standards.[5] Our experience has been comparable during the past 18 months, as we completed more than 20 strategic plans for municipalities.

Clearly daily fee golf courses are outperforming their municipal brethren, despite the cost handicaps.

What is ironic is that 1,315 of the nation's municipal golf courses are located within the Top 100 statistical areas where demand for golf is strong, and that those golf courses have the advantage of pricing power should they choose to exercise it. In other words, if they are providing value, they shouldn't be losing money, but they are.

Why?

---

5 National Golf Foundation, "Maximizing the Economic Benefits of Municipal Golf Courses," October 2012, Slide 25.

The Death Spiral

The financial and capital challenges that municipal golf courses are currently experiencing can be tracked through four distinct phases during the past decade. These phases are detailed below:

- Phase 1—Profitable operation.

- Phase 2—Competitive forces lead to declining customer base, rates fail to keep pace with inflation, and discounts given to retain remaining customers; all cause revenues to fall.

- Phase 3—Reduced profits or operating losses create deferral of capital expenditure, resulting in deterioration of course conditions, further adversely impacting rounds and revenue.

- Phase 4—General fund subsidy, privatization to independent management, sale, or closure of courses is required to relieve the city of the draining financial obligation caused by the attempt to provide a recreational service.

Often viewed as the entry door to golf, the brand image of municipal golf courses is one of "inexpensive, affordable golf." Their historical brand image also includes the expectation of average course conditions, small clubhouses, limited food service, and catering to season pass holders, seniors, juniors, and new golfers. During the past decade, this stereotype has changed; many municipal courses now offer high-quality experiences. To illustrate, within the past 15 years, 14 municipal courses were built within 30 miles of Denver. Those municipal courses are all focused on providing a "country-club-for-a-day" experience. Thirty-eight percent of all golf courses in Colorado are municipally owned.

A few have thrived. Fossil Trace, in Golden, at the foothills of the Rockies, with a Jim Engh designed course that overlooks the Coors Brewery, is doing really well—over $2.0 million alone in just its food and beverage operation.

Nationally, however, many municipal courses are struggling.

If a golf course is losing money, the cost of water is often one of the principal causes. Other contributing factors include that the accelerated investment made and the associated cost structure to operate higher-end facilities have created a financial abyss. Try a Google Alert for "Golf Courses Losing Money" to receive a plethora of emails highlighting the challenges faced nationally.

There are four factors that are driving municipalities out of the golf course business: 1) water, 2) labor cost, particularly where labor unions are present, 3) medical costs, and 4) pension benefits.

While labor unions have a vital role in some sectors of the U.S. economy, labor unions are an anathema for the management of a golf course. The requirement to maintain the course 7 days a week dictates overtime with accelerated labor costs of time-and-a-half or double time.

We have observed at several municipalities, for example, where the maintenance crew at the golf course is prohibited from trimming a tree if a ladder is required. That work must be accomplished by the Public Works Department. When the work is completed (usually several weeks later) the course is billed at the going rate; inefficient and unworkable.

Because golf course workers are governed by the same pay scale as those who work for that municipality, the fringe benefits are far higher than those available from private enterprise, as illustrated in the golf course payroll structure shown (on right) for another municipality for an executive 18-hole golf course.

With gross revenues just exceeding $500,000, this course has no chance to

Payroll: Base and Benefits
Unsustainable

Greenskeeper		2012	2013	2014	2015	2016	
703	Retiree Health Care	9,564.92	10,245.76	11,009.46	12,014.59	13,036.17	
706	Permanent Employee	44,821.56	46,487.12	48,735.98	51,170.43	53,551.77	
712	Unemployment Compensation	62.75	65.08	68.23	71.67	75.32	
715	Employers Social Security	3,428.85	3,556.26	3,728.30	3,916.13	4,115.84	
719	Hospitalization Insurance	13,433.16	14,660.42	15,847.91	17,131.59	18,519.25	
721	Longevity Pay	.00	.00	.00	20.83	250.00	
722	Retirement Fund Contribution	9,053.95	10,836.15	13,290.30	14,077.60	14,795.49	
100% Allocated		**80,365.19**	**85,850.79**	**92,680.19**	**98,402.85**	**104,343.84**	**51.3%**

Golf Course Manager		2012	2013	2014	2015	2016	
703	Retiree Health Care	13,495.70	13,987.98	14,479.06	15,192.12	15,839.46	
706	Permanent Employee	62,866.34	62,866.34	63,495.00	64,129.95	64,771.29	
712	Unemployment Compensation	88.54	88.85	89.73	90.62	91.52	
715	Employers Social Security	4,837.96	4,855.18	4,903.27	4,951.84	5,000.90	
719	Hospitalization Insurance	13,433.16	14,660.42	15,847.91	17,131.59	18,519.25	
721	Longevity Pay	375.00	600.00	600.00	600.00	600.00	
722	Retirement Fund Contribution	12,774.75	14,794.00	17,478.71	17,800.74	17,977.10	
100% Allocated		**107,871.45**	**111,852.77**	**116,893.68**	**119,896.86**	**122,799.53**	**52.7%**

survive in the long-term with the payroll structure in place. The benefit package at most municipal golf courses exceeds 40% of base pay. That pay scale is just not sustainable and should be a warning sign to each municipality that it is time to exit from self-management of the course.

Beyond the cost factors, municipalities struggle to properly manage a for-profit enterprise. As regretful it is, they often lack the depth and breadth of professional business skills needed to manage a golf course.

Procurement practices can also be incredibly inefficient.

The concept of a request for proposal, required by all cities based on some anticipated threshold of cost (usually around $15,000) has real merit. Open bids, all vendors; best value to the municipality wins. Sounds simple.

But they often botch the purchasing decision process.

Often it starts with the appointment of a committee which numerically scores the proposals received. We have observed the actions of committees on which one evaluator gives a vendor such a low score in one category that the vendor, though obviously the best qualified, has no chance of winning. A system designed for equity is fraught with flaws. It is our subjective opinion that the most qualified candidates are selected only about 60% of the time. The margin of error is way too high.

A major multi-course West Coast municipality issued a bid in 2012 to manage one of its facilities under a 20-year lease. The winning bid was determined based on the total funds the county would receive over 20 years. Sounds like the right selection method, correct? Wrong! The municipality did not consider the present value of money. The winning vendor's bid was back-loaded so that while the compensation to be received by the municipality in the aggregate was the highest, when considered on a present value basis, it would have been in the middle of the pack. Further, the liquidated damages for breach of the contract were negligible. The concessionaire could milk the contract for the early years and then bolt when cash flow, based on rental payments required, turned negative. It is hard to believe that in 2012 a major municipality would make such a fundamental error.

To provide another example among many that are available, for an engagement for a seven-course, East Coast municipality, purchasing required each vendor to complete for every single task of the engagement a form delineating direct labor costs, indirect labor costs, profits, other direct costs including travel expenses by line items, equipment material contracts, subcontractor costs, and other expenses to be incurred. There were 37 rows of tasks on the form and 5 columns for every task to be completed by the consultant.

The low bid, $44,830, was deemed "non-compliant and rejected" because the vendor wrote,

> "We greatly appreciate the request to prepare a detailed analysis of six components via 37 line items for each of six proposed tasks with respect to the aforementioned RFP. It would present an impressive array of data by which a comparison might be made between vendors. But would it be meaningful?
>
> Truth be told, each of the vendors that completed the exercise precisely would be guessing. No vendor within the golf industry tracks by component the man hours allocated to each task.
>
> Why? Each client engagement is unique. Every golf business review becomes a custom-tailored assignment based on the initial site review, the key interviews, the local market analysis; therefore quickly gleaning the political forces in play.
>
> Consultants are hired to produce substance, not to comply with form. In Appendix A, a summary of our technical proposal is presented. In Appendix B, we have succinctly summarized the cost proposal you were seeking."

They preferred form over substance. While the decision was made by a committee, the designated buyer had no specialty in purchasing golf consulting services. Public government organizations thrust people in areas in which they have little expertise. The resulting decisions, often swayed by personal politics, have an adverse effect on the golf course achieving profitability.

This municipality accepted a bid for $101,046, wasting $56,216 based on "pride with their purchasing process," as explained by the manager of that department.

A municipality in the suburbs of Chicago, Illinois, issued an RFP in January, 2012, for which it received two responses—$19,300 and $25,000. They accepted neither, nor did they inform the vendors in a timely manner that their proposals were rejected.

The city invited a third firm to submit and thereby avoided the bid process by awarding a contract for $23,500 to a part-time consultant. They probably circumvented the law by referencing a previous contract with that consultant for work he performed several years prior, merely tacking on an extension to that original agreement. As of May 10, 2013, the report was still in draft form, supposedly, as advised by email. In the State that the golf course operates, governments can claim exemption from the state's Freedom of Information Act if a document is considered a draft, and not yet discussed in a public meeting. Citing that exemption is a good way to hide the truth from the public.[6]

Poor revenue decisions, inefficient purchasing, organizational flaws, and lack of depth and breadth in professional management have led to the accelerating trend of privatization of municipal golf courses.

The combination of public and private operations is illustrated in the following figure[7]:

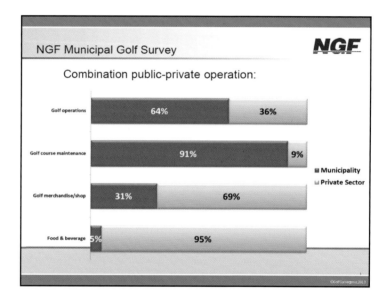

But is privatization the answer? Remember that it comes in all flavors.

The Inherent Challenges of Municipal Management

Managing a municipal golf course is a challenge, regardless of its management structure. City Council requires transparency. The golf course management and staff are well compensated, and the golfers expect low prices and a quality golf experience. Those elements don't mix well.

---

6 Identity restricted, email received from Director of Parks on May 10, 2013.

7 National Golf Foundation, "Maximizing the Economic Benefits of Municipal Golf Courses," October 2012, Slide 28.

The management of a municipal golf course usually takes one of three forms.

The first form of management uses only city employees, and in this form the swing of quality will hit both extremes, from outstanding dedicated employees to those merely "punching the clock." Monmouth and Morris Counties in New Jersey are examples of municipalities that get it largely right. I would speculate that about 15% of municipalities can manage their courses as effectively as a third party.

A second form of management is "leases." Third parties pay a negotiated rental fee to the municipality and inure to the benefit of the revenue, the gains and losses, and, if the contract is well written, are held accountable for the ongoing capital improvements. While this form of agreement provides the municipality the least short-term risk while being isolated from net operating losses, it provides the highest long-term risk if capital improvements are not made. Leasing to individual concessionaires often can also produce less than desirable results.

Concessionaires are for-profit entities, and as such they create a natural conflict of interest between scope of services and efficiency of operations. The City of Thornton, Colorado, has learned this the hard way. It has taken the city over two years, lots of effort, and much money to clean up the mess created by a management company.

The third and current most popular form of privatization is management contracts, by which the third party is paid an annual fee, currently ranging from $75,000 to $200,000, to manage the facility. Third-party management companies can usually only produce economic benefit in excess of their fees on facilities whose gross revenue potential exceeds $1,250,000. Yes, there is so much inefficiency in most municipal operations that a third party can take 10% of the gross off the top and the financial position of the municipality is in better financial condition than had it managed the course itself.

To assist in making a decision concerning the optimum form of management for a municipal course, the following chart summarizes the matrix of decisions a municipality faces as far as risk, capital investment exposure, and the right to inure to the benefit of profits or to fund loss:

Matrix of Decisions	Self-Manage	Management	Lease
Risk	Full Risk	Full Risk	No Risk
Capital Investment	Full Capital	Full Capital	No Capital, unless negotiated
Profits	Full Profits	Full Profits less a management fee	No Profits other than "rent"

There are some key rules of thumb, depending on the financial position of a golf course. If the course is incurring operating losses and lacks capital—leasing would be preferred. If the value is eroding and expenses are increasing, professional management is a viable option. If a course is breaking even and covering debt and capital, self-management remains the preferred management choice.

There are frequent debates as to the best structure, but the form of management preferred by municipalities has varied greatly over the past two decades.

Why the Flip-Flop?

Up until the early 1980s, most municipal courses were managed 100% by municipalities. With the advent of management companies in the late 1980s, these firms were retained, they paid the cities a lease fee, and they benefited from the earnings with profits shared, in some cases, above certain thresholds.

With the boom in golf in the late 1990s, municipalities opted to either self-manage or to pay management companies a flat fee while retaining the profits for the cities' coffers. Gordon Gecko's greed became their mantra—let's make the money ourselves. It can't be that hard to manage a municipal golf course.

Unfortunately, many municipalities didn't fully comprehend the difficulty of creating a value-based golf experience while generating sufficient cash flow to offset the bond payments hidden within their often inefficient organizational structure. When combined with a declining tax revenue base and softness in the golf industry, municipalities are now hoping to revert to the late 1980s model of leasing, one in which third parties assume the capital and operational risk.

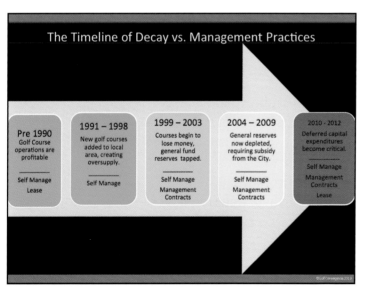

This cycle of lease to self-management to management contract to leasing is highlighted in the figure to the left.

If Third Parties Are Better, Why Isn't Every Municipality Adopting That Form of Management?

The privatization of a municipal golf course meets with resistance from many sectors. Golfers are fearful rates will go up. Golf management and staff are afraid their jobs will be lost. Parks and Recreation Department managers are fearful capital improvements will not be made. The city council is fearful the benefits received will not offset the fees paid.

Billy Casper Golf Management, one of the leaders in the management of municipal courses, understands both the myths and the realities of this subject, and presents the following reality check to municipalities during its presentations.[8]

Though golfers maintain that rates will go up, the city council usually determines price. Management companies can increase rounds and revenue through tee time yield management, guest retention and acquisition programs, promotion and public relations, and cross marketing opportunities.

Dispelling Management Company Myths

Myth	Reality
Rates will go up	Dictated by market/Approved by Owner
Residents will lose access	Locals are always #1 priority
Conditions will deteriorate	Improved conditions = more golfers
Employee House Cleaning	Employers always seek good staff
Service will suffer	Professional staff delivers results

BILLY CASPER GOLF

The argument that residents will lose access is one of the "fear arguments" that golfers throw into the debate with little support. The reality is that 90% of rounds are played by golfers who reside within 10 miles of the course, programming is directed toward residents, and, most courses are operating at less than 50% of capacity. Access to tee times is not a real issue unless the golfer is demanding a permanent prime time at 8:00 a.m. on the weekends.

It is truly a myth that course conditions will deteriorate under the care of a leading management company; these companies fully understand that improved conditions generate more golfers. By introducing agronomic plans,

8 Billy Casper Golf, "Management Alternatives," October 2011, Slide 12.

upgrading maintenance equipment and golf carts on a repair and replacement cycle, course improvements invariably improve. An example of such is Los Amigos Golf Course, a Los Angeles County property in Downey, California. New concessionaires were retained in November 2012, and they have invested over $1 million repairing a property that effectively was abandoned.

Management and staff are fearful for their jobs. While the less competent maybe at risk, management companies don't have a bullpen full of talented help. They are constantly looking to hire locals; it's good business, provides golfers a consistent touch point, and allows the management company to introduce guest-oriented employee training.

As to the argument that service will suffer, management companies are usually on three-year contracts. While the municipal employee in essence has a guaranteed lifetime contract (save for fraud, sexual harassment, or other egregious behavior), the management company is at risk of being fired. Business plans, marketing plans, agronomic plans, employee training programs, and capital improvements are crafted and implemented to ensure a mutually beneficially long-term arrangement.

You can always find examples of where these arrangements have worked well and examples of where the management company has "sucked the paint off of the wall" in a lease, as illustrated in the following figure.

Clubhouse Bathroom in Exclusive Neighborhood in Major City

There is simply no excuse for allowing golf course facilities to deteriorate to this condition, especially considering this golf course is located within the wealthiest section of one of the largest cities in the United States. Nor is there an excuse to leave a tree laying in the fairway after it had fallen in a thunderstorm, as illustrated in the following figure.

Thus, in deciding the optimum form of management for a municipal golf course, a private club, or a resort, it is important to understand the pros and cons of that decision. The pros and cons of using a management company are summarized in the following figure.

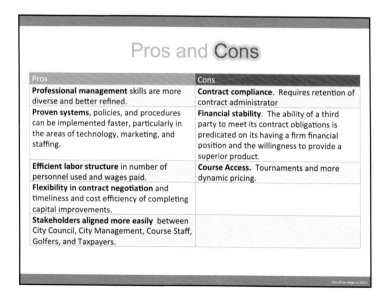

On balance, management companies bring skills and focus to golf course operations, and their influence is growing. Management companies now manage

1,653 18-hole equivalent golf courses[9] of all types, up by 21% from 2006. Here is a summary of the 20 largest, in order of size.[10]

	Company	Courses Managed
1	Troon Golf	208.0
2	Accordia Golf (Japan)	156.0
3	Pacific Golf Management (Japan)	153.0
4	Billy Casper Golf	134.5
5	Club Corp	131.5
6	Kemper Sports	105.0
7	American Golf Corp.	102.0
8	Century Golf Partners	82.0
9	Clublink Corporation (Canada)	55.5
10	Blue Green Group Saur (France)	53.5
11	OB Sports	51.0
12	Sequoia Golf Management	49.0
13	Marriott Golf	48.0
14	Lindsay Management Co.	40.5
15	Fore Golf Partners	40.0
16	Crown Golf (United Kingdom)	35.0
17	NGF Golf (France)	31.0
18	Touchstone Golf	30.5
19	Eagle Golf Group	29.0
20	Landscape Golf Group	27.0

Are There Hidden Risks for Any Course with a Third-Party Management Company?

The answer is "yes," but those risks can be by mitigated by agreement. In order to do so, there are several issues that need to be addressed. The management agreement provides the least exposure. Merely ensuring that strategic plans are created and implemented with appropriate governance should suffice.

A lease places a golf course owner at far greater risk of having assets mismanaged, resulting in a large capital expenditure to restore upon default.

---

9 http://www.golfincmagazine.com/news/features/25-largest-management-companies-2011

10 http://www.golfincmagazinemonthly-digital.com/golfincmagazinemonthly/august_september_2013#pg31

Under a lease, capital improvements requirements must be very definitive as to improvements and timetable. The ownership of intangible property needs to be defined. For example, we have unfortunately observed several leasing companies that obtained the Web site URL for a golf course, then refused to transfer the URL and access to the Web site back to the golf course owners. Amazing but true.

Under a lease, there is also the question, "Who owns the customer database?"

You might think that the question would be very simple to answer. Most golf course owners would quickly answer, "I own our customer database. Why would you think otherwise?"

Actually, if you use a third-party organization to operate your golf course or your food and beverage concession, depending on whether the contractual relationship is a management agreement or a lease, the ownership of the customer database and the associated transaction data are determined by the principles of the "law of agency."

Simply stated, whoever "owns the economics" is entitled to ownership of the customer database, unless otherwise stated contractually.

While the concept is simple, the ramifications to the "title holder" of the golf course are complex and may surprise you.

The Legal Dilemma

This issue recently came to the forefront as Golf Convergence began to undertake a customer survey as a component of crafting a strategic plan for a client who had "leased" a facility to a management company.

A standard task for this type of engagement is a golfer survey.

Because the contract with the municipality contained confidentiality provisions regarding release of financial and customer data, we naively thought that we would be able to obtain a copy of the email list from the management company to undertake the survey. All of the golfers had opted in to be contacted. Naturally, we knew our ability to use the email list would be restricted to use for the survey only, and all names would be deleted upon completion of such.

Our request for a copy of the email list was met with the following response from the management company:

> "No, we can't provide you that list. It is our intellectual property. We may be able to launch an email on your behalf depending on the advice of counsel."

That message came with the following explanation:

> "Our concerns may seem silly to outside observers, however, as a national company ... and with several hundred thousand customer e-mail addresses, we have extensive experience in matters related to privacy challenges and SPAM controls. We have to take this very seriously and be thorough in the process.
>
> Our legal department has reached out to our outside counsel. They are developing parameters that will ensure Golf Convergence can follow-up with customers. Please bear with us, privacy challenges to the use of e-mail databases is a budding area of litigation and I'm trying to find an acceptable solution that will ensure feedback and effectively and openly address any potential customer concerns."

Interestingly, the contract with the municipality and the management company was originated prior to the invention of email addresses, and the contract is silent as to the ownership of the intellectual property and the course's intangible assets.

Ultimately, the management company was supportive and launched the email survey campaign. However, there were short-term unintended consequences that have long-term implications for the golf industry.

In the short-term, the efficacy of the survey was weakened. The size of the client's email database could not be revealed to us. The open rate, click-through rate, and the ability to send targeted second emails to those categories were restricted. The ability to achieve a statistically valid survey, not knowing the size of the customer database, was limited. As a result, the ability to effectively measure the operational efficiency of the management company was hampered.

But there is a far more important consequence.

Who Owns the Economics?

Management companies believe that the individual who "owns the economics" of the course is rightly the owner of the customer database—not, by default, the golf course owner.

It is the belief of management companies we polled that if the contractual agreement is a "management agreement," the golf course and the management company have a joint and equal interest in the customer database. If the contractual agreement is a "lease," the management companies believe that the customer database is the management company's sole intellectual property.

Their belief is firmly rooted. To illustrate, we were informed by a management company that they unfortunately had to decline the request of a municipality to email a 4th of July announcement to its golfer database. It was the management company's belief that the golfers opted in merely for golf-related information, and to contact them for any other purpose would be a violation of that implicit agreement with the golfers.

This has severe negative ramifications for golf course owners. Upon the termination of a "management contract," does the management company have the right to use the golf course's customer information? To the extent that each party had a "joint and equal interest in the database," the answer would likely be "yes." In theory, the management company could then use its former client's customer database to compete against its former client if the management company represented another golf course in the local market. Unethical—yes, possible—yes, legally restricted—maybe not, especially if the rights to the intellectual property were undefined within the contract.

If the contract is a lease, even more dire consequences may result. The golf course owner is left with no information regarding its golfers' playing frequency and spending habits. The owner will lack any demographic information regarding the course's customers and be unable to contact them via email. In essence, the golf course owner would be placed at a serious disadvantage in continuing to operate the golf course, whether through internal management or the retention of another firm.

In essence, if the ownership of the intellectual property is not defined in a lease agreement, the golf course owner, whether a daily fee golf course or a municipality, effectively becomes the indentured servant of the management company. The golf course owner is unlikely to be able to afford the economic loss from terminating the contract and having to create a customer database from scratch.

What About Third-Party Tee Time Firms?

One of the brouhahas used as an argument against third-party tee time firms concerns this issue of who owns the customer email addresses.

It is the feeling among tee time providers that if they create a new customer database for a golf course through their own marketing efforts, their only obligation is to provide the golf course the golfers' names and credit card information—not their email addresses. This policy frustrates many golf course owners.

Who is right? In this case, we side with the third-party tee time company. The golfers only agreed to provide their email addresses to complete a commercial transaction with the third party and did not explicitly approve its redistribution to the golf course. Would you want your email address provided to United Airlines and Starwood Hotels if you booked your flight and hotel on Expedia or Orbitz? Probably not.

It is our opinion that it is incumbent on the golf course owner to identify such customers and to train the staff to obtain the email address of each customer upon check-in. To the extent that the golf course fails to implement appropriate procedures to capture such data, frankly, it is the golf course owner's fault, whether due to lack of business acumen or due to laziness. Technology exists that renders this a simple and quick process. There is no excuse for not getting customers' email addresses. Golf course owners bear the risk and the blame of the resulting economic loss.

What Should Any Golf Course Owner Do?

The owner of the course needs to specify, in both a management agreement and a lease, the ownership of the customer database affiliated with the golf course. In a survey conducted by Golf Convergence in May 2012, golf course owners were asked the following question: "If you lost your customer database (names, spending, emails, social media friends), what impact would it have on your revenue? The following figure shows their responses.

For the typical golf course, the database would have a value exceeding $275,000. One management company indicated that it would "sell" the database back to the city, for perhaps "as little as $750,000."

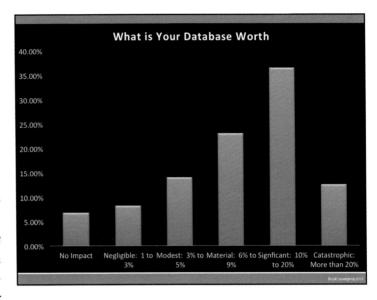

A course owner who enters into a management agreement does so to optimize the investment return from the operation of that facility, while recognizing his or her own organizational strengths and weaknesses. Management agreements provide a third party the opportunity, through that firm's expertise, to profit—but that should not be at the long-term expense or detriment of the owner. The golf course owner expects the relationship to be mutually beneficial.

The unintended consequence of the evolution of technology is that a golf course owner may be placing his course at a significant disadvantage by using a third-party management company unless the ownership of the intellectual property is precisely defined.

We believe that the golf course owner has a unilateral ownership of not only tangible assets, such as the course, the clubhouse, etc., but also the intellectual property and intangible assets, such as customer database information, brand image, etc.

Each golf course owner would be well-served to retain legal counsel for guidance in addressing the ownership of intellectual property prior to entering into any management agreement.

Management companies serve a vital role in the golf course industry. They bring a sophistication and professional management that is beyond the grasp of many golf course owners. However, we believe that their interests and those of the golf course owners should be mutually aligned both during the time the contract is in force and upon its termination.

What About Private Clubs?

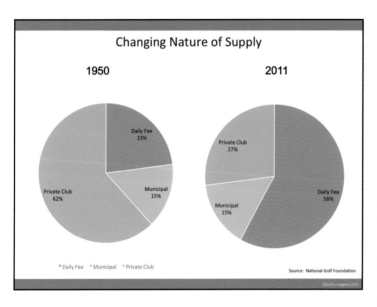

It is interesting to note that since 1950, the number of private clubs has shrunk from 62% to 27% of the golf courses in the United States.

It is a surprising statistic, but there were fewer private golf clubs in 2009 than there were in 1931, during the Depression. No growth has occurred in that area of the industry in nearly 80 years.

As would be expected, due to their higher price points, the private club industry contracted during the recent economic downturn, as shown below.

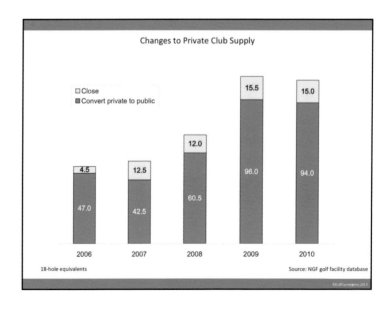

The change in these demographics makes one wonder if the private club is destined to become extinct with the changes in our culture. The answer is obviously "no." Private clubs will always have their niche for social or practical reasons. The buzzwords surrounding a private club—exclusivity, culture, service, familiarity, tradition/history, quality, convenience, consistency—will always be attractive to a certain segment of the population. However, the form of equity participation at private clubs is likely to dramatically change over the next decade.

Currently, the distribution of equity and non-equity clubs is illustrated below[11]:

Type of Private Club	Number	% of US Courses	% of Private Club
Private Equity	2,415	15.43%	60.33%
Private Non-Equity	1,561	9.98%	39.00%
Private Resort	27	0.17%	0.67%

It is important to understand the delineation between equity clubs when compared to those with initiation fees and member deposits. They are often confused.

An equity club represents a percentage ownership within a club, for example, 1/600 of a club that has 600 members. A non-equity club is usually owned by a single entity that provides members the right to use the club. Historically, both forms of private clubs provided that the initiation fee paid was refundable in total or in part, based on a transfer fee. The evolving trend is that these initiation fees are becoming non-refundable. A prestigious private club in Colorado implemented just such a policy. This movement to non-refundable initiation fee structure provides the opportunity to fund capital improvement programs.

All private clubs would be advised to offer non-refundable memberships at 40% of the current equity prices and to use such funds for capital improvements and for funding a capital reserve.

The Proper Governance

Historically, private clubs were run by committees. Structured like businesses, the clubs had boards consisting of members with diverse backgrounds and skill sets. The typical organizational structure of a private club is reflected in the chart on the next page:[12]

---

11 National Golf Foundation, "Golf Facility List," 2012.

12 Club Managers Association, *Board Resource Manual*, "Club Organizational Information," Section 2, pg. 1.

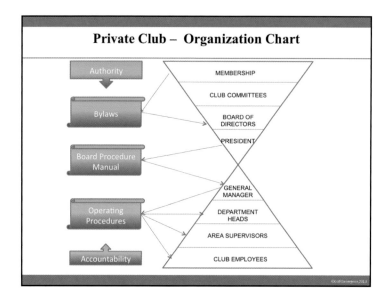

The Cacophony of Chaos

To operate a $4 million enterprise requires a lot of vision, talent, and patience.

Brad Klein, one of the leading journalists on golf course architecture, wrote in *Golfweek*, "When it comes to running a private golf club these days, most boards are overwhelmed. If the politics don't get them, the business demands will."[13]

While each person on a board may, individually, be a delight; collectively, the decision-making process in which they engage can be ineffective.

Klein echoed those sentiments by writing, "The folks who gravitate toward power at a private club tend, in my experience, to be the kind who like to set the agenda. Rarely does the self-selection process of club governance produce decision-makers of moderate temperance and firm wisdom."[14]

Why does this behavior occur? Most people seek consensus rather than discord. Most individuals will compromise their personal positions to achieve group harmony—especially in a country club board setting where they aren't

---

13 Brad Klein, *Golfweek*, "Club Politics in Era of 'the Deal,' " January 13, 2007, pg. 9.

14 Ibid.

being paid and the meetings often run late. Thus, the aggressive individual can wear down the group, resulting in consistently poor decisions.

For group decisions to be effective, the group must possess three characteristics: they must be diverse, they must be decentralized, and each member must be independent.

What is the perfect board? First, the president of the board should be required to go through the rotation of chairs from secretary (to learn the bylaws), treasurer (to understand the finances), and vice president (to learn the management and operational issues), before becoming president (having developed the vision to lead from years of serving). Second, the board members should possess diverse educational backgrounds and have skills in the basic business disciplines: accounting, customer service, food and beverage, finance, human relations, and law.

The Delegation of Decision Making

Perfectly run clubs are "benign dictatorships." For a club to run properly, the general manager needs unilateral decision-making power, as long as it is consistent with the policies of the club.

As Klein believes, "Governing boards should do little more than set basic policy, with the details of implementation, operations and rules enforcement in the hands of professionally trained management."[15]

The figure to the right shows the ideal operational structure for a private club.[16]

Private Club Management

Activity	Owner/Board	Management
Budget	Approves	Recommends & Provides Input
Capital Requests	Approves	Prepares Requests
Personnel Policy	Adopts	Recommends & Administers
Mission Statement	Adopts	Implements
Day-to-Day Operations	No Role	Makes All Management Decisions

---

15 Ibid., 9.

16 Club Managers Association, "Director's Guide for Understanding Club Governance," *Premier Club Services*, pg. 27.

Governance, Ownership, and Management

The quality and the financial stability of a municipal golf course are ultimately dependent on the actions of a city council that dictates its annual budget. For a golf course that is cash-poor but asset-rich to balance the budget, it will ultimately need to liquidate assets or privatize services.

From a "business of golf" perspective, the daily fee ownership model seems preferable. Owners make decisions that yield benefits to owners; this is the purest form of capitalism. Resorts are tied into large corporate decision-making models, and private clubs, with their ingrained committee system of member volunteers, can be ineffective.

Path to Success

1) For municipal golf courses to operate as high-end price point facilities and compete against daily fee courses is ill-advised in the vast majority of cases.

2) The role of municipal golf courses should be limited to providing playgrounds for kids to learn, places for First Tee Chapters to be operated, outdoor recreation venues for senior citizens living on Social Security, and courses where new entrants to the game can play with friends and family without the pressures of social decorum and etiquette so tightly observed at high-end daily fee courses and private clubs.

3) The vast majority of municipal golf courses in the United States are hard-pressed to operate efficiently and with a profit.

4) Of the nation's 2,415 municipal golf courses, 1,315 are located within the Top 100 core-based statistical areas. They have the advantage of pricing power and should choose to use that power by raising rates.

5) If fringe benefits exceed 40%, a municipality should consider utilizing a third party to manage the golf course.

6) There are some key rules of thumb, depending on the financial position of a golf course. If the course is incurring operating losses and lacks capital—leasing would be preferred. If the value of the course is eroding and expenses are increasing, professional management is a viable option. If a golf course is breaking even, covering debt and capital, self-management remains the preferred choice.

7) Private clubs that are operated by a member-based committee system would be well-advised to abandon such form of governance and retain a professional golf management firm to operate the club, for very few committees make a meaningful, positive difference in the success of the club.

Concluding Thought

The test of a first-rate intelligence is the ability to hold two opposed ideas in the mind at the same time and still retain the ability to function. One should, for example, be able to see that things are hopeless and yet be determined to make them otherwise.

F. Scott Fitzgerald

Chapter 5

The Geographic Local Market Analysis and Assessing Weather Playable Days

Steps 1 and 2 of the Golf Convergence WIN™ Formula

The secret is in the dirt.

Ben Hogan

Chapter Highlights

The financial success of a golf course is dependent upon both controllable and uncontrollable factors. Two of those uncontrollable factors are location and weather.

Some say that the key to making money occurs when you buy, not when you sell. Many also say that the key to success is "location, location, location." Both are so true.

It is inconceivable to think of buying a golf course without first undertaking a geographic market analysis, calculating whether the market is under- or oversupplied.

What Do Starbucks and Golf Courses Have in Common? Far More Than You Think …

How do Nordstrom, Neiman Marcus, Outback, Starbucks, Four Seasons, Ritz Carlton, and every other department store, restaurant, and hotel chain determine the locations for their businesses? They evaluate demographics. This is the first step in the Golf Convergence WIN™ formula.

To determine the location of their retail locations, they use the MOSAIC™ lifestyle database, which in 2012 had 12 lifestyle groups, as illustrated by the following table.

MOSAIC Lifestyle Data - 12 Lifestyle Groups

	Life Style Groups	Examples - 1	2	3	4
1	Affluent Suburbia	America's Wealthiest	White-Collar Suburbia	Enterprising Couples	Small-Town Success
2	Upscale America	Status-Conscious Consumers	Affluent urban Professionals	Urban Commuter Families	Second-Generation Success
3	Small-Town Contentment	Second City Homebodies	Prime Middle America	Suburban Optimists	Family Convenience
4	Blue-Collar Backbone	Neuvo Hispanic Families	Working Rural	Lower-Income Essentials	Small-City Endeavors
5	American Diversity	Ethnic Urban Mis	Urban Blues	Professional Urbanities	Mature America
6	Metro Fringe	Steadfast Conservatives	Southern Blues	Urban Grit	Grass-Roots Living
7	Remote America	Hardy Rural Families	Rural Southern Living	Coal and Crops	Native Americana
8	Aspiring Contemporaries	Young Cosmopolitans	Minority Metro Communities	Stable Careers	Aspiring Hispania
9	Rural Villages and Farms	Industrious Country Living	America's Farmlands	Comfy Country Living	Hinterland Families
10	Struggling Societies	Rugged Rural Style	Latino Nuevo	Struggling City Centers	College Town Communities
11	Urban Essence	Unattached Multi-cultures	Academic Influences	African-American Neighborhoods	New Generation Activists
12	Varying Lifestyles	Military Family Life	Major University Towns		

Having established that the game of golf is played largely by Caucasian, well-to-do, above-the-average-age people, on golf courses that are located in the lifestyle groups classified as "Affluent Suburbia, Upscale American and Small-Town Contentment," courses in these areas are likely to outperform those located in the areas classified as "Blue-collar Backbone, Rural Villages and Farms, or Struggling Societies. The majority of golfers can be classified in the top three tiers of the MOSAIC lifestyle database.

The objective of this typology is:

- To classify neighborhoods in a way that provides the most powerful description of consumers' behavior, lifestyles, and attitudes.
- To identify lifestyle groups that are as recognizable and meaningful as possible to marketers.
- To ensure that each of the named groups contain sufficient numbers of households to be statistically reliable for most analyses.

- To ensure that each cluster is homogeneous in terms of demographics and consumer behavior.

- To avoid an excessive concentration of individual U.S. MOSAIC types within particular geographic regions, except where appropriate."[1]

To illustrate, presented below is the MOSAIC profile for five cities and for the United States in the aggregate.

These MOSAIC statistics indicate that it would be far preferable to acquire and operate a golf course in Atlanta, Georgia, or Becker, Minnesota, rather than in Arcata, California; Brookings, Oregon; or Casper, Wyoming.

But the devil is in the details. While the Atlanta market appears to be quite attractive, there is a catch. Atlanta is encircled by Interstate 285, with Interstate 20, roughly cutting the city in half, north from south.

If you were trying to find a Starbucks or a high-end daily fee or luxurious resort inside of I-285 and south of I-20, you would be challenged. Why? The affluent suburbia of metropolitan Atlanta is located north of I-20, as demonstrated in the figure to the right.

	Arcata, CA	Atlanta, GA	Becker, MN	Brookings, OR	Casper, WY	United States
Affluent Suburbia	0.0%	31.3%	34.4%	0.00%	8.5%	13.90%
Upscale America	1.0%	9.1%	10.3%	0.00%	2.6%	11.10%
Small-Town Contentment	7.9%	17.5%	23.9%	1.60%	18.6%	11.80%
Blue-Collar Backbone	15.0%	.9%	0.6%	4.70%	25.3%	6.20%
American Diversity	9.8%	.9%	1.2%	23.70%	2.9%	8.80%
Metro Fringe	15.1%	10.1%	8.4%	7.20%	23.8%	10.50%
Remote America	3.4%	.4%	0.6%	9.80%	6.8%	6.30%
Aspiring Contemporaries	0.0%	17.6%	2.1%	0.00%	0.0%	7.70%
Rural Villages and Farms	25.4%	1.3%	13.0%	23.80%	4.1%	9.40%
Struggling Societies	10.8%	2.1%	2.7%	21.10%	5.1%	7.00%
Urban Essence	10.8%	7.5%	2.3%	2.20%	2.4%	5.80%
Varying Lifestyles	0.9%	1.2%	0.7%	5.80%	0.0%	1.40%

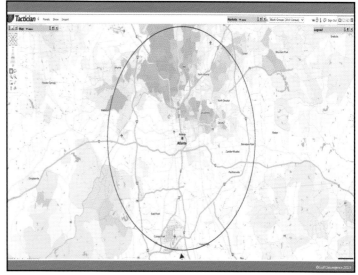

Key: The scale is yellow (low affluent) to pink (high affluent).

1 http://www.spatialinsights.com/catalog/product.aspx?product=80&content=1386

Matching the known profile of customers to the population by age and gender, households by size, median income, the composition of the labor force by industry and employment rates and the metro area size is essential for big business, and it is essential for golf courses.

Interestingly, in February 2013, the MOSAIC Clusters were divided into 12 new global categories, as illustrated in the following figure.

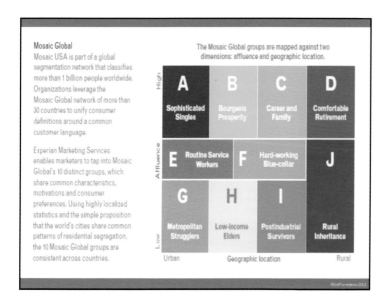

Again the vast majority of golfers fall within the "sophisticated singles," "bourgeois prosperity," "career and family," or "comfortable retirement" categories. It should be emphasized that these data are available for the vast majority of international markets, so golf courses, regardless of their locations, can use the MOSAIC model to measure financial potential.

Presented in the table below is an example of the new 2013 US MOSAIC profile applied. One will note that golf courses near Irvine, CA; Mundelein, IL, and San Antonio, TX might have the opportunity to prosper based on the demographics.

	Irvine, CA					Macomb IL	Mundelein IL	San Antonio TX	City of Sarasota FL	Thompsonville MI	Tallahassee FL
	5 Miles	10 Miles	15 Miles	20 Miles	25 Miles	10 Miles	10 Miles	10 Miles	5 Miles	5 Miles	10 Miles
Top 3 Rating	36.90%	19.10%	18.00%	15.90%	12.80%	-13.00%	38.60%	26.70%	7.50%	-17.00%	-11.00%
Power Elite	13.10%	8.10%	6.60%	4.80%	2.40%	-5.40%	19.60%	12.90%	0.00%	-5.40%	-2.80%
Flourishing Families	20.70%	7.70%	8.20%	7.70%	8.40%	-2.30%	8.50%	8.80%	-3.00%	-5.50%	-3.40%
Booming with Confidence	3.10%	3.30%	3.20%	3.40%	2.00%	-5.30%	10.50%	5.00%	10.50%	-6.10%	-4.80%
Suburban Style	-3.20%	-1.80%	-1.10%	0.70%	1.50%	-5.80%	0.20%	4.40%	-4.50%	-5.80%	-26.30%
Thriving Boomers	-2.20%	-2.40%	-2.80%	-3.00%	-2.80%	-2.50%	-2.00%	-4.30%	-1.20%	1.90%	5.40%
Promising Families	-1.40%	-2.00%	-2.00%	-1.90%	-1.90%	-2.60%	-1.20%	3.60%	-1.60%	-2.60%	-5.70%
Young City Solos	11.30%	5.00%	3.00%	2.10%	1.40%	-1.50%	1.30%	-0.60%	-1.60%	-1.80%	-1.00%
Middle-class Melting Pot	-1.30%	0.50%	3.70%	5.80%	7.60%	-4.90%	0.70%	5.50%	-0.90%	-4.70%	-9.90%
Family Union	-6.20%	5.80%	5.10%	4.30%	6.20%	-5.60%	-4.20%	-3.20%	-3.50%	-4.10%	0.10%
Autumn Years	-5.60%	-5.30%	-5.00%	-4.80%	-4.60%	4.00%	-4.50%	-5.30%	-2.60%	19.00%	22.40%
Significant Singles	3.40%	3.20%	3.60%	3.40%	2.60%	0.90%	3.70%	-0.60%	1.60%	-5.10%	-1.00%
Blue Sky Boomers	-4.90%	-4.80%	-4.70%	-4.50%	-4.50%	1.00%	-4.40%	-4.80%	8.10%	23.30%	25.80%
Families in Motion	-3.40%	-3.40%	-3.40%	-3.40%	-3.40%	2.90%	-3.40%	-3.30%	-2.40%	6.30%	9.60%
Pastoral Pride	-7.00%	-7.00%	-7.00%	-7.00%	-7.00%	5.00%	-6.90%	-7.00%	-5.80%	6.00%	11.70%
Singles and Starters	-1.30%	-2.90%	-3.40%	-3.40%	-3.40%	22.80%	-4.10%	6.60%	-3.20%	-7.10%	-22.50%
Cultural Connections	-6.30%	5.30%	5.30%	4.70%	4.30%	-7.90%	-6.30%	-5.90%	-2.90%	-7.90%	-6.00%
Golden Year Guardians	-2.10%	-2.50%	-2.70%	-2.40%	-2.90%	4.10%	-1.10%	-5.40%	11.60%	5.90%	9.10%
Aspirational Fusion	-2.70%	-2.60%	-2.60%	-2.60%	-2.40%	-0.50%	-2.50%	-2.40%	1.40%	-2.70%	-0.40%
Struggling Societies	-4.20%	-4.20%	-4.20%	-4.20%	-4.00%	3.20%	-4.10%	-4.20%	-0.20%	-3.70%	-0.20%

Every golf course is unique and every market is local. Thus, to determine the financial potential of any golf course, it is essential that you understand the demand and supply details of the market.

The following chart reflects how you can discern the potential of a market.

Demographics Provide the First Clue to a Course's Potential

Category	Centerville, MI	Downey, CA	Durango, CO	Greenville, NC	Penn Valley, CA	Sioux Falls, SD	U.S.
Demographics							
Age (Median)	35.30	34.60	37.20	35.20	46.20	35.00	37.10
Age (Index)	95	93	100	95	125	94	100
Income (Med Hhld)	$46,994	$47,758	$56,248	$37,701	$66,752	$57,094	$51,618
Income (Median)	91	93	109	73	129	106	100
Disposable Income (Med Hhld)	$40,159	$40,629	$47,273	$33,106	$58,880	$47,626	$45,301
Disposable Income (Median)	89	90	104	73	130	105	100
Ethnicity (% Cauc.)	86.10%	43.00%	86.80%	56.50%	92.60%	90.50%	73.90%
Ethnicity Index	117	58	117	76	125	122	100

At first glance, Centreville, Michigan, and Durango, Colorado, seem likely to attract a low- to mid-tier daily fee golf course. Downey, California, is probably going to be best served by an economically diverse municipal golf course at a low price. Greenville, North Carolina, would have a challenge supporting many private clubs due to the ethnicity mix. Penn Valley, California, appears appropriate to support a higher-end daily fee or a private country club in what is likely to be a retirement community. Sioux Falls, South Dakota, might do well with a family-oriented, mid-tier priced, daily fee golf course where pace of play would be important.

How does one divine those conclusions from such scant data? Centreville and Downey have nearly identical demographics (age, income, and disposable income) except for ethnicity. Caucasians would place a far higher value on having the opportunity to play golf than an ethnically diverse population. Durango's income and ethnicity would foretell the success of a daily fee golf course, if it were appropriately priced. Penn Valley's age, income, disposable income, and ethnicity statistics have the characteristics of a retirement community in which value provided will be paramount to a fee-conscious community.

While these statistics provide a foundation, they don't provide the depth of insight necessary. There is a series of reports available to golf courses through Golf Convergence's license of the Tactician and National Golf Foundation databases. The reports needed to undertake an in-depth analysis include: Demographic Trend Report, Income and Disposable Income Report, MOSAIC Adult Population Summary, Population > 18 report, NGF Demand Report, and the NGF Supply Report.

By utilizing these reports, one can construct the following matrix of insights.

The Real Potential of a Golf Course is Found in the Details

Category	Centerville, MI	Downey, CA	Durango, CO	Greenville, NC	Penn Valley, CA	Sioux Falls, SD	U.S.
Avid Golfers	1,533	53,481	680	2,137	1,163	4,410	6,887,600
Total Golfers	5,722	199,558	2,537	7,975	4,339	16,456	25,700,000
Golfing Households	3,566	162,242	2,063	6,484	3,528	13,379	21,219,240
Rounds Played	65,978	4,362,404	44,054	142,876	111,172	277,08	463,000,000
Rounds Played Locally	N/A	2,210,079	24,965	75,533	55,876	151,279	279,190,432
% of Rounds Played Locally	N/A	51%	57%	53%	50%	54.60%	60%
Golfing Fees	N/A	178,033,600	1,408,200	4,233,005	4,293,361	11,840,212	20,179,122,176
Golfing Fees per Household	N/A	1,097	683	653	1,217	885	951
Rounds Played per Golfer	11.53	21.86	17.36	17.91	25.62	16.84	18.02
Golf Fees per Round	N/A	40.81	31.97	29.63	38.62	42.73	43.58
Golf Participation	12.33%	6.65%	9.17%	6.03%	7.28%	9.75%	8.37%
Total Population +18	34,460	2,167,323	23,903	100,552	41,874	126,865	232,116,402
Population	46,412	3,002,961	27,686	132,276	51,924	168,815	307,156,296
Households	16,876	845,776	11,464	52,242	22,902	68,316	113,900,256
Population/Household	2.75	3.55	2.42	2.53	2.27	2.47	2.70
Golfers per 18 Holes	1,144	9,978	1,269	1,994	1,446	2,057	1,737
Avid per 18 holes	307	2,674	340	534	388	551	463
Avid Household Index	78	578	73	115	99	141	100

©Golf Convergence 2013

The chart to the left provides insight that golf courses in Centerville, Michigan, and Durango, Colorado, are likely to struggle, depending upon the experiences created and the relative price points. Conversely, Downey, California, and Sioux Falls, South Dakota, have positive demand for golf.

Demand Is a Benchmark That Supply Renders Relevant

The Characteristics of Supply Nationally

Category	U.S.
Premium >$71	1,313
Value $40-$70	3,893
Price <$40	6,438
Private/Public Mix	26%
Premium/Value Mix %	25%
Premium >$71 %	11%
Value $40-$70 %	33%
Price <$40 %	55%
Number of Holes - Total Facilities	264,627
Number of Holes - Public Facilities	191,916
Number of Holes - Private Facilities	72,711
Number of Holes - Resorts Facilities	24,840
18-Hole Equivalents	14,701.5
Public 18-Hole Equiv.	10,662.0
Private 18-Hole Equiv.	4,039.5
Resort 18-Hole Equiv.	1,380.0

Source: National Golf Foundation Supply Report
©Golf Convergence 2013

The question becomes "What is the supply in an individual market?"

The NGF tracks over 30 different statistics in each golf facility in the United States, including: year opened, total holes, price point, number of tee stations on range, peak green fee, and area allocated to sales. A summary of some of these key data points is presented in the table to the left.

The statistics listed earlier can be detailed for any market based on any segment radius the user selects. That analysis is extremely important. Understanding the relative price points within the market and the balance of public, private, and resort courses is a further segmentation that is required.

To illustrate, if you examine the chart below, the Greenville, North Carolina, market appears to have demand that exceeds supply. That is true. However, there are three private facilities, and the analysis suggests that only slightly more than one golf course is needed. The opportunity appears to be in the public sector. But there is a risk. To the extent that the private clubs provide public access on some basis (such as weekday play, afternoon play, waiving initiation fees, and offering discounted dues), the opportunities for the public golf course can become quickly eroded.

Are these calculations precisely accurate and infallible? Absolutely not. They provide insights and interesting perspectives, but to act aggressively based on the analysis has risks. For example, in Downey, California, the data suggests that within 10 miles of the area examined, based on the number of golfers that reside within that radius, 27 additional golf courses could be added.

Category	Centerville, MI	Downey, CA	Durango, CO	Greenville, NC	Penn Valley, CA	Sioux Falls, SD	U.S.
Total Facilities	5.00	6.00	2.00	4.00	4.00	8.00	15,869.00
If Market In Balance	3.91	34.99	1.00	4.62	3.00	11.00	14,882.00
Demand – Supply Balance	1.09	27.01	1.00	0.62	1.00	3.00	
Golfers per Public Facility	1,144	10,072	1,269	1,994	1,085	2,057	1,659.00
Public Facilities	4.00	6.00	2.00	1.00	2.00	6.00	11,603
If Market In Balance	2.79	24.91	1.00	3.29	2.00	8.00	10,593.50
Golfers per Private Facility	1,430	10,072	1,269	7,975	2,170	2,743	2,269.00
Private Facilities	1.00	0.00	0.00	3.00	2.00	2.00	4,266.00
If Market In Balance	1.13	10.08	0.00	1.33	1.00	3.00	4,288.50

The Final Answer as to the Course's Potential and Its Pricing Power

But that would be foolhardy for several reasons. First, the basis of measurement is comparing national benchmarks to a local market. The conclusions can become skewed. The demand that exists in Downey is complemented by 345 playable golf days. While national 18-hole golf courses average less than 30,000 rounds each per year, golf courses in Downey, California, frequently exceed 90,000 starts per year, reaching the facility's theoretical capacity of 102,000 rounds, as shown in the figure at the top of the next page.

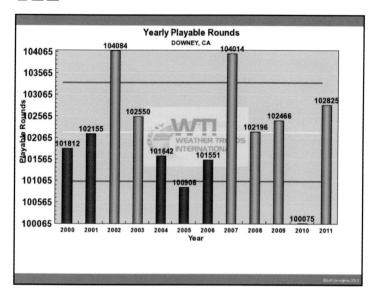

The real opportunity is to nudge prices upward, ensuring that a consistent value-based experience is provided to the golfer. But even that has a threshold based on the ethnicity reflected in previous charts and the median household income that is below national benchmarks.

Why Customer Demographics Really Matter

Location	Miles	MOSAIC #	Income	Age	Hispanic	Black	Asian	Golfers	Slope Rating
Brooklyn Park, MN	10	0.90%	$63,595	36	5.50%	12.40%	7.30%	4,129	141
Charlotte, NC	5	-6.00%	$49,410	34	17.10%	32.30%	4.20%	3,843	120
Chelan, WA	10	-11.30%	$46,900	41	37.70%	3.40%	6.00%	398	119
Columbus, OH	5	-0.30%	$41,655	33	5.70%	30.00%	4.20%	8,584	125
Irvine, CA	5	36.90%	$90,186	36	14.30%	1.90%	32.70%	3,848	133
Irvine, CA	10	19.10%	$80,752	36	36.60%	1.60%	15.90%	3,680	133
Macomb, IL	10	-5.40%	$31,694	28	2.90%	6.20%	2.20%	742	133
Mundelin, IL	10	38.60%	$87,833	40	13.70%	2.90%	9.20%	1,524	138
San Antonio, TX	5	26.70%	$76,890	31	41.50%	6.50%	6.50%	2,298	131
Sarasota, FL	10	7.50%	$50,434	49	13.80%	7.30%	1.70%	2,350	117
Tallahassee, FL	10	-11.00%	$39,789	29	6.40%	35.00%	2.90%	3,261	131

Blending the demographics with supply, as measured by golfers per 18 holes within the competitive market, defines the potential of a golf course. Shown here is this exercise from the Clemson University Strategic Planning Pilot Study that revealed the potential (Irvine, CA) and the challenges that some courses face (Macomb, IL) from uncontrollable factors.

From this information, the potential for a golf course can be ascertained.

With the data known, measuring the median household income compared to the green fee provides further insights as shown in the figure at the top of the next page.

Average	Green Fee Rate	Median Household Income	Relationship	Price Sensitivity
Bloomington, IL	33	58,307	56.60%	Great value
Brooklyn Park, MN	63	63,595	99.06%	Price appropriate
Charlotte, NC	49	47,870	102.36%	Price appropriate
Columbus, OH	40	53,937	73.70%	Great value
Fernie, BC	65	62,509	103.98%	Price appropriate
Irvine, CA	175	90,186	194.04%	Service and /or course must excel
Macomb, IL	36	31,694	113.59%	Price slightly high
Mundelein, IL	100	87,833	113.85%	Price slightly high
San Antonio, TX	50	76,890	65.03%	Great Value
Thompsonville, MI	95	41,800	227.27%	Service and/or course must excel

Note: The relationship is determined by dividing the green fee rate by the result of dividing the median household income by 1,000.

This chart clearly shows golf courses that have the opportunity to raise rates and those where the experience must excel to command the rates posted.

Understanding the unique market in which a golf course operates (the underlying demographics of its customers) is fundamental to maximizing its financial potential.

In general, 90% of all rounds played at municipal courses, private, and most daily fee golf courses are played by golfers who live or work within a 30-minute drive time from the golf course. However, regional resorts often draw their customers from a 300-mile range. And for national resorts or golf courses listed in a Top 100 in the United States or World listing, golfers travel from far greater distances.

Just the Facts: Industry

90% Rounds	30 Minutes
15% Golfers	60% Revenue
Distinct Customers	8,000 Golfers
Barrier	Time/No Barriers
Defectors	50%
Game	Caucasian, Rich, Old

Fifteen percent of the golfers generate 60% of the revenue, and the average golfer plays at seven different courses annually. Thus, because 50% of golfers play a golf course only once per year and only 13% play a single facility six or more times, identifying your customers is fundamental.

Undertaking the geographic local market analysis is the first step in the Golf Convergence WIN™ process.

Go

If you licensed the supplemental template that accompanies this Field book, call Golf Convergence to arrange delivery of the necessary Tactician demographic reports that will enable you to complete Step 1: Geographic Local Market Analysis. The Field book includes an Excel worksheet with all of the vital data elements defined as well as related statistics for golf courses in the United States.

Upon completion of the exercise, answer the following questions:

1) Is your MOSAIC profile support of a golf course in your local market consistent with the course's defined vision?

2) Is demand weak or strong in relation to supply within a 10-mile radius of your course?

3) Is the value being offered consistent with the demographics?

4) How does the suggested median green fee compare to your current rack rate?

5) How do you explain any variance that may exist?

Controlling the Uncontrollable

Mother Nature is fickle—she gives and she takes. Hot, cold, snow, blizzards, avalanches, rain, sleet, thunderstorms, lightning, hurricanes, tornadoes, drought, wind, who knew weather came in so many flavors?

How much would you pay to control the weather? How much would you pay to have the correct answers consistently to these questions? The analysis of the impact of weather is the second step in the Golf Convergence WIN™ formula:

• How many days will it rain in the next two weeks? Will it be too hot for people to golf?

- When should I choose to run promotions?

- How many employees will I need to schedule?

- How has weather impacted my sales in the past?

- How will the weather impact my business this week?

- How many golf playable days will my course have in the next 14 days?

- Will Mother Nature take care of my course watering needs?

- Will the weather be okay for the upcoming tournaments and outings?

- Do we need a back-up plan for the scheduled outdoor wedding this weekend?

Trying to efficiently operate a business that is outdoors can be exasperating. Rain minimizes water costs, but sunny skies and warm days boost business. Weather has a material impact on the financial performance of a golf course. The power of just one degree difference in temperature or one inch of rain can significantly influence the retail golf industry. Did you realize the following effects of weather change?

- 1° hotter = +1.3% beer or soft drink sales

- 1° colder = +9% increase in girls outerwear sales

- 1° hotter = +10% increase in sun care products sales

- 1° colder = +24% increase in electric blanket sales

- 1° hotter = +24% increase in air conditioner sales

- 1° colder = 1.4% increase in coffee consumption

- 1° hotter = +13% increase in hedge trimmer product sales[2]

Fortune 100 companies in 23 countries believe in the power of weather changes and of forecasting those changes. They utilize Weather Trends International to help them generate return on investments of from $10 million to $230 million annually.

Weather Trends' clients include 3M, Ben & Jerry's, Black & Decker, Coca-Cola, Hershey's, J&J, Target, and Walmart. All of these companies utilize Weather Trends International's on-demand mapping, 20-year trend, custom alerts,

---

2 Weather Trends International, "Weather Trends 360 Business," pg. 4.

sales and market planning, analytics, and sales forecasting to help them better understand how weather influences their sales. This information allows them to plan product manufacturing and shipment accordingly. Should snow blowers be put on sale in Colorado in late September or early November? Should spring flowers be available for purchase in March, April, or May?

Weather Trends provides 1- to 14-day and 3-, 6-, 9-, and 11-month global weather forecasts by Geo market or ZIP Code with 80% accuracy. Using proprietary algorithms and millions of lines of code to generate forecasts, Weather Trends' 10-year client retention rate exceeds 90%. The following figure is an example of what the company offers.

What relevance do these tools have for the golf course industry? Enormous, and the cost of these services can range from complimentary (for the basic weather alert service) to $2,500 annually per facility (for a comprehensive set of historical analysis and forecasting tools). This seems a nominal expense considering the potential of having some control over the effects of weather at your golf course.

Weather's Impact on Golf

Weather's impact on golf has been clearly demonstrated in 2013 as numerous PGA tournaments have subject to many weather delays. The importance of weather on golf was featured by Global Golf Post in its 2013 Open coverage shown on the following page.[3]

---

3 http://digitalmag.globalgolfpost.com/20130715/20130715#&pageSet=1&page=0

In 2012, for many parts of the country, 2012 set a record for maximum highest temperature, highest minimum temperature, and least precipitation—all favorable elements for golf.

To announce the rounds played in 2012, the National Golf Foundation published the following newsletter:

"2012 Rounds Played—The Largest Single-Year Jump Since the Millennium"

The most influential factor in the golf economy in 2012 was the 5.7% increase in rounds played.

Improved weather (emphasis added) was the biggest influence on rounds played. PGA PerformanceTrak reported a healthy 6.5% increase in playable days nationwide in 2012. Weather in the northern region of the country was particularly favorable compared to 2011. Playable days in these states increased 13.6%, compared to 5.5% in the rest of the country.

Nearly every state experienced a gain over 2011 statistics. The geographic engine for the improvement has been a huge section of the northern half of the country, where the year-after-year growth average was 9.5%, compared to 3.8% for the rest of the country. The area from the Dakotas to Vermont (technically, the West North Central, the East North East Central and the Mid-Atlantic regions) drove up

the national numbers, mainly because 44% of all U.S. golf courses and 47% of the country's public golf courses are located in this area as illustrated above.

It is important to note that Mother Nature probably doesn't deserve all the credit for the increase in rounds played. National measurements of consumer confidence and spending have also been slowly and consistently edging upward from dips we saw in the recent Great Recession. Feelings of personal financial well-being are undoubtedly tied to an individual's positivity toward all types of discretionary and recreational spending, including golf.

As you would expect, golf course operators have benefitted from the jump in rounds played. PerformanceTrak reported that median golf fee revenues were up 6.6% at member facilities through December 2012. However, given that 'all golf is local,' individual facility performance is driven largely by the nature of local competition, weather, and economic/socio-demographic factors."[4]

But how can we give appropriate weight to the factors that may cause an increase in rounds? Is weather the most important? The economy? Consumer confidence?

---

4 http://ngfdashboard.clubnewsmaker.org/1liec384tsf1sl9b7u4wlc?a=5&p=1012685&t=43825

What we do know is that statistically, year after year, local weather conditions repeat less than 15% of the time.

Reports and Tools That Answer the Question and Predict Future Operating Results

Weather Trends International has crafted a set of tools specifically for the golf industry that include those shown in the figure to the below.

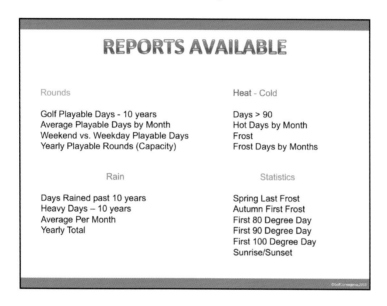

While historical data are always interesting, Weather Trends facilitates the ability to do the following:

1. Determine if management is under- or outperforming the weather.

2. Provide for efficient scheduling of events and staff.

3. Ensure optimum conservation of water resources.

Is Management Outperforming the Weather?

To ascertain management performance against the weather, a few data points are necessary.

First, determining the number of golf playable days at the facility throughout the past several years (preferably a decade).

A **Golf Playable Day (GPD)** is defined as a day (sunrise to sunset) when the maximum heat index is above 45 degrees Fahrenheit and below 95 degrees, and there is less than 0.20 inches of rainfall.

The **heat index** (**HI**) is an index that combines air temperature and relative humidity in an attempt to determine the human-perceived equivalent temperature—how hot it feels.

Total Possible Golf Playable Hours is defined as the normal maximum number of possible golf playable hours between (sunrise to sunset) when the normal maximum heat index (a combination of temperature and humidity) is below 95 and above 45, and there is less than 0.20 inches of rainfall.

While one may debate the precision of that definition, consistently applied, it is more appropriate than academic. In October 2012, Golf Convergence conducted an industry survey to determine how many golf courses tracked playable days. While 68% indicated that they did track playable days, how that day was measured varied widely. Answers ranged from "above 40 degrees," "above 50 degrees," and "above 60 degrees," to "any rounds played, April 1 to November 30, regardless of weather," "course is open," "weather permitting," "75% of tee sheet filled," "no frost or rain", and "no severe weather." It is somewhat amusing how unscientific were the criteria used by those courses that tracked playable days.

Examples of golf playable days, based on the more formal definition, are as follows:

City	Days
Arcata, CA	294
Atlanta, GA	272
Becker, MN	181
Brookings, OR	277
Casper, WY	223
Downey, CA	344
Durango, CO	246
Dubuque, IA	193
Fort McMurray, Alberta	162
Greenville, NC	259
Penn Valley, CA	302
Sioux Falls, SD	205

Additionally, gathering revenue information, preferably for the past decade, is appropriate. Those numbers are then inserted into the following worksheet to determine if a facility's management team is underperforming or outperforming the weather.

An example of that calculation is presented below.

	Base Averages	2010	Variance	2011	Variance	2012	Variance
Gross Revenue	$1,815,608	$1,975,110	$159,502	$1,730,385	$(85,223)	$1,741,329	$(74,279)
Playable Days (Weather Trends International)	214	219	5	205	(9)	234	20
Revenue per Playable Day	$8,300	$9,019	$41,502	$8,441	$(74,704)	$7,442	$166,008
Revenue Change That Should Have Been Attributable to Weather			$41,502		$(74,704)		$166,008
Under Performance by Management			N/A		($10,519)		($240,287)
Over Performance by Management			$118,000		N/A		N/A

©Golf Convergence 2013

Provide for Efficient Scheduling of Events and Staff

Weather Trends International provides a complimentary and extensive weather-forecasting tool. These alerts inform decision makers about significant events in the 1-to-14-day time window.

Using the Weather Trends short-range model, these alerts can be issued to adjust decisions pertaining to

- employee scheduling,
- revenue predictions/goals,
- course watering maintenance/timing, and
- favorable/unfavorable promotional/marketing periods.

Utilizing future weather guidance can help mitigate the sometimes volatile effects and daily fluctuations that playable hours/days can have on golf course revenue.

To illustrate, if a golf course superintendent knew for sure that it was going to rain .75 inches within 48 hours, he or she could defer using the usual 400,000 gallons dropped on the typical golf course north of I-70, and could save the golf course $800 by avoiding paying $2.00 per 1,000 golf gallons. A golf course that has 268 playable days could easily spend $214,400 annually for water. So a weather alert service offers great potential savings.

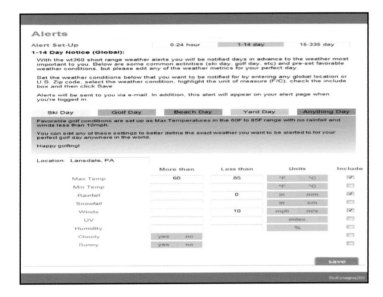

To create an alert sent to their phones via text or their computers by email, golf course operators merely need to go to wt360.com and complete the template shown to the left.

This complimentary flexible form allows you to set automatic alerts based on maximum and minimum temperatures, rainfall, snowfalls, winds, etc. You then choose the weather events desired and the advance notice time frame you want, save the template, and beginning saving money.

For those individuals seeking a more comprehensive weather forecast, Weather Trends International provides a specific custom forecast, for as little time as a week or for an entire golf season, as illustrated in the figure on the next page.

Look at Chicago and Denver to see a lot of blue (much colder) and green (far more rain) and to realize that 2013 is going to be a challenging year for the golf business. Fortunately, the weather forecast for Seattle looks promising until above-average rains are forecast for the period starting August through October.

In spring 2013, the nation has experienced the coldest conditions in 17 years and the greatest one-year drop in temperatures in over 125 years. And then there's that four letter word, SNOW, the most in two decades, delaying the start of the golf season by weeks and even months for the northern third of the

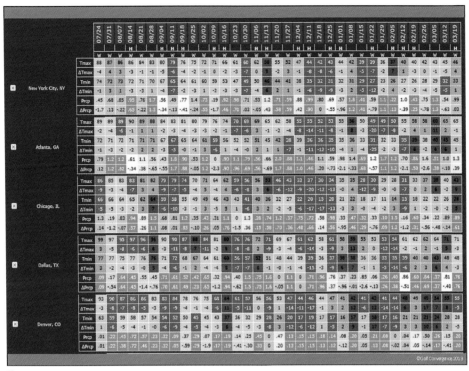

Key:
Dark Blue: much colder <= 5 degrees colder
Light Blue: slightly colder -1% to 5 degree colder
Dark green: <= 200% great precipitation
Grey: same as last year

country. In late March, as much as 49% of the country was still blanketed in snow, the most in decades, compared to only 7% in 2012.

So if you had confidence that long-range weather forecasting was accurate, and you knew the forecast for 2013, how would you change your current plans? Here are a few ideas:

1. Knowing season start timing on a by-city basis will improve revenue forecasting and enhance the strategic planning process.

2. Production profiles for clubs, balls, apparel and other golf-related merchandise could be adjusted to better manage a possible overstock scenario and soften the need for dramatic markdowns.

3. Inventory allocation could be adjusted to place the most product in areas of the country with the most favorable weather.

4. Caution should be exercised in offering off-season rates in the spring, thinking that the revenue can be made up in the summer.

5. Outings and events could be scheduled for days on which the probability for rain is low.

6. Advertisements in local media could be placed for weekends during which weather is to be favorable.

7. If a superintendent knew that in 48 hours it was going to rain 1¼ inches, using 400,000 gallons of water on the golf course could be avoided, saving as much as $800 in water expenses.

8. A superintendent could defer a fertilizer application costing upwards of $10,000 with the knowledge that it would likely be washed away by heavy rains.

Understanding the impact of the weather playable analysis is the second step in the Golf Convergence WIN™ process.

Go

If you licensed the supplemental template that accompanies this Field book:

1) Call Golf Convergence to arrange delivery of the necessary Weather Trends Playable Days report that will enable you to complete Step 2: Weather Playable Days Analysis as to whether management is over- or underperforming the weather. If you are consistently underperforming the weather, ascertain why by determining the highest yielding historical revenue days and determine if more careful scheduling based on forecasted weather would be beneficial.

2) Go to www.wt360.com and sign up for the complimentary basic weather alert service.

3) Enroll in the Weather Trends International's comprehensive set of weather tools by calling Weather Trends International or visiting www.wt360.com.

4) Review the number of playable days for the coming year. Set preliminary work schedules based on that data.

5) Examine forecasted precipitation. Determine how water resources could be optimized, and select appropriate timeframes for aerification. If you are going to have a warm fall, aerification could be postponed, permitting the golf course to charge higher daily green fees after Labor Day.

Path to Success

1) The location of the golf course and the surrounding demographics provide the foundation for the potential investment return if the tactical plans and operations are consistently executed. It is vital to understand your market: the age, income, population density, and ethnicity with a 30-minute drive time. Those demographics define the price threshold that a course can achieve based on demand. The number of golfers per 18 holes is also a fundamental benchmark to gauge relative supply vs demand. A golf course that believes every golfer is its customer will underachieve due to the lack of a proper, targeted focus.

2) Those in the industry maintain the mantra that the golf industry is oversupplied and that their woes are principally related to this uncontrollable factor and the weather. As a general statement, the golf industry has more courses than needed. But the opportunity for each golf course is defined by the local market. If a course is located in one of the Top 100 core-based statistical areas, demand will exceed supply, suggesting that holding firm on prices, if they match the experience, is appropriate.

3) While weather is uncontrollable, it is absolutely manageable. By using the historical and forecasting services provided by Weather Trends International, an astute operator can make his financial numbers dance by improving revenue through scheduling events wisely to reduce labor and water expenses. Because 50% of your peers are part of the late majority and laggards, adopting these tools will provide you a significant competitive advantage over them.

4) Weather insurance is also available for playable days lost due to rain or snow, and it should be considered for major tournaments and outings.

Concluding Thoughts

A man should look for what is, and not what he thinks should be.

Albert Einstein

We don't see the world as it is. We see it as we are.

Anaïs Nin

Chapter 6

Strategic Plan Summary
The Conclusion of Why

The greater danger for most of us lies not in setting our aim too high and falling short; but in setting our aim too low, and achieving our mark.

Michelangelo Buonarroti

Chapter Highlights

The first section of this book, concluding with this chapter, has focused on the uncontrollable factors that influence the business of golf. In essence, we have focused on the hand a golf course is dealt. From the mixed messages and the cacophony of chaos, to the competitive landscape and the diversions well-intended associations can create, distractions can lead many away from understanding the purpose and the unique qualities of their facilities.

The potential of a golf course and the unique experience that can be created there is heavily influenced by the demographics surrounding the golf course and the number of playable days the facility might enjoy annually. At its core, all golf is local, and all solutions are local. While each golf course has a unique personality, the business model to ensure a successful golf course is consistent. Thus, the vital need exists to create a strategic plan that precisely defines the vision, the opportunity, and the client base.

This chapter highlights the fact that golfers are consumers who are attracted to and become loyal to facilities that create an emotional connection with them. It is not only about the golf but also about the experience enjoyed.

The Question of "Why?"

The beauty of the game of golf is that every golf course is unique. No two of the over 33,331 facilities are identical. Even if you play the same golf course hundreds of times, each round will offer different tee marker locations, pin positions, weather conditions, and playing companions. Because of the diversity in the age, income, ability, and ethnicity of your playing companions, no two rounds of golf are identical.

What attracts a golfer to play one course versus another, particularly the same one multiple times? The simple answer is location. But that leads us down a false trail, for within most locales, particularly in the United States, you have many courses and clubs to choose from.

We believe, and have confirmed through multiple consumer surveys, that golfers or members subconsciously select where to play or join a club based on their own value systems and self-image. Would a star professional athlete play on a regular basis a local municipal golf course where getting a tee time is difficult and he or she would have to mingle with the masses while waiting to tee off? Not likely. His time is too precious or her desire for privacy would prevail. Would a blue-collar worker, with no savings or financial resources, join an exclusive private club? Not likely. A probable lack of financial resources and the discomfort of not being in a familiar social network probably would make that golfer feel uncomfortable.

In essence, individuals buy what they can afford based on the experience they seek.

The golf course owner, the management team, and the board of directors craft that experience within the expressed vision, tradition, history and governance of the facility. They define the brand promise and that leads to who is likely to be attracted to and motivated to play that course or become a member of that club.

Successful facilities are exceptional at defining their vision and brand promise. As you walk into the Karsten Creek Golf Course in Stillwater, Oklahoma, the brand of that facility is clearly expressed. The plethora of trophies won by the Oklahoma State University golf team in NCAA competition adorns the walls. It is an impressive display of competitive success, and the golf course is consistent with that theme, as it is a true test of the game.

The brand promise at Cherry Hills Country Club, in Colorado, is also clearly communicated as you enter the clubhouse, as shown.

The history of the club, with its many national championships, is prominently displayed in a "museum" that the USGA helped construct.

It is that message that enables Cherry Hills to levy a significant non-refundable initiation fee while maintaining a two-year waiting list. That message has also facilitated the club's ability to undertake respectable capital assessments in the past several years.

Down the street from Cherry Hills is the Wellshire Golf Course, another 18-hole course (shown at right). It is only one of three Donald Ross golf courses within the state of Colorado (the famed Broadmoor resort and Lakewood Country Club are the other two). Ben Hogan won the Denver Open at the Wellshire in 1948. But that course is only able to eke out $35 per 18 holes of play.

Why such a large difference between the $200 guest fee at Cherry Hills and this municipal course operated by the City and County of Denver? Because the value offered is that significantly different.

At the Wellshire, the stately clubhouse is in disrepair. While a snack bar exists, the main dining areas are operated by a concessionaire, and only for catered events. The range is a lake with floating golf balls secured by a dam that leaks, necessitating the creation of a pond in the landing area on the 10th hole. And the course, despite is $700,000 budget, is poorly maintained. Dead trees and limbs abound. The living trees encroach on the playing corridors. Where square greens and chocolate drops existed, round green are now present. Double greens with centering bunkers joining the 4th and 13th holes appeared in 1926, but now there are two greens separated by rough. While the course is profitable due to its prime location in Denver, it is substantially underperforming and lacks adequate capital reserves. The potential of the course is enormous.

Though these two courses are only one mile apart, they are light-years away from presenting golfers or members the same experience. These examples demonstrate a formula to measure the strategic vision of a golf course.

Strategic Vision = Brand Promise = Customer Attraction Quotient

Cherry Hills is a championship venue where the finest players in the game play. Wellshire is an entry-level golf course for the masses. While its potential is immense, the vision of the facility defines the experience—affordable golf, hence a lack of investment or care.

In each case, the financial performance of the course mirrors its brand promise. But defining the experience that will be provided is only one component. Ensuring that the demographics within the local market are consistent with that experience is central.

Having matched the experience to the demographics, golf course operators will find that the median financial returns of their facilities are likely to fall within the benchmarks shown in the table at the top of the next page.

It is not surprising that the EBITDA is highest at resorts and the lowest at municipalities. The low revenues and high payroll expenses toll the bell for many municipal courses.

Thus, to ensure that financial goals are achieved, stating a facility's focus via a strategic plan is fundamental. Without a defined strategic vision, effective tactical plans can't be developed, for they rest on funding and personnel requirements.

Vision Defines Investment Potential

	Daily Fee	Municipal	Private Clubs	Resorts
Rounds Played	25,000	30,000	17,343	18,291
Full Time Employees	10	6	28	33
Total Revenues	1,100,000	978,249	2,700,000	1,772,783
Membership Fee and Dues Revenues	150,000	96,500	1,400,291	75,000
Green Fees	384,625	440,548	150,000	775,775
Cart Fees	150,000	190,239	162,500	145,000
Merchandise	85,000	86,000	200,000	185,000
Golf Shop Salaries	150,000	182,908	200,000	247,848
Maintenance Salaries	200,000	250,000	400,000	320,950
Total Maintenance Costs	225,000	220,000	460,000	402,792
EBITDA	221,561	142,406	240,259	487,000

Source: PGA Performance Trak 2011 (survey conducted in 2012)

Without tactical plans, the resources required for management and staff to perform satisfactorily will be lacking, and appropriate operational execution will not occur.

Where a lack of strategic planning occurs, which is the case at about 75% of all golf courses, the results are highly predictable. Policies, procedures, and practices at these courses are based on the ever-changing whims of the owner, management, and staff, or upon the golfers' influences. Management and staff at such courses will often respond to the latest self-imposed crisis or priority. At these courses, the saying "vision without action is a dream" is inadequate. Instead, action without vision is a nightmare.

It is just as important to state what the vision is not as it is to define what the vision is. It is impossible to satisfy the needs of your golfers by starting with determining what they are willing to pay. It is often said that firing the worst 5% of your customers is a healthy practice when you're working to ensure the attainment of your long-term goals.

There is always a conflict of interest between those who own or run a golf course and the golfers who so often insist they are overpaying for the experience received. On the next page is a vision statement that might be crafted by golfers.

142

> ### The Golfer's Vision Statement
> ### This Is a Joke ☺
>
> Living in a very wealthy, well-to-so suburb of Chicago, we are accustom to enjoying the finest life offers. Therefore, we expect to be provided superior municipal golf courses with spectacular clubhouses providing excellent food/beverage/banquet facilities and a diverse array of merchandise at highly discount rates as compensation for the taxes we pay. Our courses will be perceived as the best among neighboring districts. The losses incurred should merely be considered part of our tax dollars, as the libraries, pools, and other parks activities are supported comparably.

Having a strategic plan executed by individuals who believe in the "why" of the facility is all-important. Every operational decision at a well-managed facility can be tracked upwards to the tactical plans and to the facility's strategic vision, as illustrated in the figure below.

It is this system of decision making that ensures success.

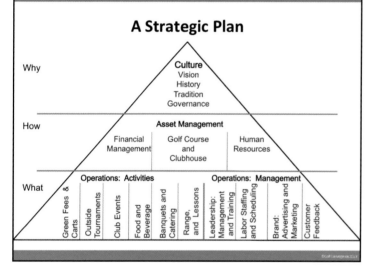

Everyone who awakens daily with the passion to ensure that his or her personal "why" statement is aligned with the brand promise of a facility has the capability to create a spark that brings to life that facility's brand promise. When your staff is imbued with a vision, as are those who work at Bandon Dunes, Black Wolf Run, Cherry Hills, Cog Hill, and many other fine facilities, a superior experience consistent with the price charged results. And that experience doesn't have to be at a high-end private country club. It can be created at a municipal golf course.

Where that vision is missing and where the passion of employees is at a low ebb or is completely absent, as is so often the case at municipal golf courses, the financial potential will not be reached.

A well-defined vision is a hallmark of the respected Ritz-Carlton hotels, where all employees carry a card in their wallets. The front of the card[1] (shown to the right) is compelling, and it very accurately conveys the strategic vision of the company and the importance of the employees' "emotional engagement" with their patrons.

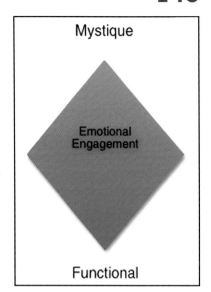

The card carries the motto "We are Ladies and Gentlemen serving Ladies and Gentlemen" with the credo of

> "The Ritz-Carlton is a place where the genuine care and comfort of our guests is our highest mission.

> We pledge to provide the finest personal service and facilities for our guests, who will always enjoy a warm, relaxed, yet refined ambience.

> The Ritz-Carlton experience enlivens the senses, instills well-being, and fulfills even the unexpressed the wishes and needs of our guests."[2]

Included are the 12 service values under the banner "I am proud to be Ritz-Carlton":

Functional

1. "I build strong relationships and create Ritz-Carlton guests for life.

2. I am always responsive to the expressed and unexpressed wishes and needs of our guests.

3. I am empowered to create unique, memorable and personal experiences for our guests.

4. I understand my role in achieving the Key Success Factors, embracing Community Footprints and creating The Ritz-Carlton mystique.

5. I continuously seek opportunities to innovate and improve The Ritz-Carlton experience.

6. I own and immediately resolve guest problems.

---

1 Ritz-Carlton, "Employee Card."

2 Ibid.

7. I create a work environment of teamwork and lateral service so that the needs of our guests and each other are met.

8. I have the opportunity to continuously learn and grow.

9. I am involved in the planning of the work that affects me.

10. I am proud of my professional appearance, language, and behavior.

11. I protect the privacy and security of our guests, my fellow employees and the company's confidential information and assets.

12. I am responsible for uncompromising levels of cleanliness and creating a safe and accident–free environment."[3]

Embedding the vision within the employee's mindset is one of the many reasons the Ritz Carlton hotels provide a special experience.

Defining the Unique Vision

The reasons that people play golf are incredibly varied.

The young are excited to discover a new sport, learn discipline, and respect the core values of a game. For family and friends, golf provides a way to deepen relationships and experience leisure in a time-fractured world. As to sportsmanship, golf provides a forum for competition and athletic prowess, and for some, it brings great riches and international fame. For businessmen and women, golf gives an opportunity (beyond webinars, emails, and teleconferences) to pierce the formal rigors and the impersonal nature that are business and connect with co-workers and customers, demonstrating that each cares about the other beyond what may be perceived in the work environment. For the senior citizen, a golf course represents the office where a seasoned golfer can regale his or her buddies with tales of days gone by and his or her many accomplishments. For the golf course residential homeowner, the course is a beautiful backyard. For the wealthy, it is place to celebrate their lineage and their fortunes, as well as the fact that they have escaped, either through inheritance or hard work, the financial bullets of life.

The reasons that attract people to a course are varied, but the emotional experience of golfers is the strongest contributor to the fiscal sustainability

---

3 Ritz-Carlton, "Employee Card."

of each course. And every golf course provides a different emotional experience.

Defining the Compelling Emotional Experience

How is that emotional experience delineated and conveyed to attract customers? What is clear is that every facility has its own unique personality.

That personality might be defined by whether the course is ranked in national magazines; the pedigree of the architect; local, state and national championships hosted; slope rating; the conditioning of the course and the type and number of grasses and flowers planted; cart and caddie policies; amenities provided both on the course and in the locker room; the number of customer touch points; whether cell phones or computer use are permitted in the clubhouse; dress codes; smoking policies; tipping policies; gift policies; whether reciprocity is available; gender/ethnic barriers, whether expressed or implied; whether members hold multiple memberships at other clubs or are first-time members of a club; other amenities available (tennis courts, exercise rooms, swimming pools, etc.); and whether the facility attracts individuals who are first-time members or first-time customers.

Beyond the course, one of the clearest ways to define the emotional experience is via the clubhouse, as illustrated in the following figure.

At the private Midland Country Club, Michigan, this 90,000 square foot facility supported largely by Dow Chemical is perhaps the clubhouse of the future. It features corporate conference rooms; it offers golf, recreational, or social memberships; and it offers a fitness area and spa, aquatics, child care, and several dining alternatives.

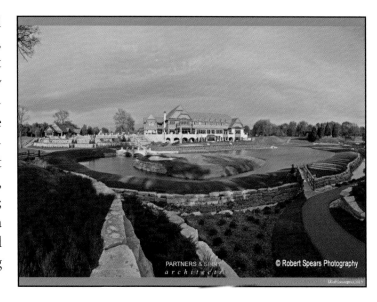

It Is About the Experience

Golf is about enjoying nature and people in a leisurely environment. Think about the people who are drawn to the "sport." When was the last time you were at a golf course or club when you didn't enjoy the company of your playing partners? How many times have you met a stranger on the first tee and, after spending some time with him, found a kinship? Golf is really unique is its ability to bond its participants.

For the golfer, the ability to hit the risk-reward shot to get on the 16th hole at Bandon Dunes or to attempt to reach the par 5, 18th at Pebble Beach is all about the experience. You seek to play St. Andrews not because the quality of the golf course ranked #1 in the world in July, 2013 by golf course architects from around the world but because of its history. Who doesn't want to pause on the Swilcan Bridge where so many great golfers have stood? For those who reach that pinnacle, it is not about the game but about life's journey and about an escape from the rigors of the daily world.

Golf courses are not successful only by what they offer but by how they make people feel about themselves; golf meets the psychological and physical needs of many.

The Formula

There is one formula that defines the success of every commercial enterprise.

Why would you pay $4 for a cup of coffee, whether at Starbucks or for my favorite scrumptious Mint Condition Mocha at Caribou? Certainly you wouldn't pay that for 16 ounces of flavored water. You buy at Starbucks or Caribou for the ambience. Starbucks today is like the bar on the old *Cheers* television series. It's the place to go, to be recognized by the barista who calls out, "Good morning, Skinny Vanilla Grande Cappuccino coming right up," before you even order. Starbucks is about asking the manager, Michelle, how her nursing school night classes are going or how Julie's last cardio session went as she prepares for the 10K Bolder Boulder in between the times she prepares coffees and fetches pastries.

People pay what they pay because the experience received, in terms of its value, equals or exceeds the price paid. The formula is

$$Value = Experience - Price.$$

Where that occurs, customer loyalty is created. Conversely, when the price exceeds the experience, customer attrition is sure to happen.

A golf course's ability to create an appropriate emotional experience is a function of its cash flow plus the investment either in equity or debt that is allocated to the business. That is the trap for most golf courses and clubs. Very few can carry and amortize debt in excess of $1 million. With the golf course being a living organism requiring an annual capital investment of more than $180,000 in funds allocated to reserves, in that the median income of a golf course in the United States is $205,435, the margin for error in operating a golf course is very slight. Hence, the essential requirement that a facility knows it vision, its why for existing, and what it is not.

History, tradition, and culture are difficult to create. None of them can be created with capital investment alone. They must develop over time with the use of a meticulous set of standards that remain consistently implemented and often are very elusive. The best experience can only be created in the long-term through positive cash flow.

The successful storied golf clubs of the world have one thing in common: they rigidly discipline themselves to follow the strategic vision for the club. The same discipline can be applied to public golf courses.

Because we make decisions based on what we think we know the facts to be, the discipline of creating and writing a strategic plan, while tedious and often times frustrating, produces riches in terms of consistency and attainment of the goals established.

Path to Success

1) People don't buy WHAT you do; they buy WHY you do it. Do you know why you do what you do? When that is known, the route to achievement will be clear.

2) A golf course is a sanctuary that provides serenity and leisure in a world in which we are over-stimulated and bombarded with messages that seem meaningful but are meaningless. A golf course provides a respite for a brief moment of time, a respite that we sorely need to balance life's forces. Hence, whether it is played on a nine-hole chip-and-putt course or on a rigorous championship course, golf represents an oasis for those seeking an emotional experience.

3) Matching the "why" of the golf course or club to a target market seeking a specific experience is central to a focused plan.

4) Without a written plan that precisely states the vision, the resources to be allocated, and the operational execution that is to occur, the results achieved will be more by accident and luck than because of expertise.

5) Understand that all golf is local and that every solution is unique.

6) Invest 2 hours to complete the strategic planning vision exercise, the local market analysis and the weather playable days exercise. By doing so, you will have established a foundation for the future prosperity of your facility.

Concluding Thought

He who wants the rose must respect the thorn.

Persian Proverb

SECTION 2

Tactical Planning
Chapters 7 through 11

7. Technology

8. Financial Benchmarking

9. Financial Modeling: The Resources

10. Yield Management

11. Valuation

All that is gold does not glitter; not all those who wander are lost.

J. R. R. Tolkien

Chapter 7

Technology—The Foundation

Step 3 of the Golf Convergence WIN™ Formula

*As the world becomes more and more complicated,
our minds are trained for more and more simplification.*

Nassim Nicholas Taleb

Chapter Highlights

Of the dollars spent building, maintaining, and operating a golf course, the lowest return on investment often seems to be the return from investment on technology. It is ironic that one of the tools designed to create simplification, to provide meaningful insights, and to facilitate the ability to effectively manage a golf course becomes one of the most frustrating aspects of managing a golf course. Such need not be the case.

This chapter names the leading vendors of technology and the unique niches they serve. Here we predict how information systems currently installed may dramatically change within the next five years, reflecting the great changes we see in other industries as we transition from computers to laptops to iPhones and iPads. These changes will dramatically alter the customer touch points within a clubhouse and greatly improve, simplify, and enhance customer service.

It Shouldn't Be This Hard

The proper installation and utilization of a golf management system and its associated integrated components serve as a foundation for a golf course to reach its financial potential; these comprise the **third step in the Golf Convergence WIN™ process.** The correct use of technology at a golf course has the prospect of increasing its net income by more than 12%. Really!

For example, knowing who your new, core, and former customers are and tailoring customized messages to each segment at an appropriate frequency is a key customer service differentiator among golf courses. And maintaining inventory levels with appropriate turn rates provides the opportunity to introduce the current fashions and equipment, consistent with the purchasing patterns of your customers.

Further, adjusting prices dynamically based on demand is a practice used by airlines, car rental companies, and hotels; it is a fundamental principle of business management, yet this practice remains in its infancy in the golf industry.

As an example, the utilization report below for an internationally famed golf course reflects the utilization at that facility from January through December and from the opening tee time to the last tee time. Weekday utilization is shown on the top half of the chart and weekend play on the bottom half.

Utilization Report

Tee Time	Jan	Feb	March	April	May	June	July	Aug	Sep	Oct	Nov	Dec	Avg
						WEEKDAYS							
7	0.31%	0.00%	0.10%	4.11%	27.32%	44.08%	49.69%	40.41%	39.07%	12.82%	1.49%	0.17%	18.10%
8	0.12%	0.00%	0.25%	14.21%	39.98%	44.54%	46.11%	47.43%	34.74%	21.85%	7.54%	0.00%	21.39%
9	1.42%	0.00%	5.19%	16.87%	31.49%	48.32%	52.92%	50.00%	45.22%	28.95%	8.20%	0.24%	24.05%
10	3.19%	0.11%	9.06%	16.08%	37.94%	44.39%	57.52%	55.13%	48.70%	27.75%	15.72%	1.54%	26.44%
11	4.02%	0.00%	10.24%	12.20%	33.15%	44.60%	48.52%	44.64%	47.13%	18.07%	10.86%	1.42%	22.91%
12	1.65%	0.11%	8.90%	11.40%	25.92%	43.56%	49.78%	46.71%	48.14%	21.30%	8.53%	1.27%	22.44%
13	0.65%	0.00%	8.04%	12.56%	21.61%	38.99%	42.19%	45.50%	38.75%	20.21%	4.35%	0.53%	19.45%
14	1.24%	0.11%	8.77%	9.51%	17.94%	28.28%	33.42%	39.27%	40.28%	25.02%	4.29%	0.49%	17.37%
15	0.21%	0.00%	7.54%	12.10%	57.21%	60.29%	62.14%	60.82%	40.87%	9.38%	1.01%	0.06%	27.65%
16	0.00%	0.11%	3.40%	31.49%	37.63%	49.17%	52.13%	48.43%	28.37%	5.27%	0.13%	0.04%	20.53%
						WEEKENDS							
7	6.11%	0.00%	3.50%	42.11%	67.35%	78.46%	65.46%	78.86%	55.15%	51.38%	5.36%	0.00%	37.81%
8	10.39%	1.16%	3.14%	53.68%	70.24%	75.42%	68.22%	75.51%	57.42%	55.00%	14.17%	0.68%	40.34%
9	15.82%	1.24%	9.47%	57.46%	79.53%	72.37%	79.12%	57.24%	57.37%	21.49%	0.93%		43.66%
10	13.61%	2.19%	17.51%	39.98%	58.19%	67.96%	65.89%	62.20%	35.81%	49.59%	13.35%	0.58%	35.58%
11	11.76%	1.02%	10.49%	43.20%	46.88%	66.60%	64.69%	70.26%	42.11%	37.13%	14.50%	1.75%	34.20%
12	5.38%	1.49%	8.62%	39.09%	54.90%	57.91%	58.16%	86.53%	51.48%	36.99%	9.50%	1.02%	32.67%
13	0.86%	0.73%	7.41%	28.01%	33.06%	41.52%	45.39%	51.93%	52.19%	26.74%	2.42%	0.00%	24.20%
14	2.37%	0.15%	5.77%	11.93%	14.89%	25.42%	35.70%	43.64%	42.80%	36.92%	8.06%	0.45%	19.02%
15	0.64%	0.00%	2.78%	33.11%	47.78%	60.54%	63.27%	65.65%	38.05%	11.96%	1.02%	0.00%	27.07%
16	0.16%	0.00%	1.11%	8.00%	28.99%	42.68%	49.26%	37.88%	11.33%	5.51%	0.00%	0.00%	15.49%
Average	3.91%	0.44%	6.66%	25.38%	41.27%	52.12%	54.14%	55.50%	42.76%	27.96%	7.65%	0.56%	26.53%
Average	8.91%	0.44%	6.66%	25.38%	41.27%	52.12%	54.14%	55.50%	42.76%	27.96%	7.65%	0.56%	26.53%

©GolfConvergence_2015

This is one of the most powerful reports that golf software can create.

The red-shaded cells in the report shown above reflect utilization of less than 40% during that hour. Cells shaded in yellow reflect utilization of from 40% to 60%. And those cells colored green, represent utilization greater than 60%.

Examine how the utilization on the weekends migrates in June to above 60% before noon, falls to 40% to 60% from noon to 2, is 25.42% from 2 p.m. to 3 p.m., only to soar back to 60.54% after 3 p.m. What is going on?

Would anyone like to guess when the twilight rate starts? That's right, 3 p.m. If this multi-course operator would offer a value rate that begins at 2 p.m., the gross revenue of the course would increase by more than $250,000.

Note the term "value rate," not the dreaded "discount." A discount would merely shift the play from 3 p.m. to 2 p.m. and weaken the noon to 2 p.m. segment. A value rate would be the same as the current rack rate. In addition to that, perhaps range balls, a coupon for a soda fountain drink, or even a $5 voucher for merchandise purchased at the time of check-in could be created to incent the golfers to play earlier. The cost to the golf course—near zero—yet the revenue, at $150 per player, has a significant upside.

The ability to efficiently manage a golf course is only available to those who properly gain the insights available from the proper use technology. But therein are the challenges.

Our Software Doesn't Work That Way

As we travel through life, we often hear statistics that remain indelibly stuck in our minds. I read one such statistic several years ago in an interview Bill Gates, founder of Microsoft. He said that 70% of all requests for new software features were already included in the software that was commercially available. Hard to believe, but familiar to Golf Convergence.

Rob Smyth, National Sales Manager of IBS, has been working in the club industry for more than 18 years. He represents the third generation in the family business—Smyth Systems—one of the early pioneers in club enterprise software. He recently shared an anecdote: A controller at a private club, upon seeing one of the features in the IBS software during a sales demonstration, stated, "I wish that feature was in our Smyth System." Though the individual had been using the Smyth software for over a decade, he didn't realize the feature desired was in the software he had been using.

Who is responsible for that misunderstanding? Was it a lack of adequate training by the Smyth representative over a decade ago? Or should the responsibility be placed on the controller who never took the time to fully learn and understand the software?

It's a catch-22. It is so easy, and unfortunately so common, that golf course personnel place the blame on the software vendor, stating that they were inadequately trained or the ongoing support is poor. This excuse exonerates them from the failure to use the software properly, for otherwise the clear conclusion becomes that they are not competent.

The picture below reflects the frustration often heard from those responsible for operating a golf course.

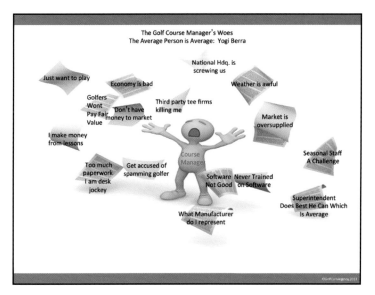

Realistically, there is no golf management software system that will precisely meet the needs and wants and desires of a municipal, daily fee, or resort course in exactly the ways the golf course personnel desire.

Unlike the general business application software to which we all have become so accustomed, (Word, Excel, PowerPoint, and Outlook), the user interface from one vendor software to another is dramatically different. Some use an icon-based approach while others use a hierarchical system reflective of a very dated DOS-based application.

I would wager that no matter the depth of your technical expertise and computer familiarity, there are very few who would be able to use any vendor's software without additional assistance and training. The proper configuration of a golf management software system, with its numerous templates, fee tables, SKU charts, report preferences, and security-level permissions reflecting the unique policies and procedures of that facility, is a daunting task to fully organize.

It is my observed opinion, from watching the selection of software by golf courses for nearly two decades, that over 25% of the golf courses select the wrong vendor, despite what may appear to be extensive due diligence and investigation through the typical Request for Proposal process. And if they acquire a system that meets their basic needs and are satisfied, every set of annual upgrades introduces a whole new round of frustrations for golf course personnel as they grapple with the changes. It is not uncommon for a customized feature designed for a client to break when the generic upgrade is installed.

Who's at fault? What's "broken"? What we are confident of is that the executives at the golf course management companies are customer-centered and committed to serving golf course owners. While one or two firms many love the courtship and hate the marriage, at their core, they are unified in ensuring that their firms' software is properly and fully utilized.

In defense of the software firms, what is demanded of them in terms of functionality and support far exceeds the amount of money paid by most golf course owners.

Buying What You Need to Buy and No More

Could any golf management software system be used at any golf course? Not a chance!

The information-system needs of a municipal golf course, a daily fee, a private club, and a resort are vastly different. For instance, even the customer database and the reports desired at a nine-hole municipal golf course like the Tony Butler Municipal Golf Course in Harlingen, Texas, differ significantly from the requirements of the five-course complex operated by the State of New York at the famed Bethpage State Park.

It could even be stated that of all of the golf facilities in the United States, perhaps as few as 5% have one vendor handling all of the information-processing requirements. From third-party tee time reservations, to tournament management, to handicapping, to food and beverage, to banquet and catering, to property management systems, to email marketing, to the creation and maintenance of a Web site, many vendors dominate a particular market segment.

So what does a golf course need? To clarify the fundamental requirements, presented on the next page is a chart highlighting the **principal priorities** at each of the varied types of golf courses.

Module	Component	Daily Fee	Municipal	Private Club	Resort
Accounting		X		X	
Food and Beverage				X	X
Marketing	Email	X	X		
	Customer Relationship Management				
	Social Media				
Hotel Interface					X
Membership				X	
Merchandising					X
POS	Computer	X	X	X	X
	Tablet				
	Wireless				
Reporting	Pre-Formatted Report	X	X		
	Open Database Query System				
Tee Time Reservations	Call Center				X
	Electronic Tee Sheet	X	X		
	Lottery				
	Online Reservations			X	
	Touch Tone Telephone				
	Yield Management				
Application Interface to 3rd Tee Time Networks		X			
Other Modules, such as Radio Frequency Identification Technology (RFID)					

While this chart is designed for the golf course looking to precisely define its needs, it is woefully inadequate.

To illustrate, the talented Jim Roschek, PGA, who oversees the Alamo Golf Trail in San Antonio, says one of his highest priorities is an open database query system that consolidates the customer transaction information from the six golf courses so that he can effectively engage in customer relationship management. It is his goal that when a golfer who is a loyalty card member approaches the first tee, the course host's (starter) iPad tablet with the RFID technology embedded in the golfer's loyalty card, will immediately display the customer's name to allow for the personal recognition of that valued customer, just as guests at the Ritz Carlton might experience.

For other multiple-course municipalities, such as Bergen County, New Jersey; City and County of Honolulu, Hawaii; City of Los Angeles; Milwaukee County, New Jersey; Monmouth County, New Jersey; Morris County, New Jersey; or Westchester County, New York, the outdated but necessary touchtone interactive voice reservation system is a primary requirement to ensure the fair and equitable access to tee times by their taxpaying citizens. While one would think that these entities would have migrated to an Internet-based application designed for booking tee times, such transition has yet to occur. Based on contracts recently signed by these entities, such transition is not in the short-term future.

Management companies such as Billy Casper Golf, Century Golf Management, and Kemper Sports Management serve courses that have a diversified set of needs. These companies focus on the consolidation of multiple courses with different owners that they manage centrally, so that they can introduce the economies of scale and also marketing initiatives that allow these courses to in many cases financially outperform the operating results of the single course operator.

Pin the Tail …

While there are many permutations beyond the simple chart, it only serves to demonstrate the difficulty of selecting the proper system, difficulty which is exacerbated by the purchasing methods used by most golf courses.

The typical evaluation process would involve the following three steps: 1) issue a request for proposal, 2) conduct a Web-based online demonstration, and 3) and perform an on-site demonstration of the short-listed vendors. This process is highly flawed, for several reasons.

First, golf course personnel rarely define precisely what they are seeking in a software system. While a municipality or a resort, through its organizational entities, may have access to IT personnel to guide them, such personnel are lacking a fundamental understanding of the business of golf and can complicate what should be a simple process.

Second, what used to be a high-end, customized purchase is now a commodity that can be had at a very reasonable and cost-effective price point. To anticipate that these vendors will engage in a protracted purchase cycle competing against multiple vendors is sheer folly. While vendors would once come to you and conduct sales demonstrations, it is becoming more common for golf course personnel to travel to the vendors' headquarters. Only a multiple-course management company or a prestigious resort (because of their national brand recognition) could effectively command an audience with a vendor. Today, most software is demonstrated within a vendor-sponsored Webinar.

As a result, the selection of a golf management system has become largely influenced by what golf course competitors are using down the street. A quick phone call to your friend or foe simplifies the process.

For example, with over 2,000 golf course installations, Fore! Reservations is considered the leading value-based golf management system, and it includes a robust marketing component. If you are thinking of any custom requests, don't bother. It is what it is, and it is very good. If you are seeking a flexible monthly lease at a competitive price point and desire some custom programming, Club Prophet would be a wise selection. If you say you're looking for a call center, EZLinks becomes a natural choice. For a private club or a small resort, seriously consider Jonas, which justifiably dominates that market segment. Operating a private community with multiple courses? Chelsea's Information Systems' lottery-based tee time reservation system is the clear choice. For a municipality looking to integrate all of their recreational services, Active Network and Vermont Systems become frequent choices.

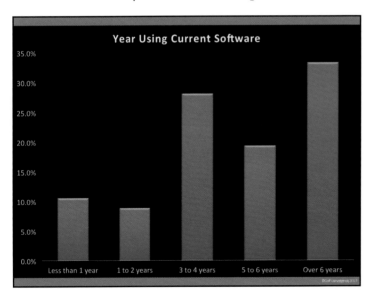

Golf courses, having selected a vendor, rarely change software providers, as evidenced in this survey (shown left) of golf course operators conducted by Golf Convergence in March 2011.

The initial decision is important. Technology provides a fabulous competitive advantage to the golf course that uses it properly.

Unfortunately, golf courses succumb to many faulty practices that fight against effective marketing. Perhaps this is because golf course owners are slow to accept change and are considered to be lagging consumers of technology. Or we have become immune to the constantly evolving promises made by advertising that we are overwhelmed and do nothing. Perhaps we are so overwhelmed by the increasingly upgraded technological promises that we don't really understand the systems, and we become immune to all the noise.

One Size Fits All—Nope!

What is regrettable is that not one golf management software system that exists today precisely meets 100% of the needs of a golf course.

Why?

The majority of software firms serving the golf industry could be classified as entrepreneurial small companies. They lack the necessary capital reserves to undertake all of the development that would be required by every golf course, for every golf course is unique. These small firms must make a simple, and prudent, financial decision, and the cost of developing exactly what is best for a particular course far exceeds the amount of money a golf course or private club is willing to pay.

Active Network and Jonas Club Management have significant financial resources, but their division is a small part of their parent company. As such, it could be debated that their golf divisions are small entrepreneurial-based businesses also, and that they will have to compete within their companies for development and marketing funds. Measured by gross revenues, it is unlikely that many, if any, golf management firms are generating in excess of $25.5 million in annual revenue from their custom software business. That revenue classifies as a small business based on the criteria formulated by the United States Business Administration.[1]

Creating a customized software program to meet a golf course's precise operational needs and graphical user interfaces is cost-prohibitive. For example, to design a dynamic yield management system that automatically adjusts the price of every tee time every day based on the supply and demand reflected by reservations on the tee sheet would cost over $1 million.

---

1 http://www.sba.gov/sites/default/files/files/Size_Standards_Table.pdf

Perhaps as many as 15% of the golf courses in the United States have management teams sophisticated enough to deploy the software, are innovators and early adopters, and would seek to adopt such software. The vast majority in the golf industry would say something like, "We don't believe that you have developed the software that will correctly adjust our prices to maximize our revenue. We don't need it, we don't like, and you are scaring us." Interpreted, read that, "We are not going to give you control of our pricing."

The marketing for this type of system, we believe, should include some of the following components:

> "If you are the golf course operator who likes to have total control over every aspect of your operation, we have a solution for you. Based on the demand for your golf course, you will be able to automatically modify your price structure in a way that will maximize your revenue, increase customer satisfaction, and conserve labor resources."

The adoption of what is perhaps the most single powerful module, yield management that has the most potential to dramatically and positively impact the net income of a facility, will closely mirror the "Innovation of Diffusion Model" in Geoffrey Moore's book *Crossing the Chasm*.

Putting it into a simple perspective, the purpose of technology is not to manage the business from a screen. Customers visit your golf course because you have a common set of values and beliefs with respect to one aspect of your lives— how to spend your leisure time. The role of technology is to help you manage and complete routine transactions faster so that you have the opportunity to establish a human connection with your customers.

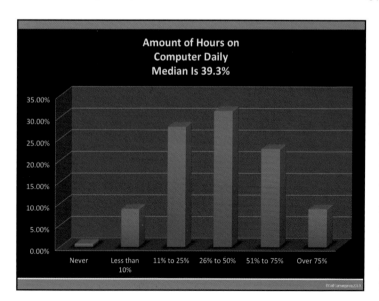

Technology will help you and your staff to **not** to sit behind your desk for the balance of the day, as illustrated by the chart to the left, which represents the results of a survey of golf course operators conducted by Golf Convergence in March, 2011.

Need a Scorecard to Tell the Players?
Picking the Right Horse to Ride

Who then will help you manage your business more efficiently? Which software company has designed a system that is most consistent with your policies and procedures, the system that will create the greatest value from your investment?

In undertaking the research for this book, we asked those vendors we believe to be the leaders in the industry to prepare an executive summary of their various software modules, including third-party application interfaces. They also provided profiles of their company and customer lists, defined their unique selling propositions, and described the depth and breadth of their staffs. These reports also included their current focus and their vision for the future development of their core products.

Presented in the following figure is a list of those vendors, along with our summary of what we believe to be their special niches and their corporate strengths. Each of these firms was given the opportunity review a draft copy of this chapter in advance, and they had varying thoughts on their niches and strengths. However, as impartial spectators in the golf software game, we believe that this chart will enable you to make the first cut in determining which of these might be the best vendor for you to partner with to guide you in managing your facility more effectively.

We were pleased that Chelsea Information Systems, Club Prophet, EZLinks, Jonas, and Vermont Systems responded to our research request in a timely manner. That speaks to their customer-service orientation and to their commitment to, and empathy for, their potential customers. They no doubt realize that selecting the proper vendor can be challenging, and they seem to sincerely

Firm	Niche	Strength – 1	Strength – 2	Strength - 3
Active Network	Municipal & Daily Fee	Public Company	Integrated system for Parks and Recreation	Interactive Voice, Yield management & Query tools with open database
Chelsea	Municipal, Residential Communities	Diversity of industries, parking, electronic signs	Web based/leased system	Lottery based tee time system with IVR Phone via VOIP
Club Prophet	Municipal & Daily Fee	Monthly fee – no contract & multi site locations	Reporting system	Custom development focus
Crescent Systems	Daily Fee and Private Clubs	Private club market in Southeast USA	Web search and marketing presence	Horizontal diversification
EZ Links	Municipal & Daily Fee	Call center with web yield management	Client list	Offer Barter
Fore! Reservation	Single course municipal and daily fee	Value based	Core functionality	Installed customer base > 2,000
IBS	Daily Fee and Private Club	Breadth of product line for private & city clubs	Support call center	Historical brand reputation
Jonas	Private	Dominate private clubs	Corporate resources	Management team
US eDirect	Municipal	Large municipal clients, i.e., City of Los Angeles, etc.	Integrated system for Parks and Recreation	Offers IVR component
Vermont System	Municipal & Military Golf Course	Very stable, well run company with 1,100 clients	Integrated system for Parks and Recreation	Handle all branches of military currently

Note: Those highlighted in green will accept payment in the form of bartered tee times.

desire to communicate their product offering and corporate history accurately to aid you in your decision-making process

There are many other software firms serving the golf course management sector. 1-2-1 Marketing, Course Trends, Cybergolf, GolfNow/Golf Channel, J2 Golf Marketing, and Legendary Marketing are leaders in building Web sites for golf courses and providing email marketing communication systems. ClubSoft and Northstar Technologies are emerging companies in the private club market. Clubessential and VCT Corporation focus on creating online communities for private clubs. Boxgroove, eGolfScore, Electronic Transaction Systems Corporation, Golf Pipeline, Golf Box, GolfNet, Handicomp, iWanamaker, and Teemaster are among a bevy of other software providers.

There are also four firms, Active Network, GolfNow/Golf Channel, GolfSwitch, and Quick18, that are focused on the third-party distribution of tee times. These firms are rocking and rolling and shaking the golf course industry to its core, creating much angst, consternation and debate about their barter-based models. They are thriving anyway.

ChaChing! ChaChing!

In May 2012, Golf Convergence conducted a survey of golf course operators' deployment of golf management software. Sixty percent of golf courses pay for licensed software and each of them pay a median $8,636 to initially acquire and $3,664 annually to support their golf management software platform from a vendor they have utilized for more than four years.

Surprisingly, the majority of golf courses use a different vendor for their primary management software, the creation of their Web site, and for communicating with customers via email (the average course maintains 3,664 emails in its database). The integration between these primary systems still lags.

While those are the averages, the first-year costs for a golf management system will start around $5,000, with second-year costs beginning at $500 for a single module. The high end of the market for a single course is $40,000 in the initial year, with annual costs approaching $20,000 for a full complement of software modules.

Because of perceived constrained cash flow strain among golf courses, for reasons most often attributed to the economy, weather, and the oversupply of golf courses in the United States, many operators have opted for the barter model. It is rumored that one software company has over 100 different contracts representing the various services it provides and the negotiation strength of the various golf course operators.

The barter concept is straightforward. With golf courses operating at near 50% of capacity nationally, the golf course is asked to provide the software vendor one or two tee times which the vendor can sell through its own sales network to regain the funds it would have received for the preferred up-front cash payment.

These firms have been able to create Web sites on which they offer local market tee times for multiple golf courses on a single Web page. The customer now has a choice of many. Many golf course owners believe that these third-party sites are encouraging their customers to play elsewhere and that the software companies are offering the tee times at a lower price than what is available at each golf course. Golfers are being trained, they say, to purchase golf based on price. Some worry that each member of a foursome made up of individuals who have never previously played together could have paid a different green fee.

The issue as to whether third-party intermediaries and bartered tee times are beneficial for the golf course owner generated perhaps even more debate in 2012 than the anchored putter ban by the USGA has brought in 2013. The NGCOA has issued several white papers on the subject, suggesting a set of guidelines for courses.

Then PGA of America President Allen Wronowski issued the following statement in February 2012 regarding this issue:

> "The PGA of America's Board of Directors decided this week to overturn a decision made at its last Board meeting that approved ongoing negotiations with a third-party tee-time provider for an endorsement by The PGA.
>
> After reviewing a number of recent communications from the employer community expressing disagreement with the practices of third-party resellers and their impact on the golf course industry, the Board concluded it is in the Association's best interests to end current negotiations with one company and engage owners on a common approach to this practice. The PGA Board acknowledges

that the benefits and risks of using the database marketing and web-enabled tee sheets are not clearly understood and will dedicate resources to improve an understanding of this subject. The PGA also has considerable marketing assets it believes can increase online purchases of tee times and pledges to bring those to bear on a solution in the future, although there is no timetable for an agreement with any reseller."[2]

Throughout the debate we ponder, from our quantitative analysis perspective, whether this issue is mostly emotional and reflective of the subconscious or silent admission by golf course owners of their inability to properly manage a golf course.

As spectators listening to the divergent views of an extremely heated argument, we offer in the following figure our synthesized analysis of this debate.

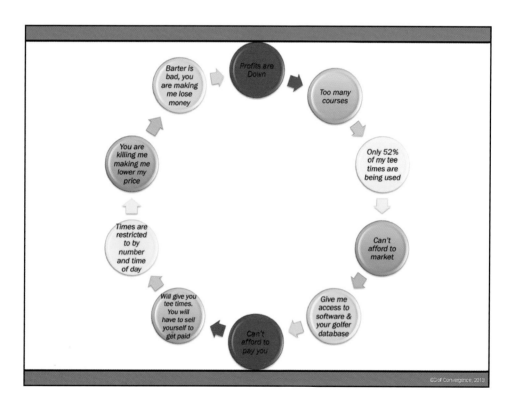

It is estimated that more than 45% of America's daily fee facilities work in some fashion with third-party resellers.

Here are some quick numbers—approximately 10% of the 424 million rounds played in 2012 were booked online, based on the NGF Demand Model.[3] Less than 1% of all tee time inventory that is made available to consumers via the Web is bartered. Putting aside the debate and running the numbers, the impact of providing third parties bartered tee times is estimated in the table to the right.

Calculating the Impact of Barter	
Number of Courses Participating in Barter	4,000
Estimated Annual Revenue per Course	$20,000
Gross Revenue from Barter	80,000,000
National Golf Industry Revenue	25,000,000,000
Revenue Paid to Third Parties?	0.32%

Third parties can hardly be the cause of the woes of the industry.

Clearly the industry (64% of the industry as confirmed in the survey conducted by Golf Convergence) would prefer to negotiate an annual fee for such a service rather than trade bartered tee times. When separated from the herd mentality fostered at national conventions like the NGCOA's, 58% of golf course operators believe that third parties either increase or have no impact on the facility's revenue, as shown in the figure to the right.

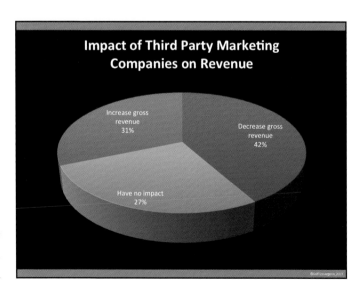

The feelings on this subject are strong. One software vendor, Fore! Reservations, issued a

---

3 National Golf Foundation, "NGF Demand Model," 2012, pg. 4.

white paper on the subject,[4] and that was still available on their Web site in January 2013.

Harry Ipema, CEO and Founder of Fore! Reservations, Inc. stated,

> "I have served the golf industry for 15 years, and am passionate about the overall financial health and success of every golf course. I want to see this industry thrive in the months and years to come, and operators profit from serving and growing this great game. I encourage every operator to maximize your software utilizations, leverage your customer database, enact best marketing practices and implement technology that helps your business increase rounds and revenue.
>
> In a golf economy where price erosion is spiraling out of control, it's critical that courses discount less and stop bartering tee times with third-party resellers that operate on a barter-for-resale model. When the Internet consumer is trained to go away from the golf course's website to find a better tee time price, the course loses. Barter is essentially creating additional competition for courses, and with an industry challenged by excess supply, increasing competition is not the right solution. Instead, I believe our industry should adopt a "commission-based" model and pay third-parties based on results of rack-rate tee time sold.
>
> Fore! Reservations elects not to engage in barters as we firmly believe the best place to see your tee times is on your website by offering the lowest price guarantee."

He does proffer a solution: "Why doesn't the golf industry adopt a 'commission-based' or 'finder's fee' model with third parties and pay those companies based on their results."[5]

It should be noted that in June, 2013, Fore! Reservations was acquired by GolfNow/Golf Channel and the white paper appears to be withdrawn from the firm's web site when searched in September, 2013.

We believe that a hybrid combination of solutions may be the answer. The cash purchase price for the software should be determined upon execution of the software license. The golf course operator should have the flexibility of paying cash or offering to barter tee times subject to controlling the times for which they are offered and the price for which they are sold. If the vendor is unable to liquidate the times based on the course-controlled parameters, the difference between the value of the tee times liquidated and the contract cash value is due to the software firm.

---

4 http://support.teeitup.com/archives/harrys-blog/the-harmful-effects-of-barter-white-paper-january-2010/

5 Ibid.

What's Next?

Apple, Nordstrom, and Microsoft retail outlets have one thing in common: they have replaced the POS counter with wireless tablet-based terminals that allow the employees to roam the stores to serve their customers. Swipe your credit card, enter your email address, and your receipt is zipped right to you, as illustrated in the following figure.

Recently I asked a Starbucks cashier in Carlsbad, California, what percent of her users pay for their beverages with a mobile application on their phone. Her answer? "75%." I was stunned, and while my subsequent observations would place that number closer to 25%, it can absolutely be envisioned that within a short period of time, our cell phones will replace our wallets. Google "mobile wallets" and a plethora of technology alternatives emerge, including Visa v.Me, and Square wallet, as illustrated in the following figure.

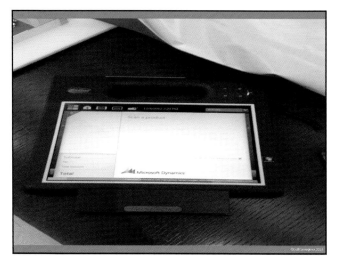

These evolutions in technology will be adopted in the golf industry, albeit slower than in commercial business. New applications to the golf industry in the short term will likely include the following:

- Golfer Technology: Apps to order food on course.

- Course Technology: iPad on 1st tee, carts with music systems and iPad and cell phone chargers, RFID on loyalty cards.

- Facility: POS counters are likely to be gone as mobile transaction terminals are adapted. Expect to see these at high-end resorts first.

- Management: An "alert system" will emerge. Managers will be alerted when transactions occur beyond the parameters they established, transactions discounted, arrival on property, etc.

These solutions are likely to be Web-based. From call centers, to RFID loyal customer recognition, to tablet POS software, to yield management, it is likely that some software firms will form consulting divisions to monitor the real-time financial performance at a golf course and recommend and implement changes as mutually agreed.

At the 2013 PGA Merchandise Show, Club Prophet announced its mobile starter application, as illustrated in the figure to the left.

There is a feeling held by some industry professionals we have interviewed that the existing software firms will not be able to adapt quickly to the accelerating technological changes in our society. Many seem to think that future software applications (the technology the customers expect) should become customer-focused rather than facility-focused. The theory supporting this thinking is that if golfers receive better service, they will play more frequently. In turn, golf course revenues will rise and owners will be willing to pay a share of that increased revenue to software vendors for the superior technology.

Political and consumer wordsmith, Dr. Frank Luntz, highlights what consumers are seeking in his book *What Americans Really Want ... Really: The Truth About Our Hopes, Dreams, and Fears*. He says they want more money, fewer hassles, more times, more choices, and no worries. The successful software of the future will embrace these themes and create marketing messages for golf courses and golfers, as illustrated in the next figure.

Marketing Themes Dr. Frank I. Luntz, Author "Words that Work"		
Consumer Desires	**Golf Course**	**Golfers**
More Money	Increasing your revenue by generating the most golfers at the highest yield	Save on your green fees.
Fewer Hassles	Staff is relieved from the monotonous and troubled to handle repetitive phone calls from golfers. Golfers get the time they want at the price you want.	Three clicks to book
More Time	Service is able to serve golfers more personally at the course.	Fast booking create greater leisure
More Choices	All the technology you need at the most effective value you would hope.	All the courses, all the time.
No Worries	Introducing you to golfers you never knew but always wanted to have them play your course.	The best tee times at the lowest prices

Consumer applications in the golf industry will dramatically change during the next several years with smart phone applications, mobile Web sites, tee time bookings by email, and email toolboxes and texts. Even now, as shown to the right, there are the impressive offerings of GolfNow/Golf Channel.

Tips, Tools, and Traps

While some of the academic discussion about the future can be overwhelming, there are some easy, small progressive changes that can be made now that will have immediate benefit.

It's amazing how difficult some golf courses make the process of reserving tee times on the Internet. For example, through 2012, the City and County of

Denver's golf courses had a convoluted set of reservation policies that were so daunting they discouraged customer use, as shown in the next figure.

Can you imagine walking up to a Neiman Marcus, Nordstrom, or any retail store and being required to demonstrate who you are and whether you have the ability to pay before being allowed to enter the store to purchase?

In this case, those who were able to navigate the three entry doors to attempt to book a tee time but were seeking to modify, cancel, or delete that reservation were faced with the dreaded "CAPTCHA" code data entry field shown in the next figure.

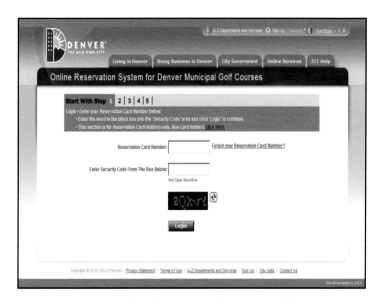

Using the City and County of Denver's Web site, we booked a reservation for a foursome at 9:20 a.m. Since we were merely testing the accuracy and efficiency of the software, and are very conscious about not creating a no-show, we attempted to cancel the reservation 1 minute later. Amazingly, the software system could not find the tee time.

Fortunately, the City and County of Denver implemented EZLink software on its seven golf courses in May, 2013.

Regarding tee time reservations, there is a lesson offered by the airlines that every golf course should adopt. The real estate on the home page of your Web

171

site has different values. As people read from left to right and from the top down, the most important items should be in the upper left corner Web site. If you go to the Web sites of Orbitz, United Airlines, and most car rental companies, you will see their booking engines on their home pages in the upper left corner.

At most golf courses, to book a tee time, at best, you've clicked a minimum of three times before the available tee times are displayed. You most often see "book a tee time" as a link on the home page, as illustrated on the Eagle Mountain screenshot that follows. Astute golf course owners will ensure that their Web sites enable customers to book on their home pages, as shown on the Walters Golf Web site in Las Vegas.

With rates an increasing concern of golfers and golf courses along with the growing perceived influence of third-party tee time companies, adroitly managed companies are doing what they can to create loyalty and trust. For instance, OB Sports includes on the Web sites of each of the courses it manages a Blue Ribbon, Best Rate Guarantee that the lowest prices offered anywhere will be available at that Web site. And, as shown here, OB Sports has created a live link showing the current NFL football scores.

How Good Are You at Leveraging Technology to Your Advantage?

There are many tools available to management that evaluate how effective a firm's Web site marketing efforts are.

MarketingGrader (formerly Website Grader), a free tool offered by Hubspot, measures the marketing effectiveness of a Web site and provides an inbound marketing score (on a scale of 0 to 100) that incorporates Web site traffic, SEO (search engine optimization), the blogosphere, social media, and other inbound marketing factors. Marketing Grader has been a very helpful site at providing basic advice on how a Web site can be improved and how the site is faring against the competition. It also measures a firm's Web site content creation, optimization, and Web site promotion skills, as well as measuring how well a Web site is doing at converting traffic into leads and then to customers. The grade assigned provides insight as to whether the Web activities are effective.

Following is an example of the Hubspot Web site grader for Golf Convergence.

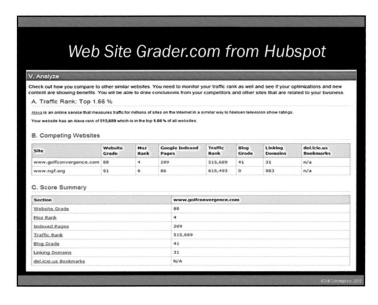

Another interesting tool is Open Site Explorer, which gives you the ability to compare your Web site to the sites of other firms, showing your page and domain authority along with how many other Web sites link to your site.

Senderscore.org by Return Path, provides insights into your inbox placement and sender reputation. ISPs make millions of filtering decisions based on senders' reputations. Knowing your score is the first step to improving email delivery and response rates.

We Are Going for Launch

Where that leave does today's management team at a golf course? If increasing attention is not being placed on technology, they are floating in the vast seas without a paddle and reacting to the winds of the consumer and the perils of capitalism.

And for those who are overwhelmed by this chapter, you may want to throw in the towel when you learn about the incredible demonstration of sixth sense technology[6] being developed by Pranav Mistry, a PhD student in the Fluid Interfaces Group at MIT's Media Lab. Mistry has developed a wearable device that enables new interactions between the real world and the world of data. The Web site biography highlights his talents as "Some previous projects from Mistry's work at MIT include intelligent sticky notes, Quickies, that can be searched and can send reminders; a pen that draws in 3D; and TaPuMa, a tangible public map that can act as the Google of physical world. His research interests also include Gestural and Tangible Interaction, Ubiquitous Computing, Machine Vision, Collective Intelligence and Robotics."[7]

Technology is a great asset for the golf course operator when properly deployed.

Go

If you licensed the supplemental template that accompanies this Field book, Step 3: Technology is an excellent exercise that will give you a grade on your use of technology.

It asks the extent to which the latest software and social media have been integrated into your operation.

It is unlikely that any golf course will be designated at the post graduate level.

---

6 http://www.ted.com/talks/pranav_mistry_the_thrilling_potential_of_sixthsense_technology.html

7 http://www.ted.com/speakers/pranav_mistry.html

Path to Success

1) The purpose of technology is to allow you to complete routine transactions faster so that you have more time to create a personal human connection with your customers when they are visiting your golf course.

2) The role of technology is to improve your customers' experiences, making it easier and faster for them to do business with you while satisfying their preferences.

3) Knowing who your customers are is essential to being able to serve them correctly.

4) Each of your customers is unique. Their needs, wants and desires all vary. Your ability to create a customized experience for each individual determines their loyalty. That connection starts with a handshake, the foundation of human interaction in our culture.

5) The Sinek motto is "People don't buy what you do. They buy why you do it." As a golf course operator, your WHY is your passion for creating a superior entertainment and leisure experience for your customers. Passion is contagious. Technology allows you the freedom to become passionate.

Concluding Thoughts

In order to succeed, your desire for success should exceed your fear of failure.

Bill Cosby

The great pleasure in life is doing what people say you cannot do.

Walter Bagehot

Chapter 8

The Key Financial Benchmarking

Step 4 of the Golf Convergence WIN™ Formula

A wise man recognizes the convenience of a general statement, but he bows to the authority of a particular fact.

Oliver Wendell Holmes, Jr.

Chapter Highlights

Would you consider flying a plane without an instrument panel, driving a car without the speedometer, determining if you have a fever without a thermometer, perhaps cooking a prime rib without a meat thermometer?

If you've answered "no" to most of these, why would you manage a golf course without comparing your operating performance to the national, state, and local benchmarks made available by Golf Datatech, the National Golf Foundation, the PGA of America, and many other reputable research firms?

This chapter covers the importance of utilizing these reports and information on how to become an active participant in submitting your information on a confidential and highly secure basis to these national research efforts.

The Real Scoreboard in the Business of Golf

It can seem puzzling and even amusing that the same activity, playing 18 holes of golf, can result in a golf course generating revenue of less than $300,000 in a year or earning more as $20 million. How do you compare the performance of your facility to others in your local market and to courses throughout the nation? Can you in some way identify what factors are adversely affecting your net income?

Financial statements are the goalposts of business. Financial statements (balance sheet, income statement, cash flow) and budgets can often serve as the foundation to provide a framework for the performance of a golf course, but it is our opinion that developing and monitoring key performance indicators are of equal value to the financial health of a golf course.

There are a limitless number of financial ratios, but those that are key include profitability ratios, liquidity ratios, activity ratios, and debt ratios. These traditional indices are often used to provide an overview of financial health, because they are prepared monthly, quarterly, or annually, and they provide a report on how the business did.

These historical indicators are very much like a school report card. While some indicators may make you feel good if you've done well, if you haven't performed to the level of your goals, they provide very little indication as to what to correct. Following the platitudes of "work harder, work smarter, and surround yourself with the better team" merely fall to the floor when you realize the course's performance still should have been better. Thus, most within the industry cite uncontrollable factors as the cause of poor performance, when in truth they're just playing poorly the hand they've been dealt.

Wouldn't you like to have automatic adjustments or text alerts made within your information systems that have the potential to positively impact current transactions and future revenue streams? Would you enjoy putting your facility on a kind of autopilot?

While such software is in its infancy and being introduced to the golf industry incrementally, there exist now 14 operational reports, 6 that analyze the customers and 8 that provide yardsticks of the facility. These provide a flexible and deft management team the opportunity to make real-time and updates that have the potential to positively influence operational results.

Presented in the following figure are these reports.

While the eyes of the un-
initiated and the cynic may
glaze over with all the numbers, in a dynamic and ever-
changing business, we have
observed that some innovators can make the numbers
dance.

The Key Reports

Customer Analysis

Customer Distribution: stratifies golfers into 10 segments by number and spending
Customer Demographics: age, income, and ethnicity of your customers
Customer Retention: core, new and lost customers
Customer Spending by Class: SKU generates highest yield per transaction
Customer Spending by Individual:
Zip Code Analysis: residential and business location of customers

Facility Analysis

Merchandise Sales by Vendor: rank vendors orders by inventory, sales and turnover
Reservations by Booking Method: customer reservation preferences, .i.e., phone, internet
Reservations by Day of Week: highlights demand by day to facilitate proper pricing
Revenue Benchmarks: benchmarks (green fees, carts, etc.) to compare to competitive norms
Revenue per Available Tee Time: established net rate per round by time slot
Revenue by Department: focuses on revenue centers
Rounds per Revenue Margins: customer frequency versus yield per customer
Course Utilization: demand vs. supply by time slot

©Golf Convergence 2013

Mirror, Mirror on the Wall—Who Is the Fairest Customer of All?

Customer Analysis

The **Customer Distribution** report, nationally, reflects that just a few of your customers have the greatest impact on revenue. Usually, 15% of your current customers generate 60% of the revenue. Most courses invest a lot of energy and money in serving all of their customers and fail to target their key clients. The revenue generated by outings, tournaments, and leagues often generates up to 40% of the gross revenue of many public golf courses, whether they be municipal, daily fee, or resorts. Leagues, north of I-80 and in the Midwest of the United States, are essential revenue components. It always amazes me that in the off-season, from November through March, full-time staff members are passive and do little to nothing to solicit recurring revenue for the upcoming season. It is our belief that a city's public golf course should have booked at least 25% of its green fee income before the season starts. This report identifies the location of the low-hanging fruit that should be picked.

The **Customer Demographics** report identifies the spending potential of cur-
rent customers and their price sensitivity. A median household income above national averages would suggest that demand is inelastic, that prices could be raised, and that the experience being sought would require an additional

178

investment in the course and in the service levels to ensure customer satisfaction meet customer expectations. On the flip side, if the median household income is low and the age of the population is older, there will be tremendous resistance to price increases. At one community golf course we observed, the patron cardholders defiantly maintained that their $400 season passes were the appropriate price for the course, even after learning that the average unlimited season pass play rate in the United States is $1,250 and that the deferred capital expenditures at the golf course (which was worn, tired, and in need of attention) exceeded $3 million.

The **Customer Retention** report reveals the turnover in the customer database. Although 30,000 rounds may be played at a facility, the unique number of customers served ranges from 3,500 in smaller communities to more than 11,000 in major metropolitan markets. With 50% of the customers who play the course one golf season not returning the next, replacing them with new customers and communicating uniquely to the core, acquired, and lost customers is valuable. We observed a Kansas City golf course that generated $45,000 in revenue in August and September by sending out an email to golfers that had played their facility in April but had not returned during May, June, or July. That reconnection with the customers generated a return visit, and it was simple, effective, and possible because the course captured salient golfer information at the time of the reservation. It should be noted here that the utilization of a call center or having an easy reservation wizard on the home page of your Web site is the optimum process to clean customer data. Attempting to obtain this information at the point-of-sale counter during check-in is fraught with operational challenges. That is why, even in the most efficiently managed facilities, customer data is gathered only on up to 75% of the customers. Having a Web site that offers online reservations facilitates the creation of a customer database. A golf course that gathers no customer information or transaction data is clearly being poorly managed.

Customer Spending by Class indicates which SKU generates the highest yield per transaction. Usually that is the prime time rate. This knowledge facilitates creating the appropriate "buckets—time slots" on the tee sheet to optimize revenue. For example, should a prime time on Friday afternoon be available to all golfers or restricted by the class? At a municipal golf course, if there is a differential in rates between residents and nonresidents, it is often advantageous to reserve an appropriate percentage of tee times during the prime time specifically for nonresidents. About 70% of municipal and daily fee courses offer unlimited play passes. Reserving prime tee times for pay-as-you-go customers is an effective strategy to increase revenue.

Customer Spending by Individual identifies your best customers by their frequency of play and by their spending. This information is often very revealing. As we met with the management team in Abu Dhabi, this report was being reviewed by the General Manager, who was stunned that one customer has visited the course only nine times but has spent $45,000 during the past year. His comment was, "I know the gentlemen, but I had no idea that he was that important a customer to our facility." The clubhouse is shown below.

It was immediately suggested that the Director of Golf that create an "amenity package" and have it delivered to the customer with a note of appreciation. It is in the DNA of all of us to be attracted to those who acknowledge our presence, celebrate our uniqueness, and appreciate our patronage.

ZIP Code Analysis: While email marketing is the most effective advertising, many golf courses advertise in other media. Which are the appropriate publications in which to advertise; a local publication like the *Castle Rock News Press* or *The Denver Post*? The answer would usually be "the more targeted the placement, the more effective the result."

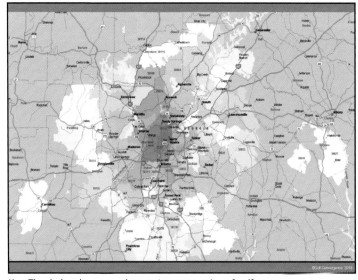

Presented to the right is an analysis of public golf courses in and near Atlanta, Georgia. Would your preference be to own and operate a golf course shown in the top center section of this map, which represents the geographical boundaries north

Key: The darker the green, the great concentration of golfers.

of I-20 and between I-75 and I-85, or a golf course that is located in the lower half this diagram? Clearly, the upper section has far greater potential.

At some well managed courses, it might seem that there are few reasons to make the dynamic updates we suggested; however, they have alternative systems in place to ensure superlative customer service.

At the exclusive and privileged Castle Pines Golf Club, perhaps one of the best locker room attendants in the United States, Tommy, takes time every night to review the members and guests scheduled to play the next day. He has expanded the service to such a fine level, that he commits to memory the drink preferences of members and guests. At the nearby Colorado Golf Club, Bill, the locker room attendant, maintains a similar level of attentive service.

At the incomparable Bandon Dunes resort, return guests will often find in their rooms monogrammed chocolates, caps, and perhaps even golf balls, along with a personal note from Hank Hitchcock, the general manager.

Reviewing the tee sheets and noting the scheduled customers can create memorable moments that result in repetitive revenue. Even at less glamorous courses, personalization at a reasonable cost can begin with staff focusing on customer name recognition and courtesy.

Also important is the practice of creating appropriate rate buckets starting 60 days before the actual day of play, a prudent practice that allows management to update tee sheets to reflect the evolving patterns.

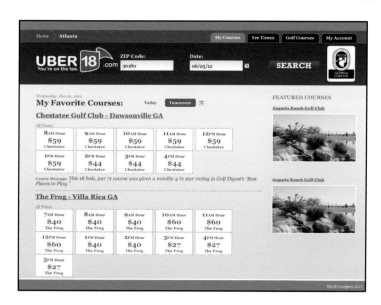

Note, in the figure on the left, how one golf course, The Frog, in Villa Rica, Georgia, is offering dramatically different rates throughout the day.

The Frog's prices change constantly and automatically based on the volume of advanced reservations occurring that day and within each hour.

One price undoubtedly doesn't fit all.

Facility Analysis

Merchandise Sales by Vendor: provides for efficient ranking of vendors by sales, turnover rates, and levels of current inventory on hand. It is our observation, from reviewing the inventory of many golf courses, that the vast majority order only a few items from many vendors, hoping to create a diversified selection of merchandise. If the 80/20 rule ever applied it would certainly be with respect to merchandise sales. Twenty percent of the vendors generate the vast majority of sales. It is always amusing how buyers will hang on to merchandise that is not selling throughout the season and will only offer a substantial discount at the end of the season to liquidate the slow-moving items. Reducing the price of an item, starting at the 30th day, a certain percentage for every day it remains unsold, up to the cost, would provide capital that could be invested in other faster-moving merchandise.

Reservations by Booking Method: evaluates customer reservation preferences, such as calling center, phone, Internet, etc. If I were operating a golf course, I would offer golfers a discount for reserving their tee times over the Internet if they completed a customer profile and entered a credit card that was chargeable in the event of a no-show. This report would provide the flexibility, through pricing, to encourage customers to use the medium that provides them the best customer service and the course the greatest amount of customer data.

Reservations by Day of Week/Hour: highlights demand by day to facilitate proper pricing. Should there be a weekend rate? Should Sunday afternoon be heavily discounted? What about creating incremental pricing by day? Monday is usually the slowest, and Wednesday usually does well. This report is a valuable tool to determine demand and pricing.

Revenue Benchmarks: (green fees, carts, etc.) are used to compare your revenue to competitive norms. There is only one price that matters in forecasting revenue: the yield per time. Carts (70% of purchases), Merchandise, and Food and Beverage (a known, small percentage of the revenue per time can be established). As will be seen, the rates realized at your facility can be compared real time by month to those of your competitors.

Revenue per Available Tee Time: the established net rate per round by time slot, becomes an accurate predictor of likely gross revenue. If you ask at a golf course how many rounds ("starts") the course is likely to achieve that year, you can accurately forecast gross revenue. A golf course will typically net 55% of its rack rate; this information is supported by the Golf Convergence survey shown below.

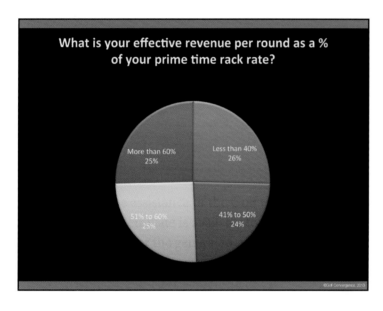

We are always humored at the PGA eavesdropping on conversations between golf professionals. The conversation goes, "How did you do last year?" "Great, rounds were up 5%." That information, while it may be socially courteous, is meaningless.

We demonstrated the forecasting power of the effective yield on a recent business trip to a very popular Hawaiian resort. Management there indicated that the course rack rate was $275 and 78,600 rounds were played last year. Gross revenue we calculated was likely about $11,444,160. It is not uncommon for Hawaii resorts to achieve merchandise sales that bring in income equal to 40% of the green fees and to earn an amount equal to 20% of the green fees in food and beverage sales. We guessed that this 36-hole course was doing around $18 million in annual revenue. Our guess was within $250,000 of the actual revenue. From learning the cost of water and utilities to knowing the increasingly important variables, benchmarks, and standards in operating a golf course, we could predict the profitability of this resort.

Revenue by Department focuses on revenue centers; the relationship between green fees, carts, merchandise, food and beverage, and other (range, instructions, etc.) is predictable. By knowing the yield on green fees, it is easy to forecast the yield per round at a specific golf course after ascertaining the following: 1) Are carts required? 2) What is the green fee walking? 3) How hilly is the golf course? 4) How large (in square feet) is the pro shop? 5) Is it well merchandised? (Think Sea Island Resort in Georgia and Grayhawk Golf Club in Arizona.) 6) How large (in square feet) is the clubhouse? 7) Is there a snack bar separate from the restaurant? 8) How many items are on the menu? and 9) Is beer and/or alcohol served on the course? Knowing these variables makes predicting revenue fairly accurate. I know I'm in a great golf shop when I feel compelled to buy something unique for my wife that she would not be able to find at a department store. Most frequently, though, I hear something like, "We carry a very limited line of understated women's clothes, just basic staples, but sales aren't good."

Rounds per Revenue Margin: This report contrasts how many rounds are played by category with the yield of that category. To illustrate, at a university golf course, students and faculty are likely to dominate the tee sheets during prime time, playing on highly discounted passes. They are likely to play 30% of the rounds while contributing only 15% of the revenue. Alumni and those with an affinity for the university who are visiting as a one-time event may play only 10% of the rounds but generate 40% of the revenue. But this is possible only if university logo apparel is properly marketed. There is simply no reason that a university golf course should lose money if it is properly marketed. With that stated, I was chagrined to learn of a university in the Southeast that is losing $1 million per year. With a few questions, I learned that the clubhouse was operating as a high-end restaurant with an incredibly diverse menu—a quick way to lose a lot of money.

Course Utilization: demand versus supply by time slot. The power of this report was illustrated in the previous chapter on technology, where we presented the fact that the opportunity to increase the yield in a 1-hour slot (the hour before twilight rates) had the potential to increase revenue by $250,000. It is clearly my favorite operational report because it has the greatest potential to increase revenue. And for those using yield management software, this report provides the information needed to create initial targets.

A Confession

There's a confession that I need to make regarding my intellectual bias in writing this book, in the strategic approach to Golf Convergence, and more broadly in life. Having served as a CPA at one of the national accounting firms, I believe that numbers provide 60% of the solutions to most problems. While qualitative issues, the touchy-feely stuff, the quality of communication, the passion, and the crispness of execution are all vital, the ultimate scoreboard in every business is a set of key performance indicators that measure the ultimate financial success of the business.

To illustrate, presented on the top of the next page are the 2012 National Football League/American Conference financial standings.[1]

---

1 http://www.nfl.com/standings

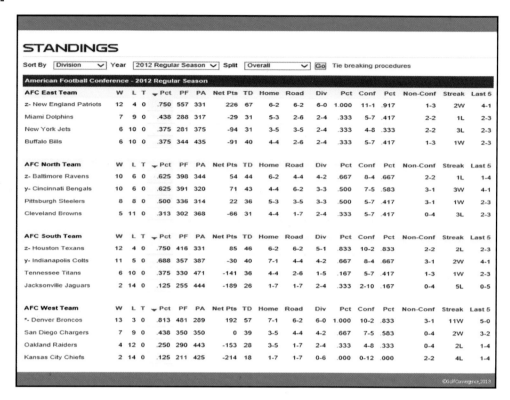

Look at the net points differential. It tracks almost exactly each team's standing in the league. In baseball, the key statistic would be the runs differential, or in National Basketball Association, points differential would again be most important. That is shown below in green (positive) and negative (red).

Group: League | Conference | Division
Season: 2012-13 Regular Season

Standings   **Expanded Standings**   **Vs. Division Standings**

Eastern Conference

	EASTERN	W	L	PCT	GB	HOME	ROAD	DIV	CONF	PF	PA	DIFF	STRK	L10
1	z - Miami	66	16	.805	-	37-4	29-12	15-1	41-11	102.9	95.0	+7.9	Won 8	9-1
2	y - New York	54	28	.659	12	31-10	23-18	10-6	37-15	100.0	95.7	+4.2	Won 1	8-2
3	y - Indiana	49	32	.605	16 ½	30-11	19-21	13-3	31-20	94.7	90.7	+4.0	Lost 3	5-5
4	x - Brooklyn	49	33	.598	17	26-15	23-18	11-5	36-16	96.9	95.1	+1.8	Won 2	7-3
5	x - Chicago	45	37	.549	21	24-17	21-20	9-7	34-18	93.2	92.9	+0.3	Won 2	5-5
6	x - Atlanta	44	38	.537	22	25-16	19-22	11-5	29-23	98.0	97.5	+0.4	Lost 2	4-6
7	x - Boston	41	40	.506	24 ½	27-13	14-27	7-9	27-24	96.5	96.7	-0.2	Lost 1	4-6
8	x - Milwaukee	38	44	.463	28	21-20	17-24	7-9	24-28	98.9	100.4	-1.5	Won 1	3-7
	Philadelphia	34	48	.415	32	23-18	11-30	7-9	22-30	93.2	96.5	-3.3	Won 1	5-5
	Toronto	34	48	.415	32	21-20	13-28	5-11	22-30	97.2	98.7	-1.5	Won 5	7-3
	Detroit	29	53	.354	37	18-23	11-30	8-8	25-27	94.9	98.8	-4.0	Lost 1	5-5
	Washington	29	53	.354	37	22-19	7-34	5-11	15-37	93.2	95.8	-2.5	Lost 6	3-7
	Cleveland	24	58	.293	42	14-27	10-31	3-13	18-34	96.5	101.2	-4.7	Lost 6	2-8
	Charlotte	21	61	.256	45	15-26	6-35	6-10	18-34	93.4	102.7	-9.2	Won 3	4-6
	Orlando	20	62	.244	46	12-29	8-33	3-13	10-42	94.1	101.1	-7.0	Lost 3	2-8

Western Conference

	WESTERN	W	L	PCT	GB	HOME	ROAD	DIV	CONF	PF	PA	DIFF	STRK	L10
1	z - Oklahoma City	60	22	.732	-	34-7	26-15	10-6	39-13	105.7	96.5	+9.2	Lost 1	7-3
2	y - San Antonio	58	24	.707	2	35-6	23-18	12-4	33-19	103.0	96.6	+6.4	Lost 3	3-7
3	x - Denver	57	25	.695	3	38-3	19-22	11-5	38-14	106.1	101.1	+5.1	Won 3	8-2
4	y - LA Clippers	56	26	.683	4	32-9	24-17	11-5	35-17	101.1	94.6	+6.5	Won 7	7-3
5	x - Memphis	56	26	.683	4	32-9	24-17	10-6	34-18	93.4	89.3	+4.1	Won 2	8-2
6	x - Golden State	47	35	.573	13	28-13	19-22	9-7	28-24	101.2	100.3	+0.9	Won 2	6-4
7	x - LA Lakers	45	37	.549	15	29-12	16-25	8-8	28-24	102.2	101.0	+1.2	Won 5	8-2
8	x - Houston	45	37	.549	15	29-12	16-25	6-10	24-28	106.0	102.5	+3.5	Lost 2	6-4
	Utah	43	39	.524	17	30-11	13-28	9-7	26-26	98.0	98.1	-0.1	Lost 1	7-3
	Dallas	41	41	.500	19	24-17	17-24	7-9	24-28	101.1	101.7	-0.6	Won 1	6-4
	Portland	33	49	.402	27	22-19	11-30	6-10	18-34	97.5	100.7	-3.2	Lost 13	0-10
	Minnesota	31	51	.378	29	20-21	11-30	4-12	17-35	95.7	98.1	-2.4	Won 1	5-5
	Sacramento	28	54	.341	32	20-21	8-33	7-9	14-38	100.2	105.1	-4.9	Lost 4	2-8
	New Orleans	27	55	.329	33	16-25	11-30	5-11	15-37	94.1	97.9	-3.9	Lost 5	2-8
	Phoenix	25	57	.305	35	17-24	8-33	5-11	17-35	95.2	101.6	-6.5	Lost 1	2-8

The doubter would say that these statistics measure only the results of success and are not predictors of it. But when you examine the golf industry, there are many indicators that can guide improved performance. Shown below is a 2011 report on a municipal golf course, one whose financial data is released to the public. The course is generating $2.6 in revenue and losing six figures. When viewing the data in comparison to national statistics, we can see that the maintenance costs provide a data point for further research.

When examining the course conditions with trained agronomists, the golf course is getting $750,000 in value at a cost of $1,524,000. There are many reasons for this, including the involvement of a labor union. The City is only one of four municipal golf courses in California that still use labor union employees. Most municipalities have contracted the management of their golf courses to third parties, because private companies can better control these current and future costs and reduce the potential pension liability.

Comparison to the National Municipal Golf Course

Maintenance Department	California Course	National			
		Bottom 25	Median	Top 25%	Top 10%
Full Time	9	3	4	7	11
Part Time	0	4	7	10	16
Payroll	$821,084	$167,000	$251,085	$400,000	$587,000
Other Expenses (Supplies/Repairs)	206,000	110,000	179,262	285,000	401,800
Maintenance Expenses (Fertilizer, Seeds, Gasoline)	86,000	100,000	160,000	293,820	443,066
Other Expenses (Building repairs, cleaning supplies)	411,733	10,000	35,000	84,500	163,015
Total Maintenance Expenses	$1,524,000	$387,000	$625,347	$1,063,320	$1,594,881

It Could Be So Easy

In golf, the key performance indicator for the public golf course is revenue per round purchased (RevPUR) or the revenue per available tee time (RevPATT), especially when these are measured for one set of local competitive golf courses.

Developing meaningful benchmarks is a struggle. Through Performance-Trak, about one-third of the golf courses in the nation participate in the PGA's monthly key performance indicators reports or the annual operating survey. While these are a great foundation for meaningful analysis, if one looks at a section, like the Minnesota PGA (which encompasses North and South Dakota), so few courses participate that the results are mostly labeled with asterisks which signify that insignificant financial data has been provided. Golf course managers or owners who don't contribute information to this repository or access its data operate in the dark, in spite of the fact that light and insight are available for free.

Despite these noteworthy efforts, only 33% of golf courses participate. These low numbers are surprising, especially considering that PGA professionals can earn member service reports, which are part of the associations' educational requirements to maintain certification.

The NGCOA Canada has invested six figures to implement a benchmarking system for its more than 1,000 golf operators. Committees were formed and the appropriate indices were crafted, or so they thought. The minutia of some benchmarks a few operators thought were important, such as the number of handcarts rented, caused many professional managers to deduce that the investment of time it takes to complete monthly reports far exceeds the benefit.

In 2012, The Royal and Ancient abandoned a benchmarking service that focused on maintenance costs. In February 2013, a new benchmarking tool (tracked system) was introduced there. It's titled "Course Tracker,"[2] and its goal is to accomplish the following:

- Monitor, analyze, and evaluate your course's progress.
- Identify where your business can make money and save money.
- Track income and expenditures and plan for the future.
- Generate illustrated reports to help you make informed decisions.
- Anonymously benchmark with other similar courses in your country.

Graham Duncan comments, "CourseTracker is structured so that data can be entered quickly and simply. Information is then reported in a clear and concise, but also extensive, manner."[3]

Hamish Grey, Chief Executive of the Scottish Golf Union, commented, "We ultimately aim to have a 'tracker system' as good as the USA. We know from the USA that it takes a while to get people on board, and our low-key basic attempts now are making breakthroughs—171+ clubs registered now. At this stage we

---

2 https://www.coursetracker.org/
3 Ibid.

don't have the comparative data, but we hope in two years' time the position will have changed!"[4]

Why are the participation rates of golf course so low? Sadly, the root cause is a lack of sophistication on the part of many golf course owners as small business entrepreneurs. Because their livelihood is dependent upon the cash flow generated by the course, they hold a false belief that protecting their "trade secrets" is beneficial. In contrast, throughout the airline and hospitality industry, vital operational benchmarks are shared for the collective welfare of the industry.

Implementing such a system, we believe is like a term paper; it is a very iterative process. While many golf course owners and managers would like to have comprehensive comparative data on a local basis, the innovators and the early adopters get quickly frustrated as the results from such exercises produce sample sizes too small to be meaningful. Then do you publish the survey data that would indicate general national trends, hoping that those who review the report will be motivated to participate in future surveys, or do you just give up?

The solution to creating meaningful data depositories is readily available and would be simple to implement, but because of parochial boundaries and defined territories, it is not likely to occur in the short- or intermediate-term.

The root of the problem is lack of trust. It would be very easy for software companies to create an interface in which the key performance benchmarks were automatically uploaded monthly into a national database. For this to occur, the association managing the data would confidentially and independently sign a nondisclosure agreement with the software vendors that they would not come to market with a competing product. The risk for the software vendor is that by participating in the automatic uploading of the data, in this trusted transaction, they would be disclosing your client list. As such, they put their own economic security in jeopardy with the release of that information.

In a survey conducted by Golf Convergence in 2012, 82% of golf course owners and managers believe that national associations should enter into non-compete agreements to facilitate building a meaningful financial benchmarking service.

While there was agreement with the software vendors on the confidentially of their client lists, another hurdle, as shown on the next page, is exposed.

---

4 Hamish Grey, "Email to Author," February 24, 2013.

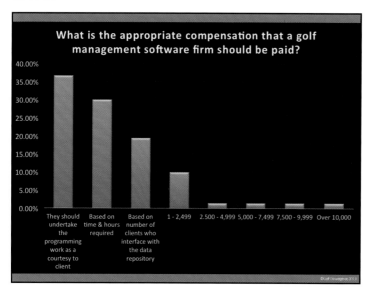

Not surprisingly, the core of the issue is money. Golf course owners and managers feel the software companies should do this as a service to their clients. Naturally, for the incremental work necessary to create and maintain the interface to what is likely an ever-changing database structure, the software companies are appropriately seeking compensation.

With less than 5% of the respondents believing that a fee in excess of $2,500 per year is appropriate, it's unfortunate that the benchmarking services performed will largely remain voluntary and dependent on the innovators, the early adopters, and, eventually, the early majority to lead.

That makes one wonder, if the information being supplied is accurate, do the consolidated results represent a median performance or perhaps the upper 10% to 25% quintile of golf course operations?

In Spite of Themselves

Despite the resistance received, Golf Datatech along with the National Golf Course Owners Association, the National Golf Foundation, and the PGA, via its PerformanceTrak, in a cooperative alliance, are doing an outstanding job creating meaningful and timely insights to help those within the industry efficiently manage their facilities. Some examples follow:

> "PerformanceTrak, in Cooperation with NGCOA, is the largest single source of rounds-played data in the industry. Primary contributors of this monthly data are PGA Professionals and NGCOA members along with other allied partners. This PerformanceTrak data is shared and combined with data from other industry contributors, including Golf Datatech, to prepare the National Rounds Played Report. Unique to PerformanceTrak, current year and prior year volume

figures for monthly and year-to-date rounds played are provided along with percent change.

In addition to rounds-played-monthly data, PGA Professionals, employers, and other registered users of PerformanceTrak also provide revenue data for four key performance indicators (KPIs). These include golf fee revenue, merchandising revenue, food and beverage revenue and total revenue. Comparative reports are generated for revenue per round with drill-down segmentation by facility size and by state, local markets and for PGA of America, by PGA Section.

NGCOA members may use the PGA PerformanceTrak service at no cost through the link below. Individual course data is maintained under the strictest security and password protection. **The NGCOA and PGA of America maintain a number of security and reporting procedures to ensure that individual facility data is kept confidential. Data about a specific facility is not available to any users other than those at that specific facility** [emphasis added]."[5]

The reports available provide fabulous insight.

The competitive market analysis enables golf course operators to compare their financial performance against their direct local competitors. The first report shown below indicates the golf courses that are included in the competitive rate set.

Monthly, based on data provided by the golf course, the golf course owner, manager, or PGA Professional can measure performance in rounds played, revenue, revenue per utilized rounds (RevPUR), and revenue per available tee time (RevPATT), illustrated in the top figure on the following page, in a 12-month rolling report.

5 http://www.pgalinks.com/index.cfm?ctc=1778

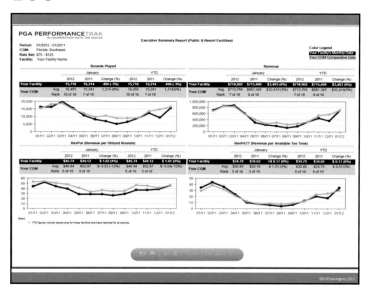

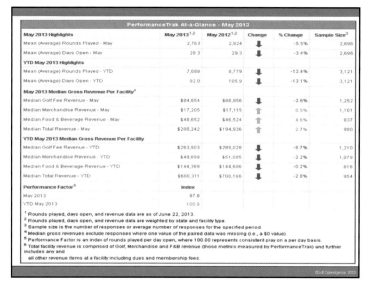

The golf course is also provided a report comparing its performance with the same period for the prior year. This golf course is in the middle of the pack.

In addition to the local market analysis, PGA PerformanceTrak publishes a monthly newsletter with national trends. The May 2013 report is shown in the bottom figure.

Though many golf courses were closed well into 2013 due to weather, based on the courses reporting, 2013 is lagging the strong financial performance of 2012.

Another valuable contributor to key performance indicators is Golf Datatech, which provides "the golf industry with specialized market research covering retail sales, inventory, pricing and distribution, along with consumer attitude and usage studies and strategic sales and marketing consulting as follows."[6]

"The Golf Datatech Retail Market Reports provide timely and accurate data on market share, unit sales, dollar sales, average pricing, inventories and distribution for: golf balls, golf clubs (woods, irons, putters and wedges), footwear, bags and gloves.

In addition, Golf Apparel Reports are available covering the categories of men's and women's shirts, tops, bottoms and outerwear.

6 http://www.golfdatatech.com/

Sales data for all Retail Reports is accumulated monthly from hundreds of retail outlets and projected to the total market based upon proprietary models created by Golf Datatech.

Sales and inventory data is transmitted to Golf Datatech through each shop's point-of-sale software system and includes: units sold, actual selling price and inventory remaining. Individual shop data is collapsed into totals within the database to insure confidentiality.

Golf Datatech reports are currently produced monthly for the United States, the United Kingdom, Germany and Sweden."[7]

These reports are insightful and invaluable, as illustrated in the men's shirt report shown below.

Would you go to Walmart to buy a Zegna Italian suit or a Robert Graham shirt? For an entry-level golf course with green fees under $25, would you carry Peter Millar or Fairway & Greene? Nope. The appropriate price category for that facility would be in the $0.00–$49.99 price point, which would suggest that Nike, Greg Norman, and Adidas golf shirts are more appropriate.

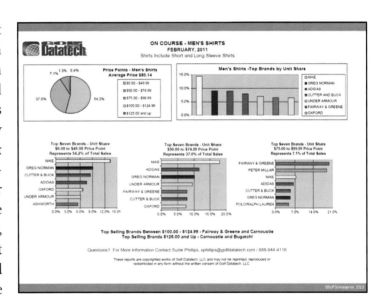

With the plethora of FREE standard reports that Golf Datatech publishes monthly, a golf course can easily determine which brands they should be carrying in each line of merchandise carried. These reports are available for golf balls, woods, putters, and irons, as shown in the figure on the next page.

7 http://www.golfdatatech.com/research-products/retail-market reports/overview/

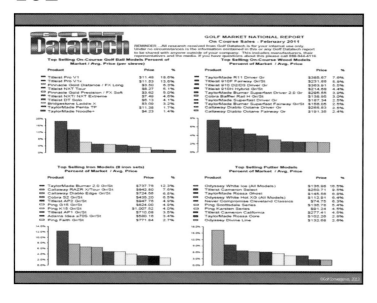

Golf Datatech provides the insights and perspectives that can guide the golf course operator or manager to increased profitability. It remains a mystery why the majority of the industry doesn't utilize the PGA PerformanceTrak or Golf Datatech reports. The good news is that if you are using them, you will be outperforming the financial returns of your direct competitors, increasing your customer loyalty, and ultimately gaining significant market share advantage.

My Food Operation Is Eating Me Alive. Any Benchmarks?

Profitable Food Facilities (PFF) is a food and beverage consulting group that specializes in operations evaluations for captive market venues, including Private Country Clubs and Catering Operations. Established in 1991, PFF has a client base numbering over 370 projects in 48 states, and has reviewed and designed more than 140 private club operations worldwide.

They are frequently asked, "What should our food costs and labor costs be at a private country club?" To answer that, we must differentiate between a snack bar and a full-service restaurant. There are two distinct businesses at a club: a la carte dining and banquets and special events.

A typical full service restaurant not associated with a golf course targets overall food costs at 30%, labor costs at 30%, and other costs at 30%, for a profit of 10%. Some operations are more profitable than others, and these numbers vary slightly depending on the concept.

As Michael Holtzman, President of PFF, highlights so adroitly,

"A club has a unique set of challenges that make this harder including:

- Open on slow days

- Big pours at the bar

- Free items given away (coffee in the morning, ice cream at dinner, etc.)

- Member privileges (I belong to a club, so the food is less)

As a result, the average private club loses $250,000 annually in F&B. There are slightly over 4,000 clubs. The private club food and beverage business loses 1.25 billion dollars annually … which is truly staggering, as these loses are ultimately assumed by the members as part of their dues or assessments."[8]

What is the fix? Daily fee golf courses and private clubs have higher food and labor costs. The first step is to set the following benchmarks that Michael Holtzman has advised:

- "Current sales for banquet, a la carte, beverage and % of sales

- Current food costs and % of sales

- Current labor costs and % of sales

- Current F&B management cost and % of sales"

The challenge right now is we see clubs with food costs averaging 45% and labor costs averaging 65% or more. Here are some solutions:

- Food and beverage payroll is by far the highest expense. Management of this number on a daily basis by the entire food and beverage team will reduce these costs.

- Calculate payroll on a daily basis. Most golf facilities can reduce labor costs by 15%.

- Stagger the "start" and "end" times.

- Eliminate overtime.

---

8 Michael Holtzman, "Food Service Club Benchmarks", March 21, 2013 (letter to author).

- Banquet servers should not make more than $15–20 per hour.

- Service charge for banquets should be added to the facility's revenue with the serve being compensated based on the prevailing wage.

- Cost out every menu and catering item. Target 20–25% banquet cost and 30–33% a la carte dining cost. If anything is over 40% food cost, change the portion, the ingredients, or the price. If it is still over 40%, don't sell the item.

- Re-engineer the menu and bold and highlight the more profitable items. Less description and smaller text for the less profitable items."[9]

What About Private Clubs?

A software company, Club Benchmarking, has emerged with a platform that is impressive. Currently, over 1,000 of the more than 4,000 operational private clubs in the United States have entered their financial data to create a reliable repository of valuable insights and perspectives.

Club Benchmarking is a business intelligence tool with strong ties to the Why, How, What model. According to its founders, Club Benchmarking is grounded in the core belief that when club leaders elevate fact over opinion, the result is healthier clubs with more empowered general managers, as well as boards that are properly equipped to focus on the key strategic and operating issues.

Club Benchmarking provides 24/7 online access to accurate "apples-to-apples" club industry data, key performance indicators and reports for every area of the club, and powerful filtering tools that let subscribing Club Benchmarking members control their comparison sets by many criteria (including, but not limited to, revenue, geography, and dues).

Automatic graphic reporting provides credible, standardized club industry data for use in strategic planning, for the budgeting process, or for routine periodic analysis of a club's strengths and opportunities for improvement, as illustrated in the figure at the top of the next page.

---

9 Ibid.

Developed in cooperation with club general managers, board members, committee members, and audit firms, the platform has been adopted by the Club Managers Association of America as the industry's central database of standardized data. Club Benchmarking now powers all of CMAA's annual Club Industry Reports (Finance & Operations, Policies & Procedures, Compensation & Benefits and the Economic Impact Report).

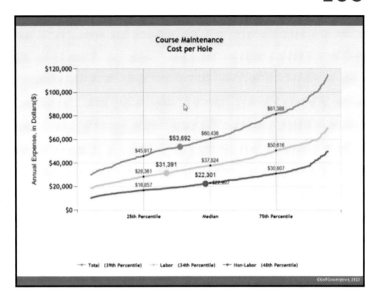

One of the key insights developed as a result of aggregating data from over 1,000 clubs across North America is the business model of the club business, referred to as The Available Cash Model. The Available Cash Model shows clearly that the proportionate sources and uses of cash to operate clubs do not vary based on where a club is or the size of the club. The model provides keen insight into the true financial drivers of a club, as shown in the figure below.

As this book goes to print, Club Benchmarking is working with certain multi-course operators and management companies to extend both the benchmarking platform and The Available Cash Model into the broader golf course industry, including resort and daily fee facilities. The powerful filtering capability and graphic reports have proven as valuable in those segments as they have in the private club segment.

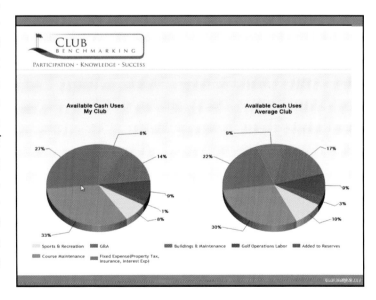

The End Game

Gathering the benchmark data and then implementing the changes indicated will begin the process of turning a struggling club into a profitable club.

Go

If you licensed the supplemental template that accompanies this Field book, you are encouraged to do the following:

1) If you are not currently subscribing, register as a participant for PGA Performance-Trak and Golf Datatech, which includes several reports, including rounds and golf playable days, along with the retail reports.

2) Have your PGA Professional print the PGA PerformanceTrak Annual Operating Survey of 44 reports for the nation, by PGA Section and local market. Compare your operating results to those shown.

3) The course's retail buyer should compare and contrast merchandise product lines to the median household income within 10 miles of your golf course (if a municipal or daily fee course) to determine if the most optimum product lines for that course's customers are being stocked.

Path to Success

By understanding the financial statements of a golf course, facility managers can undertake tactical planning designed to enhance strengths, address weaknesses, exploit opportunities, and deal with threats.

The lessons of this chapter are the following:

1) Financial statements are the goalposts of business.

2) It is vital that operators acquire localized benchmarks to evaluate themselves as operators.

3) Golf Datatech, PGA PerformanceTrak, and Club Benchmarking provide credible valuable data repositories which can be used to compare the financial performances of golf courses.

This chapter has provided a bevy of benchmarks to select from; each one of them is unique and valuable for your golf course.

Concluding Thoughts

All of knowledge has its origins in our perceptions.

Leonardo da Vinci

Some people learn by words, some people learn by consequences, some people can't learn.

Nick Saban, football coach, University of Alabama
February 27, 2013

Chapter 9

Financial Modeling
Step 4 of the Golf Convergence WIN™ Formula (continued)

You've got to be very careful if you don't know where you're going, because you might not get there.

Yogi Berra

The only place success comes before work is in the dictionary.

Often attributed to Vince Lombardi also said by Mark Twain, Vidal Sassoon, and Donald Kendall, co-founder of PepsiCo

Chapter Highlights

In Chapter 8, we addressed in detail the key management reports that are available to guide decision making at a golf course and the leading key performance indicators fundamental to evaluating the operation of a golf course.

This chapter builds on that foundation and provides operating templates that allow the golf course operator to undertake revenue and expense-module simulation to determine the mix that will optimize the financial performance of the golf course.

Is This a Waste of Time?

Is creating financial forecasts and undertaking revenue modeling a productive budgeting exercise? It seems that owners and managers most often insist on revenues increasing and expenses being cut. Thus, the probable approach of the staff person preparing reports—how can I mask or hide problems and create rat-hole accounts that will ensure that we meet the budget and protect me, so I can get my bonus? It doesn't often seem that employees within a company are working with mutually aligned goals and objectives.

In many cases, a comprehensive and detailed budgeting process doesn't produce the hoped-for value for the time invested. The ability to forecast the future with any certainty is hazardous. Beyond salaries, rent, debt payments, and other fixed costs, the variable costs are just a guess.

Perhaps the guideline for budgeting is that the time invested should equal the attention span of those responsible for meeting the budget on an ongoing basis. In other words, it is sheer folly to invest a significant amount of resources to analyze each component of the financial statement by general ledger account if that management tool is only going to be given an occasional glance.

We live in a world where attention to detail is rare. Thus, the focus on a few key performance indicators is essential to effectively manage a golf course.

Golf's Rubik's Cube

Golf Rubik's Cube

Green fee - WE - 18	FB - Labor	Instruction	Tournaments	Range
Mtn - Labor	Season Pass	Capital Invt	Senior Rates	Herbicides
F&B CGS	Carts	Green fee - 9	Club Fitting	Green Fee - WD- 18
Merchandise - Vendors	GS - Expenses	GSO - Labor	Water	F&B Expenses
Administration	Electricity	Pesticides	Merchandise - CGS	Leagues

©Golf Convergence 2013

There are many variables in running a golf course. Which are leading indicators and which are trailing indicators? Presented to the left are 25 of the components, many of which are central in influencing the net income at a golf course.

How do you solve the puzzle and line all the elements up correctly? It looks a little overwhelming doesn't it? That is understandable with the limited time that we all now have. We become distracted as to the bigger issues because we are busy solving what are often emotionally charged immediate problems.

The first step is to line up the common elements: revenue versus expenses and the classification into departments.

In the operation of a golf course, there are several revenue categories that influence all the others. For example, the rounds played statistic, as reflected in individual green fees or season pass play, is an accurate predictor of carts sold, merchandise bought, and food and beverage products consumed.

From an expense perspective, as a generality, the restaurant operations at a municipal golf course are little more than snack bar operations. The vast majority of that revenue center and the associated costs often are contracted to a third-party under lease. However, for daily fee and resort golf courses, the restaurant operations become more complex and they are challenged, at best, to break even. Therefore, monitoring those costs, especially with respect to labor hours and the margins in food and liquor, draws increasing attention. At a private club, the dining experience can easily be a popular and profitable amenity equal to golf, tennis, swimming, and other activities.

The largest cost center in operating a golf course is (or should be) maintenance. The accurate answers to only two questions regarding expenses will provide you with 80% of the information you need to identify the type of experience that course will deliver: How many labor hours are incurred annually in maintaining the golf course? How much do you spend on water?

It can be stupefying to review the financial statements of golf courses around the world.

While there has been a little more standardization in the general ledger accounting used and in the departmental reporting in the United States, the variances between courses are often unexplainable.

Why consolidate the labor from the golf shop, maintenance, and food and beverage under one general ledger account with no allocation to those cost centers? Why allocate the electricity costs for the entire golf course to the golf shop when the largest part of the electricity is used by maintenance? How could any manager not record the rounds played by season pass holders when determining the average revenue per round? How can the golf course still be using a paper and pencil to record revenue? I know that even today cash registers are still used at golf courses, particularly those with lower price points. You have to wonder about the variance between cash collected and the revenue reported to the IRS.

The inconsistencies in the preparation of income statements from golf course to golf course are vast. Presented below is what would be deemed to be "generally accepted."

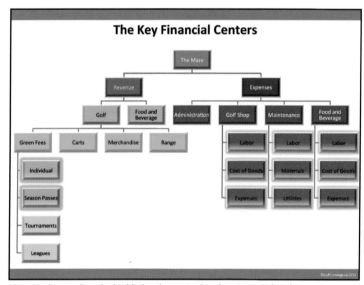

Note: Understanding the highlighted areas in this chart is crucial to the management of the course.

Depending on the type of operation (municipal, daily fee, resort, and certainly, private club), you could debate the relative dependency of one department's revenue on another's. To illustrate, merchandise sales at the famed golf courses in Scotland are likely to have gross revenue from tourist purchases greater than the fees earned from visitor green fees. Who doesn't spend 100 pounds to play Royal Dornoch and drop another 250 pounds on shirts, sweaters, hats, and logoed golf gloves? A close look at the financials of those famed courses would no doubt reveal that their merchandise sales are impressive and far exceed the revenue from membership fees paid annually by the locals.

While the rankings of the Top 100 golf courses in the world by *Golf Magazine*, *Golf Digest*, and *Golf Week* provide very interesting reading for golfers and create many debates as to their accuracy, those rankings have a great financial impact on the revenue stream of the courses named, particularly those in Europe and Asia, and to a lesser extent in the United States.

Conversely, when a well-known and respected professional golfer criticizes the renovation work of the architect of a famous course like Cog Hill Golf and Country Club, the collateral damage is in the brand hit the golf course may take in the eyes of golfers, and whether that facility remains on their bucket list of courses to play.

For a municipality, financial statements and the departments that management can influence are illustrated below. The revenue generated in the rest of the departments is largely influenced by the green fees and season passes. With respect to expenses, labor and general administrative costs are really the only two areas where variable costs can be cut, as presented in the following figure.

For those unfamiliar with municipal golf courses, the municipal service charges represent an allocated cost from the general fund to the enterprise fund for accounting, legal, purchasing, and other services performed by the city on behalf of the course. While these fees can range from $0 to over $500,000, the normal expense allocated is $50,000.

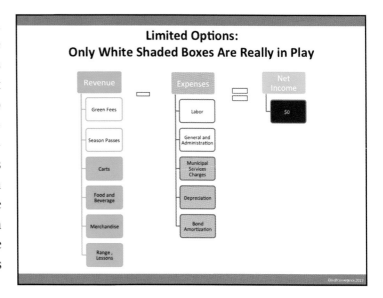

Around and Around the Wheel Goes, Where It Stops Does Anybody Know?

Managing a golf course can seem daunting. Having now spun the Rubik's cube to align like activities into comparable general ledger accounts with departmental and sub-departmental reporting, there are several departments for which templates that can easily assist the golf course manager are available.

Individual green fees, season passes, maintenance labor, equipment and materials, capital expenses, food and beverage labor, and food and beverage expenses lend themselves to modeling to determine the appropriate fees or expenses that should be posted or incurred to achieve the objectives desired, as highlighted above.

To illustrate, a municipal, daily fee, or resort golf course can have more than 80 posted rates, depending on the day of the week, the time of the day, the season, and the type of player (senior, junior, student, etc.). Of those rates, one rate, the 18-hole green fee rate during prime time, determines and influences all others.

PRIME TIME SUMMER RATES
OFF SEASON RATES: 25% DISCOUNT, NON-RESIDENT: 10% PREMIUM, IF IMPLEMENTED

COURSE #1

Day of Week	Golfer Type		Holes	Industry Standard Percentages	Rule of Thumb	Enter Your Current Rate		
Weekend	Green Fee	Walking	18		Base	$ 95.00		
		Per Seat - Every Day of Week	18		Base Rate	$ 28.00		
	Carts Required on Weekends		18		Is Cart Required on Weekends	No		
	Weather Playable Days	Weather Trends International - 10 Year Average			Number of Playable Days	214		
				Discount from Rack Rate		Rate Calculated	Enter Your Current Rate	Variance
		Early Bird	18	10%	Discount from Prime Rate that Day	$ 85.50		$ (85.50
	Regular	1st Twilight (Early Afternoon) - walking	18	30%	Discount from Prime Rate that Day	$ 66.50		$ (66.50
	Regular	2nd Twilight (4 hours before sunset) - walking	18	40%	Discount from Prime Rate that Day	$ 57.00		$ (57.00
	Regular	3rd Twilight (2 hours before twilight) - walking	18	50%	Discount from Prime Rate that Day	$ 47.50		$ (47.50
	Regular	Walking	9	40%	Discount from 18 Hole Rate that Day	$ 57.00		$ (57.00
	Regular	Walking	18	30%	Discount from Weekend	$ 66.50		$ (66.50
	Regular	1st Twilight (Early Afternoon) - walking	18	30%	Discount from Prime Rate that Day	$ 66.50		$ (66.50
	Regular	2nd Twilight (4 hours before sunset) - walking	18	40%	Discount from Prime Rate that Day	$ 57.00		$ (57.00
	Regular	3rd Twilight (2 hours before twilight) - walking	18	50%	Discount from Prime Rate that Day	$ 47.50		$ (47.50
	Regular	Walking	9	40%	Discount from 18 Hole Rate that Day	$ 57.00		$ (57.00
Weekday	Senior	Walking	18	30%	Discount from Weekday Base	$ 66.50		$ (66.50
Weekday	Junior	Walking	18	30%	Discount from Weekday Base	$ 66.50		$ (66.50
Punch Tickets - Cart Included		Rounds	Holes	Percentage of Rack Rate	Rule of Thumb	Rate Calculated	Enter Your Current Rate	Variance
5 Day	Regular	25	18	75%	Discount from Weekday Rate	$ 1,496.88		$ (1,496.88
7 Day	Regular	25	18	75%	50% Playday, 50% Weekend	$ 1,764.06		$ (1,764.06
5 Day	Senior	25	18	60%	Discount from Weekday Rate	$ 1,247.50		$ (1,247.50
7 Day	Senior	25	18	60%	50% Playday, 50% Weekend	$ 1,461.25		$ (1,461.25
Punch Tickets - Walking Only		Rounds	Holes	Percentage of Rack Rate	Rule of Thumb	Rate Calculated	Enter Your Current Rate	Variance
5 Day	Regular	25	18	75%	Discount from Weekday Rate	$ 1,246.88		$ (1,246.88
7 Day	Regular	25	18	75%	50% Playday, 50% Weekend	$ 1,514.06		$ (1,514.06
5 Day	Senior	25	18	60%	Discount from Weekday Rate	$ 997.50		$ (997.50
7 Day	Senior	25	18	60%	50% Playday, 50% Weekend	$ 1,211.25		$ (1,211.25
Unlimited Play Pass - Cart Included		Rounds	Holes	Percentage of Rack Rate	Rule of Thumb	Rate Calculated	Enter Your Current Rate	Variance
Unlimited	Regular	64	18	75%		$ 4,530.11		$ (4,530.11
Unlimited	Senior	64	18	60%		$ 3,752.49		$ (3,752.49

©Golf Convergence 2013

The chart to the left can be used at any public golf course. To do so, enter the desired rack rate in the first row, and it will automatically calculate all the other rates instantly, with no debate, discussion, or consternation over whether the relationship between the rates is appropriate.

There are certain relationships between the price of prime time green fees and all other rates. The 9-hole rate is about 60% of the rack rate. Seniors are accorded a 27% discount. Shoulder-season rates are usually 25% lower and are differentiated from off-season rates that may offer much as a 50% discount. Cart rates are fixed within a range of $12 to $25, representing up to 50% of the green fee cost at the less expensive facilities.

This template, which is available for license at www.golfconvergence.com, has all of these relationships outlined to make it possible for a golf course to immediately update its fee schedule.

Go

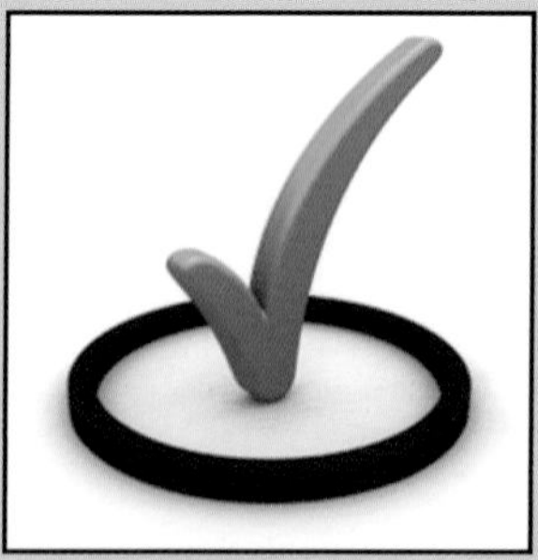

If you licensed the supplemental template that accompanies this Field book, open Green Fee Calculator-Qualitative (Step 4) and Customer Value Experience (Step 6).

1) First complete the Customer Value Experience template. A model for establishing green fees might be comprised of six variables: slope rating, strategy (difficulty and shot values), conditioning, playing

texture variety, ambience, and customer amenities. Each of these components and its effect on the appropriate price for the green fee is presented in this template. By completing the Customer Value Experience, you will have an estimate of the value currently created at your golf course, and you can than compare it to your current green fees.

2) Once you have established the proper fee for 18 holes during prime time, proceed to open the Excel workbook for the Green Fee Calculator-Quantitative. Merely enter the price determined in the first row, and all the other recommended fees will be automatically determined: weekend, weekday, hours within the day, carts included or excluded, type of golfer, and time of year. It can be just that easy.

3) The final step in this process is a review of the competitive prices in the marketplace, which may lead to subjective adjustments made to capitalize on the strengths and the perceived weaknesses of the course.

Want to Pick a Fight?

The easiest way to get into an argument is to tell golfers with unlimited play passes that their passes were significantly underpriced. Hell hath no fury like senior citizens listening to a presentation at a city council meeting that reveals that their median income exceeds $85,700 and that the three-figure amount they are paying for each season pass is substantially underpriced. There may not be a more self-indulgent or privileged class in America the season pass holders at a golf course.

The theory behind season passes actually has some merit. A golf course is always looking for cash infusion. The ability to deposit significant revenues in advance offers desired cash infusion and is also an emotional comfort. What remains uncertain is how many different passes should be offered and at what prices (5-day weekday,

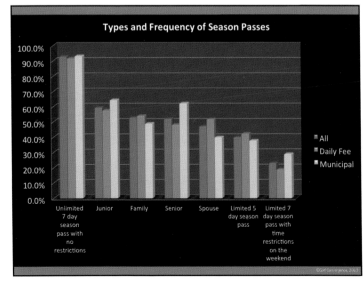

7-day weekend, 7-day with weekend times, restricted to after a designated time, seniors, couples, families) and whether carts are included or offered as a separately priced season pass. The chart shown on the previous page illustrates the types and the frequency of season passes offered.

Golf Convergence conducted a survey of golf courses in April 2012. Of the courses responding to our survey, 78% offered unlimited season play passes. In an independent survey conducted by the National Golf Foundation,[1] 70% of municipal golf courses offer a season play pass.

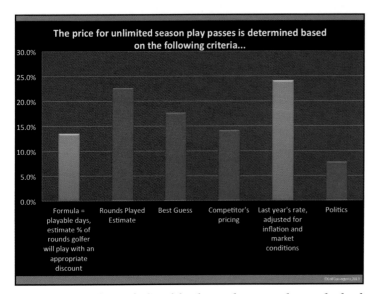

What was alarming in their response was that 79% of the golf course respondents had no rational basis for how they calculated their annual season pass prices, as shown to the left.

There is a very logical methodology to assist in determining what the proper unlimited season play pass is. The formula consists of four components: the number of playable days, the rate charged, the breakpoint based on the number of rounds a golfer is likely to play, and the discount to which they should be truly accorded for prepaying a nonrefundable fee at the beginning of the golf season.

In the survey conducted, the respondents answered that they anticipated a golfer who purchases a season pass will play 30% of the playable days. They also indicated that season pass holders are entitled to a 32% discount from the prime-time rack rate and that the season pass should be based on 42 rounds played. That number is debatable, especially in warm weather climates where 75 rounds may be a more appropriate benchmark.

If we apply those parameters to golf courses located in both warm and cold climates, an estimate of the appropriate rates for season pass is shown in the table on the next page.

---

1 National Golf Foundation, "NRPA 2012, Maximizing the Economic Benefits of Municipal Golf," October 16, 2012, Slide 26.

To include carts in this formula, increase the rack rate for the base value of the cart. But the manager needs to ask, "What is the right breakpoint?" A breakpoint is defined by identifying what percentage of the season pass holders will not receive the full value from the purchase of the pass versus the percentage of golfers who will use the pass so often that they are in

The Average Annual Season Pass: A Fair Fee?

	Warm Weather Climate	Cold Weather Municipal
Holes	18	18
Playable Days	300	180
Playing Frequency	30%	30%
Rounds Played	90	54
Rack Rate	60	30
Frequency Discount	32%	32%
Annual Fee	3,672	1,468

essence paying less than five dollars per round. As in a Las Vegas casino, it is astute to set the breakpoint at the rate that 40% may play more often but 60% will not. The differential represents the convenience of prepaying and is similar to insurance; you always buy it but seldom use it.

It is our opinion that these frequent users of the pass should pay a rate that at least equals the cost of producing the round of golf with respect to maintenance cost. It is always humorous to listen to those who advocate that we need to get season pass holders to play more because their incremental purchases of merchandise and food and beverage will sustain the golf course. Instead, these value-conscious golfers often buy season passes because they are frugal, and their on-course purchases are significantly lower than those of many casual golfers.

Season passes are an anathema to many golf courses. Responding courses to the April, 2012 survey were charging an average of $1,250 for a season pass, but rates ranged from a low of $400 to a high of $2,300. In cities like Casper, Wyoming, and Durango, Colorado, where season pass prices hover around the minimum price points, it isn't hard to figure out why breaking even is an annual challenge or why deferred capital expenditures are increasing. Those courses are trapped in the death spiral, with customer demands trumping financial logic. Yet debates about rates are rooted in each person's self-interest.

We can say with a great degree of confidence that the financial crisis faced by many municipalities in the operation of the golf courses is rooted in the pricing of season passes. Because the members of city councils and mayors are elected officials whose compensation is based more on prestige than remuneration, often their votes on issues of fee increases are based on what provides the greatest opportunity for them to be reelected and not on what is in the best interest of the golf's enterprise fund. A harsh but true reality.

One of the really interesting exercises is to counter the arguments that if we raise the rates, golfers will go elsewhere. A season pass price sensitivity analysis is illustrated in the following figure.

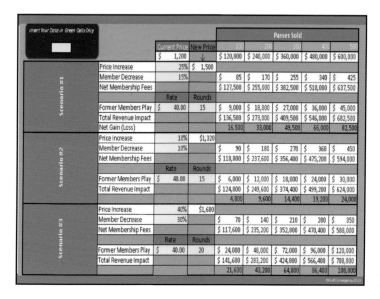

Getting customers to agree to a fair value for green fees or season passes isn't possible. If you are looking to update rates at the beginning of a season, ask, "What is the appropriate rate?"

To get customer support or diffuse their protest in advance is a wise strategy. Let them in on the series of questions regarding the underlying methodology of the rate calculation. For example,

1. If we were to raise our rate by 25%, what percentage of the membership do you think will not renew their season passes? Enter the percentage provided by the customer.

2. Do you think that those individuals who don't renew will give up the game? The answer usually takes two forms. Respondents will either say that those who don't renew will play all of their rounds elsewhere, or that they will play far less rounds at this course as a personal protest because they're upset.

3. How many rounds do you think you will actually play at this course paying the rack rate? Again, enter the number provided by the customer.

Having obtained the input of the customers on the critical numbers that project a decrease in the purchase of season passes and how many rounds they are likely to continue to play at the rack rate, the impact on gross revenue can be measured.

In over 85% of the multiple times we've seen this exercise conducted, the impact on revenue is positive for the golf course. To achieve customer buy-in from the golf advisory committee or from frequent customers, remind them that this additional revenue will allow the facility to begin making the capital investments that have long been sought to improve their playing experience. This usually achieves their full buy-in, because they can see the promised tangible benefit from a slightly higher investment.

In Michigan, we observed a group of 40 golfers who dominated the tee sheets Monday through Friday. They hollered and screamed and said that if the rates were raised, all of them would be taking their business elsewhere. More often than not, it is good gamble to call their bluff.

Golf is a social game. Courses customers play are part of their psychological identity. While they will put up a formidable and vocal protest, ultimately, they will continue to play at the same golf course because the life change of switching courses is uncomfortable. In the case of the Michigan course, only a few departed and the net operating loss was reduced from the increase in season pass income received.

The purpose of this research was to test the following hypotheses regarding season passes across the United States. Here are the insights obtained.

Hypothesis	Results
Season pass rates are determined based on a defined formula.	No
The breakpoint would be determined based on the number of playable days. Thus, annual pass rates in warmer climates are higher than colder climates.	Correlation exists.
The definition of a playable day is standard throughout the industry.	No
A standard rack rate discount percentage would be applied throughout the industry.	No. The discount % accorded is rarely calculated.
Annual season passes at municipal golf courses are lower than at daily fee courses.	Yes
Annual season pass rates are directly correlated to the green fee; i.e., a $20 green fee course has a lower season pass rate than a golf course with an $80 green fee.	Correlation exists.

The bottom line of season passes is that they should be avoided for someone always loses.

If the customer purchases the season pass and doesn't use it, they hold a grudge against the golf course. If a golfer buys the pass and uses it far being the course's calculated break point, management of the course begins resenting that golfer. Eliminating season passes at public golf courses is the path to increased profitability.

Go

If you licensed the supplemental template that accompanies this Field book, and offer a season pass or membership at a semi-private club, open Step 4: Season Pass-Fair Fee, and Season Pass Sensitivity Analysis.

1) Calculate the proper rate for your season pass or seasonal membership based on the number of playable days (obtained from Step 2 in the Golf Convergence WIN™ process), utilizing the industry benchmark that a golfer will play 30% of the playable days and should be accorded a 32% discount from the rack rate. How does your current rate compare?

2) If your rate is significantly lower than the national average of $1,250, determine the underlying assumptions that are embedded in your current price regarding the frequency the golfers play and the discount they are being accorded.

3) Enter your current season pass rate, the number of memberships that you have outstanding, and a range of memberships you are likely to sell.

4) Begin experimenting by increasing your season pass rate, estimating the number of members that will drop out and their reduced frequency of play in the upcoming season.

5) If you believe the increase in revenue forecast is worth the emotional heartache, consider implementing the new rate in the upcoming season. It is important to be mindful that while your success is measured in numbers, the customer's success is measured by the quality of the experience. As in all things, there must be balance.

A Screw Is Loose

Is it harder to increase revenue or to decrease expenses?

A story told to me about Henry Ford, the founder of the long-standing U.S. automobile company, remains locked within the recesses of my brain. The company was struggling during its infancy, and expenses were exceeding revenue. Everybody at a meeting of company executives was offering ideas as to what could be cut. Finally, in exasperation and frustration, Henry Ford said, "I got the answer. We can cut all the expenses and just shut this place down. Obviously that won't work. So let's determine **where we need to make investments that will achieve our goals.**"

Whether that story was true, who knows? But it illustrates a great point.

Increasing revenues is dependent upon making assumptions with no certainty as to their realization. Because it is easier to address that which is known, expenses become the focus.

Golf, like the manufacturing of a car, can be viewed as an assembly line process. Each of the functions performed in the golf shop, in maintaining the golf course, or in operating a restaurant represent a number of repetitive tasks.

The condition of the golf course is one of the primary determinants as to how golfers select one course over another. With respect to maintenance, the appropriate cost centers are labor and maintenance. Because maintenance costs are about 33% of the total expenses of operating a golf course, they always draw close attention. Highlighting the utility costs separately is important, too, because they have the potential to represent over 25% of the maintenance budget. There is not a greater threat to the financial sustainability of a golf course than the accelerating cost of water, fuel, and electricity.

We have personally seen adequately maintained courses in North Dakota (the Links of North Dakota and Bully Pulpit Golf Course) whose maintenance costs are less than $400,000 and golf courses whose maintenance budgets exceed $3.0 million. A great variable observed in that analysis was the price point of the green fee or the exclusiveness of the private club.

With respect to the maintenance of a golf course, there are 29 different tasks that superintendents perform. The results of a survey conducted by Golf Convergence during May, 2012, indicated that the hours required to maintain a golf course vary widely depending on location, from a low of 12,000 to more than 30,000 hours.

Shown below is the template prepared by a superintendent in the St. Paul, Minnesota area. It reflects that only 12,228 hours are required to maintain the golf course during its 8-month, 32-week season.

Season Length – Weeks/Months		32	8			
Task		Daily	Monthly	Yearly	Hours per Task	Total Hours
Administration	Record Keeping	7			1	224.00
Bunkers	Rake	7			4	896.00
Cart Paths	Cart Paths	7			1	224.00
Clubhouse	Clubhouse Grounds	7			1	224.00
Course	Ck. Irrigation	7		5	0.25	57.25
Course	Irrigation Repairs				20	0.00
Course	Trimming	3		2	16	1,568.00
Course	Overseed/Topdress Areas	0		2	25	50.00
Course	Fungicides			2	25	50.00
Course	Herbicides			2	25	50.00
Course	Insecticides				25	0.00
Cutting	Greens	7			3	672.00
Cutting	30" Collar	3			1	96.00
Cutting	Tees	3			6	576.00
Cutting	Fairways	3			4	384.00
Cutting	First Cut	2			1.5	96.00
Cutting	Roughs	1.5		1	30	1,470.00
Cutting	Native Areas	0			100	0.00
Cutting	Aprons	3			1.5	144.00
Cutting	Driving Range	3			4	384.00
Cutting	Verticut Greens	0	2		30	480.00
Equipment	Cleaning	7			0.25	56.00
Equipment	Maintenance	7			0.25	56.00
Greens	Pins	7			3	672.00
Greens	Ball Marks	7			2	448.00
Greens	Topdress Green2X Month	0	2		30	480.00
Greens	Rolling Greens	2			3	192.00
Greens	Brushing Greens	2			2	128.00
Maintenance	Soil Testing	1		2	10	340.00
Maintenance	Aerification	0			50	0.00
Maintenance	Fertilization	0	1		16	128.00
Ponds	Ponds	0	2		10	160.00
Shop	Cleaning	7			1	224.00
Shop	Maintenance	7			1	224.00
Shop	Gardens	7			3	672.00
Tees	3X Markers	21			1	3.00
Tees	Overseed Tees	0	2		10	800.00
Tees	Topdress Tees	0	2		10	0.00
Training	Training	0	1		1.5	0.00
Trees	Trees/Ornamental			2	50	0.00
Total Man Hours Required						12,228.25

The median hours reported by the respondents from colder climates was 18,500 hours, but those from warmer climates averaged closer to 25,000 hours. There is always a debate as to how many full-time employees are required on a maintenance crew: the head superintendent, the assistant, perhaps a mechanic, and maybe an irrigation specialist. Those four positions consume approximately 8,320 hours annually. If the course had an 18,500-hour budget, that would only leave room for 10 seasonal workers who clock 1,000 hours each.

Some golf course superintendents prepare the maintenance budget on a weekly basis to determine projected payroll. Using the template illustrated below, which was created by Del Ratcliffe, of Ratcliffe Golf Services, a Charlotte, North Carolina, management company, achieves that objective.

WEEKLY ESSENTIAL GOLF MAINTENANCE TASK SCHEDULER

Course Name: Edinburgh USA
Date: Monday, July 15, 2013

Total Weekly Task Dollars	Day of the Week →	Sat	Sun	Mon	Tue	Wed	Thu	Fri	Task Freq.	# of Staff Needed	Task hrs.	Total Daily hrs.	Total Weekly hrs.	Position Abbreviatio
	I. Mowing													
$ 328.50	A. Greens	✓	☐	✓	✓	✓	✓	✓	6	2.0	2.5	5.0	30.0	EO I
$ 186.90	B. Approaches/Tees/Par 3's	☐	☐	✓	☐	✓	☐	✓	3	2.0	3.5	7.0	21.0	Labor
$ 525.60	C. Fairways	☐	☐	✓	☐	✓	☐	✓	3	2.0	8.0	16.0	48.0	EO I
$ 630.40	D. Roughs	☐	☐	✓	✓	✓	✓	☐	4	2.0	8.0	16.0	64.0	EO II
$ 197.00	E. Intermediate Rough Cut	☐	☐	☐	✓	☐	✓	☐	2	2.0	5.0	10.0	20.0	EO II
$ 213.60	F. Clubhouse Grounds	✓	☐	✓	☐	☐	✓	☐	3	1.0	8.0	8.0	24.0	Labor
$ 642.50	G. Trim Mowing	☐	☐	✓	✓	✓	✓	✓	5	2.0	5.0	10.0	50.0	AGCS 2
$ 157.60	H. Roll Greens	✓	✓	☐	☐	✓	☐	✓	4	1.0	4.0	4.0	16.0	EO II
$ 88.00	I. Driving Range Fairway	☐	☐	✓	☐	✓	☐	☐	2	1.0	4.0	4.0	8.0	Tech.
	II. Bunkers													
$ 788.00	A. Rake Bunkers	✓	✓	☐	✓	☐	✓	☐	4	4.0	5.0	20.0	80.0	EO II
$ 427.20	B. Bunker Maintenance	☐	☐	✓	☐	✓	☐	✓	3	2.0	8.0	16.0	48.0	Labor
	III. Set Up													
$ 495.00	A. Change Hole Cups	✓	✓	☐	✓	✓	✓	✓	6	2.0	2.5	5.0	30.0	AGCS
	IV. Syringing													
$ 924.00	A. Hand Water Greens	✓	✓	✓	✓	✓	✓	✓	7	3.0	4.0	12.0	84.0	Tech.
	V. Greens Periodic Maintenance													
$ 99.00	A. Ball Mark Repair	☐	☐	✓	☐	✓	☐	☐	2	1.0	3.0	3.0	6.0	AGCS
$ 205.60	A. Chemical Application	☐	✓	☐	☐	☐	✓	☐	2	1.0	8.0	8.0	16.0	AGCS 2
	II. Miscellaneous													
$ 577.36	A. Carts	✓	✓	✓	✓	✓	✓	✓	7	1.0	8.0	8.0	56.0	Cart Att.
$ 142.40	B. Range Divots	☐	✓	☐	☐	✓	☐	☐	2	1.0	8.0	8.0	16.0	Labor
$ 440.00	C. Equipment Repair and Maintenance	☐	☐	✓	✓	✓	✓	✓	5	1.0	8.0	8.0	40.0	Tech.
												Total Weekly Hours→	617.0	

Populate with your staff positions and wages →

Position	Abbreviation	Rate
Golf Course Superintendent	GCS	$ 35.00
Assistant Golf Course Superintendent	AGCS	$ 16.50
Second Assistant Superintendent / Spray Tech	AGCS 2	$ 12.85
Technician	Tech.	$ 11.00
Equipment Operator I	EO I	$ 10.95
Equipment Operator II	EO II	$ 9.85
Labor	Labor	$ 8.90
Mechanic I	MECH I	$ 20.71
Mechanic II	MECH II	$ 13.89
Seasonal / Labor	Seas. Labor	$ 7.85
Cart Attendant	Cart Att	$ 10.31

Weekly Total Labor Dollars →	$ 7,069	Weekly Average Hourly Wage →	$ 11.05
Average Dollars For Maintenance Day →	$ 1,010	Weekly Full Time Equivalents →	15

©GolfConvergence,2013

Another valuable template available to superintendents is a deferred capital expenditures estimate. The golf course is a living organism that requires an average of $281,810 annually in investment or capital reserve allocation, since the cost to renovate a golf course is likely to exceed $3 million. Note that the cost to build a new golf course today is likely to exceed $8.0 million, exclusive of the land and clubhouse costs.

Based on estimates provided by the Golf Course Builders Association and the current replacement cost of the components, the funds needed to bring the course current can be quickly estimated, as shown in the table on the next page.

Golf Course - Estimated Deferred Capital Expenditures: Conservative Approach							
Golf Course Name:				Based on Maximum Life	Input Field	Automatic Calculation	
Component		Years Minimum	Years Maximum	Estimated Cost to Replace	Years Since Asset Replaced		Annual Capital Reserve
Greens	Sand based root-zone	15	30	$ 1,250,000	25	$ 1,041,667	$ 41,667
Sand Bunkers	Total Bunkers	10	15	$ 975,000	15	$ 975,000	$ 65,000
Irrigation System							
	Controls and Satellites	15	20	$ 175,000	3	$ 26,250	$ 8,750
	Pipe and Wire	15	25	$ 500,000	27	$ 500,000	$ 20,000
	Pumping Systems	15	25	$ 425,000	27	$ 425,000	$ 17,000
	Sprinklers	10	15	$ 150,000	27	$ 150,000	$ 10,000
Tees	Re-Turf	15	20	$ 225,000	27	$ 225,000	$ 11,250
Drainage		20	30	$ 870,000	27	$ 783,000	$ 29,000
Water Features	Front Nine Liners (estimate)	25	35	$ 65,000	8	$ 14,857	$ 1,857
	Back Nine Liners (estimate)	25	35	$ 80,000	3	$ 6,857	$ 2,286
Cart Paths	Asphalt (6-8 feet wide)	15	25	$ 625,000	25	$ 625,000	$ 25,000
Fairways	Re-Turf as needed	15	30	$ 1,500,000		$ -	$ 50,000
Total Deferred Capital				6,840,000		4,772,631	281,810

With the assistance of the Golf Course Superintendents Association of America, another template is available to guide the maintenance crew in demonstrating to the owner or the general manager during the budgeting process the type and cost of equipment required. Different pieces of equipment are required for the greens, tees, fairway, and rough. Including transportation vehicles, tractors and trucks, sprayers and spreaders, utility equipment, and hand-held equipment, a golf course needs an average of about $543,000 in equipment to maintain a golf course. An annual capital reserve of $90,000 would be a prudent entry in the budget process.

Go

If you licensed the supplemental template that accompanies this Field book, open Step 5: Maintenance—Annual Golf Course Labor Scheduler, Maintenance—Weekly Golf Course Labor Scheduler, Deferred Capital Expenditures Calculation and the Equipment Template.

1) For the tasks listed on the Maintenance—Annual Golf Course Labor Scheduler, enter the number of months and weeks the golf course is open annually. Then enter the frequency with which each of the tasks is performed by day, week, month, and year. That exercise will give you a quick estimate of the number of labor hours needed. What is your gut? High? Low? To fine-tune, examine the hours budgeted for each task. Upon confirming their accuracy, decide what

is the best allocation between full-time, full-season, and part-time workers to achieve the results desired.

2) If you would like an estimate of the projected weekly maintenance payroll, proceed to the Maintenance—Weekly Golf Course Labor Scheduler. Enter the number of tasks that the crew will perform that week, adjust the hourly rates (for full-time, divide the annual compensation by 2,080 hours), and determine if the projected salary expense is comparable to the budget.

3) The deferred capital expenditures template will provide you a quick estimate for budgeting purposes as to the cash reserves that should be on hand for reinvestment in the golf course. Enter the years since each component of the golf course was updated. For example, if the irrigation system was replaced 10 years ago, enter that number for each of the four components of that system. The calculated results will show that about $750,000 should be in reserve now for the replacement of that system in another 10 years.

4) The equipment template will provide you a quick estimate for budgeting purposes as to the cash reserves that should be on hand for repurchase of equipment. The typical golf course requires about $543,000 in equipment to maintain the golf course at a silver level or higher. Creating a great golf experience and charging a rate that matches that experience cannot be done without proper equipment. On the equipment template, based on the inventory on hand, enter the number of pieces of equipment (such as three walking green mowers or two triplex green mowers) in the row indicated. Then enter the age of the equipment. The template will automatically calculate the accumulated depreciation and reflect the capital that should be in reserve to replace it.

Anybody Hungry?

Operating a snack bar or a restaurant along with a golf course is a necessary evil. Of all the departments of the golf course, the food and beverage operation has the greatest probability of generating a loss. From staffing issues with hourly employees, to food spoilage issues, to sanitation inspections, there's not a lot of upside, certainly in the snack bar operation and perhaps even in a full-scale restaurant. It is always possible that outings, tournaments, banquets, corporate-sponsored events, and weddings will produce the volume necessary for potential profit.

One of the critical components to a successful operation is the scheduling of labor. Templates such as the one illustrated below represent a tool from which a manager can ensure that payroll costs are in alignment.

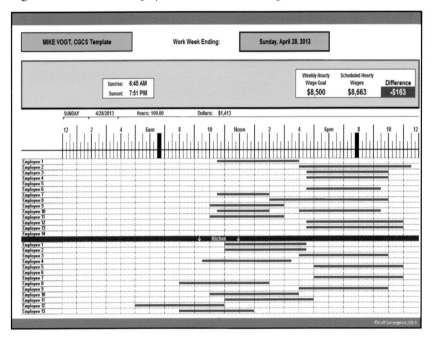

The five-tab template developed by Vogt, who is the head of the McMahon Group's Golf Division, facilitates the weekly projection of food and beverage costs shown here.

	Sunday Brunch	Food Service Closed	Lunch and Dinner Only	Lunch and Dinner Only	Lunch and Dinner Only	Lunch and Dinner Only	B-Fast, Lunch & Dinner
Daily and Weekly F & B Cost Calculator	Sunday	Monday	Tuesday	Wednesday	Thursday	Friday	Saturday
Total Food & Beverage Sales	$3,456.00	$ -	$1,234.00	$2,543.00	$3,456.00	$2,890.00	$2,345.00
Average Price per Cover	$ 17.45		$ 10.03	$ 16.84	$ 20.69	$ 23.50	$ 20.94
Total Covers per Day	198	0	123	151	167	123	112
Food Cost	45%	45%	45%	45%	45%	45%	45%
Labor Cost From Managers Detail	$1,413.35	$ -	$1,212.85	$1,173.85	$1,307.85	$1,728.23	$1,826.73
	$ 487.45	0	$ (534.15)	$ 224.80	$ 592.95	$ (138.73)	$ (536.98)

Tying It All Together

You might love to spend all day pounding the keyboard and watching the Excel spreadsheet update with numbers that would numb your mind, but what purpose would that serve? The race is won by those who are efficient, not by those who invest the most hours. Why not use a set of templates to accurately assess current operations and predict future performance?

The number of variables that exist on a golf course is actually quite small, but those managing a golf course need to consider its diverse activity centers, the number of customers it serves, and the different revenue and cost centers involved. To illustrate, shown in the following table is a five-year cash flow forecast that requires less than 15 minutes to prepare.

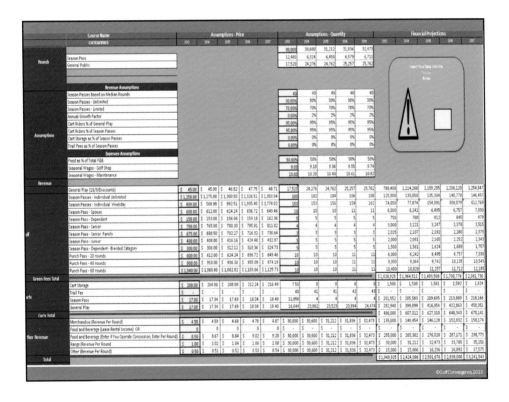

Is it perfect? Probably not. But for the time invested, is it a valuable tool to determine the revenue of a golf course? Absolutely. This template also includes the variables regarding operating expenses and capital budgets. Recently, a resort golf course that is losing money wanted to undertake to make cash-flow forecast simulations based on varying assumptions, such as hotel occupancy, member visits, outside play, and all the permutations one could think of in operating the resort. Within an hour, the optimum strategy for operating the course in 2013 was revealed. The course went from a loss of $1,161,000 in 2012 to a profit of $250,000 in 2013.

Go

If you licensed the supplemental template that accompanies this Field book, open Step 4: Five-Year Financial Projection—Daily Fee or Municipal, Five-Year Financial Projection— Resort, and/or Five-Year Financial Projection— Private Club template.

1) Select the template that is appropriate for the course you want to model. There are 60 variables. Enter the data for each variable based on last year's operating results. This comparison will provide you an indicator as to the accuracy of this planning tool for your facility.

2) Proceed to generate a cash flow forecast for the current year based on changing the assumptions in the matrix. Executing multiple scenarios will strengthen your understanding of the financial relationships in the operation and provide an accurate reflection of the future financial performance of the facility.

That Is Too Much Work

For those just wanting to cut to the chase and get a snapshot of a golf course's financial picture, there are only a few questions you need to ask:

1. What is your rack rate?

2. How many rounds of golf (starts) did you have during the past 12 months?

3. How many labor hours are invested in maintaining your golf course?

4. What is the cost of your water and utilities?

5. When was the last time you replaced the irrigation system?

Based on your intuition as to the location of the golf course and the neighborhood you observed driving to the course, you can reasonably estimate the financial potential of the golf course. A secondary set of numbers that will fine-tune your financial projection would be

1. What is your annual season pass or membership rate?

2. What is your revenue per round purchased?

3. Are maintenance expenses about 33% of total revenue?

4. Is your food and beverage principally used by golfers, or do you have extensive outside dining guests for lunch and dinner?

5. How many leagues, tournaments, or banquets and weddings do you anticipate this year?

None of those questions would be deemed to be too intrusive—merely casual conversation at the course. From knowing the answers to these questions, you could reasonably estimate the cash flow of a golf course.

Flash Cards

Golf Convergence conducted a "flash poll" of 500 industry leaders in March 2013, asking one question, "What are the five key benchmarks (key performance indicators) that you rely on to manage operations?" Shown below are the consensus responses.

Key Performance Indicator from Golf Industry Leaders		
Daily Fee - Municipal	Private Club	Resort
Labor as a % of Gross Revenue	Rounds played by members	RevPar = Revenue per Available Round
Merchandise Sales and Cost of Goods Sold	Guest Fees	Utilization percentage based on available rounds
Total Starts	Member Retention	Labor dollars per round
Revenue per round: green fee + cart fee	New Members + Waiting List	Costs per hole & per round
Net income	Change in Initiation Fee	Conversion ratio of resort golf rounds to resort room nights
Loyalty Rating from Customer Survey	Cash Requirements	Retail sales per round & per room night

These serve as a good starting point for the efficient management of a golf course.

Path to Success

Financial modeling is at the foundation of the success of a golf course. Rather than a punitive tool to hold management and staff hostages to meeting artificially derived targets, operational templates provide quick insights into the interrelationships of the various revenues and expenses at a golf course. The ability to streamline the financial forecasting process results in a deep understanding of the key drivers of revenues and expenses.

In all of sports, there is only one number that really matters—the final score. In business, there's only one number that really matters—the net income.

Why? The net income, in the long run, is a measure of customer satisfaction. In turn, customer satisfaction is a reflection of every aspect of the business, from the experience of playing the golf course (conditioning, price, etc.) to the interactions with management and staff.

To achieve maximum net income, do the following:

1) Simplify the facility's financial forecasting process by "retiring" the current tools used.

2) Incorporate a set of operational templates into your weekly, monthly, and annual forecasting.

3) Select five key performance indicators that measure 75% of your revenues and emphasize them on a "leaderboard" in a staff area of the facility.

4) Celebrate the wins weekly. Achieving financial success at the golf course is a team goal from which all should benefit.

Concluding Thought

The wise boldly pick up a truth as soon as they hear it.

Hsueh-Dou

Chapter 10

Yield Management
Step 4 of the Golf Convergence
WIN™ Formula (continued)

People will buy anything that is one to a customer.
Sinclair Lewis

Chapter Highlights

Since the advent of public golf in the late 1800s, yield management, by design or by accident, has been an integral part of pricing at golf courses. Prices that change by time of the day, day of the week, player type, season, and year are examples of the use of basic yield management theory.

While historical attempts at adjusting rates to influence demand were unscientific, more accurate adjustments are now possible due to the evolution of technology and the ability to construct a database that accurately portrays the utilization of the golf course for multiple years. Those who operate a golf course can now appropriately balance the capacity of the golf course at the highest net revenue per reservation.

Opponents of a dynamic pricing structure seem to believe that customer dissonance from strangers who meet on the first tee and discuss the varied prices they have paid will create customer service issues. But it is known, understood, and accepted that the rate structure for airfares, hotels, and even car rentals is the standard way efficient managers price business today. This chapter provides insights on how today's golf manager can implement powerful and profitable pricing.

Training Wheels

Because the golf course has a perishable inventory of tee times, fixed capacity, predictable time-related demand, and high fixed and low variable costs, it is an industry that is ideal for revenue management, whether by offering an all-inclusive one-price fee or by unbundling the various components at a golf course (green fee, cart, range balls, etc.) like the airlines do for checking bags, sitting in a row with extra room, and other such services.

Tee times are like airline seats. Once the airliner takes off, the empty seat is worthless, and once the 9:45 a.m. tee time comes and goes, it's gone forever. The goal is revenue optimization.

Revenue management has been described as "The application of information systems and pricing strategies to allocate the right capacity to the right customer at the right place at the right time."[1]

Often, it is thought that the objective of Revenue Management is to raise rates or to maximize utilization. This is wrong!

The real objective of Revenue Management is to maximize revenues and profits through the effective management of product availability in the marketplace. Customers assign value to a firm's products. When the perceived value is high, demand increases. When the value is low, demand declines. For a golf course, typical demand is reflected below.

---

1 Barry C. Smith, John F. Keimkuhler, and Ross M. Darrow, "Yield Management at American Airlines," *Interfaces*, Vol. 22, pp. 8–31.

Revenue Management is the process by which demand for products of differing value is segregated and accepted. It is the discipline that allows companies to create many, many products that attract market demand, and then manage that demand in a manner that maximizes revenues and profits, as illustrated in the following figure.

This figure might be applicable for a weekend, when demand would be higher and the desire to let seniors or coupon-holders have access to the course would be small.

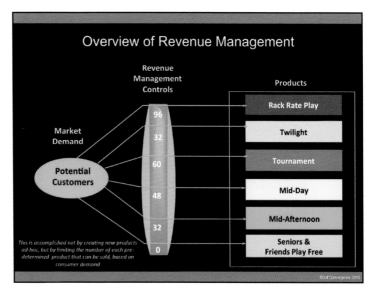

To maximize revenues, the Revenue Manager must determine the quantity of each product to make available for sale, at each course, for all days in the future. Assuming products are controlled on an hourly basis from 6 a.m. to 4 p.m., a Revenue Manager with five golf courses and an average of only five products must actively manage the availability of 250 products per day. If the product availability is managed for only the next 7 days, 1,750 controls must be checked and set each day.

While it sounds precise, without an appropriately constructed software revenue optimization module that accurately captures the historical demand at the facility, revenue management is very subjective and requires a lot of guesswork—at least initially. Understanding your sales history and improving your demand forecast requires time.

While the basic theory is simple, it gets complicated very quickly. To illustrate, on what date do you base your demand forecast on, i.e., the 1st of June, the 152nd day of the year or the 1st Friday in June. Those criteria could be, in a given year, the same day or as much as 6 days apart all generating different levels of demand for a tee time. Forecasting rounds played on the 4th of July, a national U.S. holiday, demonstrates the challenge as well. The rounds played will vary significantly if July 4th is on a weekend rather than on a Tuesday or Wednesday. And if the 4th of July is on a Friday, the demand on the following Sunday will be far less than if the 4th of July occurs during the middle of the week.

Since the various possibilities boggle the mind, it is little wonder that demand pricing has gotten very little attention in the golf industry. Some golf courses use pricing schemes such as early bird, back nine, twilight, super twilight, night out, beat the heat, and temperature (in cold markets)—all of which are examples of demand pricing in golf. Yet most golf course managers use a traditional approach to setting green fees. They set weekday and weekend prices based on a minimal amount of data. Then, to stimulate rounds, they use newspaper advertising, participation in coupon books, and providing inventory to third parties.

It is way too complex to attempt to figure out manually. And that may be why demand pricing is only now coming into vogue as more and more yield management software programs become available.

Why the Golf Industry Model for Tee Times Is Flawed

As the industry moves to demand pricing, an examination of golf's historical pricing practices provides insights in comparison to other industries. For example, the airline yield management model is shown in the figure below.

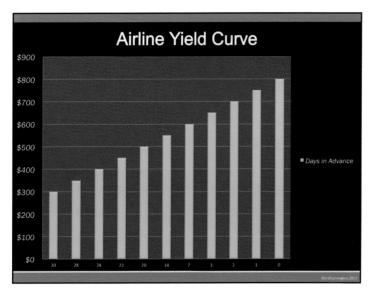

Everyone knows that the best values for airlines are obtained 14 or more days in advance on a non-refundable basis. The theory is that recreational travelers are motivated by the lower fares, and because of the certainty of their vacation, they are willing to purchase on a nonrefundable basis. Conversely, business travelers, because of less certainty as to when or where they need to be and from their increased ability to pay, are charged a higher fare for booking in the days just prior to departure.

In contrast, the majority of golf courses use a static pricing model with a tendency to discount tee times late in the booking cycle. This runs counter to supply and demand economics. While few facilities use software that would enable dynamic pricing, psychologically, many operators panic as the day of play approaches, and some engage in flexible pricing that results in the yield illustrated in the following figure.

What is ironic is that the greatest demand to book a tee time occurs when tee times first become available (40%) and within 48 hours of the tee time requested (40%). The other 20% are reserved after the first rush up until 48 hours in advance. What most operators fail to grasp is that the odds are in favor of raising prices close to the day of play, not lowering them.

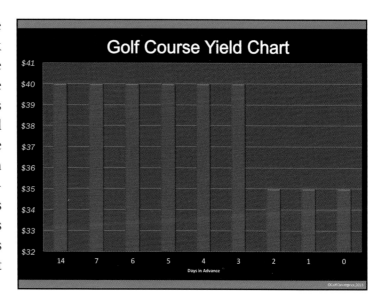

The Odds Are in the House's Favor

In Las Vegas, the odds favor the house. Over the long run, more money is lost by customers than won. It is a zero-sum game. The casinos win. Those same favorable odds are available to golf courses, if they understand the dynamics of discounting versus raising rates.

Many golf course managers are lulled into the economic trap of believing that more rounds, even at a slight discount, are financially advantageous. But discounting is a slippery slope. Presented here is a chart that highlights the perils.

Decrease in Price	Number of Additional Rounds Required to Offset Discount
5%	5.26%
10%	11.11%
15%	17.65%
20%	25.00%
25%	33.33%
30%	42.86%
35%	53.85%
40%	66.67%
45%	81.82%
50%	100.00%

Looking at this chart proves why it is sheer folly to participate in coupon books offering two-for-one green fees.

A golf course offering a 50% discount would need a 100% increase in rounds to recover the revenue lost. When you consider the additional wear and tear on the conditioning of the golf course, how can any facility offer such a discount? The logic is that if the lower rates attract a golfer to the course for the first time, he or she will be so enamored with the experience that return trips will produce a profit many times the discount given. Golf Convergence research has shown that these discount-oriented golfers spend little money at the course, bring few additional customers during their visits, and return infrequently and only when they again can play at a reduced price.

Someone who has taken the opportunity to purchase a product for $20 will seldom feel good about purchasing the product again for $40.

Raising prices annually is a practice most golf courses have gotten out of the habit of doing. Citing the economy, the competition, and the growing influence of third-party tee time purveyors, they have been locked into a mindset of paralysis. Shown here is the positive impact on gross revenue when prices are increased.

Increase Price	Decrease in Rounds That Can Occur to Generate the Same Revenue
5%	4.76%
10%	9.09%
15%	13.04%
20%	16.67%
25%	20.00%
30%	23.08%
35%	25.93%
40%	28.57%
45%	31.03%
50%	33.33%

Interpreted, if a golf course increased its prices by 50%, it could lose 33% of the rounds played yet still generate the same gross revenue, with far less work, far better course conditions, and the same bottom line. Note that a given maintenance budget determines the course conditions which, in turn, determine the attractiveness of the facility and enhance customer loyalty. Part of that equation is the tee time interval.

The odds are in favor of the golf course, as shown in this chart.

While this chart exaggerates the extreme of discounting versus price increases, it does support the theory that golf courses make a mistake discounting, believing additional rounds are the path to profitability.

If For No Other Reason, Here is Why You Should Increase Your Prices

Price Movement	Amount	Impact	To Break Even
Decrease Price	50%	100%	Need to Double Rounds
Increase Price	50%	33%	Can lose 1/3 of rounds
House Odds are In Your Favor		67%	

Creating a Winning Hand

Winning poker is not just about maximizing the pot on a good hand, for many players will generate some return with strong cards, but it's also about playing a bad hand well. As has been said about the game of golf, "It's not how many great shots you hit but how many really bad shots you don't? If the goal is to increase net income, it is only logical that dynamic pricing be implemented.

Municipal golf courses have been particularly slow to implement this dynamic. Shown here is an easy-to-understand pricing model that would benefit all public facilities, and it would be accepted by customers based on the values they would receive.

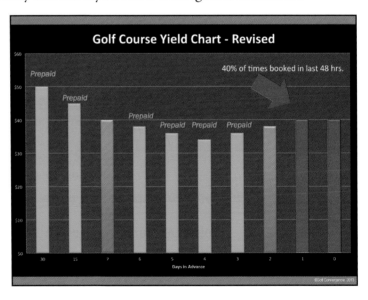

Golfers looking to secure a prime tee time, be it on a Saturday morning or a holiday weekend, are willing to pay a premium to secure that preferred time, if for no other reason than it allows them to effectively plan the balance of their day with family and friends. And charging a premium secured by credit card would increase revenue and enhance the value to the customer. Or if a tourist is traveling to a resort over a holiday weekend, paying a premium to secure a preferred time is a win-win situation.

To recognize historical practices of booking 7 days in advance, that practice can continue if you accept a credit card at the time of the reservation, with the card only charged on the day of play upon the appearance or the non-appearance of the golfer.

Closer to the day of play, the demand to play at a specific time increases. Therefore the golf course would be wise to charge a higher price within 48 hours of the time reserved.

Technology Determines Price

While the golf management software that is currently prevalent throughout the industry could accommodate the simplified dynamic pricing outlined above, with the increasing automation of the tee time reservation process and the growing use of the Web to book tee times, many golf courses have started implementing the dynamic pricing shown in the following figure.

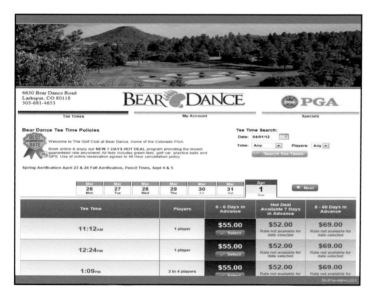

Note on this slide that variable pricing is being used and that the course offers the "best rate guarantee," calling it a "green ribbon guarantee." Please note the premium on booking 8 to 60 days in advance.

Another derivation of an alternative pricing strategy is often available in resort areas where rates may vary by tourists (at public courses), residents of a state, or those who choose to join the course loyalty club. An example of that sort of dynamic pricing is shown in the following figure.

The ability to offer different prices based on day of the week, time of the day, and time of the year has been available for over two decades.

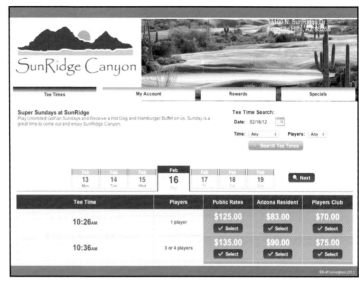

These dynamic pricing models have been made possible by the great advances in technology that are being driven by third-party tee time firms who are engaged in barter. These firms have created applications to facilitate the booking of tee times by consumers, as shown below on iPhone applications.

Interestingly, the average cell phone user downloads 40 applications on an iPhone and 25 on an Android phone, while a BlackBerry user downloads 15 applications.[2] It is only a matter of time before a golf course deploys reservation technology that can provide access to any mobile platform to drive its core business.

Golf Channel's Golfnow .com, Quick18, and EZ-Links, which offers a full suite of golf management software products, are leading in the development of software motivated to create dynamic pricing

2 http://paidcontent.org/2010/09/09/419-average-number-of-apps-downloaded-to-iphone-40-android-25/

and to ensure that the tee times obtained from golf courses are fully liquidated. It is our understanding that 33% of barter times offered are sold by these firms in addition to the tee times booked for the golf course. Active Network and Club Prophet also provide yield management modules for golf courses seeking to internally price their tee time inventory.

The applications being developed to dynamically price tee times are focused on monitoring current demand versus historical demand and providing for the automatic adjustment of the tee time rates displayed through the various distribution channels. The ability to create numerous products and to price the products based on perceived demand is shown in the following figure provided by EZLinks.

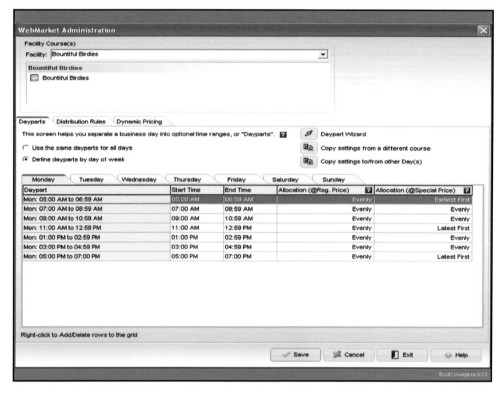

These templates enable the tee time reservation system to monitor actual bookings within the designated tee time slot and automatically adjust the prices, either up or down, based on the number of days remaining until the day of play. These applications ensure that the capacity of that time slot is reached. This top figure illustrates the ability of the golf course owner to distinguish between parts of the day, to select the appropriate channels (facility Web site for the general public, Loyalty Card deal page, iPhone, search engines, Android, Facebook, Twitter, etc.) and incorporate dynamic pricing based on trending patterns of demand.

The results of this dynamic pricing are shown in the following figure.

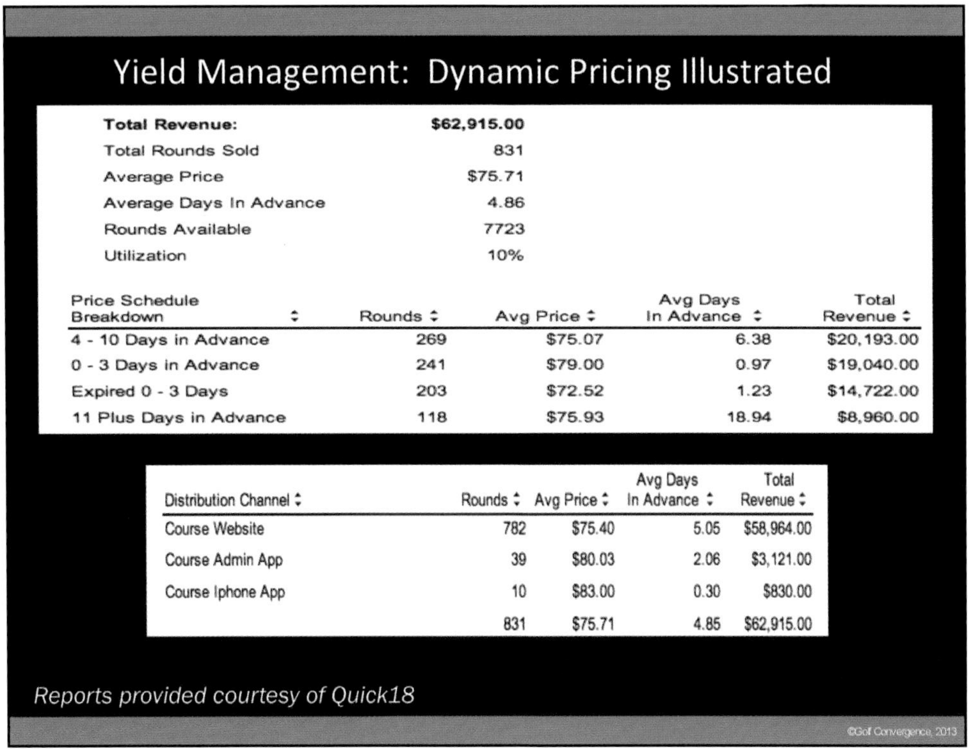

Yield Management: Dynamic Pricing Illustrated

Total Revenue:	**$62,915.00**
Total Rounds Sold	831
Average Price	$75.71
Average Days In Advance	4.86
Rounds Available	7723
Utilization	10%

Price Schedule Breakdown	Rounds	Avg Price	Avg Days In Advance	Total Revenue
4 - 10 Days in Advance	269	$75.07	6.38	$20,193.00
0 - 3 Days in Advance	241	$79.00	0.97	$19,040.00
Expired 0 - 3 Days	203	$72.52	1.23	$14,722.00
11 Plus Days in Advance	118	$75.93	18.94	$8,960.00

Distribution Channel	Rounds	Avg Price	Avg Days In Advance	Total Revenue
Course Website	782	$75.40	5.05	$58,964.00
Course Admin App	39	$80.03	2.06	$3,121.00
Course Iphone App	10	$83.00	0.30	$830.00
	831	$75.71	4.85	$62,915.00

Reports provided courtesy of Quick18

©Golf Convergence, 2013

This report only reflects a slice of the reservations that day. It is estimated that 12% of tee times booked at golf courses today are reserved via the Internet or through mobile applications.

How Much More Money Would You Like to Make?

To begin to implement dynamic pricing at a facility, you need to undertake a few fundamental steps:

- Determine the demand versus the supply of golf courses near the facility.
- Measure the potential to increase rounds based on the age, income, and ethnicity of your golfers.
- Develop insights on the strength of your customer franchise.
- Evaluate potential resurgence from former customers.
- Ascertain demand by hour, by day, by week, by season, and by year for the past two years.
- Determine the number of products to be offered and the price point for each.

- Identify golfers' price sensitivity by rate and time of day.

- Determine revenue per available tee time (REVPATT) compared to published rate, to monitor incremental gains.

Go

If you licensed the supplemental template that accompanies this Field book, open Step 4: Green Fee Yield—Revenue Modeling Exercise template:

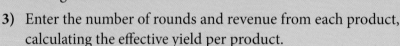

1) Select a busy month from the prior year.

2) Ascertain how many "products" were sold during that month.

3) Enter the number of rounds and revenue from each product, calculating the effective yield per product.

4) Undertake revenue modeling, changing price points and projected rounds based on the assumptions made.

5) Conclude whether updating pricing for the upcoming season is viable.

By undertaking this exercise, you can quickly determine the impact of rounds and price changes on projected revenue, as shown here.

Product	Rounds	Historical Average Green Fee	Actual Revenue	# of Rounds % Change	# of Rounds	Fee % Change	New Green Fee	Projected Revenue	Difference
18 Hole	9,801	$69.00	$676,269	-10%	8,821	12%	$77.28	$681,679	$5,410
9 Hole	21	34.00	714	-2%	21	20%	40.80	840	126
Twilight	389	45.00	17,505	-22%	303	15%	51.75	15,702	(1,803)
Yearly Ticket	65	50.00	3,250	9%	71	8%	54.00	3,826	576
Juniors	77	26.26	2,022	-23%	59	25%	32.82	1,946	(76)
Super Twilight	99	30.75	3,044	10%	109	12%	34.44	3,750	706
Tournaments	336	65.00	21,840	10%	370	10%	71.50	26,426	4,586
Comp	115	-	0	0%	115	12%	-	-	-
Men's League	223	25.00	5,575	5%	234	0%	25.00	5,854	279
Women's League	176	16.00	2,816	0%	176	0%	16.00	2,816	-
Kid's Camp	345	12.00	4,140	19%	411	0%	12.00	4,927	787
Kid's Camp (9)	134	5.00	670	0%	134	5%	5.25	704	34
Early Birds (Mon. & Tues.)	345	45.00	15,525	14%	393	5%	47.25	18,583	3,058
Couples Sunday pm (9 holes)	298	48.00	14,304	0%	298	10%	52.80	15,734	1,430
Total/Avg →	12,424	$61.79	$767,674	1%	11,515	7%	$67.98	$782,787	$15,113

Brave New World

It's a beautiful day, the tee sheet is largely empty, there are only a few groups on the course, and in walks a foursome. They confirm that the rack rate is $75, including cart. They offer to pay $50 per player with lunch included. Do you take their offer?

The need for golf course operators to maintain rate integrity by properly conditioning a course, developing a customer database, and deploying integrated TTRS/POS technology to efficiently market to the core, acquired, and defectors has been chronicled. However, those practices have only been implemented by the adroit to stem the tide of falling rounds and fractured yield throughout the industry.

With supply forecast to exceed demand for the next decade, until market forces become balanced, golf course operators may be subject to a new trend—negotiated pricing of individual tee times. Which offers do you take or decline?

Negotiated Transactions Dominate the Commercial Landscape

Consider how prevalent negotiable pricing has become. Cars, houses, airline tickets via Expedia or Orbitz and hotels via Priceline are merely a few purchases for which negotiation/bargaining is commonly used. While haggling dominates in the U.S. for infrequent high-end purchases, it is common on most purchases throughout the world. Would you ever pay retail for any item in Asia? Not likely.

Discounting, affinity, and customer loyalty programs are pervasive in nearly all industries.

Ranging from the Starbucks Gold Card (one free drink for every 12 purchased), to Office Depot's quarterly credit on purchases, to merchandise and travel rewards from American Express, or cash back on Costco and numerous other credit cards, paying the asking price for a commodity is the exception rather than the rule.

Readily Accessible Information Will Accelerate Negotiated Pricing

The thought that golf will become a negotiated transaction is perhaps an inevitable result of current price pressures that will be compounded by another market force—greatly enhanced information available to the consumer.

Evolving technology is enabling the consumer to find the lowest price for a commodity instantly. Recently, BlackBerry launched shopsavvy.com. A consumer merely scans the bar code or the QR code of the product, and the price of that item at neighboring stores is displayed.

iPhone applications, such as savebenjis.com or redlaser.com, provide a comprehensive price comparison in your hands. The strength of this app is its ability to compare a product across multiple vendors. You can search by product name, bar code, manufacturer, keyword, and a half dozen other criteria. It also has the ability to add product reviews. Google Search offers an identical service.

Thus, superior information is allowing the consumer to make an informed decision. Currently, the numerous third-party tee time sites are, in essence, providing a comparable service by displaying the price of various golf courses on a single screen. Thus, golfers can learn instantly the pricing within their market.

One of the key tenets of capitalism is based on the inefficiency of the market place. The informed can leverage superior information to the disadvantage of the uninformed. With the introduction of new technology, the balance of power in purchasing decisions is switching from the vendor to the consumer.

Why Negotiated Tee Times May Become a Reality within Five Years

Golf course managers and staff are largely reactive, rather than proactive. In their defense, perhaps they are so consumed with operational tasks that the more valuable strategic and tactical planning tasks get shortchanged.

However, even though it will be challenging to train counter staff on which deals to accept and how to record them within the industry's POS systems, negotiated tee times are likely to dominate soon.

Golfers will have superlative information as to current rates in a local market and a plethora of choices, while golf course operators will become even more focused on rounds at the expense of revenue. Golfers will control prices by voting with their feet.

Golf course operators would be wise to know the value of the experience they create and take all offers that equal that price.

Determining the Proper Rate

Fair market value is defined as "the price for which property can be sold in an 'arm's length' transaction; that is, between informed, unrelated, and willing parties, each of whom is acting rationally and in its own best interest."[3]

In theory, if the green fee were properly set for each individual tee time, it is logical to assume that 100% of the available times would be sold.

Some golf course owners establish green fees based on cost plus desired return on investment. Others set the green fees based on the market value of nearby courses. Still others base their fees on a subjective perception of the value of the golf experience. This subjective valuation method results in one facility charging over $125 per round competing against another course that charges less than $30, yet both are between 6,000 and 7,400 yards, have 18 holes, and take roughly 4½ hours to play.

None of these three methods works well long-term. None of these will give you any clue on whether you should accept a negotiated price from a golfer.

A Golf Course's Proper Focus: Matching the Price to the Experience

Golfers are very astute and value-driven. They subconsciously decide where to play based on a simple formula: value = experience – price. Golfers measure their experience based 90% on the course (slope, strategy, conditioning, grass texture, ambience, and amenities) and 10% on the service standards encountered.

---

3 http://www.cisco.com/warp/public/csc/about_financing/glossary.html

A golf course's ability to create a consistent experience, while manageable, is limited by the positive cash flow available for reinvestment plus additional capital, debt, and personnel committed.

What is totally controllable by the golf course operator is the price. The green fee can be adjusted instantly based on numerous subjective or objective factors.

The golf course operator who adjusts the rate subjectively or intuitively is likely to do so at the expense of yield per round. The correct price based on value created can be measured in advance of the golfer's based on an objective standard that measures the key components a golfer subconsciously considers in assessing value.

The success of this process was evidenced by Quintero Golf Club in Peoria, Arizona. That club began using the yield management software in January 2013. Though rounds were down 10%, revenue increased by 14% over 2012, which was an impressive gain.

Go

If you licensed the supplemental template that accompanies this Field book, open the
Step 6: Customer Value Experience or review the exercise you completed with the template in Chapter 9.

1) Reexamine, to support the calculation, the value the facility generates reflected in the rack rate green fee.

2) Prepare a list of your competitors' prices.

3) Compare the results of your team's pricing estimate to actual market value and determine if a rate adjustment at your facility is warranted.

Path to Success

1) There is perhaps no more subjective area in the business of golf than determining green fees. Prices for green fees are sometimes said to be based on the ego of the management team and not on supply and demand.

2) Oftentimes, prices are set based on what competitors are charging.

3) Prices should only be set based on the value of the experience created. Once the baseline rate has been established, the ability to adjust based on demand becomes viable.

4) The progressive golf course owner will begin a search for software that will provide for yield management and facilitate negotiated pricing of tee times. With these tools, the golf course owners are in complete control reserving tee times and accepting or rejecting offers based on established criteria.

Concluding Thought

The young man knows the rules, but the old man knows the exceptions.

Oliver Wendell Holmes

Chapter 11

Golf Course Valuation
Step 4 of the Golf Convergence WIN™ Formula (continued)

The street-smart person realizes that the painful part in deciding to do something is that you are really deciding not to do everything else.

David Mahoney

A weak person has doubts before making a decision; a strong person has them afterwards.

Karl Kraus, Austrian author and journalist (1874–1936)

Chapter Highlights

The axiom often heard regarding real estate transactions is that you make money when you buy, not when you sell. The components of buying and selling a golf course are actually complex. From title surveys, appraisals, transfer of permits and licenses, determining status of habitat and wetlands, structural issues (HVAC, utilities, and irrigation), employees and independent contractor agreements, hydrology study, and community-controlled covenants are all issues that need review.

Because this is a transaction an individual or entity makes infrequently, knowledge of the nuances of how a golf course is valued and the pitfalls of purchasing is essential. For the seller, just as a home seller prepares a house for showing, preparing the golf course for sale can help to ensure that fair value is received and that deductions for deferred capital expenditures are minimized.

This chapter focuses on the dramatic changes that have occurred in golf course real estate transactions, in a market in which prices have fallen by as much as 33% during the past six years. We will also address current industry benchmarks, the reasons why historical valuation methods are no longer applicable, and the information you need as a buyer or seller to receive a fair price.

Abracadabra—Poof: The Money Disappeared

During the last five years in the United States, the weak economy and the fact that golf course supply exceeds demand have changed the landscape of golf course real estate transactions. As the selling prices for residential housing have fallen, so have the prices for golf courses. The major lenders focused on the golf market (such as Capmark, GE Capital, and Textron), have vacated the market, liquidating rather than expanding their golf course portfolios.

For seven consecutive years, more golf courses have closed than opened. These changes in the dynamics of golf course real estate are reflected in the contrast of new course openings to closings shown in the following figure.

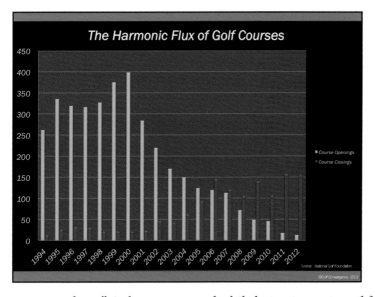

When demand exceeds supply, prices rise. The opposite has been occurring between 2006 and 2013; 932 golf courses have closed. They represent 5.9% of the industry.

Larry Hirsh, President of Golf Property Analysts and one of the industry's leading appraisers, estimated that nearly 500 other golf courses are "eligible for purchase." As he commented while being interviewed for this book, "The golf course industry is akin to the Republican Party. Both have lost their constituencies and need to attract women, minorities, and focus on the family if they are to prosper."

And it gets worse. As Hilda Allen, an industry leader in the sale and auction of golf courses and residential communities, stated, "I would speculate that 25% of the existing courses are for sale on some basis." She continued, saying,

"With so many facilities losing money, the net income multiplier or the income/capitalization rate valuation methods are no longer applicable. If there is a positive net cash flow (NCF), then the industry appraisers say 7 to 10 times multiple. If the cash flow is negative, then a gross income multiplier with consideration given to each profit center is used and is from .675 to 1.6 times the gross income multiplier.

Owner financing is the key component; most buyers/investors have equity sources with debt participation. There are a group of new buyers with Wall Street hedge funds and some capital sources who are the 'kings' at this juncture as they are able to negotiate discounts from 10% to as much as 50%.

In some cases, buyers have paid ten cents on the dollar. In the Atlanta market, Echelon Golf Course was listed with our firm for over $12M three years ago. The property, including a few existing lots and a golf course, sold for under $2.0M in the last 12 months."[1]

There are clearly some negative factors that weigh heavily on golf course values:

1. Lack of financing.

2. The size and scope of the courses and clubhouses built starting in the 1990s are very expensive physical assets to maintain, thereby impacting cash flow.

3. The second-home vacation market has vanished, with individuals preferring to pay a small premium for staying in luxury hotels rather than the constant cash outflow of second-home ownership.

Many developers of golf course communities had projected that 70% of residents would be golfers, when in fact only 20% to 30% of residents are golfers, according to Dennis Hillier, J.D., Greenberg Traurig, who is "recognized as the pioneer in the industry of equity club conversions and membership programs. During the past 30 years, he has designed more than 1,800 membership programs throughout the United States, the Caribbean, Europe and the Pacific Rim."[2]

Hillier stated, however, that "the residential market is getting stronger. In the spring of 2013, 950,000 new houses are projected for construction, up from 500,000 units in 2010. Note that the residential construction benchmark is 1.3 million units a year. Much of the problem was due to

1 Hilda W. Allen, "Email to Author," March 19, 2013.

2 http://www.gtlaw.com/People/Dennis-W-Hillier?tab=fullBio

the industry building in excess of 2.2 million units per year for many years fueled by low interest rates, easily obtained credit and flexible paybacks for the developers. The correction has required that this excess inventory be absorbed, resulting in lower numbers of units being built. If a second vacation home market is to revive, i.e., Martis Camp, it will be the exception rather than the rule. To be attractive, units will be priced between $350,000 and $500,000, far lower than planned a decade ago."[3]

4. Private clubs are saddled with refund liability on equity memberships (those who own stock in a club) and deposits (corporate-owned private clubs). The negative impact of this liability on the brand image of a private club is evidenced by this article about a lawsuit against a club in Naples, Florida:

"A saturation of golf courses in Naples may be a dream for golfers in the nation's top golf spot, but it often can turn into a nightmare for members who quit and demand membership refunds.

The Naples area's recent ranking by the National Golf Foundation as No. 1 in the nation for its 1,530 golf holes—a per-hole population of 212—also has led to a series of lawsuits filed by golfers seeking refunds after many years on clubs' waiting lists.

With more than 91 golf courses to choose from in Collier alone, many waiting lists remain stagnant in providing refunds to those who want them. Basically, no one on that list is ever going to get a refund," Callahan's lawyer, William Dillon of Fort Myers, told jurors during closing arguments. "It's a graveyard where memberships continue to die."

Steve Graves, chief executive officer of Creative Golf Marketing, which creates membership promotions, said the contracts popular in Florida, Nevada, California, Arizona and Washington are like Ponzi schemes, meaning one or several must join for those on a waiting list to get a refund.

"It's like the line in the song Hotel California. 'You can check out any time you like, but you can never leave," Graves said. "The developers wove this wicked web into their documents, frankly, as a way to protect themselves. There are people on those boards who love the fact that members are held hostage."[4]

---

3 Phone conversation, March 15, 2013.

4 http://www.naplesnews.com/news/2013/mar/11/collier-abdundant-golf-courses-refund-member-suits/

5. National weather forecasts also have an impact. As covered in Chapter 5, the cold and rainy 2013 forecast may dampen values.

In the past few years, due to the economy, many clubs slashed initiation fees or began to offer non-equity memberships at far lower prices. With the redemption of a membership on the waiting list redeemed on a 4 to 1 ratio, the lower fees collected make it improbable that the higher initiation fee charges of a decade ago can be redeemed.

These anchors have a major negative impact on value. The average price of a golf course has fallen 33.6% since 2006, as shown in the figure below.

The National Golf Foundation has said the following about golf course sales activity:

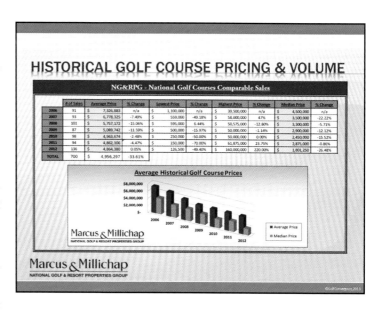

"While new golf facility openings are few, golf course transaction activity has been vigorous over the last six years. From publicly available sources, NGF has tracked nearly 1,300 golf facility transactions since the beginning of 2007, and this number is almost certainly understating actual sales." The release indicated that, "Privately owned public golf courses made up nearly 80% of courses sold since the beginning of 2007."[5]

A Glimmer of Hope for Stabilization

A glimmer of hope has surfaced in 2013, with partially developed real estate projects with amenities attracting renewed interest, especially the interest of

5 http://ngfdashboard.clubnewsmaker.org/Newsletter/1ehoffw2rtc118g6mneb4l?a=1&p–128357 5&t=43815

those buyers with cash who require no financing. Attractive opportunities are available for buyers as many sellers seem to have a willingness to negotiate with the increased certainty of closing.

Underneath the broad trends of openings and closings, there is a shift in the types of golf courses in use that is impacting value. The chart below reflects the changes in facilities from 2006 to 2012, as reported by the NGF.

		TYPE			Total
		Daily Fee	Municipal	Private	(by size & length)
SIZE	9 holes	-135	-28	-161	-324
	18 holes	121	60	-244	-63
	27 holes	-3	4	-9	-8
	36 holes	-4	-1	-20	-25
	45 or more holes	-9	-2	-2	-13
	Total	-30	33	-436	-433
LENGTH	Regulation Only	57	13	-437	-367
	Executive Only	4	22	9	35
	Par 3 Only	-83	-1	-4	-88
	Regulation & Executive	-3	1	-3	-5
	Regulation & Par 3	-1	-2	0	-3
	Executive & Par 3	-2	1	0	-1
	Regulation, Executive & Par 3	-2	-1	-1	-4
	Total	-30	33	-436	-433

The net change in the number of private clubs and the number of regulation courses from closures (temporary and permanent) and conversions is not surprising.

The increase in the number of executive golf courses supports the theories previously advanced herein that golfers are seeking shorter courses and that golf for the majority is about having fun rather than an athletic challenge.

In an article titled, "Where Golf's Growth Model Went Horribly Wrong," Dr. David Hueber stated,

> "The gist of my research is that the golf courses built or renovated during the 1990s were costly, difficult, and took longer to play than new golf courses built in the 1920s and 1960s, which may have contributed to the decline in golf participation and rounds played. Consequently, the golf course industry has a large number of unsustainable golf courses that are not economically viable and socially responsible. This suggests that we are offering a golf course product that our customers don't want to buy."[6]

Former PGA of America president, M. G. Orender echoed those thoughts, stating,

---

6 Global Golf Post, "Where Golf's Growth Model Went Horribly Wrong," February 18, 2013, pg. 12.

"I see courses all the time that are going to lose $300,000 to $400,000 until the end of days. The industry is not going to get out of this mess with those courses until either those courses go to seed or become parks or something else."[7]

The need now exists for more golf courses that are shorter, easier to play, and less expensive; they must require less money spent on water, chemicals, and maintenance. To that end, "there is a great deal of redesign and redevelopment work in transforming the unsustainable inventory into something that makes business sense."[8] That is the belief of famed golf course architect Bobby Weed.

But the question is, "Will the cost of that redesign and redevelopment produce a positive return on investment?" And for golf to again become vibrant, the cost to play will have to come down, the time required to play will need to be less, and clubs must become family-friendly. Solutions for private clubs may include creating tiered membership by age: 25, 30, 35, 40, and 45, with non-refundable deposits (perhaps 40% of the historical equity fee) and an increasing dues structure by age.

Regarding the future growth of the industry, the National Golf Foundation has said that

> "Golf course openings remain at historic lows, but given the condition of the overall economy many would be surprised that there are any new golf courses opening. Equally surprising to those who feel new course development has come to a complete halt may be the number of golf course projects under construction.
>
> In 2012, NGF recognized 199 courses (18 hole equivalents (18 HEQ)) in development (either under construction, in planning, or proposed projects). Roughly 73% of these projects are new facilities, with the remainder representing expansions to existing golf facilities (e.g., 9-hole addition).
>
> As the real estate market continues to recover, we may see more closures and fewer developments under construction. High residential inventories and low commercial occupancy rates, combined with a tightening of credit, have stymied some developers who would otherwise be building new courses or eying distressed golf courses for

---

7 Ibid., pg. 13.

8 Ibid., pg. 13.

potential re-development. NGF predicts a net change of negative 100 to 150 18 HEQs in 2013, and for at least a few years thereafter; a gradually improving ratio of supply and demand."[9]

While the net liquidation of golf courses will continue, it is kind of ironic that the value of golf courses will likely rise, not for the intrinsic value of the investment return as golf courses, but for the value of the land for alternative uses.

Government Gives, Government Takes

One area that is drawing increased scrutiny is the property taxes being assessed golf courses. A potential reduction in real estate tax assessments is a fertile area in which golf courses can improve their bottom line.

The methods for calculating property tax assessments can vary widely between governmental jurisdictions. Some many use replacement costs while others may establish the annual tax based on fair market value, which could use comparable sales or income as alternative methods of valuation. With such a diversity of methods used, and with each often applied differently, the annual assessments can vary widely creating the opportunity for golf courses to review and protest property tax assessments.

A private country club in the Denver metropolitan area was awarded a six-figure rebate because its initial assessment included vacant land adjacent to the golf course that was zoned for future real estate development. We also know of farmland in the middle of nowhere in Nebraska that was valued as residential real estate, with a $150,000 annual property-tax bill on a golf course that generates $2.5 million in revenue per year. Left unchecked, and with governments seeking additional sources of revenue, property taxes are a likely source of government income, and the appeal process is complex and often requires the retention of specialists.

The process of protesting property taxes involves: 1) assessment evaluation, 2) preparation of appeal, and 3) negotiation or litigation.

---

9 http://ngfdashboard.clubnewsmaker.org/1490nvl84121sl9b7u4wlc?a=5&p=1138375&t=43825

Golf Property Analysts recommends that golf course owners consider the following when appealing property taxes[10]:

1. What is the current assessment?

2. What is the operating trend of the club for the past three years?

3. Are there any items of deferred maintenance?

4. Are there bids to address these items?

5. Has the club been sold recently?

6. Has the property been marketed for sale?

7. Does the club have inadequate, adequate or super-adequate equipment?

8. Is the club efficiently managed?

9. What is the appeal deadline, and has an appeal been filed?

10. If private, does the club have a full membership?

11. Is there a waiting list?

12. Are there any easements, covenants or restrictions precluding alternative development of the property?

13. Is your state a "highest and best use" state, or are tax assessments based on the property's current use?

Appraisers can be retained based on a flat fee or on an hourly basis to appeal property taxes.

Specialists (such as Complex Property Advisors Corporation) reviewing a club's property tax assessment may represent the course on a contingency-fee basis. Note that members of the Society of Golf Course Appraisers are precluded from accepting such contingency fee assignments, as they are perceived to perhaps compromise the independence of the appraiser in determining the valuation.

Other specialists, such as National Golf & Resort Properties Group, underwrite golf course sales. During the past two years they have underwritten over $500 million in sales. Underwriting (determining where a golf course will trade if sold today) is different than appraisals. The appraiser's view is often historical, while an underwriter usually leans more on prospective.

---

10 http://www.golfprop.com/LinkClick.aspx?fileticket=6wLd5NcQJVM%3D&

Common mistakes in appraisals include valuations determined by price per hole, price per acre, replacement costs, discounting cash flow during the first year with the assumption of gaining members at a rate that is not feasible. In addition, comparative quotes may be two to three years old, using gross revenue methods of valuation. That is why it is important to use an appraiser who specializes in golf courses.

How Will Future Real Estate Transactions Be Valued?

The interesting twists of the most recent economic challenges have changed the benchmarks on which golf courses are valued.

Historically, there were seven valuation methods: book value, liquidated value, excess earnings, multiple models of revenue or net income, cost, comparative market value, and discounted cash flow.

Of the seven valuation techniques, the two most frequently used are discounted cash flow (income approach) and comparative market value.

These valuation methods are incorporated into appraisals to determine value. Golf course values are a mix of real estate and business, and to come up with a proper valuation, you have to understand the mix of the two.

Components that influence the value of a golf course include location, site configuration, population, topography, scenic appeal, course features, amenities, and access to major highways and expressways. A comprehensive appraisal also looks at things like irrigation pumping systems, cost and availability of irrigation water, drainage, ADA compliance, food and beverage operation, safety issues present resulting from poor golf hole design, maintenance equipment, chemical and fuel storage, bridges, cart paths, utilities, clubhouse, and maintenance.[11]

At a minimum, the value of a golf course is the value of the land. Appraisers look for the highest and best use, which is a bit of a wild card that can have a significant impact on determining value. Thus, a golf course valued at $3.5 million may be valued at a much higher dollar amount if the land were redeveloped where commercial zoning is already in place.

11 Gorman Group, "Golf Course Appraisals," www.gormangrp.com/golf_course_appraisals.html

Appraisals are a subjective process. The appraised value of golf course hinges on the numbers attributed to three factors—income stream, capitalization rate, and market value. These three are interrelated. Knowing two of the three components makes it possible for you to calculate the third. For a golf course, one of the most common methods of determining value is to use the following formula: market value equals the income divided by the capitalization rate. The capitalization rate is the yield from the investment that is necessary in order to attract investors.

With numerous golf courses losing money, this standard formula for valuing a golf course, which hinges on the income stream, is currently not applicable.

Today's Benchmarks: The Art of the Deal

The method of valuing of golf courses is gravitating toward a combination of discounted cash flow models, using capitalization rates and the creation of pro forma forecasts based on the probable income results with new management.

The capitalization rates are constantly changing in response to economic conditions and alternative investment opportunities. One of the reliable sources for current rates is provided by The Society of Golf Appraisers, an organization that provides information about financing and investment criteria, information that is instrumental in the evaluation of golf course-related investing and lending activity.

In their 2013 survey, the Society of Golf Course Appraisers indicated that

> "Current or 'going-in' Cap Rates ranged from 6% to 14.5%, and averaged 11.1%, reflecting a relatively flat trend since 2010. The average terminal or residual cap rate was 11.8%, similar to what was found in 2011.

> The results indicate that most investors still focus returns on recent historical financial performance rather than on "Proforma," or potential performance.

> However, investors in clubs that are considered to provide probable opportunities for repositioning, vis-à-vis management and/or significant capital improvements, tend to focus on the returns they expect after the facility is improved."[12]

---

12 http://ngfdashboard.clubnewsmaker.org/1s8yofy32wl1sl9b7u4wlc?email=true&a=2&p=1138375&t=43825

Steven Ekovich, who is Vice President, Investments, of Marcus & Millichap National Golf and Resort Properties Group in Florida, closely tracks every golf course-related real estate transaction, including the benchmarks utilized to value the transaction. Shown below are his cap rate comparisons for the years from 1990 to 2011.

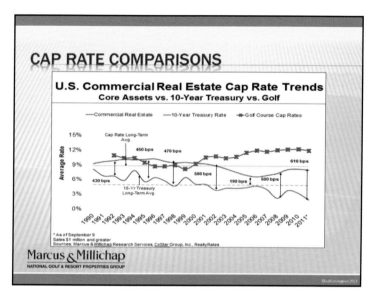

The increase in the capitalization rate from under 9% in 1999 to over 11% in 2012 reflects the increased risk and diminished prospects from the investment in a golf course during the past five years until 2013.

When interviewed for this book, Ekovich stated,

"Golf course real estate transactions are beginning to percolate nicely again. In residential communities where the amenities were completed and only a minority of lots were sold, these projects are attracting investor interest due to the upside potential of real estate from the resurgence in the residential market. Interested buyers in real estate are golf operators, international buyers, private equity funds, residential opportunity funds as well as horizontal and vertical developers.

Golf course demand for courses not in residential communities is also gaining traction as yields on core real estate have dropped precipitously.

For our clients, we look at the historical performance of the asset and carefully develop pro forma projections based on the opportunities that the current ownership and management missed. Those projected cash flows are then appropriately discounted for the risk involved to protect our clients."[13]

---

13 Steve Ekovich, Conference Call, March 12, 2013.

Other valuation methods are net income multipliers and gross income multipliers, which are appropriate for clubs with weak or negative margins. The gross income multiple is a more accurate barometer. Many buyers know exactly the investment required to operate the club. Thus, based on their confidence levels, they can determine the appropriate investment that will generate a profit.

For those golf courses where net income is being generated, the 2013 SGA Survey reports "the average Net Income Multiplier (the inverse of the Cap Rate) at 8.1, is comparable to the 2011 average of 7.9." Where a gross income multiplier is used, the following benchmarks serve as reference points.

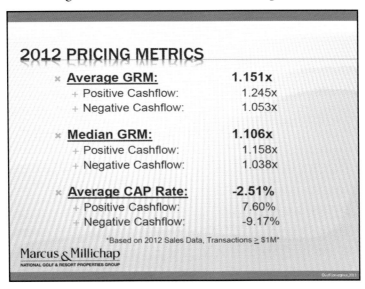

Other relevant benchmarks in determining the value of a golf course, as published in the 2013 Society of Golf Appraisers survey,[14] included those listed below.

Benchmark	Current Index
The average management fee	3.6% of gross income
Capital reserves / allowances (excluding equipment leases)	3.0%
The average time a golf course remained on the market	12.2 months, representing a 2-month+ decline compared to the 2012 average of 14.5 months
Broker commissions averaged	3.5%
Average lending interest rate	7.4%
Prime lending rate	3.5%
Average debt coverage ratio	1.41
Average loan to value	63.0%

---

14 http://www.golfappraisers.org/

To participate in or to subscribe to the SGA's Investor & Lender Survey, go to www.golfappraisers.org. By frequenting that site or by contacting Marcus and Millichap, you can remain current on industry lending and real estate transaction benchmarks.

The Process

Though not used in determining value for real estate transactions, two benchmarks serve as an effective frame of reference as to the size and scope of a potential transaction: cost and replacement value.

When asked what it costs to build a golf course, the first question that must be addressed is, "What component?" The construction budget, land costs, water sources, power, clubhouse, parking, maintenance building, and the cost to grow the course between seeding and opening; these are the principal components. Add the variables of the types of soil (sandy sites are less expensive), clearing and earth moving on the site, irrigation requirements, and the owner's vision for the course. With 140 to 180 acres of land being used to build a course, the cost of building a golf course can vary widely.

The American Society of Golf Course Architects[15] advised those desiring to build a course to proceed as follows:

1. Ascertain project feasibility
2. Choose an Architect
3. Site Selection
4. Land Planning
5. Land Entitlement

6. Financing
7. Construction Documents

8. Course Construction
9. Course Maintenance
10. Ownership and Operation

---

15 http://www.asgca.org/course-design

The process from concept to first tee shot can take more than two years: 6 to 12 months for permits, 3 months to select a contractor through a bid process, and 6 to 12 months to grow in the course before it can be opened.

The cost per hole can vary from $50,000 to more than $175,000 for some upscale courses. The Golf Course Builders Association of America has constructed a cost template that will estimate the cost of the following: a full 18-hole renovation, a USGA green surface renovation, tee renovation, bunker renovation, irrigation renovation, and the cost to build a new golf course, as shown in the following figure.

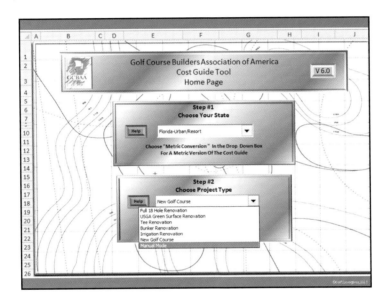

This template can be purchased at www.gcbaa.org for $100. It was crafted based on a member survey. Recognizing the varying soil conditions and geographic climates in which a course might be constructed in the United States, it segments the estimated cost by 84 different regions (for instance, Oregon coast, Oregon resort, and Oregon rural).

The template provides for the manual entry of other estimated costs, such as sediment traps, practice range netting, builder's risk insurance, growth in costs, architectural fees, restroom facilities, engineering fees, demolition of existing buildings, maintenance facilities, maintenance equipment, sand capping import, and topsoil import.

The estimated cost to build a new course in the United States is about $8 million as illustrated on the next page.

Category	Amount
Mobilization	$117,059
Clearing	285,000
Existing Grass Removal	221,400
Earthwork/Excavation	732,500
Shaping	185,000
Drainage	318,625
Storm Drainage	300,000
Irrigation System	2,343,000
Greens Construction	503,400
Tee Construction	402,575
Bunker Construction	445,825
Cart Path Construction	577,875
Seed/Bed Preparation	315,000
Soil Amendments	101,250
Grassing	504,230
Specialist Items	168,750
Miscellaneous	399,500
Subtotal	7,920,989
Bonding	79,209
Total	$8,000,188

In undertaking a feasibility study, incorporating this forecasting tool is invaluable. The line-item detail the template provides is superlative; it provides for an additional line-item entry to allow the analyst to create a customized forecast, and it quickly summarizes the estimated costs, as shown in the following figure.

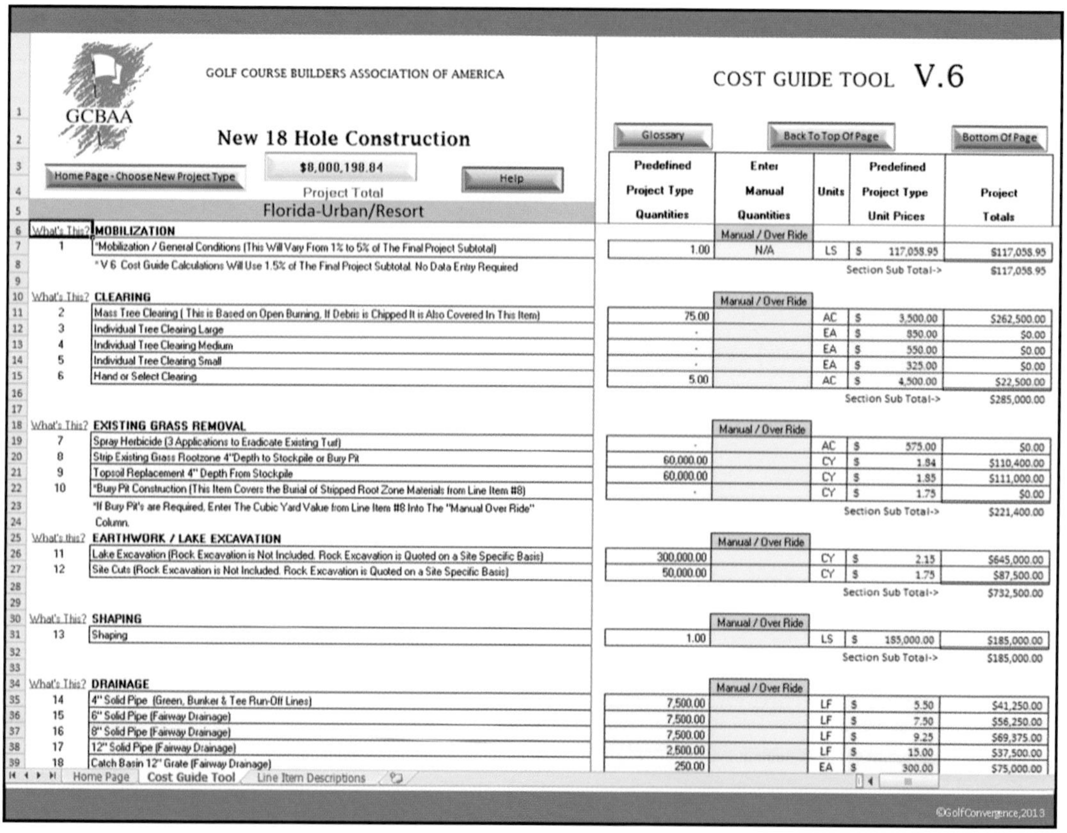

GOLF COURSE BUILDERS ASSOCIATION OF AMERICA

GCBAA

New 18 Hole Construction

$8,000,198.84

Home Page - Choose New Project Type

Project Total

Florida-Urban/Resort

COST GUIDE TOOL **V.6**

Glossary | Back To Top Of Page | Bottom Of Page

Help

			Predefined Project Type Quantities	Enter Manual Quantities	Units	Predefined Project Type Unit Prices	Project Totals
		MOBILIZATION		Manual / Over Ride			
7	1	*Mobilization / General Conditions (This Will Vary From 1% to 5% of The Final Project Subtotal)	1.00	N/A	LS	$ 117,058.95	$117,058.95
8		*V 6 Cost Guide Calculations Will Use 1.5% of The Final Project Subtotal. No Data Entry Required				Section Sub Total->	$117,058.95
10		**CLEARING**		Manual / Over Ride			
11	2	Mass Tree Clearing (This is Based on Open Burning. If Debris is Chipped It is Also Covered In This Item)	75.00		AC	$ 3,500.00	$262,500.00
12	3	Individual Tree Clearing Large	.		EA	$ 850.00	$0.00
13	4	Individual Tree Clearing Medium	.		EA	$ 550.00	$0.00
14	5	Individual Tree Clearing Small	.		EA	$ 325.00	$0.00
15	6	Hand or Select Clearing	5.00		AC	$ 4,500.00	$22,500.00
16						Section Sub Total->	$285,000.00
18		**EXISTING GRASS REMOVAL**		Manual / Over Ride			
19	7	Spray Herbicide (3 Applications to Eradicate Existing Turf)	.		AC	$ 575.00	$0.00
20	8	Strip Existing Grass Rootzone 4"Depth to Stockpile or Bury Pit	60,000.00		CY	$ 1.84	$110,400.00
21	9	Topsoil Replacement 4" Depth From Stockpile	60,000.00		CY	$ 1.85	$111,000.00
22	10	*Bury Pit Construction (This Item Covers the Burial of Stripped Root Zone Materials from Line Item #8)	.		CY	$ 1.75	$0.00
23		*If Bury Pit's are Required, Enter The Cubic Yard Value from Line Item #8 Into The "Manual Over Ride" Column.				Section Sub Total->	$221,400.00
25		**EARTHWORK / LAKE EXCAVATION**		Manual / Over Ride			
26	11	Lake Excavation (Rock Excavation is Not Included. Rock Excavation is Quoted on a Site Specific Basis)	300,000.00		CY	$ 2.15	$645,000.00
27	12	Site Cuts (Rock Excavation is Not Included. Rock Excavation is Quoted on a Site Specific Basis)	50,000.00		CY	$ 1.75	$87,500.00
28						Section Sub Total->	$732,500.00
30		**SHAPING**		Manual / Over Ride			
31	13	Shaping	1.00		LS	$ 185,000.00	$185,000.00
32						Section Sub Total->	$185,000.00
34		**DRAINAGE**		Manual / Over Ride			
35	14	4" Solid Pipe (Green, Bunker & Tee Run-Off Lines)	7,500.00		LF	$ 5.50	$41,250.00
36	15	6" Solid Pipe (Fairway Drainage)	7,500.00		LF	$ 7.50	$56,250.00
37	16	8" Solid Pipe (Fairway Drainage)	7,500.00		LF	$ 9.25	$69,375.00
38	17	12" Solid Pipe (Fairway Drainage)	2,500.00		LF	$ 15.00	$37,500.00
39	18	Catch Basin 12" Grate (Fairway Drainage)	250.00		EA	$ 300.00	$75,000.00

Home Page | Cost Guide Tool | Line Item Descriptions

©GolfConvergence,2013

The typical golf course generates slightly more than $1 million in revenue, with about $150,000 in earnings before interest, taxes, depreciation, and amortization. The cost of new course construction has accelerated to $8 million, even before considering the cost of the clubhouse and land. If for no other reason than the growing cost, it is understandable that new course construction in the United States has ground to a halt.

It should be noted that costs vary around the world. Golf course architecture firm Turner Macpherson, based in New Zealand, estimates that the minimum cost for a golf course is $521,000, the average cost is $2,218,000, and the cost to build an upscale course would be about $5,914,000.

In any event, owning a golf course is not for the faint of heart.

Path to Success

The focus of this chapter has been to demonstrate how golf course owners can maximize their return in the short term. Only by properly managing the business in the short term is its long-term value maximized, and that value is determined only when the golf course is sold.

A golf course owner should always have an exit strategy, even if he or she never plans on using it. Whether it be to sell the golf course to another operator or to a real estate or commercial office park developer, knowing the alternative that will produce the highest investment return is advised.

Knowing the value of your golf course provides a useful snapshot of the current financial health of the course, what options it has, and how it can improve in the long term. Evaluation of your golf course is, in essence, a reality check.

The value of the golf course can be determined much more accurately if the owner keeps a frequent tally of the market. A golf course appraisal can cost from $5,000 to $50,000, while the cost of a strategic plan starts at $20,000. Both services will generate five-year cash flow forecasts from which the owner will have the fundamental benchmarks to determine an appropriate value for the golf course.

This is an exercise that golf course management should undertake at least once every five years, whether for a municipal course, a daily fee course, or a private club.

Concluding Thought

Pay no attention to what the critics say. A statue has never been erected in honor of a critic.

Jean Sibelius

SECTION 3

Operational Execution
Chapters 12 through 18

From a board overview of the golf industry in Section 1, we transitioned in Section 2 to understanding the numbers at a golf course, as well as learning how to increase and maximize revenue, increase operational efficiency, and enhance customer service.

In Section 3, we narrow the focus even more to the golf course itself, its daily operations, and the golfers. The factors that influence the financial success of a golf course are as follows:

12. The Playing Field: Architecture, Agronomy and Maintenance

13. Marketing

14. Game Time Objectives

15. Customer Preferences

16. Customer Loyalty

17. Customers: A Future Perspective

18. Applying the Lessons Learned

There are three classes of people: those who see, those who see when they are shown, those who do not see.

Leonardo Da Vinci

Chapter 12

The Playing Field
Step 5 of the Golf Convergence WIN™ Formula

A championship course is not a championship course until a championship has been played upon it.

Michael Bonallack, former Secretary of the Royal and Ancient Golf Club of St. Andrews and five-time British Amateur Champion

Golf is not a fair game, so why build a course fair?

Pete Dye, Golf Course Architect

Chapter Highlights

There are 33,331 canvases of golf art in the world—golf courses created by artists who saw a vision of how to transform the land to entertain. No two canvases are the same.

But unlike the great art works of the world that are on display in the Louvre, the Metropolitan, the Tate, the Uffizi, or the Prado, golf courses are in need of daily maintenance. They are living organisms with personalities of their own, and they change day by day.

That leads to the question, What is the next evolution in golf course design likely to be? More importantly, how are these works of art to be preserved, protected and maintained? Should a course evolve, as the trees grow and stream banks change, or would it be better to restore each course to its original design?

That question becomes complicated, because as golf equipment changes, the experience changes, and what was safe and enjoyable may now be hazardous. What are we to do?

The Last Round

If you had only one more round of golf to play, where would you tee it up and with whom?

While many would answer with the name of a famous course that they always longed to play (Pebble Beach, Augusta National, St. Andrews, or Pine Valley), and some might say they'd want to be joined by celebrities as playing partners, in a poll conducted by *Golf Magazine*, we recall that 25% answered that they'd want to play the course that they grew up on and play with family.

That answer speaks to the core of the connection between golfers and the course, of the bond that is formed.

Golf is a game of evolution; in architecture, in equipment, and in the cost of maintaining the playing field. It is this evolution that we celebrate. In Chapter 2, we detailed the 15,647 golf courses in the United States. For comparison purposes, to illustrate that golf playing fields evolve nearly identically from country to country, presented to the left are the playing fields in Canada: 2,310 courses. The distribution between 9-hole, 18-hole, and 27+-hole golf courses is quite comparable to the United States.

PROVINCIAL	Public/Semi-Private/Resort	Private	9 holes	18 holes	27+ holes
British Columbia	297	14	117	176	18
Alberta	291	22	127	163	23
Saskatchewan	162	3	108	51	6
Manitoba	126	7	72	57	4
Ontario	715	126	250	484	107
Quebec	331	36	96	215	56
New Brunswick	55	1	19	34	3
Nova Scotia	68	4	24	45	3
PEI	30	0	12	17	1
Newfoundland	21	1	9	10	3
	2,096	214	834	1252	224

©GolfConvergence,2014

The Evolution of Architecture

The course is like a painting created by an architect in concert with construction teams who blend the green grasses with the blue water features, the white sand bunkers, the flowers with their different hues, and the trees that change colors throughout the season, creating a picture of unparalleled beauty. Golfers who take the time to appreciate their surroundings see a kaleidoscope that is constantly changing. A golf course can be like a walk through a botanical garden, not just "a good walk spoiled," as Mark Twain supposedly said. Golf wraps together nature, friends, and competition.

Over the years, the artistic interpretations of golf course design have evolved like the ever-changing styles of popular art that have defined periods in history: the Renaissance (1400–1600), Baroque (1600–1700), Rococo (1700–1750s), Neo-Classicism (1750–1880), Realism (1830s–1850s), Impressionism (1870s–1890s), Modernism (1880–1945), Abstract Expressionism (1945–1960), New Realism (1970–1980), Neo-Expressionism (1980–1990), and Computer Art (1980s–1990)[1] as part of the modern era.

Today, the style of golf course architecture that is in vogue features the following:

- Minimalist Design (natural and sustainable types of golf courses sporting strategic and playability options)
- Bunkers with fescue and Scottish broom
- Shots repelled from perched greens
- Closely cropped chipping areas
- Massive greens with many undulations and few areas for pin locations

These modern preferences make us wonder what were the primary factors influencing the architects as they crafted the works of their day. Golf courses in the United States were built as shown in the following figure.

As these courses were built, what defined their style?

What was the land like, the functionality of the construction equipment available, the performance characteristics of the clubs and balls, the architect's ego, his understanding of the purpose of the game, or her belief in what the golfers were seeking in terms of entertainment and sport?

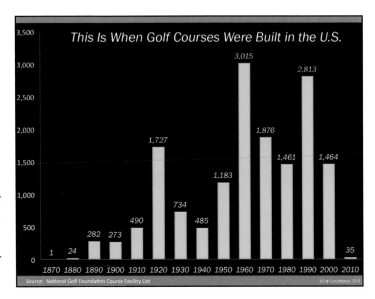

This Is When Golf Courses Were Built in the U.S.

Source: National Golf Foundation Course Facility List

---

1 http://www.arthistoryguide.com/

Was the modern era that introduced the aerial game and golf courses of grand style and length the architects' response to the growing abilities of golfers, the advances in equipment, the failure of the USGA to properly define the game, or a reflection of society and its self-indulgence?

The evolving styles in golf architecture in the United States are fascinating. Shown here is a chart representing the growth of the game in the United States by decade and the unique styles of 16 architects subjectively chosen by Bradley Klein, noted golf historian and frequent author, and by me. We chose some who painted their canvases differently than did their peers, some whose vision was clear, and some whose enlightened understanding of the game represented the sport for what it is meant to be: entertainment. Joe Passov, *Golf Magazine* Travel Editor, summarized the artistic style of each in five words or less.

The Influential Artists of Golf Course Architecture

	Courses	Era	Joe Passov, Golf Magazine Travel Editor
Donald Ross	382	1890s-1940s	Strategic, Natural Designs, Domed Greens
Robert Trent Jones Sr.	226	1930s-1990s	Heroic Design, Emphasized Aerial Game
Jack Nicklaus	213	1970s--	Hard appraoches, later designs softer
Thomas Fazio	201	1970s--	Gorgeously shaped, few perpendicular hazards
Geoff Cornish	159	1940s-1990s	Playable, handsome designs, modest budgets
Pete Dye	136	1960s--	Dramatic, sharp-edged, retro-British brutes
Tom Benedelow	98	1890s -1930s	Unsophisticated, Brought Golf to Masses
A.W. Tillinghast	86	1900s-1930s	Artfully sculpted bunkers and greens
Dick Wilson	49	1940s-1960s	Blend of strategy and forced carries
C.B.Macdonald & Seth Raynor	80	1890s-1920s	British template holes, geometric patterns
Willie Park Jr.	33	1890s-1920s	Pioneered natural, strategic inland designs
Tom Doak	27	1980s --	Angles, contour, imaginative green complexes
Coore and Crenshaw	24	1980s --	Modern minimalism, ground game emphasis
Alister MacKenzie	18	1900s-1930s	Subtlety, deception, multiple approach routes
Gil Hanse	14	1990s --	Superior shaping in the field

Source: National Golf Foundation Course Facility List – Courses built by Architects   ©Golf Convergence, 2013

Note: Number of courses pursuant to NGF Golf Supply Report.

According to the NGF Supply Report, of the 17,816 golf courses built in America since the first course was built in 1870:

- An architect is not identified with 4,321 of the courses.
- There are 775 18-hole golf courses of less than 5,000 yards.
- There are roughly 1,698 "unique" individuals designated as being golf course architects.
- Courses that are identified as having been built or renovated by members of the American Society of Golf Course Architects number 5,386.

- 9,942 of the 17,816 courses built in the U.S. have been renovated at some time.

- Forty-seven architects are responsible for constructing 25.8% (4,038) of all golf courses in the United States.

Although many of these architects are respected and admired for their work, lists that reward their designs provoke debate. These include rankings such as the "Top 100 Golf Courses" as ranked by leading golf periodicals. But the lists are informative and entertaining for many of us.

Those who discuss what makes a great architect would likely never reach a consensus. If you can play a course and name its architect by the style of the course, is that good or bad? Should the signature of an individual be so pronounced as to transcend the experience, or can that signature define the experience?

For me, the opportunity to play any of Seth Raynor's courses, with their fascinating green complexes, is always a treat, one that includes trying to understand the riddle of the green's function in relationship to the approach shot value to the hole. But all in all, his courses create an enjoyable experience.

In contrast, it might be debated that the work of Mike Stranz, who died in 2005 at the age of 55, was one of the Top 10 architects of all time, because each project he completed was so vastly different in form and function: Caledonia Golf and Fish Club (South Carolina), True Blue (South Carolina), Bulls Bay (South Carolina), Tobacco Road (North Carolina), Tot Hill Farm (North Carolina), Royal New Kent (Virginia), Stonehouse (Virginia), Silver Creek Valley (California), and Monterey Peninsula Country Club–Shore Course (California). The ability to craft something so vastly different each time is a testament to an architect's creativity.

The cost to maintain a golf course has evolved based on changes in design, construction, and grassing. What golf historian, Bradley S. Klein, wrote a decade ago remains insightful today:

> "In earlier years, if the proposed sites proved unsuitable, the architect would select an adjoining parcel. Older, traditional layouts were done by handwork and by animal drawn labor. Little earth moving was

possible, and the occasional blind shot was accepted as a sporting part of the game.

Features were built from existing grade, with putting surfaces 'pushed up' from native soil. Routings—the sequence of holes—were intimate and easily walkable owing to the close proximity of greens to tees. Real estate and cart paths were non-factors. No ground needed to be bypassed because no regulatory agencies controlled wetlands (they were called 'swamps' back then) and developers were free to drain or fill them.

The design business changed rapidly around 1960. That's when national television, Arnold Palmer, bulldozers, and suburban real estate helped reshape the golf market. Robert Trent Jones, Sr. led the way in creating new designs that favored power golf, the aerial game, and the deployment of bunkering on the flanks of holes rather than diagonally or in the middle of fairways.

At the same time, the U.S. Golf Association Green Section introduced a more technically sophisticated method of layered greens construction that enabled a new generation of fine-bladed bent grasses and Bermuda grasses to survive on greens at lower cutting heights than were imaginable two decades earlier.

Soon, wetlands were granted protected status, so the permitting process took considerable more time and land formerly usable for golf had to be circumvented. Architects found a solution to this routing problem in the form of the golf cart and tee-to-green paved paths. By the 1990's, anything was possible, a trend typified by the 'heaven and earth' approach of Fazio, Pete Dye and Jack Nicklaus, who were not averse to moving millions of tons of earth in the course of creating layouts on land ill-suited to building a golf course.

In recent years, the Modern Era has seen the rise of an alternative model of architecture that evokes traditional design principles. These courses are built with high-tech machinery and maintained with state-of-the-art, multi-row irrigation systems and small hydraulic mowing units. And yet they look decades old."[2]

---

2 Bradley S. Klein, *Golfweek*, "A Matter of Rank: Restorations, Renovations Prominent in Courses' Upward Movement," March 1, 2003, pg. 32.

The Evolution of Golf Equipment

One of things presumed in designing or renovating a golf course, but rarely expressed, certainly not among the players, is the influence of today's golf equipment on new course construction and renovations with respect to the safety of the players.

Golf course architects create safety corridors for each hole which start at the tee and encompass an area on either side of the fairway centerline and continue to beyond the green.

Kevin Norby, Principal of Herfort-Norby Architectural firm, in being interviewed for this book, wrote,

> "As golf course architects, we need to consider not only the safety of other golfers but also safety as it relates to surrounding properties.
>
> In the 1990s, we were designing golf holes with landing areas at 250 yards off the back tees of most public golf courses. Today, we are typically positioning landing areas at 270 to 310 yards from the back tees.
>
> It is my belief that, not only are today's golfers bigger and stronger than 20 years ago, but the impact which technology has had on the game is profound. Today's golfers are not only hitting the ball further but they are hitting the ball further off line. As a result, golf course architects today are being forced to design courses with increasingly wider corridors to insure public safety.
>
> So, on a perfectly straight par 5 hole, a safety corridor might total some 350 to 400 feet wide. Beginning at the tee, that corridor extends approximately 100 feet either side of the middle of the tee and widens until it becomes some 170 to 200 feet wide on each side of the landing area in the fairway—usually 250 yards from the tee. To measure that another way, we use an angle of 15 degrees off of the centerline.
>
> From the landing area, the 100 feet corridor continues up both sides of the fairway towards the green and parallel to the fairway centerline. The safety corridor should continue beyond the center of the green some 150 feet depending on the length of the hole. For a par three, the distance might be somewhat less, while for a par four or par five, more distance is required to account for shots over the green.

There are a number of other factors that can influence the width of the corridor, including the length of the hole, topography, elevation, prevailing winds, and the presence or lack of trees and vegetation.

In addition, on a dogleg par four or par five, we need to consider the possibility that there may be an alternative line of play that differs from the intended line of play. Also, since the majority of golfers are right-handed and since the majority of golfers tend to slice the ball, we typically increase the width of the safety corridor on the right hand side of the fairway.

Every situation is different but it's possible to have corridors in excess of 400 feet—particularly on short par fours or par fives where the golfer may not exercise good judgment."[3]

It should be emphasized that there are many variables and that it is impossible to design a golf course which accounts for every conceivable poorly struck golf shot. In addition, many older golf courses have holes with corridors which are much narrower than these guidelines would suggest. As technology continues to impact and change the game, many courses will need to adapt or face growing concern for public safety.

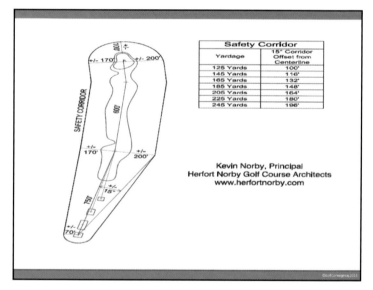

Safety Corridor	
Yardage	15' Corridor Offset from Centerline
125 Yards	100'
145 Yards	116'
165 Yards	132'
185 Yards	148'
205 Yards	164'
225 Yards	180'
245 Yards	196'

Kevin Norby, Principal
Herfort Norby Golf Course Architects
www.herfortnorby.com

Shown here is Herfort Norby's current representation of appropriate safety corridors for golf courses.

A recurring theme throughout this book is that golf courses should be shorter. Safety is certainly one important factor that leads to this conclusion.

Another important factor is cost savings. In a survey done on 26 golf courses in Melbourne, Australia, it was confirmed that "the cost of maintaining the golf course increases by about 2% percent for

---

3 Kevin Norby and Herfort Norby, "Safety Corridors for Today's Golf Courses," email, March 15, 2013.

each 100 meters of additional length, which is about the distance of two 'extra' holes."[4]

Conversely, if courses were shorter, savings would be likely. Jeff Brauer, ASGCA, President of GolfScapes, believes, "It may be time for golf courses to re-think the one-size-fits-all mentality moving forward. If we admit that we have all the championship courses we need for the 40-something men's pro tournaments annually, we would nicely accommodate more than 97% of the players on courses with maximum yardage of about 6,800 yards. In this age of belt tightening, wasting resources on so few in so many places just doesn't make sense."[5]

Kevin Norby agrees: "Today, we have plenty of 7,000-yard courses. What we really need are shorter courses that appeal to the average golfer. These shorter courses are not only less expensive to maintain and less expensive to build, but they take less time to play. Often, that translates into a course that is more affordable for the golfer and more profitable for the owner."[6]

The Acceleration of Costs

The acceleration of costs in maintaining a golf course to the level shown on television, with lush manicured fairways and slick putting surfaces, is a formula that, if it is followed by the vast majority of golf course owners, is sure to lead to diminished profits.

It is always folly to listen to a superintendent boast that the stimpmeter readings (device used to measure the speed of a golf course putting green by applying a known force to a golf ball and measuring the distance traveled in feet[7]) is approaching 13 feet or U.S. Open conditions. When single-digit handicap golfers create a local rule that that the third putt is automatically conceded (on a Nebraska course that featured severely contoured greens that were maintained at U.S. Open speed), the architect and the superintendent failed to grasp why people play golf. Only a small portion of golfers are into masochism and sadism, and appealing to that element will not produce profits.

---

4 Jeffrey D. Brauer, "Golf Course Industry.com: Should Future Courses Be Shorter?," June 2010, pg. 26.

5 Ibid., pg. 26.

6 Kevin Norby, email May 2, 2013.

7 http://en.wikipedia.org/wiki/Stimpmeter

What is ironic is that there is a "correct" speed for every golf course. Armen Suny, consultant at Castle Pines Golf Club and partner in the architectural firm of Suny-Zokol, believes that you merely need to go to the most severe pin placement. After mowing, measure the green speed. If a ball on the stimpmeter doesn't stop with three feet of the cup, the green speed is too quick.

Suny continued, saying, "Most golf course architects are missing the single most important facet of golf course design—golfers. Anyone can create a golf experience that is extremely difficult; it takes little skill to do that and has been part of the ruination of our sport ever since Pete Dye popularized the notion that difficult equates to great. What takes skill is to embrace golfers of all skill levels while challenging the best."[8]

What is for sure is that when golfers are polled on the criteria for selecting a golf course, conditioning always ranks among the highest attributes. And the investment to maintain the course annually, as shown here,[9] contains many elements that vary greatly based on geographic location.

	18 Hole Facilities			18 Hole + Facilities		
	PUBLIC	PRIVATE	ALL	PUBLIC	PRIVATE	ALL
Total Maintenance Budget	458,071	848,961	651,392	1,173,164	1,752,183	1,387,918
Line Item Components:						
Water	12,484	20,390	16,499	27,387	50,884	36,258
Fuel	22,260	33,876	28,174	40,161	5,925	47,401
Mowing Equipment	25,335	50,649	37,644	70,484	105,303	82,464
Handheld Equipment	1,702	4,419	3,066	3,187	6,331	4,345
Course Accessories	3,804	5,294	4,561	5,182	8,963	6,550
Electricity and Natural Gas	17,990	20,088	19,046	35,238	46,537	39,357
Shop tools	1,878	3,284	2,568	3,482	7,922	4,962
Irrigation Parks, heads and maintenance	5,948	9,876	7,918	12,904	16,741	14,409
Fungicidies	22,163	44,476	33,461	40,821	58,461	47,251
Herbicides - Preemergent	5,109	7,603	6,369	11,854	22,308	15,787
Herbicides - Post emergent	3,613	4,144	3,869	5,221	10,577	7,269
Insecticides	3,694	6,570	5,141	8,128	14,883	10,645
Granular fertizlizers	15,203	20,244	17,723	31,472	48,368	37,587
Liquid fertilizers	7,315	13,088	10,231	12,903	20,635	15,736
Wetting agents	3,129	5,669	4,399	6,113	7,854	6,764
Plant Growth regulators	4,309	5,982	511	5,122	12,905	8,140
Seed	4,127	5,138	4,620	10,639	10,637	10,638
Aquatic weed contro/water quality issues	1,635	2,145	1,890	2,754	4,385	3,370
Total Line Item Components	160,063	260,790	205,800	330,298	455,234	395,563

©GolfConvergence 2013

Go

Benchmarking Barometer: It is recommended that you review your golf course's maintenance budget by general ledger account compared to the *Golf Course Industry* survey. The entire survey provides insights on the top budget challenges: labor budgets, staffing levels, capital budgets, the use of generic products versus brand-name products, over-seeding practices, equipment, leasing, and golf carts.

---

8 Armen Suny, "Email to Author," March 21, 2013.

9 Golf Course Industry, "How Do You Measure Up?," February 2012, pg. 19.

An annual survey by *Golf Course Industry Magazine* survey pointed out three challenges facing the industry: The costs of fuel, energy, and electricity are uncontrollable.

Demonstrating that all golf solutions are local, water is a significant uncontrollable cost throughout the Midwest, the Rocky Mountain region, and the southwestern part of the U.S. Water costs are a factor in many golf courses losing money. Water conservation, turf disease, overseeding, lake levels, stressed turf, pipe breaks, electricity costs, run-off, weather, overspray, mowing patters, quality of cut, height of cut, water quality, weeds, grow-in, and tree limbs can all affect the quality of turf conditions.

Shown is the water expense for the seven-course city of Aurora, Colorado, golf course operation.

Water: Uncontrollable Expense Contributes to Losses

Aurora Golf System
Water / Irrigation Use and Expense 2010

Course	System Type	Irrigated Acres	Total Water Expense	Water Type	Water Rate	Total Annual Use (gallons)	Annual Gallons per Acre	Annual Water Expense per Acre	Key Improvement Recommendation
Saddle Rock	VIH	105	$182,580	Surface	$2.96	61,682,432	587,452	$1,739	Native
Murphy Creek	VIH	160	$206,643	Re-Use	$1.77	116,747,458	729,672	$1,292	Heads, Native
Meadow Hills	Block	115	$252,423	Surface	$2.96	85,278,041	741,548	$2,195	Lining, Heads, New
Aurora Hills	VIH	140	$144,032	Re-Use	$1.77	81,374,011	581,243	$1,029	Native
Fitzsimons	Block	80	$109,422	Re-Use	$1.77	61,820,339	772,754	$1,368	Native, Heads
Springhill	Block	76	$72,299	Re-Use	$1.77	40,846,893	537,459	$951	Native, New
Centre Hills	Block	27	$12,083	Re-Use	$1.77	6,826,554	252,835	$448	New
		703	$979,482					$1,393	

Abbreviations: VIH = Valve in Head; Native = Expand native (un-irrigated) areas, Heads = Upgrade irrigation heads to allow for better central control of areas to be irrigated; Lining = Line the lakes and ponds on property to reduce seepage loss; New = Replacement of irrigation with newer system

The city is paying a very expensive $1.77 per thousand gallons to an unsustainable $2.96 per thousand gallons for water. The financial impact of that expense on Aurora's financial statements is quite obvious when contrasted to the neighboring six-course municipality, the City and County of Denver.

Category	City of Aurora	City & County–Denver
Revenue	$8,655,710	$8,874,230
Expenses	8,966,425	7,795,455
Net Income	−310,715	1,078,775
Water Cost	979,482	371,693

What are the alternatives? First, education; understanding how much water is actually consumed by a golf course. The cost is usually per thousand gallons. Typical water use for a golf course would be determined as follows.

Category	Typical Golf Course
Gallons per Acre Feet	325,891
Cost per Thousand	$1.20
Gallons Used Daily by Golf Course	480,000
Cost per Day	576.00
Days Course Watered	220
Playable Days	280
Annual Water Cost	$126,720

That is expensive when you consider that the gross revenue for municipal golf courses slightly exceeds $1 million. It should be noted that some southwest U.S. golf courses utilize nearly 500 acre feet (162,945,500 gallons) of water per year to irrigate.

Here is where an ounce of prevention is worth a pound of cure.

Weather Trends International has a FREE weather alert service (wt360.com), as illustrated in Chapter 5. Its customizable templates allow the user to define the period (0 to 24 hours, 1 to 14 days, 15 to 335 days) as well as the various weather criteria, such as maximum temperature, minimum temperature, rainfall, snow-fall, wind, etc. When the forecast is beyond the parameters defined by the golf course, a text message is sent from Weather Trends International alerting you to changing weather conditions.

If a golf superintendent knew, for instance, that within 24 hours, the course would receive two inches of rain, the decision would be to save as much as $576 by not dropping 400,000 gallons of water on the course overnight.

To Preserve and Protect: Agronomy 101

Also, there are very sophisticated irrigation control systems that can monitor the amount of water the soil needs to remain healthy via weather stations, pump stations, sprinklers, intelligent field controls, and soil sensors. An example is shown at the top of the next page.

The importance of water conservation cannot be understated. First, because it is a precious resource, conserving water is environmentally appropriate. Of equal importance, water's escalating costs in many parts of the United States has the risk of financially undermining many courses.

To help the industry gain a deeper understanding of energy and water efficiency in golf, Staples Golf created the "The Energy Snapshot™." This iPad tool provides golf courses a complete analysis of their energy and water bills. It uses a survey-style layout with a series of questions about energy and water use on your golf course. The Energy Snapshot™ for Golf automatically calculates the overall efficiency of a course and provides a "Snapshot" PDF report of your potential dollar savings in both energy and water costs. The report includes the following:

1. Overall opportunity for energy and water use reduction (Low, Medium, High)

2. Estimated savings in dollars for both energy and water costs

3. Estimated reduction of carbon emissions

4. General tips on specific steps you can take to immediately begin saving

5. Contact information for Staples Golf to assist in implementation of the savings

The tool can be downloaded at http://staplesgolfdesign.com/ and is illustrated in the figure below.

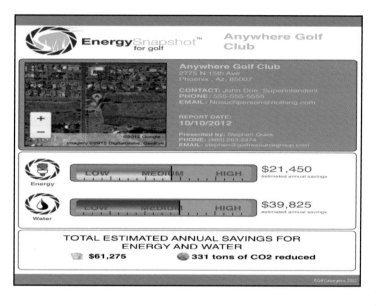

Superintendents are not only the stars of the golf course industry but perhaps the most unheralded group of industry professionals. As a group, their technical knowledge is rooted in chemistry, physics, agronomy, and other scientific disciplines.

One of the lacks in the industry is the understanding of what is required to properly maintain a golf course. Many people outside the industry and probably many golfers water their lawns, see the grass grow, and mow it. Such a simple process, it seems. Not really.

Leaves of grass collect energy from sunlight through photosynthesis, a chemical process that converts carbon dioxide into organic compounds using the energy from sunlight. The photosynthesizing **chlorophyll** in the leaf gives grass its green color.

Attend a Golf Industry Show and see how many different types of grass seed there are and the growing characteristics of each. Golf courses can have many different types of grasses with wildly varying growing tendencies.

There are two major methods of reproduction in grasses. Some grasses have additional stems that grow sideways, either below ground or just above it (bent). Stems that creep along the ground are called **stolons**, and stems that grow below ground are called **rhizomes, as follows.**[10]

---

10 http://home.howstuffworks.com/grass.htm

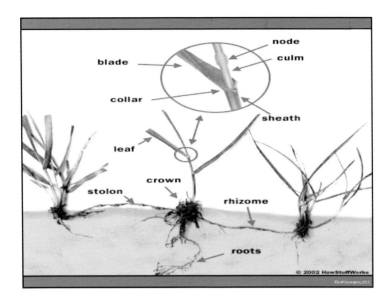

The varieties of grasses used on a golf course are diverse, but each offers different playing characteristics. Illustrated below is a chart highlighting the grasses typically found on golf courses in northern climates.

Feature	Bent	Blue Grass	Fine Fescue	Poa Annua	Poa Triviallis	Rye
Best use	Greens	Fairway	Fairway	Greens	Noxious	Fairway
Color	Gray to Blue green	Mid Green	Dark Green/ Brownish	Light Green	Light Green, shiny	Dark Green Stripe Fairway
Height	.12	.50	.50	.15	.15	.50
Blade	======	||||||||	||||||||	======	======	||||||||
Ball	Tight Lie	Ball Sits Up	Ball Sits Up	Tight Lie	Tight Lie	Ball Sits Up
Strength	Moderate Weak	Strong	Strong	Weak	Weak	Strong
Weather - Hot	Dies	Thrives	Thrives	Struggles, especially if kept wet	Can go off color. Dies.	Thrives
Weather - Cold	OK	Excellent	Dies	OK	OK	OK
Challenges	Crowds out bluegrass in summer	Long germination period	Crowds out bluegrass	Vibrant and patchy	Vibrant and patchy	Crowds out bluegrass

This chart indicates that bent grass greens are a poor choice for courses in the Deep South. The hot weather kills the blades. Courses in transition areas in the country, such as North Carolina, find that bent grass is a preferred putting surface February through June and September through October, but that it often burns out in the height of the summer.

This chart is also a gross oversimplification of the cultivars (grass types) that might be used on a golf course. For bent grass alone, selections for greens, tees, fairways, winter seeding, and overseeding might include a limitless combination of 16 varieties: "Pure select, PureFormance, Crystal Blue Links, Penneagle II, PennLinks II, Penncross Pennway, PennTrio, Pure Distinction, Penn A-1, Penn A-4, Penn G-1, Penn G-2, Penn G-6, Nu-Penn or Seaside."[11]

The goal of a superintendent is to ensure a natural playing surface, whether on greens, fairways, or tees. Every element of a course is fraught with challenges, as shown in the bottom figure on the approach to a green at a Top 200 golf course in the United States.

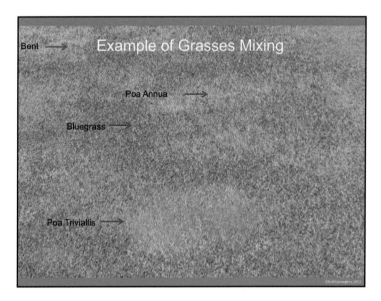

There is always a story. In the case of the grass pictured to the left at this course, the greens were to be bent grass and the fairways Kentucky bluegrass. A collar that was installed around the circumference of the green was insufficient when a heavy rain storm came right after the green was seeded. The seed washed into the fairway, causing the problem noted here.

What's the problem? A club and a ball will react differently based on the grass on which the ball rests. The goal is to provide a consistent playing surface.

Each type of grass reacts differently to the environment. Bent grass thrives with much more water that bluegrass needs. Bluegrass has a 21-day germination period while rye has a 4-day germination period. Which grass would you prefer to plant on a heavily used range? Rye is often the choice for tees and ranges, to facilitate the repair of divots. Poa annua and Poa triviallis are difficult to selectively kill in Kentucky bluegrass and bent grass. Fescue grass uses 80% fewer

---

11 Tee2Green Produce Line.

chemicals than bent. Seaside Paspalum, the drought-resistant strain, thrives on saltwater and provides a surface almost as smooth and fast as bent grass or rye. Bermuda grass is popular in the warmer climates of the southern U.S., due to the fact that its coarser blade provides heat tolerance.

One area of maintenance that significantly affects the quality of the putting surface is thatch. Thatch accumulates on the surface of the soil just below the grass line and usually out of sight, as shown below.

Thatch is described as a "layer of grass stems, roots, clippings, and debris that settles on the ground and either slowly decomposes and/or accumulates over time. Thatch buildup is commonly found on courses where grass has grown tall, mulch is frequently left, and that have never been aerated. Thatch is most common in warm weather and with creeping grasses such as Bermuda, zoysia, bent grass, and Kentucky bluegrass."[12]

To prevent thatch from occurring, golf course superintendents aerate, punching holes in the surface to allow deeper root growth that should reduce soil compaction. Shown at right is an example of a fairway that was verticut in June, 2013.

Once aerated, the root system has better access to air, water, and nutrients. One of the big

---

12 Dawn West, http://www.allaboutlawns.com/lawn-maintenance-care/aerating-and-thatch/what-is-thatch.php

differences in the maintenance practices of low-end courses when compared to elite golf courses is how often they aerate, verticut, and top dress the greens. An elite golf course will top dress bi-weekly and may even drill press the greens annually, removing up to 20% of the underlying surface matter on a green. The goal is to improve the quality of the putting surface and reduce the cost of watering by improving drainage, reducing soil compaction, and controlling thatch development.

Aerating is merely one technique in the arsenal of a superintendent. Fertilizer, herbicides, and pesticides are the magic chemicals that can be used to create great and consistent playing conditions. They are defined as

> "Fertilizer:[13] a chemical or natural substance added to soil or land to increase its fertility.
>
> Herbicide:[14] a substance that is toxic to plants, used to destroy unwanted vegetation.
>
> Pesticide:[15] substance used for destroying insects or other organisms harmful to cultivated plants or to animals."

You can't be around two superintendents for long before one asks the other, "How much 'N' are you dropping on the greens." Nitrogen, phosphorus ("P"), and potassium (K") are the primary ingredients that are mixed and mingled in what seems to a laymen to be a witch's brew to stimulate the growth of grass. Its volume is expressed in pounds, perhaps three pounds per 1,000 square feet. These major nutrients, known as NPK, usually are lacking from the soil as grass requires large amounts for its growth and survival. Each play a major part in the health of turf, described as follows:

> "Nitrogen (N) is a macronutrient and is the basis for proteins which are the molecules within plants that perform photosynthesis, making food for the plants. If plants do not have enough nitrogen, they turn yellow.
>
> Phosphorus (P) is an essential nutrient for plants and is an essential part of the process of photosynthesis growth.
>
> Potassium (K) promotes increased root growth and greening."[16]

Depending on the time of the year and the location of the course, the mixtures can vary. It is fascinating to view field laboratories of agronomists like

---

13 http://oxforddictionaries.com/definition/english/fertilizer?q=fertilizer

14 http://oxforddictionaries.com/definition/english/pesticide?q=herbicide

15 http://oxforddictionaries.com/definition/english/pesticide?q=Pesticide

16 http://www.lawncare.net/nitrogen-fertilizer-for-your-lawn/

Dr. Brian Horgan, a turf grass extension specialist and PhD at the TROE Center (Turfgrass Research, Outreach and Education), at the University of Minnesota, St. Paul. Dr. Horgan maintains a 12-acre plot of ground as a laboratory where he attempts to balance the stimulation of plant growth with the appropriate choices and amounts of fertilizers on the most cost-effective basis.

The faculties at Colorado State, Michigan State, North Carolina State, and many other fine universities have similar programs.

Maintaining a golf course is a challenge. Dr. Horgan's explanation of winter kill is an eye-opener:

> "There are four causes of winter kill: desiccation, low-temperature kill, crown hydration and anoxia. Desiccation, as it implies, is death brought on by exposure to winter winds. Low-temperature kill occurs when plants are exposed to a lethal drop in temperature. With crown hydration, the plant virtually explodes after a snow or ice thaw and suddenly refreezes. And anoxia is the toxic buildup and trapping of poisonous gasses under an impermeable layer, like ice, that kills the plant. Conditions for toxic buildup include shallow frost, warmer soils, long ice cover, and more bug activity."[17]

In the South, the Top 10 weeds include "annual bluegrass, dallisgrass, nutsedges, perennial kyllinyas, non-tuberous sedges, Virginia buttonweed, torpedograss, goosegrass, crabgrass, and doveweed."[18]

Beyond the weeds, there are all kinds of fungal diseases that attack, discolor, and kill grass. On a tour around a golf course, you can often spot many diseases, including those listed in the following table.

Category	Disease	Susceptible Turfgrass
Algae	Algae	All turf grasses
Ectotrophic Root-Infecting Fungi	Necrotic Ring Spot	Bluegrass, Fescue
	Spring Dead Spot	Bermuda grass and buffalo grass
	Summer Patch	Bluegrass, Fescue
	Take-all Patch	Bent grass

(Continued)

17 http://www.mngolf.org/turf_class_with_brian_horgan_ph_d
18 Scott McElroy, Associate Professor, Auburn University, "Control of the Top 10 Most Common and Troublesome Weeds of Southern Grass," http://www.gcsaa.tv/webinars/education/archive-files/tenweeds.wmv

278

Category	Disease	Susceptible Turfgrass
Fairy Rings	Fairy Ring	All warm- and cool-season
	Superficial Fairy Ring	All warm- and cool-season
Mildew Diseases	Powdery Mildew	Bent grass, bluegrass, fescue, ryegrass, Bermuda grass
	Yellow Tuft	All turf
Other Foliar Fungal Diseases	Anthracnose	Bluegrass and creeping bent grass
	Bent grass Dead Spot	Creeping bent grass and Bermuda grass
	Dollar Spot	All warm- and cool-season
	Fusarium Patch	Most species of cool-season turfgrass
	Gray Law Spot	St. Augustine grass, rye grass, fescue and centipede grass
	Leaf Spot/Melting-Out	Red rescue, bluegrass, rye grass, fescue
	Red Thread/Pink Patch	All turf grasses
	Southern Blight	Bent grass, bluegrass, Bermuda grass, rye grass, fescue
Pythium Diseases	Pythium Root Rot	Species grown on putting greens
	Pythium Blight	All turf
Rhizoctonia Diseases	Brown Patch	All warm- and cool-season
	Rhizoctonia Large Patch/Zoysia Patch	Zoysia grass
	Rhizoctonia Leaf and Sheath Spot	All warm- and cool-season
	Yellow Patch	Bent grass, Bluegrass, Rye Grass
Rust and Smut Diseases	Rusts (Crown, Leaf, Stem)	Bluegrass, ryegrass, old bent grass, zoysia grass, Bermuda grass, fescue
	Stripe Smut	Bent grass, Bluegrass, Rye grass
Snow Molds	Gray Snow Mold	All species of cool-season turf grass
	Microdochium Patch	Most species of cool-season turf grass

For the novice, acquiring the knowledge of what is required to run a golf course may be overwhelming.

Drugs That Kill

Even if you understand a little about fertilizers, the language of herbicides spoken by superintendents is truly a foreign language for 95% of others in the industry. And I wouldn't be surprised if there are superintendents who have bobble heads in their offices labeled with the names of the mayor, the city council, the general manager, or the board president. These are the stakeholders most likely to nod as they make a game attempt to understand the language of herbicides.

An imaginary conversation must sound like this:

> "We are doing barricade with beacon with certainty for the roundup and rodeo with lots of tenacity and velocity."

They may as well be talking about bull riders at the fairground getting ready for an upcoming event, and they might add to the herbicide vocabulary by spouting these terms—Foley reels, bed knife, bench settings, and single or double cuts, all part of their foreign language.

Actually, they are merely talking about the brand names of the herbicides and the terminology for the equipment they use to maintain the golf course. Some of their "foreign" words are named and defined.

Chemicals	Purpose
Barricade	Pre-emergent herbicide broadleaf weeds and grassy weeds: crabgrass, goosegrass, and Poa annua
Beacon	Post-emergent grassy and broadleaf weeds for agriculture
Certainty	Post-emergent grassy and broadleaf weeds with excellent control of both purple and yellow nuts edge
Echelon	Pre-emergent control for Poa annua
Primo	The purpose of pre-stress conditioning is to prepare turf grass for extreme conditions before they hit. Using Primo growth regulator prior to the onset of stresses like heat, drought, disease and traffic can strengthen the turf, and therefore allow it to withstand ongoing stresses throughout the season
Rodeo	Top choice for emerged aquatic vegetation control, i.e. cattails. Broad-spectrum grass, broadleaf weed, and brush control
Roundup	The most commonly applied weed killers in use today. These herbicides are used by everyone
Tenacity	Kills creeping bent in bentgrass
Velocity	Velocity can gradually eliminate both Poa annua and Poa trivialis from creeping bent grass at tees and fairways and effectively transition a Poa-dominated mixed stand of turf to pure bentgrass

The top bent grass diseases include dollar spot, brown patch, tracnosis, fairy ring, algae, summer patch, leaf spot, and moss, so maintaining a bent grass golf course can be an expensive endeavor.

Illustrated in the top figure is the impact of using some of these chemicals to restore bluegrass that had become contaminated.

When Poa annua (Kentucky bluegrass) is found to be encroaching on a green, some golf courses try to eradicate the Poa annua, as seen in the bottom figure at a private club that was testing a new fertilizer, POA Cure, in late 2012.

Tenacity – Eight Weeks for Blue Grass to Restore from Bent Contamination With Pre/Post Seeding and Aeration

The licensing requirements to use these herbicides are understandably extensive. But they make us wonder if we have become a society that is so politically correct that we give everyone an equal position on the rostrum, even though many lack the knowledge or the experience to speak.

Speaking against the environment or about liberally drawn environmentally sensitive areas, or listening to the ongoing debate at Sharp Park about protecting a red-legged frog and a garter snake, makes you wonder if have we lost the balance between serving man and protecting the environment.

Perhaps that is so:

"The **Sharp Park Wetlands** are home to the endangered California Red-Legged Frog and San Francisco garter snake, as well as numerous bird species. Unfortunately, in 1931 the City of San Francisco built a golf course on top of the wetlands. The 146-acre golf course has been killing endangered frogs and costing the city's taxpayers money ever since. SAVE THE FROGS!, along with Wild Equity Institute and the Center for Biological Diversity, are calling on the city of San Francisco to turn over Sharp Park to its neighbor, the National Park Service."[19]

The same Web site posted the following:

"SAN FRANCISCO MAYOR GIVES ENDANGERED FROGS THE DEATH SENTENCE

On December 13th, the Board of Supervisors of San Francisco voted 6-5 in favor of legislation to save the Sharp Park Wetlands and the endangered California Red-Legged Frogs that live there. However, on December 19, 2012, the San Francisco Mayor Ed Lee vetoed the legislation after receiving over 4,000 letters from SAVE THE FROGS!"[20]

The environmentalists lost. Should they be held financially liable when they lose these battles for the costs incurred by a city, the hit taken in the brand image of the Alister MacKenzie golf course, and the defendant's legal fees? The answer to that would make for an interesting discussion of the U.S. tort system.

Ironically, the Wild Equity Institute filed a motion requesting the award of $1.3 million in legal fees and were awarded $326,000 on July 1, 2013 even though Judge Illston noted that "Plaintiffs lost every single motion," including a motion for a preliminary injunction to halt golf operations. There is a provision in the Endangered Species Act that authorizes the courts to award legal fees when the court determines such an award to be appropriate. This is a great example of government and the legal system gone amok.

We humorously wonder if such marginal efforts to save the frogs will follow the introduction of the Goosinator.[21] This remote-controlled airplane, after three years of testing, has been introduced as a simulated predator for geese. With goose control taking up an increasingly larger percentage of maintenance

---

19 http://www.savethefrogs.com/actions/sharp-park/index.html

20 http://www.savethefrogs.com/actions/sharp-park/index.html

21 *Avid Golfer Magazine*, "Removing Goose Impediments", April 2003, pg. 9.

budgets as year-round access to grass and water attracts flocks of migrating and residential waterfowl, this device was designed to eliminate the daily clean up required from the average Canadian goose that poops 28 times per day on the course. The Goosinator encourages the geese to fly away rather than consider the golf course their home. Also causing damage to golf courses in Florida are the sandhill cranes.

What is known for sure is that if golfers truly understood the effort that goes into maintaining a golf course, they would be more respectful of it and be willing to pay more for the investment required to maintain it properly.

Go

If you licensed the supplemental template that accompanies this Field book and have yet to open the exercises to calculate deferred capital expenditures, appropriate equipment, and labor budgets, take a moment (1 hour required) to complete these exercises.

Path to Success

The most important asset of a facility is its golf course. It is the reason for being. It is our opinion that the most important employee at the golf course is the superintendent. And the most influential contractor is the architect. If the product isn't created correctly and maintained properly, everything else becomes an uphill battle.

In creating the golf course, there is a legitimate concern for the balance that must be achieved for the trees, animals, birds, etc. with the economic benefits of a golf course and the proactive recreational use of the land versus having it sit idle.

The golf course is a living organism. The course exists as it was designed by the architect only on the day it opens. Thereafter, it is essential that trees are trimmed, that the shapes of the green complexes are preserved, and that bunkers and pond edges are maintained throughout the season.

A great iPod application, Sunseeker can help the superintendent.

This application will show the sunlight that a tee or green will evidence throughout the year and highlight which trees should be trimmed or removed.

The key to success is making the superintendent an active participant in all management and board meetings. From discussing market segmentation, to the customer profile, to marketing, to finances, all management needs to understand and execute the vision of the golf course and its unique niche.

We often brand golf as a multi-million dollar industry focused primarily on professional competition, and certainly the majority of the media's focus is on what is not of great importance for the vast majority of golf course owners and golfers.

With maintenance budgets ranging from under $300,000 to over $3 million for maintaining the same amount of acreage, the money at a golf course is "made in the dirt."

Concluding Thought

Why does the eye see a thing more clearly in dreams than the imagination when awake?

Leonardo da Vinci

Chapter 13

Marketing, the Internet, and Social Media

Step 6 of the Golf Convergence WIN™ Formula

Wear the right costume and the part plays itself.

Ely's Law

Most would prefer to live in familiar misery than unknown hope.

Unknown

Chapter Highlights

Most golf courses market the "what," but few golf courses market the "why." There are so many ways to convey the brand message of a course that many courses use a shotgun approach to marketing, causing their efforts to be diffused and ineffective. The key to marketing is creating a brand impression through a repetitive and consistent message.

This chapter explores the more effective marketing alternatives and provides guidance regarding the application of evolving social media to a golf course's arsenal of marketing tools.

If Not for That, It Would Be This

Marketing is about product, placement (distribution), price, and promotion—the 4 P's of marketing.

The vast majority of golf courses focus on price and overlook promotion, placement, and product, in that descending order.

Rich Katz, Managing Director of Buffalo Communications, summarized it best:

> "Businesses frequently impart too many conflicting messages about their products, services, value proposition, culture and more. Audiences are left feeling burdened and confused. If you can relate, the time is now to develop an easy-to-understand and compelling core message. Identify three simple points of distinction that elevate your brand to world class, and support them with succinct sub-messages and attention-grabbing imagery."[1]

With so many alternatives, all costing time and money, a course often defaults to a shotgun approach of trying too many of the alternatives, as shown below.

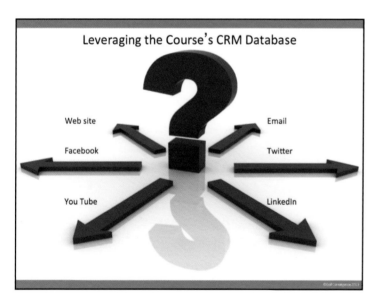

When you add to the mix coupon books, advertising in local and regional golf periodicals, billboards, highway directional signs, radio spots, television promotions, and participation in golf consumer shows, the options become overwhelming. With a limited budget that should equal, but rarely does, 5% of revenue, the disappointing results are not surprising.

The process of marketing begins with the course's name. And, out of the gate, this is where most courses begin their path to failure. The vast majority of

---

1 Email, May 7, 2013, "*Golf-Lifestyle* PR Update," May 2013.

courses are identified by either color, land feature, type of tree, direction, or location, as shown here. It is hard to believe, but true, that 28 words are used to identify 7,176 of the 15,647 golf courses in the United States, as shown in the next figure.

Feature: Color	Frequency	Feature: Direction	Frequency
Green	356	West	186
Black	88	North	142
White	87	South	133
Red	85	East	55
Feature: Land Feature	**Frequency**	**Feature: Tree**	**Frequency**
Hill	1019	Oak	440
Lake	856	Pine	368
Creek	703	Cedar	93
Ridge	507	Willow	92
Valley	496	Maple	49
River	389	Elm	41
Brook	212	Cherry	25
Feature: Animal	**Frequency**	**Feature: Miscellaneous**	**Frequency**
Eagle	165	Old	175
Deer	94	Indian	119
Fox	90	New	105

I can't wait to play Green Valley, Black Lake, West Creek, Pine Ridge, Oak Hill, and Old Eagle. We can hope that the jovial nature of the previous sentence transcends the standard words chosen. Fortunately, so far, Native Americans aren't insisting that golf courses change their names from Arrowhead, Mohawk, or Indian, not unlike the famous university and professional sports team mascots, such as the Florida Seminoles, the Washington Redskins, or the North Dakota Fighting Sioux, who relented to the political pressure to abandon that name. When that name was changed, there was a run on the remaining merchandise to preserve a piece of that school's history. Being politically correct often comes at the expense of overlooking common sense.

Names that convey emotion or images are much more effective at creating interest in a facility. The Bandit, Battenkill, Cape Kidnappers, Coffin, Colonial, French Lick, Galloping Hill, Hermitage, Man of War, Powderhorn, Rainmaker, Sanctuary, Starfire, Tuckaway, Volcano, Wildhorse, and Wizard—all of these are names of golf courses in the United States and all are names that would be likely to entice golfers—site unseen. For a client in Watford, North Dakota, in the heart of the Bakken Oil field play, we suggested changing the course name from Fox Hills to Dakota Gold; this as they expanded from 9 to 18 holes.

Web Site: It Starts Here

In today' electronic world, marketing often starts on a facility's Web site. And that is indeed a great place to craft a compelling "why."

Surprisingly, Walt Disney World's golf-related Web site leads with the "what" on what is, to me, an uninspiring Web site that has a rotating flash banner with innocuous messages. The Disney World "What?" statement is shown here:

> "Walt Disney World has four 18-hole golf courses and one 9-hole golf course on the property. Two great 18-hole architects, Joe Lee and Tom Fazio, will present you with various challenges in design and course strategy on championship caliber courses.
>
> Combined with Disney's world-renowned level of service, you will have a great experience playing these courses, whether staying at a Walt Disney World resort on vacation or for a business trip in the area.
>
> The three Joe Lee courses (the Magnolia, Palm and Lake Buena Vista) harken to the original days of Walt Disney World and more traditional Florida golf course design. Through 2012, the Palm and Magnolia courses hosted an annual PGA Tour professional event in the fall of each year, which had been a part of Disney World golf tradition since 1971.
>
> The Tom Fazio designed Osprey Ridge course brings an updated approach to course design with interesting challenges and elevations in the midst of the more remote parts of the Walt Disney World property."[2]

Can't believe they don't convey the message of "a magical journey through an enchanted forest crafted by the leading wizards of golf course sorcery, Tom Fazio and Joe Lee. While you may be tricked often, Mickey and his friends will ensure that you are charmed and treated to a memorable experience at the Kingdom of entertainment—Disney World."

The "Why?" speaks more to the emotional experience you are likely to feel when playing at a course. The marketing messages by many golf courses are rarely consistent, and they largely represent a "broadcast" message for everyone

---

2 http://www.wdwgolf.com/

to come play our course. Each course is unique and appeals to a narrower set, not to "everyone."

Let's explore possible "why" statements. They might include the following:

A municipal or daily fee course:

Option 1: "We deliver a convenient and affordable recreational experience for those who play just for fun." The subtle message here is that frequent customers who act as though this is their private club should sense the equality in the message and perhaps play elsewhere if they don't want to encounter beginners. And conversely, beginners and many women might feel more welcome reading this "why."

Option 2: "We are here to provide a cauldron to allow you to learn how good you are at golf and how you much you appreciate the traditions of the game." This would be appropriate wording for a course with a slope rating greater than 140. The subtle message here is to bring your game, and that this is not the facility for rank amateurs who don't appreciate the challenges golf offers and the traditions so respected in golf that shape the culture of the game.

Exclusive private club:

Option 1: "We celebrate the privileged lifestyle of those who have achieved success in their personal and business lives." The not-so-subtle message is that this is the enclave for generational wealth and blue-bloods.

Option 2: "We welcome families and encourage them to share their diverse recreational and social interests in a warm and engaging community environment." The subtle message is that this is a home away from home for you and for your family.

Resort:

Option 1: "We offer an oasis from the daily hassle of life, a place to restore your soul." The subtle message is that this is a vacation hideaway where you can decompress and focus on what is important in your life.

Option 2: "Every day we provide the opportunity to form new friendships, strengthen old friendships, and add to family bonds." The subtle message is that this is a comfortable, friendly environment that encourages social interaction.

The "why" is simply a well-crafted vision statement that conveys to the customer the experience offered. There are perhaps as many as 100 different "why" statements for golf courses. The success of each course is dependent on their execution of the "why" as they compete against similar promises in the local market.

A location that understands its "why" is Las Vegas, with the marketing moniker, "What happens in Vegas, stays in Vegas." The message implied is provocative and engaging: Be naughty and no one will know.

In its simplest form, a golf course could market value, experience or price—the three components in the formula that determine customer loyalty.

Most golf courses attempt to compete on price. The more astute golf courses market the experience: the history, the architect, the course layout, the course conditioning, the clubhouse, amenities, practice facilities, GPS, etc. Golf is about entertainment.

The best place to convey the "why" statement is on the home page of the Web site and on the email banner. Note how a famed resort golf course, a municipal course that hosts the PGA Tour, and a municipal course that hosts the masses define their experience:

Bandon Dunes: "This is golf as it was meant to be."

"Bandon Dunes is true to the spirit of Scotland's ancient links. Here, players immerse themselves in the traditions of a timeless game and the grandeur of Oregon's rugged coast. Sweeping, untamed shores stretch for miles. Primeval grassy dunes roll to the sea. Five distinctly different courses have been conceived in harmony with the natural environment. They combine with all the essential elements to reveal a new golf experience every time you play. The soul of the game resides here. Players walk. And at the end of the day, gracious hospitality comforts each guest like a warm, friendly embrace. This is Bandon Dunes. This is golf as it was meant to be."[3]

---

3 http://www.bandondunesgolf.com/

Torrey Pines: "Welcome to the nation's foremost municipal golf course."

"Situated atop cliffs towering above the Pacific Ocean in San Diego, California, golfers marvel at the views of the coastline, deep ravines, and classic championship golf holes.

Torrey Pines is the beautiful site of one of the most memorable battles in golf's history—the 2008 U.S. Open. While taking in the views and gorgeous weather, discover our award-winning golf shop where you can take home some of the magic.

Live close by and want to improve your swing? Or perhaps you're visiting San Diego on your dream golf vacation. In either case, our popular player development programs will get you smiling about your game in no time. To learn more, please follow the links below."[4]

Tenison Park, Dallas: "Welcome to the Online Home of Tenison Park Golf Club! Click here and register today to receive club emails and eSpecials!"

"Only 10 minutes from downtown Dallas, Tenison Park offers the best in public golf with different experiences on each of its 18-hole courses. Tenison Highlands is a remodeled upscale public course with tree-lined fairways and picturesque elevation changes. Tenison Glen is a classic public course over and around White Rock Creek, and has been a favorite of Dallas golfers since 1924.

Tenison Park can be the perfect site for your tournament, weekly foursome, or family outing. The clubhouse offers a well-supplied golf shop including rental clubs and a cafe with big screen TVs to relax after your round. The driving range is perfect for warm-up, practice or lessons from a staff of PGA and LPGA instructors." *Golf in Dallas begins and ends at Tenison Park...*"[5]

The utilization of a "why" statement on a Web site is well executed by Streamsong resort, as shown on the next page.

---

4 http://www.torreypinesgolfcourse.com/_tpgallery/gallery.htm
5 http://www.tenisonpark.com/index.htm

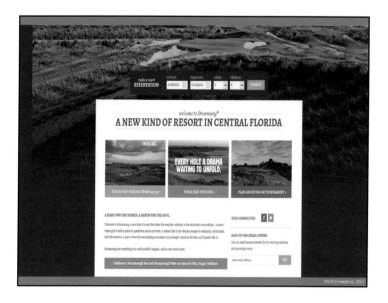

It is probably no coincidence that Bandon Dunes and Streamsong are managed (in 2013) by the same company: Kemper Sports Management.

Another Web site, below, is compelling.[6]

While you might question the commercial advertising on the home page above, with references to Callaway and Allianz, the St. Andrews Web site is elegant

---

6 http://www.standrews.org.uk/

in its simplicity. "The Home of Golf," "You've arrived" and the minimal "play, learn, shop, relax," all in contrast to the cluttered site shown below on the Robert Trent Jones Trail Site.

Almost 50% of the home page is below the fold and not seen by public viewers unless they scroll. If they scroll, they see six additional boxes promoting various offers and promotions. Leading with a title line emphasizing price is ill-advised. These golf courses that are fabulous should be on the avid and core golfer's bucket list and provide a superior experience—regardless of price.

Equally disappointing are Web sites created by templates from third-party firms. Many of these look identical. While a golf course may save a few thousand in development costs, they cost themselves tens of thousands in revenue by not having a compelling Web site. The easiest path is rarely the best.

In the spring of 2013, the management team of Pennsylvania's Honeybrook Golf Club was so frustrated that it switched its Web development from one company to another. As the season approached, basics such as phone number, readable fonts and more were missing on the home page. The home page included the dreaded "add photo," and 50% of the content was below the fold. To add to the misery, the firm it was using was having server problems. Our sympathies are with a golf course owner who is relying on a third party that disappoints just as the bears are coming out of hibernation eager to play golf in the spring. Why risk today's revenue based on a third party's promised potential for tomorrow?

Web sites need to be designed to contain the functionality sought by golfers on their desktop computers or cell phones.

That is why sites, like the Links of Glen Eagles in Calgary, Canada, shown here are so appreciated as they incorporate the "Why" message (creating memories worth repeating), facilitate on-line booking and accelerate customer segmentation.

Ultimately, the effectiveness of a facility's Web site can be measured by various indices. One of the most basic tools to determine the popularity of a Web site is Alexa. Alexa (www.alexa.com) provides traffic statistics and search analytics, identifies the audience and linked sites, and provides reviews and contact information. By using Alexa, you can compare your Web site's ranking with those of your competitors very quickly.

For instance, Alexa identifies the top Web sites in the world, as of this writing:

1. Google
2. Facebook
3. YouTube

4. Yahoo!

5. Baidu

6. Wikipedia

7. Windows Live

8. QQ.com

9. Amazon

10. Twitter

Shown here are the Alexa Rankings for the some popular courses in the United States and Scotland.

Golf Courses – Alexa Ranking

Course	Ranking Worldwide	Regional (Country)
Bethpage Black	8,515	1,506
TPC - Sawgrass	11,330	1,975
Crandon Park	25,431	4,847
Doral Resorts	93,348	28,993
Whistling Straits	418,006	59,544
Pebble Beach	256,071	72,909
St. Andrews	787,332	85,911
TPC - Scottsdale	490,660	122,162
Torrey Pines	616,740	153,222
Bandon Dunes	785,362	165,667
Harding Park	524,007	178,378
Bay Hill	1,359,042	190,354
Robert Trent Jones	1,359,042	190,354
Trump International – Scotland	1,557,551	No Data
Chambers Bay	2,987,632	No Data
Tenison Park	8,449,291	No Data

Note: Ranking is measure of web site activity. Due to the seasonal nature of golf, the rankings fluctuate throughout the year.

Alexa Ranking: March 15, 2013 @ 9:25 p.m.

©Golf Convergence 2013

Go

Alexa Ranking: Go to www.alexa.com and enter your facility's URL and that of one of your Top 5 competitors. If your ranking isn't the highest, your marketing efforts should be reviewed to include an analysis of your site's title and meta tags, traffic analytics, the entry and exit pages customers use, and the average length of the time users spend on the site using Google Analytics.

The Web Is the Spider. The Email Is the Fly.

From surveys conducted by Golf Convergence in 2012, it was interesting to note that a facility's Web site and emails remain the primary ways golfers find information about the course and the specials that may be offered.

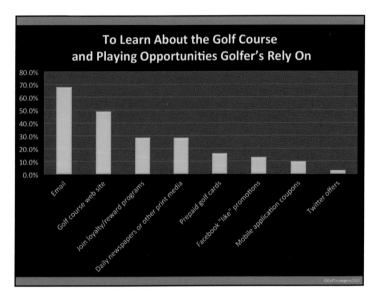

What was also interesting to note was the disconnect between the number of golfers that are using Facebook and Twitter to learn about the golf course and the resources being allocated by golf courses to such social media, as shown in the following figure.

In our fast-paced society, we are prone to want to adopt the newest, the fastest, and the best.

It is our belief that allowing others to be on the bleeding edge of social media is the optimum strategy, for I have yet to visit a golf course where there isn't some very low-hanging fruit available that would increase revenue, bolster operational efficiency, or enhance customer service. It is my humble opinion that a focus on the basics would produce far greater returns than chasing the latest craze.

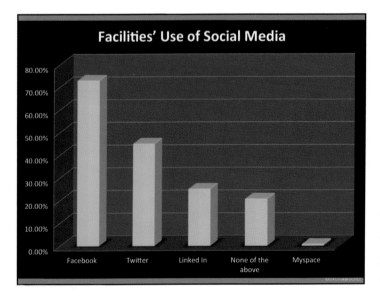

Our 2012 surveys indicate that golf courses were actually outpacing golfers in their use of social media. Seventy-four percent of golf courses have created Facebook pages but only 57% of golfers have done so. More amusing is the statistic that 35% of golf courses tweet while only 14% of golfers have Twitter accounts. Both of these examples underscore the fact that course operators are investing in social media at a faster pace than their clients are adopting social media.

In answering the surveys, golfers provided other valuable insights from which golf course owners can benefit. Eighty-four percent have made a tee time reservation online, and they spend 24.89% of their day at a computer, primarily a desktop or laptop. Typically, 12% of all tee times are made online.

Golfers prefer email messages, appropriately spaced—preferably every two weeks. The core tag line should be consistent, while the subject line may vary as it features promotions.

The theme of "Why?" becomes a consistent message through all communication media used, including email.

The subject line is tricky. First, it should be written with less than 100 characters; that to pique the reader's curiosity enough that the email is opened and to ensure that the subject line can be posted to Facebook and Twitter, since the latter limits the message to 140 characters, including the embedded link, as shown here.

It is estimated that only 80% of readers actually read the subject line. A reader who is familiar with the sender merely clicks on the email to open it without reading the email. Thus, it is a prudent practice to enter the subject line as the first sentence of the text.

On the Vertical Response send page (on the previous page), note that the process of posting an email message to Facebook, to Twitter, and to your facility's Web site is automatically integrated. You merely need to check the box and the software automatically posts your message to the designated social media forums.

The Rules of Thumb

There is a science to the madness of email marketing. Here are some statistics regarding email marketing tactics and trends:

- "The average email open rates have risen from 18.35% to 21.47% in the last 12 months.

- Click-to-open rates fell from 16.2% to 14.4%.

- Average bounce rates declined from 3.1% to 2.3%.

- Commercial emails account for 70% of spam complaints.

- The average person checks his or her smartphone 34 times per day.

- Emails sent on Saturdays and Sundays had higher open, click, and transaction rates.

- Subject lines with 30 or fewer characters performed above average.

- Personalized subject lines are 22.2% more likely to be opened.

- 64% of recipients open an email based on the organization that sent it.

- 47% open an email based on the subject line.

- Only 26% open the email based on the offer."[7]

Here are the basic rules of thumb:

> **Lesson 1: Repetition ad infinitum is vital.** If you are so sick of the message you want to barf, it is just beginning to become effective. "Just Do It," "The Friendly Skies," "The Pause That Refreshes," "Squeezably Soft" are brand messages that will resonate in our minds—forever—testaments to the power of repetition. Repetition of the time sent is also recommended. Choose a standard day of the week and time of day for release (perhaps Wednesday at 6:00 a.m.) to set a standard of consistency that customers can anticipate.

---

7 http://www.business2community.com/email-marketing/23-tweetable-stats-on-email-marketing-tactics-and-trends-0453475

Lesson 2: Fine tune your marketing message using A/B testing or multi-variant testing. The essence of this method is that the call to action (the enticement for the customer to act) is different even though the all other elements of the email's copy and layout are identical. By monitoring which campaign produced the highest click-through rate, you will be able to communicate more effectively in future campaigns. Shown on this page is an example of multi-variance testing.

Name	Type	Launch Date	Sent	Open	Click	Bounce	Unsub	Conv.	Revenue	
Asbury - Meadows - 2nd - Did Not Open	Canvas	Mar 26, 2013 5:16AM	99	22.22%	16.16%	1.01%	0.00%	0.00%	0.00 USD	Actions
Asbury - Meadows - 2nd - ODNC	Canvas	Mar 26, 2013 5:11AM	48	66.67%	27.08%	0.00%	0.00%	0.00%	0.00 USD	Actions
Asbury - City List - 2nd - Did Not Open	Canvas	Mar 26, 2013 5:05AM	187	19.25%	10.70%	0.53%	0.00%	0.00%	0.00 USD	Actions
Asbury - City List - 2nd - ODNC	Canvas	Mar 26, 2013 5:00AM	63	50.79%	11.11%	0.00%	0.00%	0.00%	0.00 USD	Actions
Clemson Golf 2.0 B - Study - DNO	Canvas	Mar 20, 2013 6:19AM	7,666	4.83%	0.20%	0.52%	0.26%	0.00%	0.00 USD	Actions
Clemson Golf 2.0 B - Study - ODNC	Canvas	Mar 20, 2013 6:12AM	1,057	56.67%	1.51%	0.47%	0.76%	0.00%	0.00 USD	Actions
Clemson Golf 2.0 A - Study - DNO	Canvas	Mar 20, 2013 6:08AM	7,710	5.62%	0.29%	0.54%	0.36%	0.00%	0.00 USD	Actions
Clemson Golf 2.0 A - Study - ODNC	Canvas	Mar 20, 2013 6:00AM	1,121	52.81%	1.25%	0.80%	1.69%	0.00%	0.00 USD	Actions
City of Asbury - City List	Canvas	Mar 20, 2013 5:20AM	297	35.02%	17.51%	0.00%	0.34%	0.00%	0.00 USD	Actions
City of Asbury - The Meadows	Canvas	Mar 20, 2013 5:11AM	252	55.56%	49.21%	5.95%	0.40%	0.00%	0.00 USD	Actions
Copy of Clemson Golf 2.0 Study - B - Tes	Canvas	Mar 14, 2013 5:51AM	10,953	12.43%	0.44%	3.17%	0.51%	0.00%	0.00 USD	Actions
Clemson Golf 2.0 Study - A - Testing	Canvas	Mar 14, 2013 5:36AM	10,938	13.14%	0.49%	3.11%	0.48%	0.00%	0.00 USD	Actions

©Golf Convergence, 2013

Two different email messages were being sent on behalf of Golf Convergence, the other from the city of Asbury, Iowa.

The Golf Convergence email message was regarding a Webinar to review a Clemson University pilot program and contained two different subject lines:

Test A—Subject Line: "Webinar March 21, 2013: Golf Management Made Easy, A Simplified System to Ensure Consistent Execution"

Test B—Subject Line: "Webinar March 21, 2013: Why the Financial Performance of Your Course Will Improve in 2013"

The Test A Message was opened by 77 more individuals, with 5 more individuals clicking the link and registering for the Webinar.

A multi-variant test was then executed on a follow-up email to those who opened the email and did not click (ODNC) and to those who did not open the original email (DNO). The subject lines were then changed to read as follows:

Original Message "A"

Test 1 (Open Did Not Click)—Subject Line: "Webinar March 21, 2013: Golf Management Made Easy, A Simplified System to Ensure Consistent Execution via Clemson University Study"

Test 2 (Did Not Open)—Subject Line: "Webinar March 21, 2013: Clemson University Study to Boost Your Profits in 2013"

Original Message "B"

Test 1 (Open Did Not Click)—Subject Line: "Webinar March 21, 2013: Boost the Profits at Your Golf Course in 2013 with Clemson University Study"

Test 2 (Did Not Open)—Subject Line: "Webinar March 21, 2013: Increase Your Profits in 2013 with Golf Management Pilot Study by Clemson University Study"

For those who originally opened and did not click, Original Message "B"—Test 2 was more effective as 19 more people clicked on that message than did those who received Original Message "A."

With respect to those who did not open the original message, Original Message A—Test Line 2 was slightly more effective, as 5.62% opened the message compared to 4.83% for Original Message B, Test Line 2. In both cases; however, more than 350 recipients opened the message the second time when they didn't open it initially. Go figure.

Wondering about the high unsubscribe rates in Original Message "A", Subject Line 1 (Open Did Not Click). There was a "trick" in that message. The email read as follows:

Castle Pines, CO (March 20, 2013): Click here to register.

We noted that you opened our email on March 14, 2013 but elected not to register for the forthcoming Webinar.

We review our email database very carefully every quarter to ensure that we contact only those who may receive value from our insights and perspectives. If somehow, via opt-in or sending us an email, you have been incorrectly categorized in our golf course management database category, we apologize and **we encourage you to opt-out** by simply clicking on the link below this email. We have too much respect for your time and the clutter we all suffer to burden you with unnecessary emails.

However, if you manage a golf course, we encourage you to join us on March 21, 2013, at 11:15 E.S.T. for a Webinar being conducted by Rick Lucas, PGA Golf Professional and Program Director of Clemson University's Professional Golf Management program, along with me, Jim Keegan, to introduce to you a simplified golf management system designed to ensure that your golf course achieves its goals. Click here to register. A few seats remain.

Based on the call for those to opt-out in the Original Message "A" Test 1, the unsubscribe rate soared to 1.69%; 19 people opted out. The lesson— if you show concern for your customer, it will reap rewards. Those who were not the target market for the emails shouldn't be pestered by needless emails, as they only tarnish your brand. We can assume that this is an indication of the importance of correctly mining your email list and segmenting it properly into core (frequent golfers), acquired (new golfers that year), and defectors (former customers who haven't returned).

Whether your email communication program is one such as Vertical Response, Constant Contact, or one embedded in your golf management software, analyzing the opens, clicks, bounces, and un-subscribes is fundamental to building a successful email program, as is having it cued for release 5 days thereafter utilizing multi-variant testing.

Lesson 3: The World Is Flat. Thomas Friedman's book *The World Is Flat 3.0: A Brief History of the Twenty-First Century* is an essential update on globalization and on the opportunities it provides for individual empowerment. I didn't realize when I began to read it how the words he so adroitly espoused would connect to my personal world. However, with a modest email campaign and $6,650 invested with a really good PR firm (Hunter Public Relations), the original edition of *The Business of Golf—What Are You Thinking?* has been purchased in 16 countries.

You don't think Friedman's globalization pitch is applicable to a golf course? Fossil Trace Golf Course in Golden, Colorado, with a $79 green fee (non-resident, prime time), has a map that tracks the residences of their golfers. Golfers from 34 countries have played that course since the facility opened. As with Fossil Trace, even if 80% of your golfers come from within a 30-mile radius of your facility, don't discount the possibility of attracting incremental rounds by creating an enticing marketing campaign.

Most avid golfers have a subconscious desire to play every course in the world. What unique marketing slogan will make those golfers want to play your course? For me, the mention of a chocolate milk-shake or turtle soup reinforces the brand image of Castle Pines and Pine Valley. What unique difference at your facility will compel golfers to visit? Conveying that "why" message is fundamental.

Not Only "What?" but also "How?"

Email requires work. Every time an email is sent, you and your system need to manage the bounces and unsubscribes and reclassify the prospects who purchased. The chart below illustrates the response rates to Golf Convergence emails during the first 24 hours after release with respect to opens, click-throughs, and the percentage who responded, bounced, and unsubscribed.

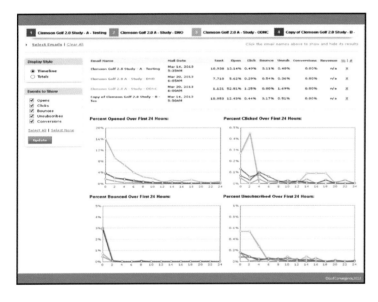

"The Science of Email Marketing," a Webinar by Hubspot's Dan Zarrella, produces many insights for the golf course owner:

- "Eight-eight percent of individuals with email accounts do not maintain separate business and personal email accounts.

- 58% maintain a separate junk inbox to trap "blast" emails.

- 80.8% read email on mobile devices.

- 65.0% prefer html image based emails."[8]

One of the interesting dilemmas for golf course owners is when to send email messages. A survey conducted by Golf Convergence in March 2012, found that the majority of golf course owners send a weekly email to an average database of 3,474 names on Tuesday between 9 a.m. and 11 a.m. Unfortunately, that is

---

8 Dan Zarrella, "The Science of Email Marketing," 2012 Edition, Slides 7, 8, 9, and 33.

the worst time to send these emails; those times have the lowest open and click-through rates and the highest unsubscribe rates.

But there is wide disparity in the email databases that golf courses have been able to aggregate, as shown in the following figure.

It is disappointing, but not surprising, that 44% of daily fee and municipal golf courses have fewer than 1,000 email address.

In studying more than 9 billion email messages delivered by Mail Chimp, Dan Zarrella[9] noted the following regarding the time the most email messages were opened.

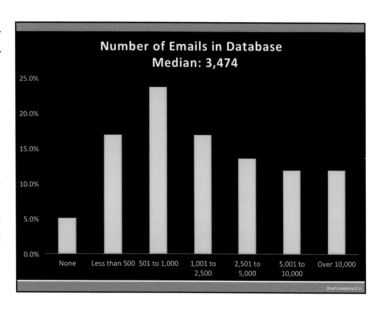

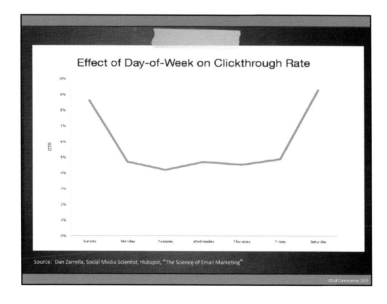

---

9 Dan Zarrella, "The Science of Email Marketing," 2012 Edition.

The highest unsubscribe rates were on Tuesday and the highest click-through rates were on emails sent between 5:00 a.m. and 6:00 a.m., as illustrated here:

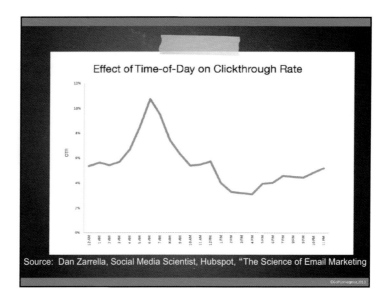

Coupons

Golf courses have long used coupons, but they continue to be one of the most ineffective marketing methods. The time needed to create and monitor coupon use is debilitating. Further, the consumer is so inundated with coupons, special offers, and other junk marketing that they really get lost in all the noise.

Historically, charity coupon books are accompanied by sports section advertising, golf magazine discount cards, PGA Tour Player's passes, and Groupon promotions, to list a few.

Often issued in bulk, these coupons are rarely tracked at redemption by a golf course to determine which publications they should be placed in to achieve the greatest effect. Courses seem to be even less likely to track the impact of coupon marketing on the Revenue Per Round. Most coupons offer at least a 25% discount, and that discount means a course would need to attract 33% more golfers to generate the same revenue. The benefit of these coupons is typically unknown and at best debatable.

Interestingly, "The number of coupons used by Americans…plummeted in 2012—down 17 percent. Coupon industry insiders disagree on whether the drop is an aberration caused by a poor mix of coupon offers in 2012 or whether it signals the beginning of the end of the paper coupon era. Last year, U. S. consumers redeemed 2.9 billion coupons … from a total of 305 billion coupons made available."[10]

Is there any upside to golf course participation in coupon books? This type of marketing program is merely one way to market, and it might be considered helpful as long as the redemption rates are low, the offers can be structured for off-peak times, and it can be shown to attract new golfers. However, these programs often favor the publisher over the golf course.

Groupon

A recent phenomenon that is drawing much attention is Groupon, a coupon emailed to and ordered by subscribers. According to Joe Assell, President and CEO, Co-Founder and CEO of GolfTEC, "The jury is still out."

GolfTEC has used Groupon in 49 different markets, offering only a 30-minute swing diagnosis for $35 (59% discount), or a 60-minute swing evaluation for $60 (60% discount). For each promotion, about 350 coupons have been purchased. Despite proactive follow-up with coupon purchasers, the redemption rate has been amazingly low; only 10 to 15%.

The key for GolfTEC is that Groupon is selling introductory programs during the fall/winter when they have plenty of capacity. Only 30% of GolfTEC lessons occur from September to February. The additional revenue has been welcome during the slower part of the year. The coupon offered does not offend other customers, many of whom purchase 25+-lesson packages.

The downside, according to Joe Assell, is that "Groupon is very difficult to work with. They bump you if they have another promotion they believe will generate greater revenue, and they pay you over 60 days."

Though Groupon has assembled massive databases in nearly every metropolitan market, extreme caution is recommended if you utilize Groupon's services.

---

10 *The Denver Post,* "Savings Tool Losing Favor," March 24, 2013, pg. 3K.

Groupon requires the golf course to sell its goods or services with at least a 50% discount from the rack rate. Groupon's commission is 50%. Thus, the golf course nets only 25% of retail. If a golf course were selling rounds of golf, play would have to increase by 400% for the course to break even—highly unlikely.

The Groupon promotion illustrated here is baffling.

The benefit is the up-front cash, and the prayer is that the redemption rate is low.

There is another challenge with these types of marketing programs—loyal customers who miss the promotion.

Highland Pacific Golf is a newer course in Victoria, British Columbia. Seeking to attract customers, the owners tried Groupon with amazing success—sort of. Their coupon was for 50% off two green fees plus power cart and range balls. The program was suspended when 600 had sold on the morning of the second day. A small group of Loyalty Program members complained that the course did not let them know so they could participate—a customer-service problem out of the gate.

Are rounds at any price a solution? Clearly not. Discounting, while a short-term fix, is a long-term path to failure and is a common component of the death spiral.

Social Media—Much Ado about Nothing?

The buzz today is all about social media. Facebook, Twitter, You Tube, Instagram, Pinterest, and more—all command the attention of the masses in varying degrees. And Medium, Whisper, and Sina Weibo are on the edge of breaking through.

The first concept to grasp is that Social Media has not killed off email. As reported,

> "Active email users far outnumber users on any social network. For example, 3 billion people use email. Now compare that number with one billion Facebook users, 200 million Twitter users, and 200 million LinkedIn users.
>
> Social media-loving age. The click-through rate (CTR) of an average email is 2.4% without social sharing capabilities. Add social icons in the email, and the CTR jumps to 6.2%.
>
> In 2012, 29.4% of email marketers included social sharing icons in their emails, up from 18.3% in 2011 (a 61% increase)."[11]

In 2012, Golf Convergence conducted a survey of the interest in social media by golf courses and whether these alternative forms of marketing were being readily adapted. Only 51% understood these forms of marketing and embraced them. Forty-two percent that were using social media were doing so only because they feared they were missing opportunities, and 7% weren't participating or didn't care, seeming to feel that social media was not useful for marketing their courses.

Golf courses are not alone in their confusion as to how to use and leverage the new digital marketing alternatives. In a research study, the Boston Consulting Group found that

> "The small-to-medium enterprise community faces a myriad of digital marketing and digital advertising choices and … most of these businesses do not have a professional marketing person whose job is to drive marketing," said John Rose, senior partner at BCG. "It's pretty hard for them to winnow their way through the 20 to 40 unsolicited requests they get a month to use digital marketing product A versus digital marketing product B. When it comes to making ad decisions, small business owners lean heavily on their peers for advice."[12]

Rose highlighted that less than 3% of their total advertising dollars flow online.

---

11 http://www.marketingprofs.com/chirp/2013/10708/social-sharing-boosts-email-results-infographic

12 http://www.adweek.com/news/advertising-branding/small-businesses-are-slow-digital-party-148029

This study provides some insight on where a golf course should concentrate its efforts and where it would be wise to minimize its efforts—the use of social media when marketing to golfers older than 40.

Experian Marketing Services surveyed email marketers across eight verticals about their email-marketing initiatives, including their strategies for subscriber acquisition, mobile and social marketing, testing, and creative design. Social networks used to display or promote emails are shown in the figure.

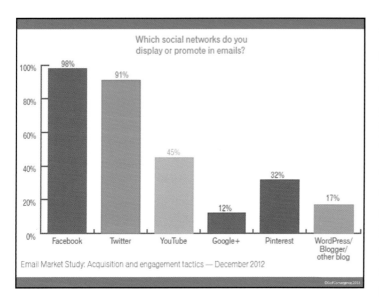

Considering the demographics of golfers, you have to question the propensity to invest time in the social media forums dominated by younger generations. While some courses, such as Treetops in Michigan, as shown in the bottom figure are doing exceedingly well in this arena, it is likely because of the intense focus and professional guidance they have received from Andrew Wood, of Legendary Marketing.

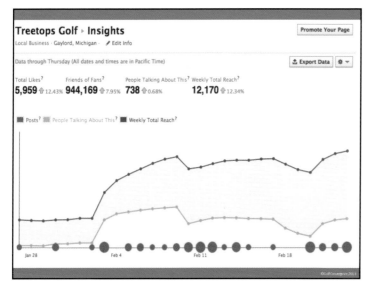

Of all the techie tools, one of the most valuable is Google Analytics, which reflects the geographic location of individuals viewing a Web site. The Google Analytics tool identifies how long customers remain on a site, the pages on the site that are being viewed the most frequently, how users enter and leave the site, what Internet browsers they are using, and many other meaningful metrics.

Google Analytics also keeps track of the number of site visits, the number of new and returning visitors to the site, and how many viewed only one page (the bounce rate). Google Analytics provides a world map that allows you to click through to learn your site's traffic by country, state, and city.

Especially for a resort, this information is invaluable in determining the source of its customer base. Shown here are Google Analytics' results.

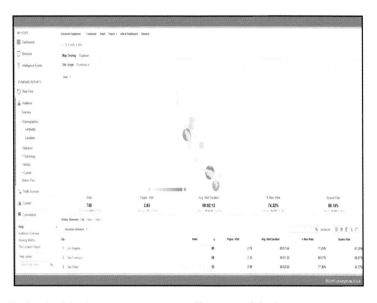

Despite all the hubbub about Twitter, illustrated below is a snapshot of that community if were 100 people.[13]

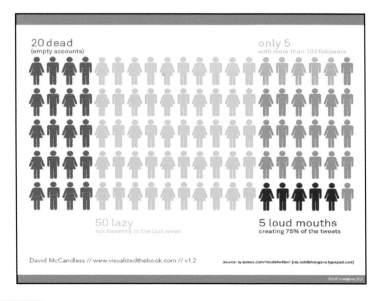

---

13 http://www.flickr.com/photos/25541021@N00/3706760751/

It's hard to get excited about allocating a lot of resources to a social media forum on which 20% are registered, 50% are lazy and haven't tweeted in a week, and five loudmouths generate 75% of all the tweets.

Other Forms of Marketing

There are many new ways to market a golf course: Google AdWords, Google AdSense, Instagram, and eBay are additional venues for golf course marketing.

Google AdWords has attracted the attention of the leading management companies like Billy Casper Golf Management and OB Sports, to name two.

Google AdWords is a pay-per-click advertising in which course operators can determine how many searched for golf or discounted golf in their local market. Rick Katz, Managing Director of Buffalo Communications comments that "You can turn on or off Google AdWords based on weather, time of the day, day of the week, and month of the year and on and on. That way, you can mitigate your risk of waste."[14]

There is a risk. In bidding for placement, the quality of the golf course's Web site determines its position in the sponsored results section.

Nevertheless, many firms are adopting pay-per-click advertising. It is common for a golf course operated by a management company to invest between $300 to $900 monthly on this form of promotion via Google AdWords or Facebook.

According to Kris Strauss, former VP of Sales and Marketing with OB Sports, now VP of Sales and Marketing with Troon Golf, the return on pay-per-click advertising is five-fold. The best return from these activities, Strauss says, is from reservations made by groups, leagues, banquets, and weddings.

All of these programs have the single focus of trying to capture the attention of golfers and motivate them to play a specific course. A few of these programs are prudent. The rest represent a slow death for the golf course operator. How do you determine which ones to choose?

---

14 Steve Eubanks, Golf Business, "Marketing Mix," April 2013, pg. 30.

According to Kris Strauss, "To properly market, adopting a holistic approach, balancing social and commercial interests, is appropriate. The key is ensuring that one's marketing efforts and technology are in sync. The use of third party platforms creates challenges in ensuring that the promotions, i.e., Facebook only or Twitter offer campaigns, when purchased by the consumer, are correctly integrated into the various point of sale platforms at the golf course. Ensuring that integration is one of our biggest challenges requiring a large allocation of our resources to ensure that all the widgets available integrate to our core platforms."

Unfortunately, most marketing programs by golf courses are created without accurately answering a simple question, "What customer segment are we trying to target?" Golf courses have historically used a shotgun rather than a rifle approach to target the various unique segments. This shotgun approach has been necessary because few courses effectively identify golfers by marketing segment.

The message and the medium for each one of these customer segments vary greatly. When golf course operators fail to identify the target market, discounting programs applicable to all become the marketing program by default.

What a golf course operator must realize is that privacy no longer exists in our lives. Every customer transaction comes with the risk that it will be immediately broadcast on Facebook, Twitter, or YouTube. When a course is intent on branding its message, the consumer, through his or her social networks, also has the potential to broadcast a message about your facility.

While caution is advised, the importance of social media to driving revenue at a golf course is clearly understood. Just ask Siri on your iPhone, "I would like to play golf. What golf course would you recommend?" The response by Siri is "I found 10 golf courses…8 of them are fairly close to you. I have sorted them by **RANKING**" (emphasis added).

The ranking, by the way, is based on the social media interaction about the golf course.

The ultimate key to marketing is realizing the long-term value of the relationship. Focusing on the customer experience and providing a personal touch should drive the message. The benefit will be influenced by the quality of personnel engaged in marketing.

Path to Success

The strategic vision for a golf course operation creates awareness of its brand image—**a unique selling proposition that is based on its "Why?" statement.**

Tactical planning for marketing focuses on the allocation of resources between advertising, public relations, and promotion.

Operational execution is dedicated to measuring the efficacy of each marketing effort as it relates to the return on investment.

To ensure that a golf course's marketing efforts are effective, accomplish the following:

1) Has a compelling "Why? statement been created and consistently articulated in all advertising, public relations, and promotional efforts?

2) With the assistance of the accounting department, create a matrix of each expenditure that is related to marketing.

3) Measure the rate of return on each marketing initiative qualitatively in terms of community brand recognition and incremental sales.

4) Select three marketing activities that produced a low rate of return or for which the rate of return cannot be measured. Sunset those expenditures, and reallocate those dollars to new promotional efforts.

Concluding Thoughts

The greatest deception men suffer is from their own opinions.

Leonardo da Vinci

Twitter is a gun without a safety release.
You have a great chance of killing yourself if you don't use it carefully.

Jim Rome, Sports Broadcaster

Chapter 14

Game Time
Step 6 of the Golf Convergence WIN™ Formula (Continued)

The quality of an organization can never exceed the quality of the minds that make it up.

Dwight David Eisenhower, as quoted by
Harold McAlindon

*It is not the same thing to talk of bulls
as to be in the bull ring.*

Spanish Proverb

Chapter Highlights

Another day begins. The uniform and the name tag go on. All the work you have done to create a vision, to determine the resources you need and to secure them—all of this is wasted unless and until you execute the plan you have laid out.

The numerous customer touch points on the "Assembly Line of Golf" will define the experience as you proceed. Although perfection in execution is probably not achievable, you can set a goal to consistently execute in an outstanding manner.

But how can you reach that goal? Is excellence merely a habit begun by good training?

This chapter focuses on training for and encouraging consistent execution to ensure that a valuable customer experience is created.

Changing Habits

What seems somewhat backwards on the Assembly Line of Golf is that the lowest-paid workers largely form the customers' opinions of the customer service received. You spend $8 million to build a course, and an $8 per hour worker can create a negative brand message that is likely to reverberate throughout the community. And … that ultimate moment of truth can be broadcast to the world instantly by your connected customers.

What is truly scary is that "Forty percent of the actions people perform each day aren't actual decisions, but merely habits."[1]

When we see the word *habit*, we presume "bad habit"—can't quit smoking, drinking, or eating, perhaps. A habit is repetitive action without thinking.

But habits can be good. Reversing a habit is usually neither easy, nor quick, nor simple. Habits are neurological processes that have become programmed into our brains. Habits are formed because the brain is constantly looking for ways to save effort. In *The Power of Habit*, Charles Duhigg points out that habits "are so strong, in fact, that they cause our brains to cling to them at the exclusion of all else, including common sense." Duhigg noted that habits can be so powerful that they create "neurological cravings" that can result in obsessive behavior.[2]

What does this have to do with forming a winning management and operational team that can ensure consistent execution at a golf course? Everything. Creating and encouraging positive habits for each member of a golf facility's team are worthy and rewarding goals. But how can management accomplish this task?

As Tony Dungy, the famed Indianapolis Colts coach and TV football analyst, says, "Champions don't do extraordinary things. They do ordinary things, but they do them without thinking, too fast for the other team to react. They follow the habits they've learned."[3]

Mike Kelley, former Executive Director at the famed PGA West complex of nine golf courses, believes that consistency is the foundation of excellence and that achieving that comes from forming consistent habits.

---

1 Charles Duhigg, *The Power of Habit*, 2012, pg. xvi.

2 Ibid., pg. 25, 47.

3 Ibid., pg. 61.

To illustrate, at a Golf Inc. presentation, Kelley outlined that he had his team do a detailed time and motion study on setting up the golf range correctly. The process was documented on laminated cards with photographs of each step of the process. From driving into the resort, to punching the time clock, to walking to the area where the range cart and supplies were always in their designated areas—step by step, the process was outlined. Defining the hitting area, setting up the tee markers to ensure safety, stacking the balls in an ornamental array, yardage signs updated, water buckets to clean the clubs, and the amenities (tees, ball markers, sun tan lotion)—all were described. Once the time and motion study was completed, Mike had his two young daughters, without any training, follow the instructions to ensure that the procedures could be precisely executed.

Mike then adds a secret ingredient—selecting employees that are passionate about serving his upscale customers with grace and aplomb.

Most golf courses retain employees to perform certain tasks, such as working behind the counter, selling merchandise, teaching lessons, serving as a starter, preparing food, serving food, and more. These repetitive tasks are often boring, and very little training is provided for those who perform them.

Most golf courses develop and continue to update a manual that explains the step-by-step execution of the various jobs at a golf facility. These are the foundation of creating consistent execution, and the Table of Contents of one of them is shown here.

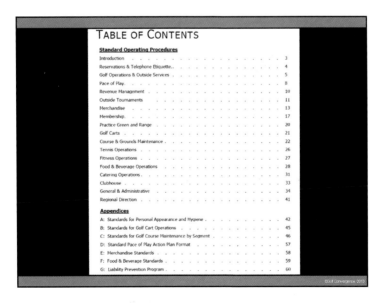

The following is the guide list used by a regional director to check on compliance with the firm's procedures, which divide the process of taking a tee time reservation into several components, all of which need to be properly (and positively) performed.

Reservation Call by Supervisor to Ensure Compliance with Corporate Standards	Date Call Was Made			
	Co-Worker Answering			
1. Phone is answered by the third ring and with the standard greeting.				
2. Co-worker asks the number of players before offering a tee time.				
3. Low demand times are offered before high demand times.				
4. Co-worker asks for a credit card and/or phone # to reserve the time.				
5. As part of the reservation script, co-worker explains the cancellation policy.				
6. If requested tee time is not available, co-worker asks to put caller on the Wait List.				
7. Prior to the end of the transaction, the caller is thanked for the business.				

Cancellation Call by Facilitator	Date Call Was Made			
	Co-Worker Answering			
1. Phone is answered by the third ring and with the standard greeting.				
2. Co-worker offers to rebook the caller for another day or time when canceling tee time.				
3. Were the appropriate cancellation penalties applied, if applicable?				
4. Prior to the end of the transaction, the caller is thanked for the business.				

Such a checklist, while it names the tasks to be performed, is quantitative and doesn't capture the qualitative aspects of the facility's vision or the positive messaging that should be communicated by the tone of voice of the staff member.

No matter how good they may be at the task, if the employee doesn't subscribe to the "why" of the facility and the experience to be created, the customer reaction is that the service is likely to be judged as ordinary, and certainly not exceptional.

The best golf course businesses begin with empathy, through identification of and agreement with the wants, needs, and goals of golfers. This process involves the following steps:

1. Determine where you are.

2. Address key touch points.

3. Understand the experience your customers are seeking.

4. Translate your "why" into effective communication.

5. Achieve buy-in within the organization.

6. Put the knowledge to work as a team.

7. Create a consistent brand experience.

Where Are You?

The launch point for evaluating operations features measuring, understanding, and improving the customer experience. How well you do is measured by touch points that include static objects (the entrance, the pro shop layout, the range, the carts, the course, the locker rooms, etc.), customer interaction with the staff and other customers, and interactive experiences via your Web site and social media.

The customers' perceptions drive future sales to them and to their peers, as illustrated below.

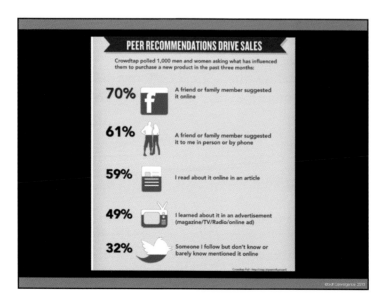

The customer experience is the competitive battleground in a golf course's search for market share.

What always amazes us are the constant changes at the top of the "food chain" among the major corporations in the United States, as illustrated here.[4]

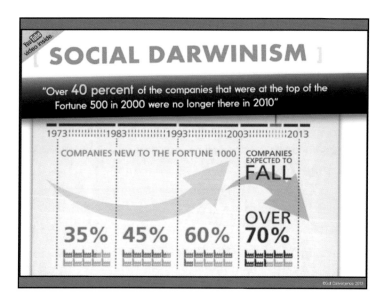

It is hard to believe that 40% percent of the companies in the *Fortune* 500 in 2000 were not there a decade later.

These companies lost their customers, and we can assume that before losing their customers, they lost their focus on serving their customers. A poor customer experience is the leading contributor to customers abandoning a business. "Eighty-seven percent of customers will not return from a bad experience."[5]

Very few golf courses define what a great customer service experience is, and even fewer measure customer service on a consistent basis.

One of the things we find surprising is how few golf courses employ professional secret shoppers to review the customer experience. In a 2012 survey

---

4 http://www.slideshare.net/briansolis/official-slideshare-for-whats-the-future-of-business?utm_source=slideshow&utm_medium=ssemail&utm_campaign=weekly_digest#btnPrevious

5 http://www.slideshare.net/Michael_Hinshaw/measure-understand-and-improve-customer-experience-mcorp-consulting?utm_source=slideshow01&utm_medium=ssemail&utm_campaign=share_slideshow, Slide 3.

conducted by Golf Convergence, golf courses reported that they rarely have their customer experience "secret shopped," as shown in the following image.

Focus and clarity only come from knowing the final destination with a singular vision. Try photographing each of the customer touch points, and you will no doubt find staff members who are in the habit of serving customers in a certain way react by noticing their lackluster service and react by saying something like, "Holy Cow!—I didn't know that was the impression we were creating."

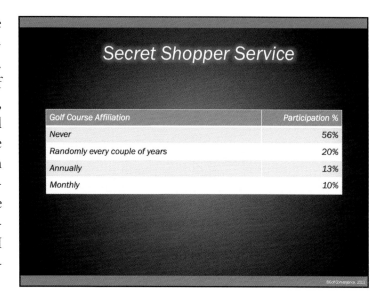

All customer reactions are a reflection of the golf course brand—from the quality of the toilet paper to the quality of the wine to the course conditions. Every customer touch point is a seed from which your brand experience grows.

Addressing Key Touch Points

Each golf course operation is part of a series of interconnected processes, the end product of which is a challenged, entertained, and satisfied customer. Each game of golf your customers play is a story; you are responsible for supplying the place for them to create their stories. Course personnel, like those at Disneyland, should be viewed as "characters," with roles to play to meet customers' expectations. When you understand and meet and even exceed your customers' unique needs and desires, customer loyalty will be created, and that will lead to the thrill ride of operating a business—financial success.

Depending on type of golf course you operate, the number of opportunities to favorably impress your customers can vary from 9 to 14. As expected, the higher the price per round of golf, the greater the number of touch points a golfer will expect. Thus, the exclusive private club, the high-end daily fee course, or exclusive resorts are likely to take the greatest advantage of the many opportunities to enhance the overall impression of their facilities.

The Assembly Line of Golf

Touch Point	Municipal	Daily Fee	Military	Resort	Private Club
Reservations					
Club Entrance					
Bag Drop					
Locker Room					
Pro Shop					
Cart					
Range					
Starter					
Course					
Beverage Cart Attendant					
Half Way House					
Cart Return					
Locker Room					
Bar/Restaurant					
Likely # of Points of Contact	9	11	9	12	14

©GolfConvergence,2013

Note: Each golf course is unique. While the number of contact points may vary slightly from facility to facility, this concept means that each course has only a certain number of opportunities to make a favorable impression.

Each customer touch point provides the opportunity to define the experience of your customer. Customers weigh each touch point based on the value they perceive they get from it.

Go

If you licensed the supplemental template that accompanies this Field book, open Step 6: Secret Shopper Service Checklist.

This template provides a list touch points divided into the sections listed in the illustration above.

It is highly recommended that every golf course retain a secret shopper at least annually, but preferably semi-annually:

1) Have an individual with a camera secretly shop your facility, taking pictures of each step on the "Assembly Line of Golf." As part of this process, have that secret shopper shop your competitor's also. It is often advantageous to have a foursome of women serve as secret shoppers. Not only are they likely to be very observant, but they unfortunately also have a greater probability of being treated dismissively and will definitely recognize poor service. During

a management meeting, show photographs of various courses, including yours, to the team.

2) Have that individual explain the experience received and price the value obtained.

3) Review the photo essay with management and staff and determine what is immediately correctable and what should be added to an intermediate-term operational or capital improvements checklist.

From the secret shopping reviews we have seen, we usually find management and staff have been living with and have been responsible for many negative messages that they have been unaware of. One example of this was the sign shown here.

What is the value of the number of golf balls this that will be stolen from this course in a year? $3,000? What is the value of the balls that won't be stolen because the "thieves" read this sign? What is the value of the customers who will be lost because of negative messages? We recommend counting "lost" balls as a cost of doing business.

Messages sent by a course create an impression of a facility in the customers' minds that they mention to family and friends.

Translating the "Why?" into Effective Communication

How do we transform a series of repetitive tasks on the Assembly Line of Golf into a consistently positive experience? Much of the service provided at a golf course is a reflection of general habits developed over many years. Routine provides the hundreds of unwritten rules/habits under which a golf course actually operates. There are no golf courses that don't have institutional habits.

Several friends have described going into a golf shop as comparable to buying chewing gum at a convenience store. The staff is reactive rather than anticipatory.

In the book *Outliers*, author Malcolm Gladwell advances the notion that it takes 10,000 hours of practicing a specific task to achieve success. To support his thesis, he examined

> "why the majority of Canadian ice hockey players are born in the first few months of the calendar year, how Microsoft co-founder Bill Gates achieved his extreme wealth, how The Beatles became one of the most successful musical acts in human history, how Joseph Flom built Skadden, Arps, Slate, Meagher & Flom into one of the most successful law firms in the world, how cultural differences play a large part in perceived intelligence and rational decision making, and how two people with exceptional intelligence, Christopher Langan and J. Robert Oppenheimer, end up with such vastly different fortunes."[6]

Gladwell's book is very compelling reading, and it highlights the opportunities and challenges of running a golf course, especially working with the seasonal, part-time, and volunteer workers that are the majority of golf course employees. Can a golf course handbook teach a golf employee excellent customer-service skills? Should the first step in redefining a facility's "brand" be to throw away the company handbook?

Here are two examples from Clayton M. Christensen's *The Innovator's Dilemma* that provide a clue to the solution to this riddle regarding staff training:

> "**IBM:** IBM's success in the first five years of the personal computer market was in stark contrast to the failure of the other leading mainframe and minicomputers makers to catch the disruptive desktop computing wave. How did IBM do it? It created an autonomous organization in Florida, away from its New York state headquarters. The organization was free to succeed along metrics of success that were relevant to the personal computer marketing. The evidence is strong that such efforts rarely successfully

6 http://en.wikipedia.org/wiki/Outliers_(book)

position in one market will suffer unless two separate organizations, embedded within the appropriate value networks, pursue their separate customers."[7]

"**Hewlett-Packard:** Rather than place its bet exclusively with one or the other, and rather than attempt to commercialize the disruptive ink-jet from within the existing printer division in Boise, Idaho, HP created a completely autonomous organization unit, located in Vancouver, Washington with responsibility for making the ink-jet printer a success."[8]

The applicability to golf course management? It is nearly impossible for a golf course to internally redefine its brand without starting over and obtaining the buy-in of all employees to a vision that everyone can focus on. Incremental change, small wins.

Today, people want control over their lives at work and at home. Therefore, provide guidelines for employees, not necessarily policies; they probably won't have additional work hours, but they can learn to work smarter.

To find success, keep it simple. With this in mind, it is my belief that the management and staff of a golf course should embrace three principles to enhance their customers' experience:

1. Welcome each guest by name and with a handshake, conveyed along with the facility's "why." Say something simple like, "It's great to have you here today"; "We appreciate your spending some time with us"; or "We're in the business of fun; let us know how we do." Any of these would create a culture of positive reinforcement.

2. Smile. Every staff person can create a friendly and respectful environment and be empowered to take responsibility for fulfilling the customers' needs.

3. Thank each customer.

Wouldn't any golf course benefit by adopting these principles as habits? Charles Duhigg has a suggestion about how to do that in his book, *The Power of Habit*.

---

7 Clayton M. Christensen, "Innovators Dilemma," 1997, pg. 110.

8 Ibid., pg. 116.

He says that new habits are created by putting together a cue, a routine, and a reward and then cultivating a craving that drives the loop."[9]

While the cues would be fairly comparable between golf courses on the Assembly Line of Golf, the routine and rewards would not. Following is a possible cue-routine-reward system for a mid-priced to high-priced daily fee course.

Touch Point	Cue	Routine	Course Reward	Employee Reward
Reservations	Call received.	Hello, welcome to (fill in course name). It is great you're calling. How may I serve you?	Tee time booked.	1. Personal satisfaction from positive customer feedback.
Club Entrance	Customer drives past entrance sign.	Flower garden with welcome sign conveying "why" theme.	Mission statement reinforced.	2. Feeling of accomplishment in fulfilling brand.
Bag Drop	Golfer's clubs are unloaded from car.	A personalized bag tag is affixed to their bag.	Identification of customer facilitated at upcoming customer touch point.	3. Monetary incentives from gratuities received.
Locker Room	Enters locker room.	An account is created with charging privileges and locker assigned. Offer to shine street shoes; leave facility logo in shoes with customer name.	Incremental spending facilitated.	4. Monetary incentives for incremental sales. 5. Monetary incentives from positive feedback provided by customers to management or via electronic surveys.
Pro Shop	Enters pro shop.	A greeter recognizes customer by name, shakes his or her hand, and asks if customer needs any assistance.	Personal shopper available to stimulate retail purchase.	6. Year-end bonus pool.
Carts	Approaches golf cart.	Golf bags put onto cart and golfer asked if they needs balls, tees, water, etc.	Incremental merchandise sales.	

---

9 Charles Duhigg, *The Power of Habit*, 2012, pg. 49.

Touch Point	Cue	Routine	Course Reward	Employee Reward
Range	Walks onto driving range.	Golfer asked if would like to demo clubs of the leading manufacturers that are selected by asking, "How far do you usually hit the ball?"	Incremental equipment sales.	
Starter	Approaches 1st tee.	The history of the course (architect, yardage) and unique conditions for the day provided while offering sunscreen.	Reinforce fun experience about to be enjoyed.	
Beverage Cart Attendant	As encountered on course.	Customer purchases throughout day, and same beverages are offered on 2nd loop through course, recognizing customer by name.	Incremental beverage sales.	
Half-Way House	Upon arriving at the turn.	Provide complimentary pretzels and chips when ordering drinks and food.	Incremental beverage and food purchases.	
Cart Return - Club Cleaning	Upon completing the round.	Ask if expectations were met, thank for coming, invite to come again by offering to make another tee time.	Mission statement reinforced with incremental booking facilitated.	
Locker Room	While freshening up after round.	Offer to shine golf shoes.	Customer service level reinforced.	
Bar/Restaurant	When orders drinks and food.	Ask if enjoyed the round and what the facility could do to improve the experience.	Feedback obtained about golfer's experience.	

What do you think the appropriate routines and employee rewards should be for your facility? An off-season team meeting of all staff might produce some interesting debate that will help the group focus on differentiating your facility from the competition.

What this method of cue-routine-reward represents is a constant communication system engaging the customer. For example, here is an illustration of how the GPS system on the carts could be leveraged to a facility's benefit by enhancing the experience, as offered by Jeff Cline, Visage Group Regional Manager—Visage Technology Group East Club Car, Inc.:

> "The GPS system is a way for a golf course to have 'total' control over the golfer's experience and the golf car during their round. Most clubs see golfers for 15 minutes in their golf shop. Then they send them out on the course for 4–5 hours with no way to communicate, monitor or affect their experience. They have to leave it up to chance that the golfer has a good experience, hears about their specials, and maybe learns about other amenities the golf club offers.

> With GPS the club can tell them about their specials, offer them food at the turn, tell them about upcoming events and even let them know that they have open dates for weddings or events. Even if the club only sees $1.50 increase per round, Walgreen's built a successful business getting $1 more per person who entered their doors. Golf courses [that] 'Own the Relationship' with their customers and can affect their golfing experience, will be the ones who get more of their business."

By achieving buy-in within the organization, the team putting the knowledge to work with a consistent brand experience can be created. That is why at Bandon Dunes, the creation of the labyrinth with the following message is so special; like Disney's properties, the course has staged a show to create an emotional experience around this memorial to the course's late environmental steward:

> *"The Labyrinth is a metaphor for our journey through life. Its path leads toward an inner light, to the center of our self and the center of the sacred; one and the same. Its direction, at times, is confusing, taking us around, and then back again. Yet, it is through the circular journey of discovery and growth that we reconnect to where we once began.*

In memory of Howard McKee, whose own journey through the labyrinth contributed to the vision and experience that is Bandon Dunes.

This is a replica of the labyrinth in Chartres Cathedral, France 1194–1220."

Path to Success

Simple is better than complicated. Guidelines are better than rules. Formulating exhaustive lists of policies and procedures and inculcating the staff with formality dampens enthusiasm and curbs decision making.

Empowering employees to fulfill the vision of the facility as they see it will create mastery in time and heighten the customers' brand experience. The goal is simply to deliver a burst of pep, warmth, and sincerity to every customer interaction.

Developing positive habits based on cues, routines, and rewards contains the power to attract a more diversified client base of those seeking fun and entertainment in a friendly and respectful atmosphere.

With the staff setting the example of gentle people serving gentle people, the staff can transform customers to heighten everyone's experience.

The key is figuring out the balance between "come and have fun" and "we offer a true challenge to your golfing skills."

Consistency of message begins with product placement. That decision is then reflected in everything in the Assembly Line of Golf.

Concluding Thoughts

We judge ourselves by what we feel capable of doing, while others judge us by what we have already done.

Henry Wadsworth Longfellow

Ten percent of your clients give you 90 percent of your grief.

Mendelson's Law

Chapter 15

Who Are Our Customers?

Step 7 of the Golf Convergence WIN™ Formula

There are some people that if they don't know, you can't tell 'em.

Louis Armstrong

Insanity is rare in individuals, but in groups, parties, nations, and epochs, it is the rule.

Friedrich Nietzsche

Chapter Highlights

This chapter explores golfers' habits and their psychology and how these can be studied.

Choice is everywhere, and barriers are prolific. There are at least five potential barriers to playing golf—lack of need, money, desire, time, or trust that the experience will be enjoyable. Why do golfers make the choices they do? How do they differentiate between all of the alternatives? What influences them?

Understanding consumer behavior provides the insight and predictive intelligence that is essential to making informed strategic decisions. Gathering the leading indicators of each golfer's future consumer behavior provides valuable guidance.

Although "time" and "cost" have often been considered the most common of the reasons for not playing golf, recent studies indicate that most of those who choose this sport play because of the level of connection or affiliation or engagement they derive. Social connection drives choice.

An X-Ray of Who Plays Golf

Identifying just who plays golf begins with knowing their ages, their incomes, and their ethnicities.

We have chronicled through NGF research that the average male golfer plays 18.6 rounds per year, is 41.7 years of age, and has an annual household income of $85,700. Those statistics are in contrast to the average female golfer, who plays 15.5 rounds per year, is 40.7 years of age, and has an annual household income of $82,400.[1]

Beyond these summary statistics, a further analysis of golfers reveals, as illustrated here, that those who play eight or more rounds per year, while comprising only 57% of golfers, play 94% of all rounds and generate 93% of the industry revenue.[2]

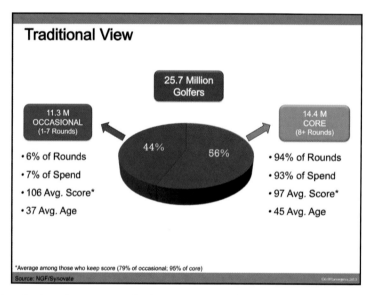

But who is playing those rounds, by generation?

If you examine the number of rounds played by age, the dramatic increase in annual rounds played by those older than 55 certainly emphasizes the importance of the availability of time. The participation rate of those 65+ has remained relatively unchanged from 1990 at 7.4% compared to the early 2010s at 7.2% of the population.

It should be noted that the impact of the recession resulted in fewer rounds played, more business at inexpensive courses, shifting the times played to the

---

1 National Golf Foundation, "Golf Participation in the US," 2012, pg. 4.

2 National Golf Foundation, "The Committed Golfer," April 2012, Slide 2.

lower-priced afternoon tee times, and deferring purchases of clubs and balls.

Furthermore, while there has been a generation shift, the participation rates of golfers by age have only changed significantly for Generation Y during the last 30 years.

The average golf participation rate of 18- to 34-year-olds in the late 1980s was 13.5%, while it was 10.8% in the late 2000s, a drop of 1.8 million rounds of golf. The boomer participation rate (10.9% in the late 1980s compared to 11.6% in the late 2000s) and the junior (ages 6 to 14) participation rate are higher, but the increased participation of these populations is insufficient to offset the decline in rounds. It should be noted

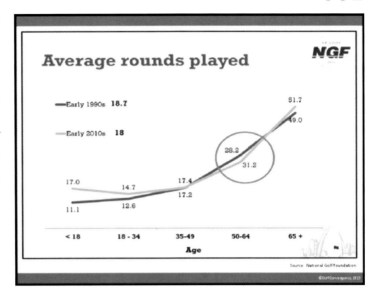

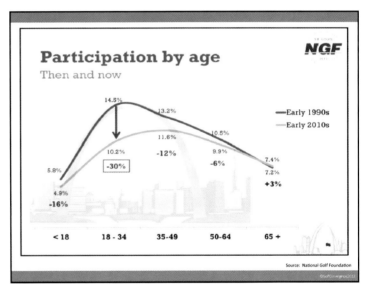

that junior participation starting at age 15 is less today than it was 30 years ago, raising the question of whether the emphasis on and dollars allocated to junior golf will reap a long-term positive investment return. The futility experienced in playing golf is also evident in the numerous attempts to grow the game.

What has attracted Gen Y away from golf? The Internet and video games are likely culprits, but lack of interest and time are real barriers, too.

In 2012, the National Golf Foundation examined what attracts individuals to commit to the game. Identifying those essential motivations is essential if the golf industry is to grow.

The NGF redefined the standard classifications of golfers from occasional, core (8–19 rounds) and avid (20+ rounds) into the following segmentation[3]:

- **Nuts:** I'm a "golf nut"; I love the game and it's my favorite activity.

- **Hooked:** I guess you could say I'm hooked. It's certainly *one* of my favorite things to do.

- **Fun:** It's fun—one of several ways I like to spend my recreational time.

- **OK:** Golf is okay, but I often choose to do something else with my recreational time.

- **Nots:** I don't really consider myself a golfer; I play rarely and usually only at the urging of others.

The research indicated that the majority of golfers are introduced to the game by a family member or a friend. It also seemed to indicate that the most productive way to create golfers who become committed is to introduce the sport through junior programs. Starting with a coach rather than from just their own personal motivation resulted in future commitment to the game also.

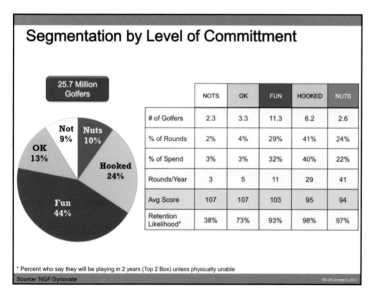

And, not surprisingly, the better the individual played, the higher the likelihood of retention to the game, as shown in the figure to the left.[4] There is clearly a correlation between competence and comfort in those attracted to the game. This underscores the need for affordable lessons, appropriate course design, playable course set-up, and the permitted use of equipment at the recreational level that enhances the enjoyment experienced.

---

3 National Golf Foundation, "The Committed Golfer," April, 2012, Slide 3.

4 Ibid., Slide 5.

The research by the NGF also measured the correlation between the fun the golfer had in playing and the perceived value of the experience. The question was asked, "All things considered, how much FUN is golf for you? (0-10 Scale; 10 = Really Fun)." There was a direct correlation between fun and commitment.[5]

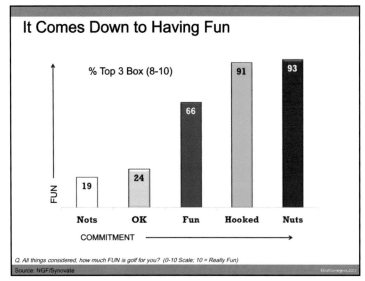

Interestingly, it was reported by the NGF that the common turnoffs within all groups that were not committed included the difficulty of the game, embarrassment, the effort required to lessen stuffiness, and rude golfers. Instruction to improve player competence and better equipment might fix the ills identified by the NGF.

The conclusion of the NGF's study was that fun = commitment and commitment = perceived value and that value determines frequency of play.

Thus, it seems that the best revenue enhancer might be to ensure hospitable customer service that encourages customers to find ways to improve their golf game.

In 2012, the National Allied Golf Association (consisting of the Canadian Golf Superintendents Association, Canadian Society of Club Managers, Golf Canada, the National Golf Course Owners Association Canada, and the Professional Golfers Association of Canada) sponsored an extensive golf consumer behavior study conducted by Navicom. The purpose of the study was to

- "Uncover findings related to consumer behavior characteristics in Canadian golf.

- Uncover actions which offer an opportunity to sustain the game of golf in Canada.

- Improve key performance indicators that impact consumer behavior as it relates to golf in Canada."[6]

---

5 Ibid., Slide 16.

6 Navicom, "Canadian Golf Consumer Behavior Study," September 12, 2012, pg. 4.

Realizing that past performance of a golf course (rounds played) is a poor predictor of future performance, the study was focused on leading indicators that would guide golf course operators. The focus was on why consumers choose what they choose. Just as in Simon Sinek's Ted Talk, the critical question was, "Why?"

The study was segmented by: market dynamics (what is the market), market drivers (what drives consumer behavior), implications (opportunities and risks), and market actions (what will drive success).

Market Dynamics

The study revealed that Canadian golfers are much like golfers in the United States[7]:

- The game has a focused appeal to males who are well-educated and have higher incomes, and there is very little ethnic diversity among this group.

- The majority of rounds are played by 26% of the golfers.

- The number of people entering the game is equal to the number of people leaving the game (18%).

- The number of golfers playing fewer rounds (38%) is greater than the number of golfers playing more rounds (14%).

- Forty percent of golfers took up the game between the ages of 6 and 17. An interesting finding is the fact that only 16% of these young golfers were introduced to the sport by their active golfer parents.

There were some stark differences between Canadian and U.S. golfers:

- Only 25% of Canadian golfers are engaged (playing, following, supporting, and endorsing the game). Seventy-five percent of them instead call themselves "casual" golfers. In contrast, in the U.S., 56% of golfers say they are engaged.

- There is limited interest in the sport outside of those who already participate. In the U.S., a large TV audience exists.

The conclusion was that "the game is still currently successful but may be vulnerable if nothing changes, and there is no way to remove the vulnerability

---

7 Ibid., pg. 13–15.

without significant innovation. The simple answer is deliver more value to more golfers."[8] To sustain the game, the innovative ways for players to overcome the time and money challenges are the following:

- "Shorten courses; take less time to play.

- Simplify the golf courses for beginners; introduce beginner times and encourage playing fewer holes.

- Lower costs."[9]

While the NGF and the NAGA studies help golf course owners understand the underlying motivations of golfers, each golf course must understand the real reasons a consumer decides to play a course. Is it for sport, for competition, for exercise, for leisure, for networking, or merely to enjoy the outdoors? By understanding the motivations of the golfer, products and services can be tailored to conform to specific needs, wants, and desires.

Billy Casper Golf Management,[10] a golf course management company that serves more than 150 public golf courses, has identified certain predictable characteristics as to the volume of individual customers are a golf facility and their behavioral tendencies:

1. A golf course, on average, has 8,000 distinct customers, from a minimum of 3,500 to a maximum of 11,000. Many believe, incorrectly, that a golf course may serve upwards of 17,500 customers.

2. 10% to 20% of those customers are "initiators" and reserve the tee time for their group.

3. Only 13% will play six or more times.

4. 50% of those customers play the course only once per year.

5. 50% of those who play will not return next year.

6. A golf course will have a 20% wallet share of core golfers who each play 40 rounds per year.

Information about customers can be obtained in several ways, among them customer surveys, volunteer programs, and advisory councils.

---

8 Ibid., pg. 17.

9 Ibid., pg. 27.

10 Peter Hill, Billy Casper Golf Management, "Programming for Profit," presented at NGCOA Multi-Users Conference, February 4, 2009.

The easiest and most comprehensive surveys are those that are electronically distributed from one of the many Internet survey sites (Survey Monkey and Survey Gizmo are two). For reasonable fees, these sites make the creation of the survey simple, filtering by various respondent collectors and tabulating the results.

Framing the Survey

The purpose of a survey is to be able to draw conclusions about a population sample with a reliability and credibility that will facilitate decision making. The process involves the following:

Step 1: What Is Your Population?

For a golf course, the population would consist of two subsets: those golfers that frequent your golf course and golfers within a 30-mile radius, whether or not they have visited your facility. The ability to compare and contrast the view of your patrons with the views of area golfers is often very informative.

Step 2: How Accurate Would You Like to Be?

The answer to this question has two components: the confidence interval and the margin of error. What you are trying to determine is how much risk you are willing to take that the answers you get on the survey are not totally accurate because you haven't surveyed the entire population.

And the related "confidence interval" is an indication of how representative the answers of the survey respondents are of the population not surveyed. Stated differently, if you were to conduct 25 random-sample surveys from the population, how often would the results differ between surveys. While 95% is the most commonly used confidence interval, decreasing it to below 90% is not recommended.

The margin of error is the risk you are willing to assume that the answers reflect the views of the population. For example, if the survey responses indicate that the typical golfer plays six different courses per year, with a margin of error of 5%, the range of golf courses played would be between 5.7 and 6.3 different courses per year.

While 5% is the most commonly used margin of error, depending on the size of the population, you might come up with between 1% and 10% for a margin of error.

Step 3: Determining Sample Size?

Having determined the population size, the confidence interval, and the margin of error desired, the required sample size can be determined, as illustrated in the chart below.[11]

Population	Margin of Error Confidence Interval					
	90%/10%	90%/5%	90%/1%	95%/10%	95%/5%	99%/1%
100	41	74	99	50	80	99
500	60	176	466	81	218	476
1,000	64	214	872	88	278	906
5,000	67	257	2876	95	357	3289
10,000	68	264	4036	96	370	4900
100,000	68	270	6336	96	383	8763
1,000,000+	68	271	6719	97	384	9513

To determine the sample size required, there are numerous complimentary Web sites to guide you, including Raosoft, Inc. at http://www.raosoft.com/samplesize.html.

Step 4: Response Rate

The response rate represents those who actually return the completed survey. A certain percentage of those surveyed must return their surveys for the surveying entity to achieve the level of accuracy sought.

In conducting the Canadian financial benchmarking survey, the challenges to achieving an appropriate response were evident.

It was hoped that the survey would reveal meaningful financial information by which courses could compare their operating performances to their peers, both regionally and locally. For that to happen, sufficient responses needed to come from each province. While a confidence level of 94% with a 6% margin

---

11 http://www.raosoft.com/samplesize.html

of error was achieved on 325 respondents from a population size of 2,310, as illustrated below, parsing the data further could have easily produced some incorrect conclusions regarding the population.

PROVINCIAL	Population (Number of Courses Located in Province)	Actual Sample Size	Statistical Sample Required to Achieve 90%/10%	Actual Confidence Level and Margin of Error
British Columbia	311	56	56	90 | 10
Alberta	313	43	56	90 | 12
Saskatchewan	165	11	48	90 | 25
Manitoba	133	14	47	90 | 21
Ontario	841	149	62	95 | 7.5
Quebec	367	10	57	90 | 26
New Brunswick	56	8	31	90 | 28
Nova Scotia	72	13	35	90 | 21
PEI	30	4	21	90 | 18
Newfoundland	22	1	17	90 | 90

Response rates vary widely depending on a number of factors such as the relationship with your target audience, the length and complexity of the survey, incentives, and the topic of your survey.

For online surveys in which there is no prior relationship with recipients, a response rate of between 20% and 30% is considered to be highly successful. When sampling golfers, a response rate of upwards of 40% is common, but the relationship of the target audience to the survey greatly influences the outcome.

The golf course in Asbury, Iowa, had gathered an email database of slightly over 250 golfers, which is too small a sample size to produce meaningful results. In such cases, extending the sample size to the city's Parks and Recreation Department is often done to capture the fringe golfers. That database had over 300 email addresses. Illustrated on the next page is the response from the survey.

The golfer response rate was 44.6%, while the Parks and Recreation database response rate was only 22.3%. The difference obviously was influenced by the interest of the respondents in the survey topic. The aggregate response provides some insights, but unfortunately the results were not statistically valid.

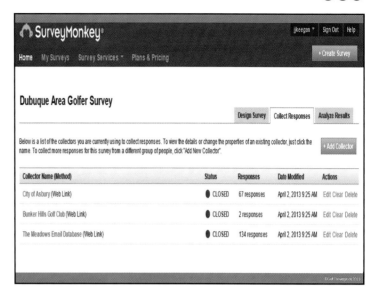

Step 5: How Many People Should the Survey Be Sent to?

Divide the sample response desired by the anticipated response rate. If you are seeking to achieve a 95% confidence level with a 5% margin of error, and you anticipate a 20% response rate, the survey should be sent to 1,795 individuals (357/.20%). Contests and awarding some complimentary rounds to respondents can stimulate the response, though those efforts may slightly compromise the validity of responses received.

There are a couple of "catches" in undertaking surveys.

First, the completion rate. The goal is that 90% of the respondents will complete all questions on the survey. The probability of achieving that completion rate is dependent upon the length of the survey and the form of the questions. After 25 questions, that completion rate starts to drop. Yes, No, and Multiple-Choice questions are preferred over essay questions for two reasons: easier to answer and far easier to tabulate the responses in a meaningful format for analysis. Also, when the survey is released, there will be an initial surge of respondents who believe they can answer the questions quickly to qualify for the prize. They tend to drop out after 10 questions.

Second, while Yes, No, and Multiple-Choice questions are preferred, they can produce serious flaws as to internal validity and create a ceiling effect. The answers to some questions on a survey need to be measurable on a 5-point or 10-point scale in order to undertake meaningful statistical analysis.

Third, when you ask customers questions about policies and procedures (rates, tee time access policies, credit card guarantees, etc.), they will respond not from the perspective of what would be equitable for all parties but solely from personal self-interest. While one might be hoping that they will respond with an amount that represents the fair market value of the experience received, they don't want to look cheap but want to ensure the lowest rate possible. Their answers reflect what they hope the new rate will become.

The Questions to Ask

A customer survey should be made up of four components: learning about the golfers, their playing frequency and preferences, their opinions of your facility, and their opinions and observances about a diverse range of topics related to customer service.

A well-crafted survey will incorporate "skip logic" to ensure that the respondent can complete the survey in less than 10 minutes. For example, if they haven't played the golf course in the last two years, the logic would be to have them skip over any questions evaluating the course, the food service, and the staff.

One of the great options a survey provides is the ability to filter responses to a given answer by gender, ethnicity, income, playing frequency, etc. Some amazing insights can be obtained by drilling into the detail, if the survey has attracted a sufficient number of respondents.

Some of the questions that might be asked and some of the responses sought are provided next as an illustration.

Learning About the Golfer

Presented in the following are the questions most frequently asked to identify a golf course's customer profiles and examples of responses received from various golfer electronic surveys conducted by Golf Convergence.

Question 1: Gender

- ☐ Male
- ☐ Female

While females comprise 50.9% of the United States population, only 19.3% play golf. The NGF reported that 21 million have played the game at least once, but have "lapsed." Of these 21 million lapsed golfers, 41.3% are female.

Question 2: Age

- ☐ 18 & Under
- ☐ 19–23
- ☐ 24–34
- ☐ 35–54
- ☐ 55–64
- ☐ 65 or older

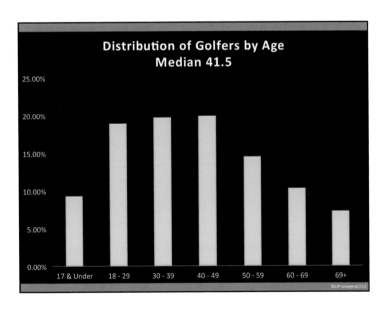

Question 3: Household Income

- ☐ 0–$29,999
- ☐ $30,000–$49,999
- ☐ $50,000–$74,999
- ☐ $75,000–$99,999
- ☐ $100,000–$124,999
- ☐ $125,000–$249,000
- ☐ $250,000 or more

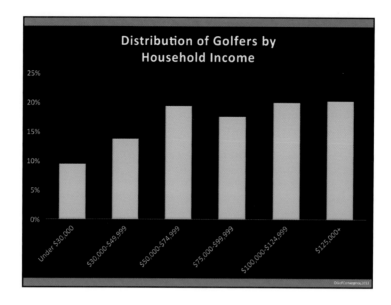

While it might seem logical that the higher the net income of the customer base, the greater flexibility in pricing that respondent might have in green fee rates, but such is often not the case.

Question 4: Ethnicity

☐ White, non-Hispanic
☐ African-American
☐ Hispanic
☐ Asian or Pacific Islander

The NGF research has documented that the participation rate of Caucasians is 11.9%, Hispanics, 7.7%, Asian-Americans 8.9%, and African-Americans 3.9%.[12]

Question 5: Education

☐ Some high school
☐ Graduated from high school
☐ Some college
☐ Associate's Degree
☐ Bachelor's Degree
☐ Master's Degree
☐ Doctorate (PhD, JD, MD)

---

12 National Golf Foundation, "Minority Golf Participation in the US," 2010, pg. 3.

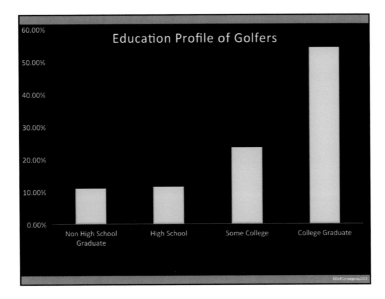

As would be expected, there is a correlation in surveys conducted by median household income and education. This question has been asked as a barometer, the thinking being that the higher the educational level of the customers, the more responsive they would be to factual discussions regarding the challenges of managing a course. But this assumption hasn't proven to be true.

Question 6: What is your postal code?

Microsoft MapPoint has an excellent software program in which the ZIP or postal codes can be inserted and graphed onto a map showing the relative distribution of respondents, as illustrated here:

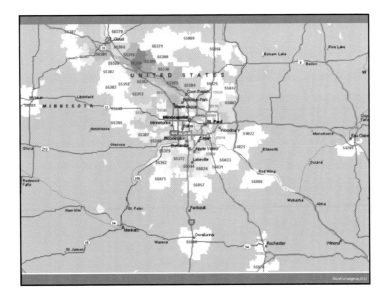

Preferences and Habits

Question 7: How many rounds do you usually play each year?

- ☐ 0
- ☐ 1–7
- ☐ 8–23
- ☐ 24–50
- ☐ 51–75
- ☐ 75–99
- ☐ 100 or more

In surveys conducted, it is not uncommon to see the median response to this question be over 30 rounds, though national averages are far less. Customers that respond to surveys are more than likely the core and avid golfers who are engaged.

Question 8: How many different golf courses do you usually play each year?

- ☐ 0
- ☐ 1–3
- ☐ 4–6
- ☐ 7–9
- ☐ 10–12
- ☐ 13 or more

The typical answer is between 4 and 6 golf courses. The response to this question often surprises golf course staff, thinking they have captured the majority of a customer's wallet share.

Question 9: What are the primary barriers that prevent you from playing golf more often? (Choose up to two answers.)

- ☐ I don't have enough MONEY
- ☐ I don't have ANYONE TO PLAY WITH
- ☐ I don't have enough TIME
- ☐ I don't have enough FUN when I play
- ☐ I cannot easily GET TO COURSE
- ☐ I am NOT VERY GOOD
- ☐ I cannot easily GET A TEE TIME when I want it
- ☐ I LOST INTEREST in the game
- ☐ NO BARRIERS; play as often as time and money permit

The leading two answers received in all studies conducted are "time" and "no barriers." These flip-flop slightly, depending on location, between a 35% and a 45% response. Money, though listed first, usually garners less than a 20% response in such surveys.

Question 10: What factors are important to you in selecting one course over another? (Select only one response per line.)

	Extremely Important	Somewhat Important	Neither Important nor Unimportant	Slightly Unimportant	Unimportant
Availability of practice facilities/instruction					
Clubhouse amenities (Food/beverage, pro shop)					
Course condition					
Course design—challenge to play					
Course design—easy to play					
Customer service					
Pace of play					
Price					
Proximity to home/work					
Rewards/loyalty program					
Social connections (leagues, where friends play)					
Tee time availability					

Course condition and price are the top two answers received in nearly every survey conducted. Interestingly, price often comes in first at the lower-priced golf courses, not at the more expensive facilities.

Question 11: What length golf course do you prefer to play?

- ☐ Short, par 3, nine-hole course
- ☐ Regulation length, par 3, nine-hole course
- ☐ Executive 18-hole golf course: 4,000 to 5,000 yards
- ☐ Regulation length golf course: 5,001 to 6,000 yards
- ☐ Regulation length golf course: 6,001 to 6,500 yards
- ☐ Regulation length golf course: 6,501 to 7,000 yards
- ☐ Regulation length golf course: Over 7,000 yards

This question was asked for the first time in 24 surveys conducted throughout the U.S. in 2012, with surprising results. While a straight average of the answers will create a skewed response understating the length of the course preferred, what was surprising was the high percentage of responses from women preferring 4,000 yards to 5,000 yards and men preferring from 5,001 yards to 6,000 yards. Short, par-3, nine-hole courses and regulation-length courses consistently received at least 10% of the vote.

Question 12: What percent of your total rounds do you play at? (Provide list of competitive golf courses within 30-minute drive time.)

- ☐ Don't play the golf course
- ☐ 1–4 times per year
- ☐ 5–12 times per year
- ☐ 13–24 times per year
- ☐ 25–49 times per year
- ☐ 50–74 times per year
- ☐ 75 or more times per year

Other

In undertaking a survey, up to 15 competitive courses should be listed. This question allows you to ascertain the "trial rate" of golfers at your facility. This question also allows you to ascertain from the respondents in the survey how many rounds they play at each course which is very valuable information.

Question 13: Which golf course would you rate as having the "BEST IN CATEGORY" with respect to the following criteria: (Provide list of competitive golf courses within 30-minute drive time.)

- ☐ Conditioning
- ☐ Course Layout
- ☐ Customer Service
- ☐ Food and Beverage
- ☐ Merchandise
- ☐ Practice Facilities
- ☐ Price
- ☐ Value

The objective of this question is to allow you to filter the responses received and to undertake a separate analysis of the opinions of customers who primarily play your competitor's courses as to what they consider best in class based on the diverse categories listed. This detailed insight help a facility determine its strengths and weaknesses.

Question 14: Based on your playing experience during the last 12 months, how likely is it that you would recommend the following courses to a friend, colleague, or family members? (Rate your likelihood on a scale of 0 to 10 with "10" being "Extremely Likely" and "0" being "Not at All Likely.") If you did not play a course, please indicate by checking "N/A."

Course List	10	9	8	7	6	5	4	3	2	1	0	N/A

Of all the questions asked in the survey, this may be the most important one. It provides insights into the loyalty of your customers both to your facility and to your competitors' facilities. By subtracting the responses received from 0 to 6 from those from 9 to 10, you can determine your facility's loyalty score, as illustrated here.

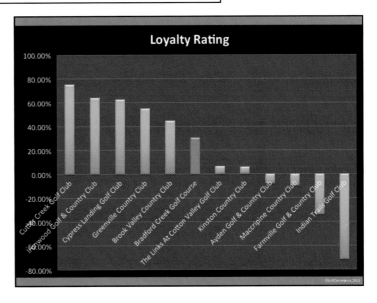

This survey above included the customer database of the municipal golf course, Bradford Creek, as well as the database of some area private clubs that participated in the survey. Interestingly, all of the clubs rated higher than Bradford Creek were private clubs. All of the courses rated lower were public facilities because of lower service, less conditioning, and less perceived value.

The national average for customer loyalty for golf courses is "26%."

Opinion of Your Facility

Question 15. How many rounds have you played at (fill in the name of the course) during the past 12 months?

(Note that this question has "skip logic" embedded. Thus, a "0" answer would result in the respondent being directed to Question 25, which addresses why he or she hasn't played the course.) Note that if question #13 is asked, this question and #16 would not be used in the survey.

- ☐ 0 If you answered 0, please skip to Question 25.
- ☐ 1–7
- ☐ 8–23
- ☐ 24–50
- ☐ 51–75
- ☐ 76–99
- ☐ 100 or more

While a good POS system will allow you to segment the customer database as to frequency paid by price segment, multiplying the answer to this question by the number of respondents provides insight as to what percentage of annual rounds (market share) the survey covered.

Question 16. What percent of your total rounds played do you play at (fill in the name of the course)?

- ☐ Less than 10%
- ☐ 10%–20%
- ☐ 21%–30%
- ☐ 31%–40%
- ☐ 41%–50%
- ☐ 51%–60%
- ☐ 61%–70%
- ☐ 71%–80%
- ☐ 81%–90%
- ☐ 91%–100%

With golfers playing 4 to 6 golf courses per year, obtaining a 20% wallet share is a great target. This question, which it may seem repetitive, is used if one is seeking to validate the answer received in Question 12.

Question 17: Please evaluate the following aspects of the golf course:

	Excellent	Very Good	Good	Fair	Poor	N/A
Affordability						
Amenities (Clubhouse, pro shop, locker room)						
Carts						
Condition of Bunkers						
Condition of Fairways						
Condition of Greens						
Condition of Tees						
Customer Service						
Food and Beverage Service						
Friendliness/ Service of Maintenance Staff						
Friendliness/ Service of Pro Shop Staff						
Golf Course Design, Scenery & Aesthetics						
On Course Services (restrooms, drinking water, beverage cart)						
Pace of Play						
Price						
Proximity						
Quality of Golf Shop Merchandise						

(Continued)

	Excellent	Very Good	Good	Fair	Poor	N/A
Quality and Availability of Practice Facility						
Rewards Loyalty Program						
Social Connections						
Tee-Time Availability						
Value Overall						

The attributes listed in this question can be adapted to each golf course's unique requirements and to the insights desired. The risk of listing too many is that you can discourage the respondent from completing the survey.

Question 18: What is the biggest challenge facing (fill in the name of the golf course)?

	1st Choice	2nd Choice	3rd Choice
Bunker renovation			
Cart paths extended, repaired, upgraded			
Clubhouse remodel			
Course design and layout			
Cultural and etiquette of golfers			
Expansion of practice facilities and driving range			
Green complexes reconstructed			
Location			
Marketing (Advertising and Public Relations)			
Modification and enhancement of tee grounds			
New irrigation system and drainage			
Pace of play			

	1st Choice	2nd Choice	3rd Choice
Patio extension and enclosure			
Player safety			
Range			
Season pass rates			
Social media adoption			
Tree removal and replacement program			

The areas listed should be custom-designed for each golf course. The list presented here is designed to begin the conversation about which elements to include.

Question 19A: To enhance the member experience and provide long-term fiscal stability for the Club, which of the following programs would you recommend (for Private Club)?

- ☐ Assessment—Capital
- ☐ Assessment—Operational
- ☐ Change the driving range location to 9-hole pitch/putt golf course
- ☐ Close the swimming pool
- ☐ Close the tennis courts
- ☐ Consolidate the clubhouse and pro shop location
- ☐ Relocate the bar in the clubhouse and enhance fine dining
- ☐ Expand the catering operation
- ☐ Increase monthly dues
- ☐ Merge with another private club to provide great golf opportunities and achieve economies of scale in management and operations.

This is a very sensitive question. Golf Convergence is aware of a client where the clear solution to cure the over $4 million in deferred capital investment was an assessment, but the Board of Directors feared a flight from the club of the "on-the-fence" members. They opted to water down the question, hoping to find a couple of short-term fixes while knowing the long-term problem would not be addressed.

Question 19B: Are you a season pass holder? (For municipal or daily fee golf course where annual passes are offered)

- ☐ Yes
- ☐ No

Seventy percent of public golf courses offer some variety of annual (season) pass. The permutations seem limitless (weekday, 7-day, couples, family, senior, junior, cart included, etc.).

Question 20. How many rounds would you play per year to consider buying a season pass? (For municipal or daily fee golf course where annual passes are offered)

- ☐ Less than 30
- ☐ 31–40
- ☐ 41–50
- ☐ 51–60
- ☐ 61–70
- ☐ 71–80
- ☐ Over 80

Question 21. For purchasing an annual pass, what discount should be accorded from the normal "rack rate," such as the Weekend Walking 18-hole rate? (For municipal or daily fee golf course where annual passes are offered)

- ☐ 10%
- ☐ 20%
- ☐ 25%
- ☐ 30%
- ☐ 35%
- ☐ 40%
- ☐ 45%
- ☐ 50%
- ☐ 55%
- ☐ 60%
- ☐ 65%

The average cost of an annual pass in the United States is $1,250. These programs are one of the biggest revenue drains in the business of golf.

The fair market value for a season pass is $2,516. The average season-pass holder plays 36% of an average 257 playable golf days, and is therefore accorded a 32% discount from the rack rate. The anticipated usage and the appropriate discount were determined by the results of an industry survey conducted by Golf Convergence in 2012.

What is fun about questions 20 and 21 is that you trap the golfer into determining what the correct rate should be. In the 24 surveys conducted by Golf Convergence in 2012, the actual rate then in effect was lower than what the respondents identified as fair market value providing evidential support to increase the rate next season.

Questions 20 and 21 usually provide leverage to raise the rates for the following golf season. One of our clients raised the rate from $400 to $675 for 2014. The golfers, even at the higher rate, will be getting substantial value, and the course will benefit from being able to create a capital reserve for its deferred capital requirements exceeding $3 million.

Question 22. Please evaluate the following aspects of our restaurant.

	Excellent	Very Good	Good	Fair	Poor	N/A
Customer Service						
Hours of operation						
Overall beverage selection						
Overall food selection						
Price						
Quality of beverage						
Quality of food						

This question is rarely asked because more golf courses have a snack bar operation. The four most popular menu items are hamburgers, club sandwiches, brats/dogs, and Caesar salads at a daily fee course offering a restaurant operation.

Question 23. Please evaluate the following aspects of our staff.

	Excellent	Very Good	Good	Fair	Poor	N/A
Golf Course Marshalls						
Golf Shop Staff						
Maintenance						
Management						
Outside Services						
Snack Bar						

This question is also rarely asked. In many cases, the customers don't have contact with all of the personnel. As importantly, implementing changes based on low ratings can be a challenge, since poorly performing staff members are not identified by this question.

Question 24. What is your opinion with respect to the trees on the golf course?

☐ Trees should be maintained in accordance with appropriate forestry practices, that is, replacement of trees in anticipation of disease or decay.

☐ Trees should be trimmed or removed only when the playability of the hole is compromised.

☐ Trees should never be trimmed or removed, and if the playability of the hole is adversely impacted, new tees should be built or the hole's site lines changed.

☐ Don't have an opinion.

This optional question is asked when the trees have become an issue in compromising the playability of golf holes. The resistance to cutting trees is amazing. Many golfers become staunch environmentalists, forgetting that a golf course is not an arboretum and that cutting trees is an integral component of golf course maintenance.

Many also forget that when a golf course is built, many trees are planted to create definition of holes without thinking what may happen 20 years hence.

Question 25. Why haven't you played at (fill in the course name)? Please check all that apply.

- ☐ Don't know where it is located
- ☐ Haven't had time so far, but I look forward to playing it
- ☐ It is too far from my home/work
- ☐ Price
- ☐ Was unaware the course existed
- ☐ Other (Please provide any other barriers to your playing including comments you may have heard about the course)

```
┌─────────────────┐
│                 │
└─────────────────┘
```

It is always surprising that upwards of 5% of golfers within the competitive market may either have not heard of the golf course or know where it is located. When the response is higher than 3%, it speaks to a marketing and branding issue at the facility.

Preferences and Customs

Question 26. What is your preferred method of paying for golf?

- ☐ Pay as you play
- ☐ Punch card
- ☐ Annual (Season) Pass

Movement away from annual passes is an ideal strategy to boost revenue. At a course where the season pass rate was $450, and some golfers were paying less than $4 dollars per round, the following was proposed by a Golf Advisory Council.

Rounds Played	Current Rack Rate: $32	Total Price	Cost Per Round
5	95%	$152	$30
10	90%	$288	$29
15	85%	$408	$27
20	80%	$512	$26
30	75%	$720	$24
40	70%	$896	$22

(Continued)

Rounds Played	Current Rack Rate: $32	Total Price	Cost Per Round
50	65%	$1,040	$21
60	60%	$1,152	$19
70	55%	$1,232	$18
80	50%	$1,280	$16
90	50%	$1,440	$16
100	50%	$1,600	$16

Question 27. What is a fair value for playing 18 holes during prime time with cart?

☐ Less than $25
☐ 25–35
☐ 36–45
☐ 46–55
☐ 56–65
☐ 66–75
☐ 76–100
☐ Over 100

This question only invokes the self-interest of golfers. They uniformly respond with the answer in the amount that is one level higher than the lowest price listed. As illustrated earlier, the likely response to this question is $32.

Question 28. What percent of your tee time reservations do you make on the Internet?

☐ Less than 10%
☐ 10%–20%
☐ 21%–30%
☐ 31%–40%
☐ 41%–50%
☐ 51%–60%
☐ 61%–70%
☐ 71%–80%
☐ 81%–90%
☐ 91%–100%

While 80% of golfers have made a reservation online, the online booking function of most golf courses takes only about 12% of their reservations. But online reservations remain one of the easiest ways to construct a customer database.

Question 29. What is your preferred method of learning about golf course special pricing, tournaments, and upcoming events?

- ☐ Check daily newspapers or other print media
- ☐ Email
- ☐ Facebook "like" promotions
- ☐ Golf course Web site
- ☐ Join loyalty/reward programs
- ☐ Pinterest
- ☐ Prepaid cards
- ☐ Twitter
- ☐ You Tube

Other

Email and the golf course's Web site routinely receive the highest responses. Surprisingly, Facebook and Twitter still lag very significantly in the surveys conducted by Golf Convergence in 2013.

Final Thoughts

Question 30. What do you like most about (fill in the name of the course)?

Other

Question 31. If you were the person in charge of managing (fill in the name of the course), what changes would you consider making?

Other

Answers to some open-ended questions at the end of the survey provide rare insights about the staff person that is excelling or vastly underperforming. Sometimes, responses have included the names of golfers who are acting like they own the place and in the process are offending other customers.

These open-ended questions usually draw about 10-word responses and can be "sorted" in Excel to determine and define the trends.

Question 32. Enter your email address to win (enter the promotion–usually a free round of golf for a foursome with cart during the current golf season). (Number) winners will be notified by email by (Date). We assure you that your e-mail address will not be sold, rented, or given to any other party.

The redemption rate on rounds won is low, thus increasing the number of prizes to be awarded comes with little risk, especially if the rounds are made available during off-peak times.

By sending an email to all respondents to congratulate and identify the winners (with their approval obtained in advance of the release of their name), you gain another opportunity for communication with the golfers and you create loyalty. They can see that the contest was legitimate and did award prizes.

Go

If you licensed the supplemental template that accompanies this Field book, open Step 7: The Golfer Electronic Survey template.

1) Using Survey Monkey, create an electronic survey. It is advised that a customer survey should be conducted at least annually.

2) Load your email database into an email marketing program provided by your golf management software company (Vertical Response - Deluxe Corporation, etc.).

3) Create a template to send an email to your database.

4) Within 5 days after sending the email, send a second email to those who did not open or opened and did not click.

5) Analyze the results in the aggregate, by collector and through filters, 10 days after survey is launched.

6) Develop a list of insights and perspectives formed from the survey results, and identify actions that can be executed.

Path to Success

Understanding who your customers are—their needs, wants, and desires—allows a management team to craft a value-based experience that will produce an appropriate financial return for the facility.

Even though survey questions regarding potential course policy changes will usually be answered in a very self-serving manner, an annual electronic survey of patrons can provide valuable insights.

While volunteers and advisory councils can be beneficial, they come with numerous risks. Thus, it is important to build and maintain a current database to obtain feedback.

Concluding Thoughts

A guest *sees more in an hour than the host in a year.*

Polish Proverb

It is not necessary to understand things in order to argue about them.

Pierre Beaumarchais

Chapter 16

Creating Customer Loyalty

Step 7 of Golf Convergence
WIN™ Formula (continued)

Human beings are distinguished from animals much more by the ability to rationalize than by the ability to reason.

Milton Friedman, Economist and Nobel Laureate

You don't have to explain something you never said.

Calvin Coolidge, President of the United States

Chapter Highlights

If a person has a habit of playing at a specific golf course regularly, can we call that customer "loyal"? If a golfer is satisfied with his or her experience playing a golf course, does that make him or her loyal? The answer in both cases is "no."

Customer satisfaction may be a short-term reaction, and it doesn't predict whether the loyalty intrinsic to a long-term relationship will be established. The fundamental characteristic of a loyal customer is their positive opinion of your business is communicated to family, friends, and associates. Loyal customers are advocates. They are uncompensated promoters of your business, and everyone they talk to knows they are expressing their true endorsements, not their paid-for opinions.

This chapter emphasizes the concept of customer loyalty and the importance of segmenting customers to enhance the brand image of the golf course and stimulate revenue.

Do Loyal Customers Really Matter?

Consider that the cost of acquiring a new customer can be "five times that of retaining an existing customer, or a 2% increase in customer retention can have the same effect on profits as cutting expenses by 10%."[1]

If customer loyalty is that important, where it does start, how is it built, and how is it sustained?

Every customer touch point provides the opportunity to build brand loyalty over the entire process of pre-purchase, purchase, and post-purchase, as illustrated in the following figure.

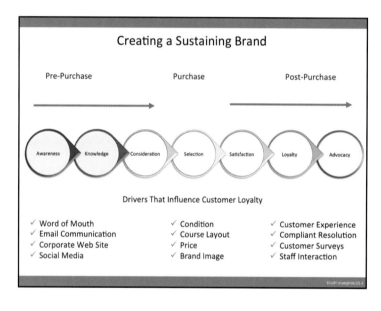

You can't shortcut the relationship. It takes time to develop customer frequency, duration, and interaction—all of which the customer controls and all of which combine to become loyalty.

A golf course achieves customer loyalty not because of what you do (sell a green fee, cart, merchandise, food and beverage) but because of why you do it, which can establish an emotional connection to your customers through every step of the purchase cycle. Their loyalty creates a brand image which becomes a sphere of influence that gets your facility repeatedly chosen over the competition, not once or twice, but consistently. Merely the name of a golf course such as Bethpage, Brown Deer, Crandon Park, Harding Park, or Trump International, immediately creates in the mind of the consumer a brand impression of the likely experience of a visit to that facility.

---

1 http://www.slideshare.net/Michael_Hinshaw/measure-understand-and-improve-customer-experience-mcorp-consulting?utm_source=slideshow01&utm_medium=ssemail&utm_campaign=share_slideshow, Slide 4.

While some may confuse the recent emphasis on customer loyalty with the evolution of social media and the connected customer, since 1993, customer relationship management came to the forefront of every smart business owner's conscience when it was introduced by Don Peppers and Martha Rogers, PhD, who are recognized as founders of that discipline. Their book *The One to One Future* revolutionized marketing when it was first published

Simply stated, customer relationship management is a system for managing a company's interactions with current and future customers. Technology is used to organize, automate, and coordinate sales, marketing, and customer service and support.

Informal methods to win repeat business have been built around marketing incentives for over 100 years, evolving from tangible goods, to cash incentives, to a loyalty system, to now virtual rewards, all illustrated by the slide shown.[2]

It is important to note that rewards programs may offer limited-time-only promotions to stimulate sales. They may give rewards or discounts at the time of purchase or point-based rewards programs based on miles flown, hotel nights stayed, dollars spent, etc.

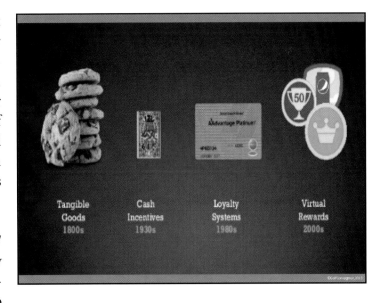

While these retention/reward programs may increase transaction frequency, it is important to differentiate between rewards programs, which stimulate additional purchases, and loyalty programs, which often cause the customer to become a promoter of the company, regardless of spending habits.

Many rewards programs merely are essentially another way of describing a discount program. The virtual rewards systems of today are so compelling

---

2 http://www.slideshare.net/alexdrozdovsky/how-game-thinking-is-changing-brands#btnNext, Slide 41.

and addicting that they create behavioral habits around which frequency of purchase, if not loyalty, is built. It becomes a game to achieve a certain status with an airline, to be rewarded with increased benefits that make travel easier, or to get "a star" downloaded while you wait for your morning Skinny Vanilla Latte or an afternoon Java Chip Frappuccino fix. As with Pavlov's experiment, when the bell rings, get a reward.

The success of Starbucks' loyalty card program is attributed to its mobile rewards app, which customers can use to pay for their orders by smartphone. Over 1 million mobile users have the Starbucks' mobile rewards app and check their loyalty program account information in real time on their phones. Additionally, the app delivers special promotions to users, and, of course, it locates Starbucks stores.

It is this stream of communication from the company to the customer that reinforces the brand and encourages purchases and loyalty. I know that system seems to work on me. I often go to Starbucks in the afternoon just to earn the additional star, especially when the time is near for me to earn an additional reward.

The process of implementing a customer relationship management system to build brand loyalty includes implementing technology to efficiently track customer transactions, measuring the customer touch points to ascertain which ones have value, and assessing the overall rating against industry peers.

Implementing a CRM System

Building customer loyalty in the golf business is straightforward. The purpose of technology is to efficiently gather data into stratified views that allow you to segment your customers by filters you deem appropriate (frequency, spending, etc.).

A customer relationship management program involves four steps: collecting data, analyzing the data, executing a marketing program, and monitoring the results. For the golf industry, those steps mean to proceed as follows:

- Install an integrated tee time reservation system that interfaces with your POS system.

- Use the software to build a customer database that tracks customer frequency, spending, and preferences. Note that developing an accurate customer database is not without challenges. One of the problems is that courses often only collect "data" from the golfers who make the tee time, especially if they check in and pay for the foursome. If the other golfers check in separately, then there's the delay of getting names (spelled correctly), phone numbers (repeated for accuracy), and email addresses, which are a pain because many are "cutesy" thus hard to listen to and type into a computer. Utilizing a registration system separate from the POS process and Web enrollment is an effective way to overcome this potential bottleneck.

- Construct a Web site that can do the following:

  1. Allow the golfer to book a tee time on the home page of the Web site or via a mobile application in three clicks. Few golf courses have Web sites or mobile applications that are this efficient.

  2. Permit the customer to self-register for tournament opportunities, merchandise specials, and tee times that are priced consistent with the course's yield management strategy. Fortunately, more courses are beginning to provide this functionality.

With the information collected, custom-tailored email and social media messages are sent to your demographically profiled customers on a bi-weekly or customer-requested frequency to win and build loyalty.

It should be cautioned that the data collection and filtering process must be accurate. Poor data will lead to poor decisions about how to manage the customer experience. Nothing is more frustrating than getting an email from a company to purchase products you already purchased from them or receiving an invitation to play in a tournament for which you are not qualified.

The key to success in building loyalty is crafting messages to golfers based on their preferences and their degree of loyalty. Identifying core, new customers (acquired), and defectors (lost customers—those who haven't played in 90 days) is essential. In Chapter 8, you have learned about the key reports that should be included in your golf management system to achieve the recommended segmentation.

Measuring the customer experience is a data-intensive effort which the vast majority of golf courses perform poorly. The best courses are only able to gather about 75% of their customers' email addresses. Less than 5% of golf courses segment their database and send tailored messages to their customers based on how often they play and how much they spend while there. Having staff dedicated to this task is a must and an expense that must be both budgeted for and measured to determine Return on Investment (ROI).

The key challenge at golf courses is understanding and believing in the power of these systems and then executing them. One of the nation's leading golf course general managers indicated to me that the system at his course provided excellent information for the owner but had little value to him or his staff.

We don't recommend a reactive philosophy of only serving customers upon their arrival. We like to see a proactive philosophy of "hand picking" your customers based on their spending profiles.

At an NGCOA Annual meeting, Peter Hill, Chairman of Billy Casper Golf, commented that at some point software may evolve to a point at which the more favorable tee times will be made available to those with the highest spending patterns per transaction, who are qualified loyalty club members, and who prove they are advocates by bringing new players to the course. That would be the ultimate in yield management.

Measuring Customer Touch Points

Secret shopper services or electronic surveys, as discussed in Chapter 15, are two effective ways to measure the perceived value the customer has experienced.

There are two different questions that can be posed to measure that value. Utilizing A/B testing, the first question would offer a five-point rating scale. Each of the touch points are listed with descriptors that are appropriate for this facility's vision, as illustrated on the next page.

367

A second question is designed to measure the relative value perceived by the golfer based on each of the touch points encountered. Asking, "Please rank (from 1 being extremely important to 10 being extremely unimportant) what is important to you in determining the value of your experience at our facility" regarding each of the customer touch points shown here would be in-

Rating the Customer Touch Points					
Touch Point	Excellent	Very Good	Good	Fair	Poor
Reservations: courtesy, efficiency and helpfulness					
Club Entrance: welcoming ambience including signage and flowers					
Bag Drop: presence of staff, greeting, assistance and guidance					
Locker Room: friendliness of staff and availability of amenities					
Pro Shop: atmosphere, appearance of staff, greeting, friendliness					
Carts: electric or gas, ball washer, beverages container, seed mix					
Range: quality of balls, turf quality, directional yardage, safety					
Starter: welcoming, playful, creates positive anticipation, helpful					
Course: conditioning, price, layout					
Beverage Cart: properly stocked, professional yet engaging					
Half Way House: good selection, quality of food, engaging staff					
Cart Return & Club Cleaning: warm, efficient, offers assistance					
Locker Room: encouraging, tidy, respectful					
Bar/Restaurant: appealing, likeable, quality					

sightful. Knowing the golfer's opinion of how you are doing and what you could be doing better has value.

Response to this question would provide insights as to value perceived measured against the cost of providing the touch points at their current level. When the customers' perceived value is low and the cost of administrating that touch point high, modifying the touch point becomes a suggested course of action.

Determining Your Loyalty Score

The value of any business to ensure sustainable growth is based on the promoters, and they can be identified by using the "net promoter score." This index measures the relative strengths of a facility's franchise. Developed by Fred Reichheld of Enterprise Car Rental, it is now a widely used measurement by many industries and companies, including Intuit and Costco. This metric of customer loyalty has shown that companies with high customer loyalty typically increase revenues at twice the rate of competitors.

To refresh this material, in Chapter 15 we covered that the question posed to the customer is as follows:

Based on your playing experience over the last 12 months, how likely it is that you would recommend the following courses to a friend, colleague, or family members. (Rate your likelihood on a scale of 0 to 10, with "10" being "Extremely Likely" and "0" being "Not at All Likely"). If you did not play a course, please indicate by circling "N/A."

Course List   10   9   8   7   6   5   4   3   2   1   0   N/A

The net loyalty score is obtained by subtracting the detractors from the promoters. With the possible range of answers from 10 (strong promoters) to 0 (strong detractor), usually those answering 1 to 6 are subtracted from those answering 9 or 10. Note that Reichheld would consider scores of 7 and 8 as "passive" respondents.

What is very revealing when conducting a consumer survey is segmentation of the database and creating unique collectors for each segment. In analyzing the data, comparing and contrasting the various filtered information can provide meaningful management insights. Presented below is an illustration of such segmentation,

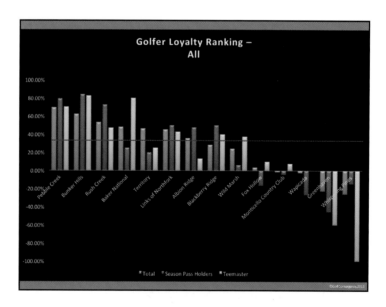

Note that a survey of season pass holders and golfers at the Pebble Creek Golf Course in Becker, Minnesota revealed that those customers gave a higher loyalty ranking to Bunker Hills. That survey insight led to an examination of the course layouts and the clubhouses, both of which are superior at Bunker Hills. The frequency of play of season pass holders at Pebble Creek, based on a ZIP code analysis, was a result of their close proximity to that course and the significantly different price points at each facility. Pebble Creek offers a superior value-based experience, while Bunker Hills as the home of the Minnesota PGA attracts special attention. Because the core layout of Pebble Creek is very solid, updating that golf course, which was originally built in 1994, became a very viable option to gain market share.

Loyalty rating can also indicate the price flexibility a golf course might have over its competitors. In southwestern Colorado there are some very fine golf courses, but they are either geographically distant from each other or they have price points that vary materially. In Durango, Hillcrest is operated under a private lease from the city, Glacier is an exclusive private club, and Dalton Ranch is an attractive real estate development. Pinon Hills, a fabulous course designed by Finger, Dye, Spann Golf Course Architects, had a higher loyalty rating. But, as illustrated below, because it was 50 miles from Hillcrest, prices, particularly for season passes, could be significantly raised because there are not many viable alternatives in the value-based segment of that market.

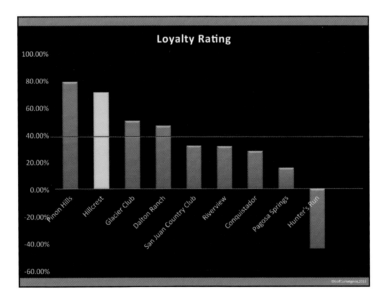

Segmentation—All Customers Don't Have the Same Value

Segmentation of customers can be based on many different criteria: demographics, geography, attitudinal affiliations, transaction value (historical recent value, historical total cumulative value, and future lifetime value), motivations (impulse, early adopter, status seeker, and bargain hunter), or lifestyle.

For golf courses, the transactional value of recent, total, and lifetime customers are the most appropriate benchmarks. For example, where segmentation beyond transaction history would be of value in the golf industry would be in identifying those who make the tee time (called "captains") versus the remaining group members and defectors (those who haven't played in 90 days).

It should be noted that for resort golf courses, the number of unique golfers who play the course is higher, and their repeat frequency is far less. Tailoring communication to those golfers at appropriate longer intervals will justify loyalty on subsequent travel.

To effectively market to these groups, Peppers and Rodgers created the Picket Fence concept shown in the figure below.[3]

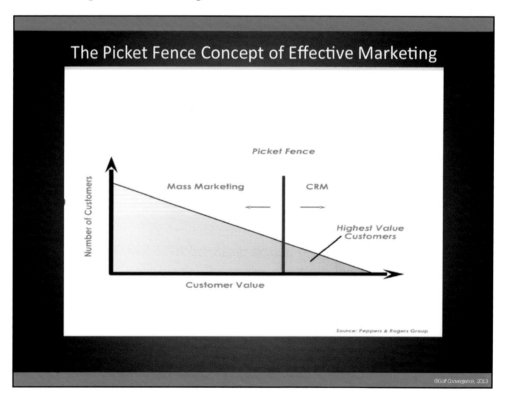

What is interesting about their Picket Fence concept is that it introduces customer segmentation to perhaps the top 33% of the customer database that

---

3 http://www.slideshare.net/vdimitroff/customer-segmentation-principles, Slide 6.

has the greatest value. Peppers and Rodgers carry that concept deeper by addressing the customers according to their differentiated value, as shown below.

The idea of dismissing customers who bring in less revenue than the cost to serve them is a good one. Unfortunately, most municipalities are precluded from engaging in the productive business practice of shooing away the season pass holders who dominate the tee sheet and behave as if they own the course. Daily fee golf courses get caught in the trap of the up-front annual revenue from season pass holders to even cash flow requirements and are reluctant to dismiss the frequent but difficult customer.

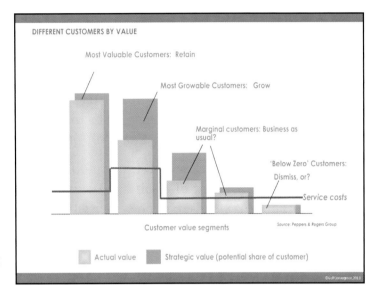

During a recent survey, a client received the following comment from a respondent:

> "I would tell that drunk 'Goosey' to quit parking in the reserved spot, stop walking behind the bar counter, and in general quit acting like he owns the place."

This pointed opinion indicates that dismissing a customer could have great value. The silent majority, who are often satisfied customers, see such behavior, don't approve, and opt to play somewhere else.

It is my belief that ethnic minorities and women are often discouraged to the point of being hazed by frequent customers that want the course to themselves. Self-interest too often takes precedence over community interests.

Thus, a course might segment its ideal customer profile as follows:

> Best Customers: enjoy the experience, interaction is good, low service requirements.

> 2nd Quartile: pay top dollar, but cost to serve is high in demands made of staff and complaints registered.

3rd Quartile: very price-sensitive but have few special demands and are easy to serve.

4th Quartile: leverage buying power to achieve low price with lots of service required.

All of this academic theory is great, but it will remain largely pointless for the golf course industry unless consistent change is achieved through execution. Change in the golf course industry seems to occur either almost accidentally or traumatically. Just as a trainer can't make someone lose weight or a counselor can't force a client to quit the excessive use of alcohol or cigarettes, it is foolhardy to think that demonstrating the benefits of customer segmentation will bring about the implementation of new management practices. The decision to implement comes from individuals.

Comprehensive customer segmentation is one of the new frontiers for golf course managers. Golf course owners and managers that invest the time in the short-term will reap financial and psychological rewards in the intermediate and long-term, knowing that they are financially stable and well-thought-of in the local community. Identifying customer segments and how to give them different value based on the growth and profit potential will increase the investment return.

How Social Media Is Changing Customer Loyalty Programs

Social media are changing the way human beings communicate, expanding the historical one-way communication (vendor to client) to two-way (vendor and client) to multi-dimensional (vendor and client and client to friends and the world).

The impact of the digital age will be felt even more in the future, as the costs of administering loyalty programs fall and the importance of customer increase is recognized, as shown in the figure on the next page.[4]

It is within the human gene that we seek to be part of a community, an entity larger than ourselves. Web pages, Facebook, Twitter, and YouTube provide golf courses with a way to improve the quality and timeliness of communication, from static pages to interactive dynamic tools of cross communication. From these communications, emotional bonds can be formed—if we only care about the customer.

---

4 http://www.slideshare.net/alexdrozdovsky/how-game-thinking-is-changing-brands#btnNext

Too often the focus is about special discounts rather than interactive collaborations. For example, soliciting input on a master plan via blog posts would attract interest. Are there golfers who don't fancy themselves as golf course architects? Not, likely. Offer a wine-and-dine, a ladies event via an alert; create that emotional bond.

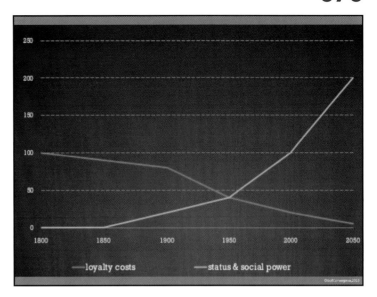

Smartphones give companies a 24-hour window through which to connect with their customer base. I'm always amazed at how the distribution of world news and sports via alerts, provides an immediate connection to that information. With mobile phones outselling PCs two to one in 2013, golf courses need to focus on not only the message and the distribution channel but also the manner of communication—shorter messages and multiple channels will prevail.

The risk of social media is that multiple-channel communications provide customers to vent not only to course personnel but also to broadcast their displeasure globally. Monitoring the "social chatter" regarding your golf course has become an important part of managing your facility's brand. Timely management of a customer's complaint is more vital than ever, to ensure that the customer is satisfied and that the problem is rectified, but most importantly before the customers' frustration level builds enough to cause them to broadcast their complaint to their social network. By really listening to complaints, by actually looking for them regularly on social media, then apologizing and implementing corrective action quickly, you may stop the bleeding, even though you may feel as though you have fallen on your sword. Simply stated, the guest experience needs to be managed with continuous guest feedback.

Creating a Coherent Strategy

There are many opportunities to implement a successful strategy aimed at creating customer loyalty. Marketing programs (outbound) and revenue strategies (inbound) enable the value chain (operations, information systems, personnel and, capital investment) to define the brand.

While plastic cards, print coupons, or punching holes in paper cards defined loyalty programs in the past, creating a multi-prong strategy of Web sites, Facebook, Twitter, and YouTube to create a community of interest now form the basis of future success. After that, a smartphone-based loyalty program can simplify the customer connection in the following ways:

- Better tracking of golfer buying behavior.

- Earning and utilizing reward points becomes hassle-free. A golfer can flash his phone at a point of sale (POS) and get instant credit in the loyalty program.

- Information captured via mobile loyalty programs can be used to strengthen customer affinity by facilitating engagement at a more personal level like the airlines and hotels do with their frequent and high-spending customers.

- Personalized incentives and offers can be delivered to complement their purchases; a club purchase might result in 50% off the price of a lesson.

- Ability to broadcast events such as last-minute tee time specials, clearance discounts on merchandise, and even Happy Birthday or Happy Anniversary wishes; all would create a great bond.

Path to Success

Customer loyalty is encouraged when you provide a positive emotional experience based on the customer's perceived value of his or her use of your facility. It is all about the emotional bond, about creating a cohesive blending of the physical attributes that the facility provides and their value to the customer. The simple formula for a customer's repeat purchase is that Motivation = Engagement + Loyalty.

Implementing and measuring the customer experience through the assembly line of golf by assessing the value the customer receives at each touch point provides a sustainable advantage. This is so if for no other reason than the fact that few in the golf industry are currently engaged in such practices.

Here are the key thoughts to remember:

1) Retaining customers is less expensive than acquiring new ones.

2) Managing the customer experience through the touch points is the most cost-effective way to drive customer satisfaction, customer retention, and customer loyalty. Not only do loyal customers ensure sales, but they are also more likely to purchase ancillary, high-margin, supplemental products and services.

3) Loyal customers reduce costs associated with consumer education and marketing and are likely to become Net Promoters for your organization.

4) Considering the highly competitive golf market today, customer segmentation is an effective way to differentiate your course from the competition.

As you create a strategic plan, the value of your golf course can be significantly enhanced by the commitment of management to understanding its customers.

Concluding Thoughts

The better you think you are doing, the greater should be your cause for concern.

Mark McCormack, "Godfather of Sports Marketing," founder of IMG

Individuals play the game, but teams beat the odds.

Navy Seal Team Saying

Chapter 17

The Industry—What Path Is It On?

A Future Perspective on How to Grow the Business of Golf

The further away the future is, the better it looks.

Finnegan's Law

Discovery consists of seeing what everyone else has seen and thinking what no one else has thought.

Albert Szent-Gyorgyi, Hungarian biochemist, awarded 1937 Nobel Prize for medicine

Chapter Highlights

What do we need to do, as an industry, to preserve the traditions of the game of golf while also offering recreational entertainment to match the evolving interests of a diverse society? Is it possible to achieve both?

This chapter explores, from the golf course owner's perspective, how the golf experience may need to evolve for the industry to grow. And it starts with focusing on golf's current customers.

The Theory of the Leisure Class

In 1899, when 307 golf courses existed in the United States, Thorstein Veblen, the author of *The Theory of the Leisure Class*, expressed his opinion that golf was a game in which individuals participated to demonstrate their conspicuous consumption of leisure.[1] In essence, people were attracted to the sport to demonstrate their superior financial position and to flaunt their lack of need for work as America transitioned from an agrarian to an industrial society.

From that meager beginning, golf in the United States has grown to a $24.8 billion industry supported by 25.7 million golfers who play around 424 million rounds while frequenting 15,647 facilities.

More than 140 years later, despite that growth, golf has not lost its elitist brand. Two-thirds of golf rounds are played are by those with a household income of at least $85,700, and their median age is 41.9.[2] The national median household income is $53,214, with a median age of 37.1.[3] For every round played in the U.S. by someone who is Hispanic or African-American, Caucasians play seven rounds. For every round played by a female, males play 5.1 rounds. Generation Y plays 58% less than do baby boomers. These statistics seem to say that golf lacks the foundation required for an industry hoping for dynamic growth.

Why is golf challenged? Our time-crunched society has created an attitude, a lifestyle, and excuses that are the antithesis to leisure. With the cultural changes stimulated by the evolution of technology and our quest to be constantly updated in this experience-based economy of endless choices, we have witnessed a lifestyle integration of work and play. This is added to the fact that we have become a child-centered society in which status is now earned by demonstrating how busy we are. However, the reality is that you always have time to do what you want to do.

With the harsh economic environment and the adverse weather during the past several years, golf is a struggling industry in which the supply of facilities exceeds demand. Since 2006, 499.5 more U.S. courses have closed than opened. Furthermore we forecast that 3,564 more facilities should close in the United States in order for utilization of golf courses to approach 80%.

---

1 Thorstein Veblen, *Theory of the Leisure Class* (Oxford, Oxford University Press), 1899, http://en.wikipedia.org/wiki/The Theory_of_the_Leisure Class.

2 National Golf Foundation, "Golf Participation in the United States," 2012 Edition.

3 Tactician, "National Golf Foundation Demand Report," February 2013.

Considering these multiple factors, we need to ask, "What does the future hold for the golf industry?"

Is it an industry worth preserving or should the massive investment made in courses, clubhouses, and equipment manufacturing facilities be viewed as sunken costs, much like a gas well in the Barnett shale, which is well advised to shut down when the cost to produce the gas exceeds $3.00 per thousand cubic feet?

Which Road Should We Take?

The future of golf is at a crossroads. It could lead in one of two directions. Or maybe it could lead in both directions. What path do you think your industry should take?

We believe the future of golf may lead in more than one direction. We estimate that 20% of golfers are traditionalists, measured by those who maintain a handicap versus as part of the total number of golfers. Tradition comes with a big price tag, and these traditionalists have the financial fortunes to underwrite their hobby.

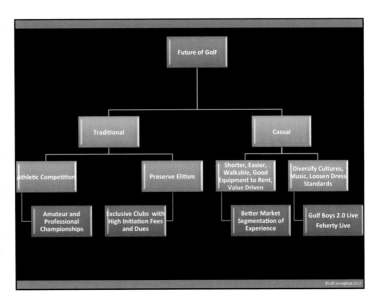

Each golf course has its own unique personality, and defining the "Why?" statement and broadcasting that message on a consistent basis to a targeted niche market is the foundation for growing a loyal customer base, even for the masses.

In crafting solutions, however, it is important to remember the distinctions between the business of golf, the entertainment product produced for the masses, and the game of golf that is overseen by various associations. These areas are often confused and muddled.

The game of golf can evolve nicely through prudent visionary leadership by golf course operators, the media, and golf industry associations.

For me, there is a list of changes that in my opinion would benefit the industry at large and golf operators, specifically. Acknowledging that, regardless of merit, none are likely to happen, because the status quo is a formidable foe. What follows are some thoughts concerning where the message and focus of each group should be centered.

Golf Course Operators: Possible Answers

At its core, golf is great **exercise**. Walking 18 holes equals a 5-mile walk or 3.5- to 4-mile run. Playing golf and walking 18 holes can burn up to 2,000 calories. Golfers exceed 12,000 steps during a typical round, meeting the guideline for daily exercise. Emphasizing golf as a key element of your health and wellness program will help drive beginner participation and increased loyalty among current members and golfers. It provides the **first solution for the future of golf—promoting the health benefits of the sport as physical exercise**.

While I understand the importance of cart revenue to the profitability of a golf course (it approaches 60% of green fees), it is refreshing that courses in Great Britain eschew carts (buggies) for pull carts (trolleys). Part of the delight of playing golf over there is the ability to walk for that exercise. The green to tee walks at most U.S. courses built since 1990 preclude such walks. Real estate developers were contributors to building extensive courses to provide greater opportunities to sell lots. While it is unreasonable to expect senior citizens and those physically challenged to walk 5 miles to play golf, using a cart still provides appropriate exercise for them.

Using a Nike Fuel band, we measured the steps required to walk some recently played golf courses. The results were startling. The courses in the British Isles, as well as U.S. courses built nearly 100 years ago are far more compact than newer courses, as noted in the following table.

Course	Country	Steps—1st Tee to 18th Green
Ganton	England	8,921
Brora	Scotland	9,563
Woodhall Spa (Hotchin)	England	10,654
Nairn	Scotland	11,179
Eugene Country Club	Oregon	11,639
Royal Dornoch	Scotland	11,754

Course	Country	Steps—1st Tee to 18th Green
Loch Lomond	Scotland	11,984
Cherry Hills	Colorado	12,321
Trump International	Scotland	12,647
Bandon Dunes	Oregon	12,914
Castle Stuart	Scotland	13,124
Hawktree	North Dakota	13,140
Colorado Golf Club	Colorado	14,567
Old MacDonald	Oregon	14,854
Links of North Dakota	North Dakota	16,694
Sanctuary	Colorado	17,142

This provides the **second possible solution—shorten the golf courses**. Notwithstanding how long many golf courses can be set up to play at full length, playing the golf courses at a reduced length (as with Tee It Forward) is a wise practice.

Using an iPod, I measured the time that elapsed while walking; less than 1 hour and 45 minutes of that 4½-hour round was actually spent playing an 18-hole round at the 7,300-yard Diamante golf course in Cabo San Lucas. It is interesting to me that over 50% of the time spent playing golf is consumed while waiting for a golfing partner to play.

If 18 holes could be played in 3½ hours, rounds would likely increase. Mine certainly would.

Are short courses the solution? Perhaps, but there is a caveat here. Short courses (par 3 courses, executive courses, etc.) are prone to losing money because their revenue potential will not offset their likely fixed expenses. Illustrated to the right is a July 2012 survey of Short Courses conducted by Golf Convergence.

Short Courses
>20,000 rounds if…
Affiliated with "regular 18 hole course"

State	Holes	Column1	Length	Fee	Column2	Rounds	EBITDA
Nebraska	9	27	1,181	$8.00	Par 3	20,000	Breaks-even
Nebraska	9	33	2,390	$12.84	Executive	15,000	Breaks-even
Colorado	9	27	1,562	$10.00	Par 3	19,454	Breaks-even - though expenses not calculdated
Montana	18	54	2,168	$16.00	Par 3	Just started tracking	Don't know - consolidated with regular 18
Montana	9	27	1,380	$10.00	Par 3	12,000	Loses Money
Montana	18	30	2,799	$20.00	Par 3	30,000	Loses Money
Nebraska	9	34	2,628	$12.00	Executive	7,300	Loses Money
South Dakota	9	29	2,636	$10.00	Executive	13,750	Loses Money
South Dakota	9	27	1,205	$9.75	Par 3	Not sure	Loses Money
Wyoming	9	27	1,187	$5.00	Par 3	2,500	Loses Money
Colorado	9	27	1,326	$11.00	Par-3	17,264	Loses Money - $25,000
Colorado	9	27	997	$10.00	Par-3	9,000	Loses Money - Over $125,000
South Dakota	9	30	2,076	$11.50	Executive	25,000	Makes money
Wyoming	9	27	1,893	$17.00	Executive	36,000	Makes money
Colorado	9	27	1,426	$11.00	Par-3	23,442	Makes money - estimate $100,000
Colorado	9	27	1,280	$9.00	Par-3	25,325	Makes money - estimate $25,000
Montana	9	30	Not on Web Site	$14.00	Executive	No Answer	No Answer
Montana	9	29	1,181	$10.00	Executive	Would not disclose	Would not disclose
Montana	9	29	1,745	$15.00	Executive	Would not disclose	Would not disclose

Like ski slopes that offer beginner, intermediate, and expert experiences, short courses would be best situated at existing regulation length golf courses.

With shorter championship courses, **the time to play is shortened, as a third possible solution,** which would be fabulous. OB Sports has it right with this great marketing concept, shown below.

Joe Riding, manager of Terrace Hills Golf Course, in Altoona, Iowa, just east of Des Moines, features his course as "Home of the 4½-Hour Guarantee"[4] as a basis for justifying his price. Realizing that these programs are dependent on the group in front of you, when the guarantee becomes 4 hours, you have my attention.

I was fortunate to be able to talk to the incredibly talented Steve Friedlander regarding his 35-year career with courses that include Loew's Ventana Canyon (Tucson), Doral (Miami), Black Wolf Run (Wisconsin), and Pelican Hills (Newport Beach). He commented that 50% of all customer complaints can be sourced to the golfers' perception as to what the pace of play should have been. He says that throughout his career, he has yet to meet a golfer who acknowledges being a slow player.

Watching the impact of the USGA's "While We're Young" Campaign, http://www.usga.org/MicroSite.aspx?id=21474854837, launched in June, 2013 should be interesting. After 2 months, less than 10,000 individual have enrolled.

Bill Yates, the Wizard of Slow Play Analysis, attributes slow play to the following factors:

1. Course management practices and policies, i.e., tee time interval
2. Player behavior

---

4 http://www.terracehillsgolf.com/new/

3. Player ability

4. Course set up, i.e., green speed, length of rough

5. Course's architectural design.

Yates is part of a major new research project by the U.S. Golf Association, whose multiyear goal is to solve golf's serious slow-play problem. "Five-hour-plus rounds of golf are incompatible with life in modern society," said USGA President Glen Nager in announcing the initiative last February.[5]

Just showing up, finding a game, and walking on, as we did at three of the Scottish courses, is such a treat. A great thing about golf is the opportunity to form new friendships by meeting strangers and enjoying pounding the pellet together, as I did with a member of Muirfield's The Honourable Company of Edinburgh Golfers, at Trump International, and with a Dell executive at Nairn.

Has the game become too hard to attract the masses? Many (perhaps most) Americans can play volleyball at the park, shoot hoops, chase a soccer ball, frolic in the pool, or play miniature golf. But the progression from miniature golf to playing on a regulation golf course is steep; playing there is much more expensive and difficult. Since 1960, the increases in slope ratings have been dramatic, as shown here.

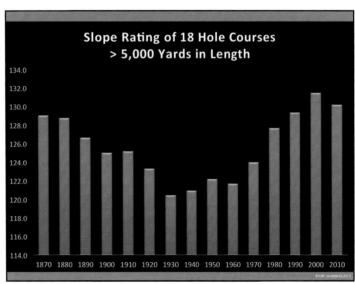

From the time of the first golf course through 1960, slope ratings averaged 122. Since 1970, the average slope rating has increased to 127. The setup of golf courses should be made easier for the vast majority of play days.

The slope rating is a critical measurement that determines the pace of play, the maintenance budget required, the gross revenue potential of the golf course, and, most importantly, the number of golfers that are likely to play. Rarely will you see a beginner on a course

5 http://online.wsj.com/article/SB10001424127887323740804578601882312192680.html?mod=itp

with a slope in excess of 145 or a foursome of accomplished players regularly playing a course sloped at 113.

Recently, in the fall of 2012, we reviewed with a U.S. golf course architect the renovation and expansion of a 9-hole course to 18 holes. The vistas are expansive. The acreage is ample. The comment was made that where there are currently six holes where there should only be three, and that there is a need to find draws, saddles, and bowls for every hole on this rolling farmland. It was suggested that a large canvas requires a large course on this 800-acre parcel. You may have guessed that this is not my perspective. Using less acreage would reduce maintenance expenses and afford the owner the opportunity to offer lower prices and attract more customers.

Today, 30% of the Top 100 Golf Courses in the World, as ranked by Travel Editor Joe Passov and his panelists at *Golf Magazine*, are located in England, Ireland, and Scotland. The pedigree of these classic venues is unquestioned—the history, the natural terrain, the bunkers faced with revetments, the gentle rolling greens, and the panoramic ocean views are compelling. In a perverse way, even the wind and rain add to the enjoyable adventure. Also inviting is the fact that a golfer is likely to end a game with the golf ball he started with, in great contrast to modern U.S. courses. There is a lesson here for U.S. golf course architects, owners, managers, and for everyone. Losing three golf balls in 18 holes increases the cost of a round by 30% on the average golf course ($12 per sleeve/$40 green fee).

The placement of tee markers should be based on ability, not gender or age, similar to the signage used on ski slopes. **Making golf courses easier is the fourth solution**, if for no other reason than it significantly reduces the cost of playing. Part of this concept is ensuring that golfers use the appropriate tee for their ability.

An increased **emphasis on service that is cordial and accommodating offers the fifth solution**. Unsure? Just ask any golfer if she feels comfortable and courteously treated consistently in many U.S. Pro Shops or if he is a fan of porta-potties. On-course bathrooms will boost play; I don't need research to state that fact.

Too many golf course employees act as though they are doing the customers a favor when serving them. When asked a question, staff members often respond, "No problem." That expression should be dropped from the lexicon of golf course staff. Instead, "It's a pleasure to serve you" should become the response.

Examples of facilities that get service right are Gleneagles in Scotland and Bandon Dunes in the United States.

Though I was neither a scheduled golfer nor a hotel guest, 30 hours after arriving in Manchester, this tired but newly invigorated golfer had played 54 holes at Woodhall Spa (Hotchiss and Bracken) and Ganton. I had driven nearly 500 miles, largely on roads that were a car-and-a-half wide, and upon approaching Gleneagles to tour the PGA Centenary course, home of the 2014 Ryder Cup, I filled my car's diesel engine with regular gasoline. Oops! With the car inoperable and desiring to be 120 miles away within 12 hours to visit the new Trump International, the hotel reservationist, the enchanting and elegant Ms. Kate Richie, and the concierge Mr. Jack at Gleneagles were incredibly attentive to my unusual needs and ensured that I would have a safe journey to my destination. I was stunned by their ability to solve my problem, and their service level far exceeded even what should be expected at this property with a 5-star designation.

As for Bandon Dunes and its minimalist approach, a visit there is always treasured if for no other reason than to chitchat with Shoe, the welcoming Ambassador for Bandon Dunes. He has talked with everyone in the game of golf. Bandon Dunes is to me the best the British Isles offers.

So should the service focus be on providing a great value-based golf experience from the 1st hole to the 18th tee or on providing numerous amenities and accoutrements that might be expected by the elite? What should be the priority for your course on the "Assembly Line of Golf"?

In America, we have gotten confused about our golf courses. We seem to think that bigger is better, that more difficult equals greater enjoyment, and that lavish amenities are a suitable substitute for warm smiles, pleasant greetings, and personalized service.

But luxury, once experienced, becomes a necessity. And golf courses would have to adopt a more simplified model to ensure that the "value = experience – price" formula remained consistent between facilities. However, I wistfully wonder whether golf course net income would increase in the U.S. if the more economical operational practices used in the British Isles were adopted.

The simplicity of the golf operations in the British Isles has an alluring appeal and is the **sixth solution.** There are no free bottles of water, no tees, no divot repair tools, and no bag tags that are complimentary and customary at

U.S. courses priced over $75. Try to find a pencil with the name of Woodhall Spa, Ganton, Cruden Bay, Royal Dornoch, or Nairn stenciled on it. Pencils with course names were only seen at Castle Stuart and Loch Lomond. The only free tees that were noticed were in a bowl by the 1st hole tee marker at Royal Dornoch and Loch Lomond. Ball markers are sold, not given away, at nearly all courses there.

What hole are you on? Don't look for a number on the flag; just yellow on the outward nine and red on the inward nine, with only the name of the course adorned on the pennant.

The hours in the pro shops are very business-like. Ganton opens at 8 a.m. and closes at 5 p.m. Woodhall Spa pro shop operates 8 a.m. to 6 p.m. The range closes at 7 p.m., though there can be daylight until after 10 in the summer. Golfers are able to play starting at 7 a.m. They merely go into the pro shop after the round to pay, as we were advised by the locker room attendants. The trust extended reaps rewards in loyalty.

Deemphasizing the need to keep score and introducing alternative scoring systems such as Stableford **is the seventh solution.** Lessening the dispersion in scores from the accomplished to the beginner is advised.

What did you shoot on that hole after the drop, the penalty strokes, and the putt that was given? Really, doesn't matter in the United Kingdom, where the Stableford system is the common scoring method among locals. There is something soothing about the Stableford scoring of 1 point for a bogey, 2 for a par, and 3 for a birdie. The BIPS (ball in pocket) posted in the U.S. seems to come with a stigma that you just aren't that good and should be able to finish the hole. Though the USGA handicap system provides for a maximum score, not completing a hole seems like you're cheating. Even a bogey feels like a reward with the Stableford method.

As previously written herein, nearly 15% of those play who play the game don't keep score. The only score that truly matters for amateurs is "Did they have fun?"

Enhancement of point of sale technology affords the eighth solution. Interestingly, air travel and golf are the only two segments of the U.S. hospitality industry where you are required to pay before receiving the service.

In Japan and Korea, golfers are issued a member number secured by a credit card, and all charges are posted to an account that is settled at the end of the day. Why can't this system be used in the United States? It seems as though the convenience of merely saying, "Charge number 6910," stimulate additional sales. Creating POS systems which facilitate and open accounts that are automatically closed upon completion of the round would enhance customer service and would certainly stimulate additional revenue. GolfNow/Golf Channel just announced the beta release of G1, POS software that is a wireless tablet based application to achieve this objective.

Yield management, customer segmentation, and CRM marketing that leverage social media will become standard business practices. To the extent that it is possible to develop software that runs the course on "auto-pilot," the industry would be well-served.

The new technology that is forthcoming in 2014 will facilitate the elimination of counters in golf shops and transform them, much in the manner of Apple and Microsoft retail locations. This arrangement creates a more welcoming and warm feeling.

Golf Convergence conducted for the NGCOA Canada a financial benchmarking study of Canadian golf courses. The results were stunning: Canada's golf courses may be outperforming their counterparts in the United States.

Canada clearly had the advantage over the U.S. in the following ways:

- The percentage of the population that plays golf (16.7% to 8.9%)

- The number of golfers per 18 holes (2,478 to 1,746)

- Average green fee per round($52.15 to $38.42)

- Food and beverage revenue ($624,008 to $355,087)

The survey revealed that in Canada golf is not about the game but about the social connection created.

What is the lesson? The success of Canada's F&B suggests that a golf course can be first "a club" and second "a golf course." That may indicated that the **ninth solution** is the **social connection and networking opportunities that**

a clubhouse might facilitate. Can you think of a better place to hang out than at a golf course?

That is what entrepreneur Donna Craig-Hoffman, President of Women-OnCourse® believes. Though not a golfer initially, an acquaintance took her to a golf course for drinks and dinner. Her thought was "Wow! What a great environment to relax in."

That thought led her to forming a "social club" for business professionals ranging from 25 to 65, and it has grown to include more than 70,000 women—1.3% of all women who play golf in the United States. More than 300 Signature and Play Day events are scheduled in cities such as Boston, Denver, the District of Columbia, Houston, Orange County, Phoenix, and San Francisco. These are supplemented with golf trips, wine tastings, and fashion trunk shows.

The events sponsored break even, and membership fees cover administrative costs. Corporate sponsorship has been obtained from firms such as Massachusetts Mutual and Callaway, companies that identify with the organization's tag line, "Golf is more than a game, it is a lifestyle," and seek an audience with this powerful group of executives. Interestingly, retired and stay-at-home women who have more flexibility with their time have been the exception within the membership, which represents a demographic very like that of women as a whole in America, both by marital status and ethnicity. In September, 2013, Women-OnCourse® was acquired by Billy Casper Golf.

In changing the function of the clubhouse, **changing a segment of the function of the golf course** might also evolve as the **tenth solution**. From opening to 2 p.m., the game should be the central focus. From 2 p.m. to 10 p.m., entertainment should be the primary focus: walking rather than riding carts, wine tasting, music, and meeting singles. The fixed orientation of an 18-hole course will lessen, and golfers should be encouraged to play only the number of holes they desire, whether 3, 6, 9, 12, or 15, with flexible rate schedules introduced.

In Arizona and Colorado, this seed has been planted in the form of "Sassy Golf." Frustrated with the rigid requirements and schedules of typical women's golf leagues, and not having enough people to golf with, Sassy Golf founder Nancy Collins thought there must be other women out there who want to play golf and don't have anyone to play with either.

That simple idea evolved into a full-fledged "league of their own" that was founded in 2008. It offers women an avenue to play and learn the game of golf in a social setting, at a great value, and with tons of variety.

The Sassy Golf Web site states that

Sassy Golf "caters to women who want to learn how to play golf for the first time or who have a love for the game, but can't commit to a set schedule because of their work, family, or personal commitments. Sassy Golf offers women how to learn the fundamentals of golf, play at multiple golf courses, become comfortable in any golf setting, and expand their social horizons all at the same time."[6]

What is really good about this initiative is how it encompasses players of all abilities, described as follows:

"FOR THE NEW AND BEGINNER GOLFER

- Players are grouped with others who have the same ability to learn at the same pace.

- There is no pressure from others in the group to win or get a certain score.

- Lessons are available before each date, so the players can learn from certified professionals.

- Golfers have the opportunity to practice at the driving range at each course.

- The reasonable cost of Sassy Golf gives women the value of learning the sport without paying exorbitant private lesson fees.

- Beginners are introduced to a number of golf courses so they can enjoy the variety of venues where the sport is played throughout the area.

- Players are able to learn the game in an enjoyable environment and meet other women to build both professional and personal relationships while golfing.

- Members are introduced to a physical game played outdoors that has great health value.

6 http://www.sassygolf.net/about-sassy

FOR THE INTERMEDIATE GOLFER

- Improve their game in a positive environment.

- Meet other women of the same skill level to advance their knowledge of personal play.

- Build relationships needed to connect with business and personal associates.

- Play as often or as little as they prefer and at a time that fits their schedule.

- Work on specific skills with a certified golf professional.

- Play with set tee times on a number of different courses so they can take their game to a new level, if they so choose.

- Take advantage of equipment and clothing offers by sponsors of Sassy Golf.

FOR THE ADVANCED GOLFER

- Learn more about what hitting yardage to expect from each club in the bag.

- Advance their strategic game so they will be able to compete at a higher level if desired.

- Get back to the reason they started playing golf in the first place—because it's fun.

- Improve their game while surrounded with players of similar skills.

- Play in a relaxed environment in addition to any leagues they may belong to.

- Have the opportunity to hit from different tee boxes at more challenging courses.

- Find a balance between enjoyment and competition."[7]

The Executive Women's Golf Association and Debbie Waitkus' Golf for Cause are two additional groups that are doing fabulous work in increasing female participation.

---

7 http://www.sassygolf.net/about-sassy

The risk these organizations take is what one industry professional calls "sizzle that leads to the fizzle." All three organizations, Sassy Golf, Executive Women's Golf Association, and Golf for Cause have reached plateaus because of the barriers discussed herein.

In an April 2013 presentation at the NGF Symposium, Stina Sternberg, Senior Editor at *Golf Digest* delivered the results of a study on women's golf participation throughout the world. Interestingly, all countries that had low female participation had one thing in common—all the countries were once British colonies, and the game was imported from there with the traditions and biases attached. Sternberg commented that the long-term solutions to women's participation in golf will be found in introducing children to the game from the ages of 6 to 13 before sexual roles evolve. She also suggested the certification of participants to ensure that they feel comfortable on the course. This would serve the industry well if applied to all potential participants regardless of gender, age, or natural athletic ability.

Another way to make everyone feel comfortable is to encourage the use of the clubhouse as a social gathering place, and to make sure the environment there is comparable to a fine restaurant such as Morton's, for instance, or perhaps a "lesser" chain that utilizes a grill typically used at most golf courses, depending on the brand image you are trying to project. You may change the brand image of the course by upgrading the clubhouse, the check-in stop on the way to the course.

Emphasizing positive messages in signage is the eleventh solution. The messages around the golf course should be positive and inviting. Have you ever counted how many messages are communicated to customers at the typical golf course between entering the property and the 1st tee? The average is six messages.

And if they are negative, they serve as a deterrent to the growth of the game and should be eliminated or changed to reflect a more positive service attitude. The signs pictured here don't have a place on a well-run golf course.

While the limitations of the clubhouse restaurant area are recognized, that doesn't send a welcoming message to a potential customer interested in golf, nor does this sign on the left:

At the home of golf, the danger of the sport is being marketed to those passing by. In this case, a limited amount of land was adapted for a needed component of the course (a driving range), in spite of the limitations of the acreage available and the risk to those who pass by.

The messages around the golf course should be positive and inviting. How comfortable would you feel playing at the Belfry, the host site for numerous Ryder Cups, with this sign (below) in the parking lot and again on the clubhouse entrance door?

It is amazing at how a staff becomes so accustomed to their surroundings that they overlook the many negative signs posted on their course. While playing the Country Club at Castle Pines, we commented to one of Colorado's leading golf professionals, George Karhoff, that the private club seemed more like visiting a high-end daily fee course because of the number of signs posted. We both chuckled at how, after many of the signs were removed, the experience was enhanced. Less is often better.

To open the entry door to the game in order to compete for the entertainment dollar, the industry should **adapt to the cultural changes in our society, and that is the twelfth solution**. Denim, T-shirts, and golf hats worn backwards might be accepted throughout public golf. It is the behavior and demeanor that is important, not the dress. Cell phones should be welcomed. Roaming beverage carts could disappear as golfers use their mobile devices to place food and beverage orders while playing—all intended to make the public playing experience more customer-friendly. Understanding what drives the buying decisions, from "cool apps" to social status, will expand the market to include new customers. Golf in 2022[8] might look like this, the image to the right.

At private clubs, **replacing high-equity initiation fees with lower non-refundable deposits and monthly membership fees** will expand the opportunities for those seeking a private club experience; **a possible thirteenth solution**. The transformation of clubhouses to sports bars, fitness facilities, and day care centers to focus on community will serve the industry well.

For a golf course owner, **membership in the Golf Course Superintendents Association of America is advised as the fourteenth solution**. Currently, only 66% of golf course superintendents are members of that organization. Membership in the **National Golf Course Owners Associates** is also advocated for the owners of daily fee golf courses for the opportunity to participate in ListServ, an internal Web-based forum for members.

The Role of Media and Associations in Growing the Game

With the PGA and LPGA on television frequently and the extensive and excellent coverage provided by the major networks, including the Golf Channel, these organizations have a responsibility and an opportunity to greatly aid in

---

8 Illustration by Dana Barak/Courtesy of Colorado AvidGolfer, J. J. Keegan, "Now and Ten," April 2012, pg. 102.

the growth of the game. They need to recognize the major disconnect between professional tour players, club professionals, elite amateurs, and regular players. There is such a wide range in attitudes of playing for pay versus not even keeping score and the focus on athletic competition rather than on exercise and social entertainment.

Having addressed the negative messages promulgated by golf course operators, TV Golf Broadcasters are also often promoters of the negative. TV Announcers have a responsibility to change the "serious, this game is so tough" approach to **make it a sport beginners would like to try, a fifteenth solution.**

Watching the tournament and playoff at Riviera this year was exasperating. The announcers were describing every shot as it were life and death, inferring that they were all so difficult that they were nearly impossible. They often send the message that golf is extremely difficult. Yes, it is very difficult to make it to the level of PGA Tour player; after all, as they say, "These Guys Are Good." But there's no need to be that good to enjoy the sport. Mike Greenberg, sports broadcaster on "Mike and Mike", humorously stated that he would compare his 77 at Muirfield on a calm day several years ago to the scores of the PGA Professionals during the 2013 Open on the same course. Naturally, he took quite a ribbing from his partner, Mike Golic.

Broadcasting events such as the Par 3 Tournament at the Masters, (on ESPN) sends a marvelous message to the public at large. Graham McDowell and

Rory McIlroy with their girl friends as caddies was heartening to watch.[9] Professional golfers were just having fun with family and friends for the sheer entertainment golf can provide.

"Fun," "energetic," and "colorful" are marketing themes for the future, and they provide the **sixteenth solution**. Fun is central to the game—hitting the long drive, then the iron, and

9 http://digitalmag.globalgolfpost.com/20130411

making the putt. In every round, regardless of ability, the player hits some shots that are pleasing. The introduction of new drivers with different color heads, new shoes with vibrant colors, and golf shirts in which one could run a 10K are all part of opening the door to the game and sustaining the business of golf.

Fortunately, today's tour players who are in their early 20s get it. The top screenshot is from a marvelous video showing a side of professional golf that is fun.[10]

Also, the concept of replacing the cart with a hovercraft is such a novel idea. Though more expensive than a cart, more difficult to drive than a cart, it is less invasive on the turf than a cart and seems like pure fun, as shown in the bottom figure.[11]

The United States Golf Association is steadfast in its adherence to maintaining tradition by applying a single set of rules and uniform equipment to level the playing field for national championships. In 2000, at the PGA Merchandise Show, then Executive Director David Fey stated, "It is from the innate difficulty of the game that enjoyment emanates and that the rules need to be consistently applied." Current Executive Director, Mike Davis,

10 http://crossover.nbcsports.com/2013/03/05/golf-boys-2-oh/

11 http://tech.fortune.cnn.com/2013/04/04/bubba-watson-hovercraft-golf-cart/

reiterated that philosophy at the USGA Annual Meeting in February 2013. We respect that.

What would be great is if **the USGA, in its advertising message to grow the game, "bifurcated" its advertising message; a sixteenth solution**. While the USGA and the kid getting the hole in one is great, that message is immediately followed by the admonition from the superintendent, "You know what this means kid. You buy the drinks."

Further, the message from the USGA could invite all to play and emphasize the progression that occurs as you learn the sport, as well as the health benefits, the social aspects, and, of course, the competition. First Tee, while laudatory, addresses a narrow audience. Creating a broader message, rather than one based solely on history and tradition, would serve the business of golf nicely.

Recruiting new players to the game by emphasizing youth, women, and minorities, **and motivating former players to return** with greater urgency, will be the hallmarks of new golf industry initiatives such as Golf 2.0, Golf Ready, Tee It Forward, Family Golf Monthly, and Play Golf America; **the seventeenth solution**.

To reflect that golf is a diversified sport, the **USGA Executive Committee might be proportionally** balanced representative to the population in America by gender, ethnicity, and private versus public golfers. While the change might be more one of form than substance, it would redefine the brand of the USGA to be more encompassing, rather than exclusive, as the **eighteenth solution**.

This balance could also be achieved at the State Association level. The USGA should recommend the consolidation of all men's and women's state golf associations to create economics of scale and efficiencies in operations. These state associations are often little more than licensed franchises of the USGA, and the USGA handicap system and grants provide them the funding to operate. While women hail equality, when operating their state golf associations, they can strongly and wrongly prefer segregation. And frankly, based on how they are often treated, they can't be blamed. How can we talk about integration where separation exists?

Regarding consolidation, I would choose that **the LPGA, at a minimum, license the PGA Education curriculum**, or even more aggressively merge with the PGA to vastly improve the experience of women professionals in the business of golf as the **nineteenth solution**.

Golf is about hospitality, and if the participation of women is to grow from its current 19%, making golf courses more women-friendly is a good first step. Anything we can do to retire the grumpy senior citizen who is working behind the counter as the starter or as the player assistant (ranger) seeking free golf, is a great move.

Note the IRS crackdown on "free golf" in an article in Jacksonville, Florida, newspaper on March 2, 2012:

> "If the message wasn't received seven years ago when the Cimarrone Golf Club was ordered to pay back wages to starters and rangers who were compensated with free rounds of golf instead of pay, it might be coming through since the Golf Club of Fleming Island had to pay more than $73,000 to 19 people last November.
>
> 'It's the law, and the government is enforcing it,' said Jack Aschenbach, president of the Northern Chapter PGA, the governing body for golf club professionals. 'We've all got to come into compliance.'
>
> The practice of paying golf course employees with free rounds of golf has always been illegal, according to Michael Young, the Jacksonville district director for the Labor Department's division of Wage and Hours. In-kind services can be paid only for volunteering at charity tournaments or for nonprofit facilities, such as The First Tee."[12]

Collectively these **19 ideas**, though implementation may be excruciatingly slow or non-existent, will redefine golf and shatter the hallowed traditions on which the industry's brand image has been formed.

In Colorado, bastions like Castle Pines Golf Club, with its properly reserved reverence from Mr. Vickers; Cherry Hills, with its championship pedigree; and Denver Country Club, with its blue-blood orientation as Denver's finest serving a small segment of society who seek to preserve an aristocratic lifestyle, will be unaffected. The remaining 90% of facilities need to undergo massive changes.

---

12 http://jacksonville.com/sports/golf/2012-03-02/story/government-cracks-down-compensating-course-volunteers-free-golf#ixzz2KnaqWZwP

Equipment Manufacturers

Equipment is expensive and the marketing messages are a barrier to the growth of the sport. Michael Berry, President of the National Ski Association, provides incredible insight into the differences between skiing and golf. He commented,

"1. Ski areas offer beginner, intermediate, and expert areas encouraging the customer to ski in the area best suited to their abilities.

2. Sixty percent of ski equipment hard sales purchases are made by the ski resorts. On a given day in Aspen or Vail, 35% of the skiers will have rented their equipment.

3. Generic national advertising promoting the sport has little to no value.

4. The key to developing new customers is developing a relationship with your best customers and leveraging that loyalty to incent them to bring family, friends and associates to the ski area."[13]

What a contrast this is to how golf is marketed. It is ironic that the equipment that novice golfers use often creates the biggest hurdle for them to play well.

Golf companies spend lots of money for player endorsements and use those endorsements in their advertising, creating identification with Tiger or Phil if you are playing with Nike or Callaway. They are selling the sizzle. The research and development process is very expensive and has resulted in making the game a lot easier for everybody, especially women, seniors, and the less accomplished or skilled.

Golf course operators would be well advised to stock the leading equipment of the year as club rentals, just as the ski industry does. The ability to rent the latest equipment at mid-priced and higher daily fee golf courses rather than being required to make an investment exceeding $1,000 for golf clubs will increase enjoyment and in turn help grow the game. If an appropriate fee is charged, the payback on the investment might be achieved after renting for less than 30 rounds, at which time the clubs could be liquidated at cost. **Facilitating the use of better equipment is the twentieth solution.**

---

13 Michael Berry, Interview, May 24, 2013.

Imagine demo clubs on the 1st tee. The starter could be quickly turned into a club salesman, as with the following dialogue:

> "How far do you normally hit the ball? 220 yards? Let me see you take a couple of swings. Looks like you have an even path angle. Would you like to try this new TaylorMade RocketBallz 10.5-degree, medium-shaft demo club today? If you don't like it, merely return it after your round."

As part of this process of education, manufacturers, in my opinion, would be advised to develop charts to explain how clubs that have 12 lofts, 7 face angles, and moveable weights should be adjusted by the typical golfer. To illustrate, the TaylorMade RBZ driver comes with a fitting guide which cites the following:

> "Using Flight Control Technology to Tune the Loft" loosen the screen in the heel, then turn the club head to line up the desired loft designation with the line on the rear-side of the hosel. For example, the standard RBZ drive lift is either 9.5°, 10.5° or HL (9° or 10.5° for Tour). Set the FCT sleeve to "higher to increase loft up to 1.5° and spin-rate up to 750 RFPM. Set the FCT sleeve to decrease loft up to 1.5° and spin-rate up to 750 RFPM. Choose from eight FCT/settings."[14]

This instruction doesn't suggest what the optimum is for the golfer based on club head speed. It is assumed the golfer understands club head speed and what setting is appropriate if playing at sea level versus in the mountains, where spin rates from the same golfer with the same club can vary due to the density of the air.

Hiring marketing professionals who are non-golfers to simplify the message would help reduce the clutter of technical terms that serve to confuse. Terms like "speed frame faced technology, optifit hosel adjustments, trajectory tuning technology, grain-flow, cavity back, u-grooves, laser and rotex milling, forged, MOI, and kick points" serve to confuse, not clarify, which clubs should be purchased by the recreational golfer.

To ensure a uniform message to the golfer, golf courses and equipment manufacturers should develop partnerships in which the names and email addresses of those customers who opt-in are provided to the equipment manufacturers'

---

14 TaylorMade™ RBZ Fitting Guide, pg. 2.

marketing departments. Most courses communicate with their clients poorly. A win-win situation would result if the equipment manufacturer communicated directly with the customers and accepted retail orders for those clients (with a commission to the course).

When golfers are fitted at the TaylorMade-Adidas Golf Kingdom adjacent their headquarters in Carlsbad, California, upon receipt of the clubs, the golfer receives from TaylorMade two postcards. One indicates, as shown below, the manufacturing process for the golfer's clubs, and the second stated,

> "You are a TaylorMade guy. You don't jump into new technology because it's new. You do your homework. You scrutinize every decision when it comes to your game.
>
> You don't follow the crowd, you prove it yourself. Your driver, fairway irons—every club earned its way into your bag. You play TaylorMade, because all that matters is performance.
>
> That's why we're sending you our new LETHAL Tour ball. This is the ball we've made for TaylorMade golfers only, and it has already won on Tour. This ball is so good that we don't want anyone else to have it.
>
> And we want you to put it to the test. Learn more at taylormade .com."[15]

---

15 TaylorMade, "The Most Innovative Tour Ball We've Ever Made."

Connecting the manufacturer to the golfer more directly would benefit the industry is proposed as **the twenty-first solution**. Social media is greatly aiding those efforts. The chart below illustrates how equipment manufacturers are connecting to the golfer directly.[16]

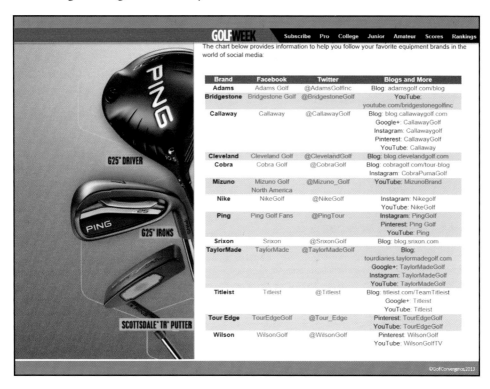

Nevertheless, manufacturers would be advised to do the following:

1. Educate the consumers on the basic principles of equipment regarding distance and loft.

2. Simplify their advertisements to be understandable by the masses and not merely the highly trained professional.

The Next 20 Years

A general malaise that unfortunately exists throughout the golf industry has been chronicled throughout this book. The industry is like a big ship in the ocean that is difficult to turn quickly. In which direction is it heading?

The National Golf Foundation believes that 50 million incremental rounds will be added to the game over the next two decades, representing growth of 5%

---

16 http://golfweek.com/news/2013/may/10/equipment-brands-tap-social-media/

to 15%. By insightful research, the NGF concluded that there are no big population drops forecast across the generations. In fact, the baby boomers, they concluded, as illustrated in the following, were a rising tide that never fell[17]:

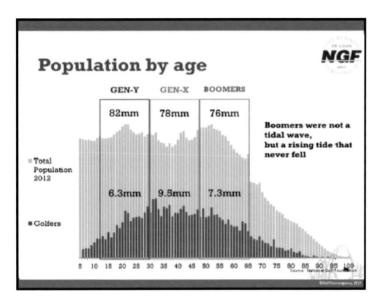

Thus, the NGF concluded that unless there is a big drop in participation rates, the golf industry will continue on a steady course of slight growth.

The key to that? Ensure that golfers have fun. And that is the risk factor for golf, since the largest demographic, 18 to 34-year-olds, just aren't having as much fun playing golf as other generations (57% report having fun compared to 78% of boomers). It seems they are likely to choose other activities that are more enjoyable for them.[18]

What Impact Will These Possible Solutions Have?

Most businesses can be analyzed by cost, by product or service, or by how the combination of those elements is marketed. As golf courses are currently maintained, the costs for golf have only one direction to proceed—up.

Regarding the product, is it possible to turn lush green golf courses to brown or to reduce the acreage required for a golf course? Changes in the ball and equipment might achieve that. Or changes in architectural design could result in shorter courses with additional hazards, with the challenge becoming accuracy rather than distance.

How do we emphasize the fun and camaraderie that this game brings? How do we create the sizzle that attracts, knowing the game will garner a following?

17 National Golf Foundation, "Big Questions on Golf Participation," April 2013, Slide 31.

18 Ibid., Slide 14.

With the industry's future relatively stable, as forecast by the NGF, for those who have considered learning the sport, it's a great time to walk through the entry door to the game, and this message should be broadcast widely. Golf course owners and PGA Professionals should emphasize providing value-based entertainment in a warm and welcoming environment.

Golf is unique. Only a very small number of individuals have the opportunity to play football at Lambeau Field, basketball at the Garden, baseball at Fenway, or hockey at the Forum. However, everyone can play golf on the course where Tom Watson won the U.S. Open at Pebble Beach Golf Links and attempt the same chip on 17 that he made to win the tournament. The handicap system allows us to play the game against anyone on an equal basis and have fun—try this with tennis.

Whether as athletic competition, exercise or social recreation, golf has many attributes.

Are these predictions likely to occur? The theory as to what should occur is well documented.

Thus, in an industry known for firmly preserving the status quo, the only thing known for sure is that capitalism creates and capitalism destroys. Golf is a business in the entertainment sector of the nation's economy. In spite of all that is financially negative about the golf industry as it exists today, I believe it can successfully adapt to the changes in our society. In that case, if the golf industry were a common stock, it would make for a wise long-term investment.

Path to Success

Golf course owners and management teams, the media, and industry associations can provide the answer to ensure the long-term vitality of the business of golf. Solutions might include the following:

For Golf Course Owners

1) Promoting the health benefits of the sport as physical exercise.
2) Shortening golf courses.
3) Ensuring rounds are played in 4 hours or less.
4) Through the course setup, warranting that golf courses play easier.

5) Increasing the emphasis on service that is extremely cordial and accommodating.

6) Simplifying golf operations and the amenities provided.

7) Introducing alternative scoring formats, such as Stableford, as the primary way to keep score, and educate golfers as to the estimated stroke equivalents.

8) Enhancing the customer experience through technology and simplifying the management of courses through an alert system of guidance.

9) Leveraging the clubhouse to provide alternative functionality focused beyond golf and more comparable to a sports bar or dining club.

10) Segmentation of the functionality of the golf course, emphasizing the game in the morning and entertainment in the afternoon and evening.

11) Ensuring signage conveys a positive message.

12) Adapting dress standards and associated behaviors to the cultural changes in our society.

13) At private clubs, replacing high-equity initiation fees with lower non-refundable deposits, initiation fees, and monthly membership fees based on market pricing.

14) Joining the GCSAA and the NGCOA.

For the Media

15) Television announcers balancing their commentary between the difficulty of the game and the enjoyment the public derives from it. Make it a sport beginners would like to try rather than one only professionals attempt to master.

For Associations

16) The USGA bifurcating its advertising message to emphasize both the casual and traditional aspects of the game.

17) Recruiting new players to the game by emphasizing youth, women, and minorities, and motivating former players to return with greater urgency (as with Golf 2.0, Golf Ready, Tee It Forward, Family Golf Monthly, and Play Golf America).

18) The USGA Executive Committee might be proportionally balanced representative to the population in America by gender, ethnicity, and private versus public golfers.

19) The LPGA, at a minimum, should license the PGA Education curriculum, or even more aggressively merge with the PGA to vastly improve the experience of women professionals in the business of golf.

For Equipment Manufacturers

20) Facilitating the use of better equipment through rentals, as the ski industry does.

21) Connecting the manufacturer to the golfer more directly via social media would open the lines of communication. Ensuring that a golfer can easily select for themselves the proper equipment through clearer product descriptions would be awesome.

Concluding Thoughts

Twenty years from now you will be more disappointed by the things that you didn't do than by any of the ones you did do.

Mark Twain

If you find a path with no obstacles, it probably doesn't lead anywhere.

Frank A. Clark, *Path to Success*

Chapter 18

The Courage to Change
The Final Exam

*All of our life, so far as it has definitive form,
is but a mass of habits.*

William James

He has half the deed done who has made a beginning.

Horace

Chapter Highlights

This book has been a journey with a simple purpose—to provide a framework (7 steps) and the tools (21 Excel and PowerPoint files) to enable golf course owners and management teams to create value that will enhance their customers' experiences and therefore ensure the highest potential return on investment.

The "why" of a facility defines its strategic vision. Based on that vision, the required resources can be identified. Based on the resources available, operational procedures can be implemented in order to reach the desired level of experience, ranging from platinum, to gold, to silver, to bronze, and to steel.

This chapters includes a checklist as your "final exam." If you have completed all of the exercises, we are confident that the process of managing your golf course will have been simplified and that you will have identified opportunities for potential higher profits.

Making the Complicated Simple

The challenges of operating a golf course aren't just about knowing the theory of what should be done, but about achieving the consistent execution of those desired principles—the daily blocking and tackling.

Whether from the lack of resources, time, or adequate leadership skills to train and manage a team, or from the constant evolution of a golf course as a living organism, it is estimated that golf courses on average reach only about 50% of their financial potential.

We believe that the fundamental cause for this disappointing level of achievement is the absence of a disciplined approach to the business of golf. It is really easy to be overwhelmed with the daily chores, and to let slide the crafting and more importantly, the adherence to a long-term vision.

While nearly every golf course creates an annual budget, and many develop marketing or membership plans (private clubs), few develop a strategic plan that serves as the lighthouse for the daily operation of facility.

The purpose of this Field book was to create a system for the management of a golf course that would create a framework by which a golf course could be operated on "auto-pilot."

Realizing that change is difficult and that plateaus are often reached by those trying to improve, Bob Sullivan and Hugh Thompson, in *The Plateau Effect— Getting from Stuck to Success,*[1] offer encouragement by defining the seven barriers to long-term success:

1. Immunity: Individuals become immune to the same techniques and solutions. Your mind and senses become dulled from the same routine.

2. Greedy Algorithms: The best short-term solutions rarely lead to long-term success.

3. Bad Timing: The ebb and flow of our circadian rhythm often says "take a break."

---

1 http://www.amazon.com/gp/product/0525952802/ref=s9_psimh_gw_p14_d0_i1?pf_rd_
   m=ATVPDKIKX0DER&pf_rd_s=center-2&pf_rd_r=0TBDT3K0PY2SCQJRWENV&pf_rd_
   t=101&pf_rd_p=1389517282&pf_rd_i=507846

4. Flow Issues: Capital, time, and the availability of skilled workers come and go.

5. Distorted Data: The wrong things are measured or risk is inappropriately assessed.

6. Distractions: Daily events change our long-term focus.

7. Failing Slowly: Clear goals have not been set.

This process of strategic planning is rooted in understanding the customers' MOSAIC profile (age, income & ethnicity) and the number of golfers per 18 holes that reside or work within competitive local market.

That information allows one to determine the potential niche in which their facility will find success as shown here:

Once the opportunity and the course's likely niche is known, the vision can be defined.

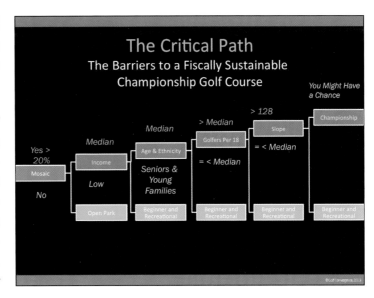

The Business of Golf—Why? How? What? provides you with seven steps. Completing the exercises in this book should take approximately 90 days. This system has been field tested and refined over the past decade. In 2013, it was field tested by 11 leading golf course managers operating 34 golf courses.

If you answer these post-test questions correctly, I am confident you will know how to use the fundamental principles of successful golf course management:

Post-Test Question 1:

Yes   **No**

☐   ☐   Have you developed a written strategic plan within the last three years; a plan prepared by management and staff and read by all?

Strategic: It Starts with "Why?"

Each one of the world's 33,331 golf courses is unique. Communicating why you do what you do, rather than focusing on what you offer, is reflected in the vision and mission statements that form your facility's brand. And your brand, as perceived by customers and potential customers, largely determines the financial success of your golf course.

The brand image is the value proposition you offer to your customers. The brand image of the experience to be received at an exclusive private club is very different from the experience expected at a low-end municipal golf course. Is your facility meant to be the entry door to the game for the masses, a park to entertain the tax-paying citizens, a forum for businesspeople to meet and greet, a private enclave, or a resort that attracts a certain clientele defined by net worth and residential location?

The components of a brand are the by-products of the course's name and logo, the facility (the course and clubhouse), the pricing, and the depth and breadth of staff—all controllable factors.

Post-Test Question 2:

Yes   No

☐   ☐   Does your strategic plan include the "Why?" of your facility?

Post-Test Question 3:

As measured by the experience provided to your customer, what market segment does your facility TARGET?

- ☐ Top 10% (Platinum)
- ☐ Top 25% (Gold)
- ☐ Top 50% (Silver)
- ☐ Top 75% (Bronze)
- ☐ Bottom 25% (Steel)

Post-Test Question 4:

What market niche are you targeting for the majority of golfers who frequent your facility?

- ☐ Accomplished (Championship: 12 handicap or less)
- ☐ Recreational (13 handicap to 25 handicap)
- ☐ Beginners (25 handicap and higher)

Note that it is not our philosophy that every golf course can be ideal for all types of golfers. We believe that differentiating the market is a healthy practice for your course and for the game. Having targeted products for different types of current and potential customers is a formula that almost always insures success.

Post-Test Question 5:

Which of the following tools (forecasting methods and reports) do you use to manage your facility?

- ☐ Competitive market share analysis
- ☐ Financial Statements
- ☐ Golf Datatech reports
- ☐ Golfer Local Market Analysis (age, income ethnicity, population density, golfers in your market)
- ☐ Mosaic Profile (demographic report)
- ☐ National Golf Foundation reports
- ☐ Operational Budgets
- ☐ PGA PerformanceTrak Annual Operating Survey
- ☐ PGA PerformanceTrak Local Monthly Competitive Golf Market Analysis
- ☐ PGA PerformanceTrak Rounds and Revenue Reporting
- ☐ Rounds—Base year analysis on the prior year
- ☐ Rounds—Linear Trend analysis on the prior three or more years
- ☐ U.S. Economic Forecast
- ☐ Weather Trends International Playable Days Report
- ☐ Weather Trends International Forecasting Data

The use of these tools provides a golf course with important perspectives on the controllable and uncontrollable factors influencing its operation.

Post-Test Question 6:

What is your revenue target from activities (tournaments, outings, food and beverage, catering, banquets, etc.), excluding green fees?

- ☐ 10%
- ☐ 25%
- ☐ 50%
- ☐ 75%
- ☐ Over 75%

Becoming independent from reliance solely on golf course revenues (green fees, carts, merchandise, range, etc.) insulates an operation from the vagaries of weather. We learned from the Canadian benchmarking study that creating a certain social atmosphere at a club can develop ongoing business not directly dependent on the golf course, even though the course may have been the initial draw.

The previous six questions form the foundation for the strategic plan. Without a vision, the course will flounder.

Step 1: Geographic Local Market Analysis

Having defined the strategic plan, the next step is a reality check to determine whether what you have planned is achievable. The answer to that question rests to a certain extent on the location of the golf course.

Post-Test Question 7:

Yes No

☐ ☐ Are the median household income and median age within 30 minutes of your golf course (municipal, daily fee, or private club) consistent with your market segment target?

If the answer is "no," as a golf course operator, it is important to import golfers beyond your local market to sustain the facility. The resort areas of Arizona, Florida, and Myrtle Beach come immediately to mind as being dependent on tourists.

Post-Test Question 8:

Yes No

☐ ☐ Is the Experian MOSAIC profile supportive of golf within 10 miles of your facility?

Post-Test Question 9:

Yes No

☐ ☐ For the market niche defined, does the number of golfers that reside within 30 minutes of your golf course exceed 500 avid golfers per 18-hole equivalent (if you are in the public market) or 2,000 avid golfers (if you seek to operate a private club)?

While you will need 468 avid golfers per public 18-hole course and 1,705 avid golfers per private course, to financially prosper you need a concentration of golfers consistent with the demographics found within the Top 100 core-based statistical areas (large metropolitan areas that create sufficient demand in relationship to the supply). Note that while there are 1,746 golfers per 18-holes, the Top 100 core-based statistical areas average 2,336 golfers per 18-holes. The non-core based statistical areas average only 1,046. Golf courses is these smaller market have a daunting challenge ahead.

Step 2: Weather Playable Days

While weather is an uncontrollable factor, weather data available today enables a golf course to determine its ideal operating season, to determine if its management is under- or over-performing in relation to the number of playable days, and to have the opportunity plan events in advance and more closely control water expenses.

Post-Test Question 10:

Yes   No

☐   ☐   Do you know how many playable golf days your course has averaged during the past 10 years?

Post-Test Question 11:

Yes   No

☐   ☐   Are you utilizing Weather Trend International forecasting tools to optimize the financial performance of your facility?

Step 3: Technology

Each individual comes to the management of a golf course with biases. Admittedly, mine is rooted in the belief that the technology that can generate operating statistics regarding the customer and the facility can be leveraged to increase net income by 20% annually. While some courses collect data, few use them proactively.

Post-Test Question 12:

Yes   No

☐   ☐   Do you know the customers (19 or more rounds per year) who played your facility in consecutive years?

Post-Test Question 13:

Yes   No

☐   ☐   Do you know the customers who played your course for the first time in 2013?

Post-Test Question 14:

Yes   No

☐   ☐   Do you know the customers who played your course in 2012 but not in 2013?

Post-Test Question 15:

Yes   No

☐   ☐   Do you engage in customer relations management by identifying segments (demographics, customer transactions, i.e., frequency, spending, etc.) to send appropriate marketing messages to each group via electronic media (email, Web site, Facebook, and Twitter) on a periodic basis?

Post-Test Question 16:

Yes   No

☐   ☐   Can a customer book a tee time reservation from your home page within three clicks, based on the date, time, and group size of the party (information located in the upper left hand side of the Web site home page)?

Post-Test Question 17:

Yes   No

☐   ☐   Do you engage in yield management by adjusting prices based on forecasted demand?

Post-Test Question 18:

Yes   No

☐   ☐   Are your prices (prime time, twilight, specials) consistent through all distribution channels (Web site, electronic tee sheet, call center, social media)?

Step 4: Financial Benchmarking

The fear that some golf course owners and managers have of participating in national financial benchmarking exercises is surprising. These national data repositories provide meaningful insights into the financial performance of golf courses. With an industry participation rate of less than 33%, when segmented into regional and local markets, the number of respondents is too small to produce meaningful data.

Post-Test Question 19:

Yes	No	
☐	☐	Do you track revenue per round by customer by year?

Post-Test Question 20:

Yes	No	
☐	☐	Do you track total spending by customer by year?

Post-Test Question 21:

Yes	No	
☐	☐	Do you know the utilization rate by hour, by day, by month, and by year?

Post-Test Question 22:

Yes	No	
☐	☐	Do you regularly participate (12 out of 12 months) in the PGA PerformanceTrak Monthly **Rounds and Revenue** reporting?

Post-Test Question 23:

Yes	No	
☐	☐	Do you regularly participate (12 out of 12 months) in the PGA PerformanceTrak Monthly **Local Competitive Golf Market Analysis**?

Post-Test Question 24:

Yes   No

☐   ☐   Have you participated in the PGA Performance Annual Operating Survey for the past three years?

Post-Test Question 25:

Yes   No

☐   ☐   Do you regularly participate (12 out of 12 months) in Golf Datatech's retail reporting regarding merchandise and equipment sold?

Step 5: Facilities

It is ironic that the asset that draws the golfers to the facility often receives the least attention with respect to the allocation of capital reserves to ensure that as it naturally depreciates it can be properly updated.

It is also surprising that though golf courses cover about 150 acres, of which 100 are typically maintained, the cost of maintaining such facilities can vary from under $300,000 to over $2 million, with differences in conditioning obviously noted but often not in harmony with the amounts spent on upkeep and improvement.

Post-Test Question 26:

Yes   No

☐   ☐   Does your facility allocate at least $200,000 annually to a reserve account for course capital improvements and equipment replacement?

Post-Test Question 27:

Yes   No

☐   ☐   Is your maintenance labor-hour budget for the year less than 80 hours per playable day?

Post-Test Question 28:

Yes   No

☐   ☐   Is the appraised value of your facility greater than 1.5 times revenue or 10 times earnings before interest, taxes, depreciation, and amortization?

Step 6: Operations

With touch points on the Assembly Line of Golf ranging from 9 at a municipal course to at least 13 at elite private clubs, the experience best remembered often involves the lowest paid employee.

Operations is about blocking and tackling—from ensuring that every employee is consistently dressed and identified by name to making sure that the public areas in the clubhouse (including bathrooms) and on the property are neat and tidy.

Post-Test Question 29:

Yes No
☐ ☐ Has your facility developed five key benchmarks that are monitored daily to ensure that its financial performance is in line with agreed-upon goals?

Post-Test Question 30:

Yes No
☐ ☐ Do you have your golf course secretly shopped?

Post-Test Question 31:

Yes No
☐ ☐ Have you developed a formula to determine the fair market value of the experience being provided at your course, independent of local competitive rates?

Post-Test Question 32:

Yes No
☐ ☐ Does your advertising, marketing, and public relations budget exceed 5% of forecasted revenue?

Step 7: Customers

With 15% of customers generating 60% of revenue and the annual turnover of those who play and don't return the following year nearing 50%, monitoring customer satisfaction is vital.

The strength of a golf course's customer franchise can be precisely measured. The customer loyalty index serves as an accurate predictor of a golf course's financial success.

Post-Test Question 33:

Yes   No

☐   ☐   Do you know your facility's customer loyalty score in comparison to that of your leading competitors?

Post-Test Question 34:

Yes   No

☐   ☐   Are your customers electronically surveyed annually as to their expectations and the experience they have received?

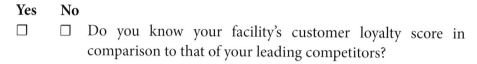

Does the Golf Convergence WIN Formula Work?

Consider for a moment what happens if the formula doesn't work. At a minimum, what would be obtained from the process would be valuable insights into methods for improved operational performance. Knowing your facility's strategic vision, developing a tactical plan, and forming some commitment to consistent operational execution would produce benefits. In other words, the process of merely working through the formula has substantial value. It represents a methodology and a discipline few achieve.

And what if the formula works? A golf course would significantly enhance its operations in relationship to its competitors, boost its profits in the short term, and increase its value in the long term. Again, great benefits result. We believe, and have proven, that application of the formula has the potential to increase your EBITDA by 12% of gross revenue.

The real question is not whether the formula works, since for over a decade it has been applied successfully at golf courses in Europe and across the United States and Asia.

The business of golf and the game of golf have in common a search for perfection that will probably never be achieved. One day, just when you think you have found the secret to the game of golf, it escapes you the next day.

The business of golf is also like that. Any time you gather a group of humans, though the goal of each may be the same, getting consistent execution remains elusive. It is our experience that between the academic theory and the reality of execution, golf courses do well if they implement 70% of these guidelines during the first golf season they are used. While we can hope to set a standard higher than organized chaos, goal setting creates focus that is beneficial.

Just before his retirement, John Zobler, Assistant City Manager for the City of Ocala spoke to us and about us. As he said, "What needed to be accomplished to provide the golf course firm financial footing was identified through this process. While it took five years to navigate the politics and allocate the resources necessary, at the end, what we needed to do was identified in the beginning. The methodology is very sound."

The City of Virginia Beach, due to labor issues and significant deferred capital expenses, went from a $233,000 annual deficit to leasing its golf courses and gaining positive cash flow. As important there is the fact that a talented management company invested over $1 million in the city's best course and is also getting a nice return on investment.

For a daily fee golf course in Sioux Falls, South Dakota, the Golf Convergence WIN™ formula suggested that a renovation of this championship golf course with an enhanced database segmentation to facilitate a rebranding would enhance the golfer experience.

For a private club that was transitioning from a developer-owned to a board-managed equity club, the process provided emotional comfort to the board as they navigated the uncharted waters of club management. Customer surveys and member meetings created solidarity of focus.

The list of success stories is long. Recently we were asked during an interview if the process had created conflict.

At every facility, there are always competing interests—owners who want to judiciously allocate resources, the management team that is seeking more resources to ensure the best customer experience, and the golfers, who are always seeking value. While self-interest dominates, to the extent that a consensus can be built, prosperity can be achieved.

The objective of this methodology is to build a consensus. We have found that good communication is the fundamental path to success. When raising fees, explaining to the golfers where the incremental money is to be invested usually achieves support. Providing management a capital budget that is funded gives them hope that they will be able to keep the customer experience at the level desired.

And for the owner, success is achieved when the steps outlined here are executed.

Challenges Beyond the Grasp of One

While the primary focus of golf course owners and managers should be on their own facilities, such focus should come with a broad perspective on understanding what the game of golf is and what it represents to our society.

There are major themes to the game of golf that each person active in the industry should comprehend. These themes direct us to the future of the golf business:

1. **Industry:** The game of golf is currently largely dominated by male, well-to-do Caucasians who are in their forties.

    Of the 23,152 members of the PGA, only 854 are minorities (3.68%). There are 364 minorities among the 4,081 apprentices. Minorities in the United States comprise 27.6% of the population. The imbalance of minorities in the sport must be corrected for the industry to grow.

    The LPGA has 1,500 members representing 5.5% of the operational work force at golf courses. Women who play the game represent 18% of golfers. The imbalance in gender employment and participation in the sport must be corrected for the sport to grow.

    Diversity is the key to the future of the game.

2. **The Game:** It is expensive to play golf, and unless you are good, frankly, it isn't much fun. Golf provides recreation and entertainment, but its real benefit is in the values developed in those who participate. Failure to attract new golfers is serious, but Public Enemy Number One is attrition. Participation rates continue to decline.

3. **The Environment:** Water is a critical resource, and its threatened supply greatly affects the golf industry. Many courses should focus on reducing the size of the playing field, thereby reducing the requirements for irrigation and fertilization. Curtailing water consumption would also reduce expenses. The industry needs to transition from emphasizing a manicured experience to allowing a natural experience.

4. **Clubhouse Facilities:** Consistent with these trends is the construction of large clubhouses exceeding 40,000 square feet, which are expensive to operate. The cost to maintain these facilities is exorbitant, and the costs are passed on to the golfers; this is another negative influence on the adoption of golf by the masses.

5. **Management and Staff:** To remain relevant, individuals within the profession and those entering the profession need to acquire the requisite business skills in accounting, management, marketing, and technology to appreciate the complexities of successfully running a golf enterprise.

Successful business operators are never satisfied with the status quo. They are often perfectionists seeking to improve operations, for leading is a journey, not a destination. Tomorrow's leaders will share their information, provide expertise, and clearly articulate their values and standards.

This Is the End

The end is the beginning, and the beginning starts with focusing on your customers. When you create a value-based experience, the foundation for your success is set.

The book's focus on why golfers play provides insights and predictive intelligence.

Understanding why golfers make choices and what factors impact those choices is necessary. The factors of cost and time so often quoted as negative factors for golf are not identified as the leading factors that impact golfer choice. Engagement with the facility, as emphasized in the Simon Sinek video, provides the key to the future successful operation of a golf course.

I hope that this analysis of the golf industry and the explanation of the formula that leads to the successful operation of a golf course have been presented in a way that will lighten the spirits of the professionals who serve the business of golf.

The value the customer receives equals his or her experience minus the price paid. To the extent that the experience equals or exceeds the price paid, customer loyalty is created. That is the goal—loyal customers.

I have written with the hope and understanding that course owners who take these words to heart and head and hands and feet will have the opportunity to bolster their investment return.

Golf is a great game, and it can be a fabulous business. It is my wish that your goals in life, as well as the goals you set for your golf course, are achieved.

Thank you for taking the time to read this book. And, as I hope you say to all of your departing customers, "I really appreciate your support, and I look forward to serving you again. Best wishes."

If you purchased the supplemental template that accompanies this Field book, confirm that all exercises have been completed and the results from each have been recorded in an assembled book for the management team to review frequently and utilize as a guiding light to ensure that the facility's investment return is maximized.

Path to Success: Your Final Grade

1) In the post-test presented in this chapter, for the 30 "yes" and "no" answers, most golf courses would answer "no" to over 20 of those questions. If you answered "yes" to:

   Less than 15: You have lots of company.

   15–20: Progress is being made. There is hope.

   21–25: You are clearly ahead of your peers.

   26–30: You are one of the industry's leaders. Congratulations.

2) For the four multiple-choice questions, if you know precisely the answers for your facility, you are absolutely on the path to success. Way to go!

Concluding Thought

What is the meaning of life? Are our lives all connected, and if so, to what and how? Such questions seem to be fundamental to the human experience.

The meaning of "my life" is different for each of us as we embark on this journey from many different starting points. Our views are drawn from our particular, and vastly unique, experiences.

Based on our culture, some of us emphasize peace in the midst of chaos. Others emphasize community, harmony, and balance. When life is good, we believe that we have dominion over nature, but then each "loss" feels like a life crisis, when in actuality only the day flow of our lives has been interrupted. We often forget that no one goes through life undefeated.

The meaning of life cannot be answered by any one person. The life experience of each of us is different. As you are reading this, our paths in this journey of life have crossed and you have made a positive impact on my life, for which I am very appreciative. I hope you enjoy the fruits of your life's harvest.

Adapted from Father Patrick Dolan's Palm Sunday Message,
April 17, 2011, Most Precious Blood Catholic Church,
Denver, Colorado

Index

1-2-1 Marketing, 162

A
Active Network, 158, 159, 162, 163, 230
Adams, Barney, 32
advanced content, defined, 9–10
aeration, 275–276
African Americans in golf, 70–71
agronomy, golf course, 270–279
Ainsworth, Eddie, 2, 59
Alamo Golf Trail, 156
Alexa, 294–295
Alister MacKenzie golf course, 281
Allen, Hilda, 240–241, 241n
American Professional Golfers, Inc. (APG), 63
American Society of Golf Course Architects, 252, 262
anchored putters, rule to ban, 68
Armstrong, Louis, 329
Aschenbach, Jack, 397
Ashley-Montagu, Montague Francis, 29
Assell, Joe, 305
associations, 59–62, 64–66
  role of, in growing the game, 393–397
Augusta National, 260
Available Cash Model, The, 195
axioms, defined, 10

B
Bagehot, Walter, 174
Bandon Dunes, 142, 146, 180, 290, 290n, 292, 327, 381, 385
Barak, Dana, 393n
bartered tee times, 83, 161
  controversy over, 163–166
Beaumarchais, Pierre, 359
Beditz, Joseph (Dr.), 48, 57, 67, 71

Beman, Deane, 64
benchmarking. *See* financial benchmarking
Berra, Yogi, 199
Berry, Mike, 398, 398n
Bethpage State Park, 28, 155
Bevacqua, Peter, 72
bifurcation, 67–72
Billy Casper Golf Management, 99, 102, 157, 310, 335, 335n, 366
Bishop, Ted, 66, 68, 72
Black Wolf Run, 142, 382
Blake, William, 37
Bonallack, Michael, 259
Boston Consulting Group, 73, 307
Boxgroove, 162
Bradford Creek, 348
brand, creating a sustaining, 362
brand promise
  defining, 138–139
  strategic vision and, 140
Brauer, Jeff, 267, 267n
Broadmoor, 139
budgets, 176
Bully Pulpit Golf Course, 211
Bunker Hills, 368-369
Bunny Slopes initiative, 35
Buonarroti, Michelangelo, 137
business of golf. *See* golf business
Business of Golf—What Are You Thinking? 12–13, 20, 301

C
Cabo del Sol - Desert Course, 275
capital expenditures, deferred, 213–215
capitalization rates, 249–251
Capmark, 240
cash flow projection, 217–219

Castle Pines Golf Club, 180, 268, 397

Chamblee, Brandel, 69, 71

change, 2–3, 34–35

Chelsea Information Systems, 158, 161

Cherry Hills Country Club, 139–140, 142, 397

chlorophyll, 272

Christiansen, Clayton M., 322–323, 323n

Cimarrone Golf Club, 397

Clark, Frank A., 405

Clemson University Strategic Planning Pilot Study, 122

Cline, Jeff, 326

Club Benchmarking, 194–195

club fitting, 78–82

Club Managers Association of America
  benchmarking adopted by, 195
  role and financial snapshot of, 65, 66

Club Prophet, 158, 161, 168, 230

Clubessential, 162

clubhouse, as social gathering place, 391–392, 393–395

ClubSoft, 162

Cog Hill Golf and Country Club, 28, 142, 203

Collins, Nancy, 388

Colorado Alliance for Golf, 2

Colorado Golf Club, 180

Colorado PGA Section, reservation system initiative by, 83–84

Colorado Third-Party Tee Time Model, 82–84

commission-based model, 166

communication, translating "Why?" into, 321–327

Complex Property Advisors Corporation, 247

Conference Board Consumer Confidence Index, 21

content levels, definitions of, 9–10

Coolidge, Calvin, 361

Cosby, Bill, 174

Couples, Freddie, 81

coupons, 304–306

Course Tracker, 186

Course Utilization analysis, 183

Course Trends, 162, 163

Craig-Hoffman, Donna, 388

Crall, Daryl, 72

Crescent Systems, 161

Crossing the Chasm, 11, 160

Cruden Bay, 386

culture, customer appeal and, 28–30

customer analysis, 177–181

customer attraction quotient, strategic vision and, 140

customer database, ownership of, 103–106

customer demographics report, 177–178

customer distribution report, 177

customer loyalty. *See* loyalty, customer

customer relationship management, 363
  implementing, 364–366

customer retention report, 178

customer spending by class report, 178

customer spending by individual report, 179

customer touch points. *See* touch points

customers. *See* golfers

Cybergolf, 162

D

da Vinci, Leonardo, 197, 257, 283, 312

daily fee golf courses
  financial performance of, 91–92
  management of, 113

Dalton Ranch, 369

Darrow, Ross M., 222n

Davis, Mike, 395–396

deferred capital expenditures estimate, 213–214

demand pricing, 224–226

demographics
  in geographic market analysis, 116–121
  importance of, 123–125
  report of, in customer analysis, 177–178

Dey, Joseph, 64

Dillon, William, 242

discounting, 225–227
  coupons, 304–306
  rewards programs as, 363–364

diseases of grass, 277–278, 280

Disney World, 288

Disraeli, Benjamin, 39

Doak, Tom, 71

Dolan, Patrick (Father), 422–423

Doral, 382

Dow Chemical, 145

Duhigg, Charles, 314, 314n, 323–324, 324n

Duncan, Graham, 186

Dungy, Tony, 314

Dye, Pete, 71, 259, 264, 268, 369

dynamic pricing, 227–232

E

Eagle Mountain, 171

Echelon Golf Course, 241

economic conditions, 21–24

economic impact on golf, 44–45
  multiplier effect of, 45

eGolf-Score, 162

Einstein, Albert, 135, 175

Eisenhower, Dwight David, 313

Ekovich, Steven, 250, 250n

Electronic Transaction Systems Corporation, 162

Ely's Law, 285

email marketing, 298–304
    response rates for, 302–303
    rules of thumb for, 298–302
    statistics related to, 298
Emerson, Ralph Waldo, 283
emotional experience. *See* experience
empathy with golfers, 317
Endangered Species Act, 281
Energy Snapshot, The, 271
Engh, Jim, 92
environment, customer appeal and, 28–31
Epictetus, 58
equipment, evolution of, 265–267
equipment manufacturers, 77–82
    financial performance of, 66
    role of, in growing the game, 398–401
equity clubs, 109
Eubanks, Steve, 310n
Executive Women's Golf Association, 390
experience
    defining emotional, 145–146
    enhancing customer, 323–326
    marketing of, 288–295
    matching price to, 235–236
    operations focused on, 317–319
    in value formula, 146–148
EZLinks, 158, 161, 163, 170, 229, 230

F
facility analysis, 181–183
    post-test covering, 416
fair market value, defined, 235
Faldo, Nick, 69, 71
Family Golf Monthly, 396
Fazio, Tom, 264, 288
fee calculation, 203–205
fertilizer, defined, 276
Fey, David, 395
Fila Korea (Titleist), financial performance of, 66
financial benchmarking
    benchmark development for, 185–188
    comparing data to national statistics, 185
    customer analysis in, 177–181
    facility analysis in, 181–183
    for food operation, 192–194
    Golf Datatech Retail Reports for, 190–192
    key reports in, 177–178
    PerformanceTrak reports for, 188–190
    post-test covering, 416–417
    for private clubs, 194–195
financial centers, 202
financial modeling
    cash flow, 217–219
    deferred capital expenditures estimate, 213–214
    fee calculation, 204–205

    food operation, 215–216
    income statement, 202–204
    maintenance calculation, 213–217
    performance indicators, 200, 219
    revenue and expense categories, 201–202
    season pass fee calculation, 203–211
financial ratios, 176
financial statements, 176
Finchem, Tim, 66, 68, 71
finder's fee model, 166
Finger, Dye, Spann Golf Course Architects, 369
Finnegan's Law, 377
First Tee, The, 24, 397
Fitzgerald, F. Scott, 113
Fitzhenry, Robert I., 12n, 90n
food operation
    benchmarking for, 192–194
    food and beverage costing for, 216
    labor scheduling for, 216
Ford, Henry, 211
Fore! Reservations, 158, 165–166
Fossil Trace, 92, 301
Four Agreements—A Toltec Wisdom Book, 10
Friedlander, Steve, 382
Friedman, Milton, 361
Friedman, Thomas, 301
Frog, The (golf course), 180–181
Frost, Gerhard, 17
Futures Company for HSBC, 40, 40n, 44n

G
Ganton, 380, 385, 386
Garcia, Sergio, 81
Gates, Bill, 153
GE Capital, 240
Gecko, Gordon, 98
Gentlemen Golfers of Leith, 61
geographic local market analysis
    demand and supply, 120–122
    demographics, 116–120, 122–124
    in PerformanceTrak, 190–192
    post-test covering, 412
Get Golf Ready, 72, 74–76
Glacier Club, 369
Gladwell, Malcolm, 322
Glen Abbey Golf Club, 66
Gleneagles, 385
Golden Circle of Communication, 3
golf
    African Americans in, 70–71
    appeal of, 25–27
    difficulty, reducing, 383–384
    elitist image of, 24–25, 378
    as entertainment product, 62–64
    future of, 56–57, 420

golf (*continued*)
  as lifestyle, 29–30, 36
  origins of, 60–61
  promoting fun of, 394–395
  promoting health benefits of, 380
  as recreational sport, 46–48
  scoring alternatives, 386
  time to play, shorten, 382
  women's participation in, 390–391
Golf 2.0, 32, 72–74, 396, 404
Golf 20/20 Vision report, 43–44, 46
Golf Box, 162
golf business. *See also* golf industry
  associations that serve, 61–62, 65–66, 393–397
  changes in, 35–36, 72–74
  consumer focus of, 25
  defined, 61
  economic impact on, U.S., 44–45
  game vs., 60–64
  impact of rules and equipment on, 66–69
  macroeconomics of. *See* macroeconomics of
    golf business
  multiplier effect of economic impact on,
    45–46
  trends in, worldwide, 41–44
  uncontrollable factors in, 20–21
Golf Club of Fleming Island, 397
Golf Convergence WIN formula
  success of, 418–419
Golf Course Builders Association of America,
  213, 253
Golf Course Superintendents Association of
  America, 65, 76–77, 214, 393
golf courses
  aeration of, 275–276
  agronomy of, 270–278
  architectural evolution of, 260–264
  average length preferred, 32–33
  building costs of, 252–255
  in Canada, 260, 387
  clubhouse as social gathering place, 387–389,
    391–393
  cultural adaptations of, 392
  daily fee vs. municipal financial performance,
    91–92
  demand vs. supply of, 53–56
  diseases, 277–278
  fertilizer, 276
  grass types, 271–273, 274–276
  herbicides, 276, 279–280
  irrigation control systems, 270
  maintenance costs, 213–217, 268–271
  municipal. *See* municipal golf courses
  number of, worldwide, 40–41

pesticides, 276
potential of, principles that define, 4–5
safety corridors, 265–266
shorter, 266–267, 382
signage on, 391–392
simplicity of operations of, 385–386
slope ratings of, 383–384
supply of, 50–53
thatch, 275–276
types of, 31, 90
valuation of. *See* valuation, golf course
verticut, 275–276
weeds, 277
winter kill, 277
Golf Convergence, 3, 5, 58, 74, 76, 103, 104,
  106, 119, 124, 130, 134, 153, 158, 160, 162,
  165, 172, 182, 183, 187, 206, 212, 219, 226,
  296, 299, 302, 307, 319, 340, 351, 353, 357,
  381, 387
Golf Convergence WIN Formula, 116, 124, 133,
  152, 210, 418, 419
Golf Datatech, role of, in financial benchmarking,
  188, 190–192
Golf for Cause, 390–391
golf industry
  barriers to success in, 408–409
  components of, 61–63
  current state of, 378–380
  growth forecast for, 401–402
  growth strategies for, 379–397
  role of equipment manufacturers in growth of,
    398–401
  role of media and associations in growth of,
    393–397
  themes related to future of, 422
  trade associations in, 65–66
  vision in, 63
golf management software system. *See*
  technology
Golf Pipeline, 162
Golf Playable Day (GPD), defined, 130
Golf Property Analysts, 247
golf rounds played 2012, 35
golfers
  attracting and retaining, 27–28
  average score of, 30–31
  behavioral tendencies of, 335
  characteristics of, 335–336, 340–343
  commitment level of, 332–333
  environment and culture determine, 28–31
  experience of, 31–34, 138–140, 144–146
  median household income of, 27
  motivations of, 335–336
  number of, 46–49

per 18 holes available, 50
survey to profile. *See* survey
wants, needs, and goals of, 317
GolfNet, 162
GolfNow/Golf Channel, 162, 163, 166, 169, 229, 369
GolfSwitch, 162
GolfTEC, 305
Google AdWords, 310
Google Analytics, 308–309
Google mobile wallets, 167
Goosinator, 281–282
grass
diseases of, 277–279
maintenance of, 275–277
mixing of, 274
types of, 273–274, 276–277
weeds in, 277
Graves, Steve, 242
Grayhawk Golf Club, 182
Grey, Hamish, 186–187, 187n
gross income multipliers, 251
Grosz, Steve, 78, 80n
Groupon, 305–306

H
habits, customer-focused, 319–325
Handicomp, 162
heat index (HI), defined, 130
herbicides, 279–280
defined, 276
Hewlett-Packard (HP), 323
Heyen, Kyle, 33
Hicks, Dan, 69
Highland Pacific Golf, 306
Hill, Peter, 366
Hillcrest, 369
Hillier, Dennis, 241
Hills, Richard, 67
Hirsh, Larry, 240
Hitchcock, Hank, 180
Hiwan Golf Club, 33
Hogan, Ben, 115, 139
Holmes, Oliver Wendell, 175, 237
Holtzman, Michael, 192–193, 193n
Honeybrook Golf Club, 293
Horace, 407
Horgan, Brian (Dr.), 77, 277
Hot Stix Golf, 78, 81
How? defined, 4–5
Hsueh-Dou, 220
Hubspot, 172
Hueber, David (Dr.), 244
Hughes, Michael, 23, 67

I
IBM, 322–323
IBS, 153
income statement
model of, 202
for municipal courses, 203
information system. *See* technology
Innovation of Diffusion Model, 160
Innovator's Dilemma, The, 322
intermediate content, defined, 9
introductory content, defined, 9
Ipema, Harry, 166
irrigation control systems, 270–271
iWanamaker, 162

J
J2 Golf Marketing, 162
James, William, 407
Johnson, Sheila, 70–71
Jonas Club Management, 158, 159, 161
Jones, Robert Trent, Sr., 264

K
Karhoff, George, 392
Katz, Rick, 286, 310
Kaufman, Martin, 69
Keimkuhler, John F., 222n
Kelley, Mike, 314–315
Kemper Sports Management, 157, 292
Kendall, Donald, 199
King, Mark, 66, 67, 71
Klein, Bradley, 110, 110n, 111, 262, 263, 264n
Kohler, David, 76–77
Kraus, Karl, 239

L
Ladies Professional Golf Association (LPGA)
evolution of, 64
role and financial snapshot of, 65, 66
role of, in growing the game, 393–394
Lake Buena Vista, 288
Lakewood Country Club, 139
Lee, Joe, 288
Legendary Marketing, 162, 308
Lehmann, Rosamond, 87
Lewis, Sinclair, 221
Lincoln, Abraham, 89–90
Links of North Dakota, 211
Little, Arthur, 32
local market analysis. *See* geographic local market analysis
Loew's Ventana Canyon, 382
Lombardi, Vince, 199
Longfellow, Henry Wadsworth, 328

Los Amigos Golf Course, 100
loyalty, customer
  customer relationship management system, 365–366
  importance of, 363–364
  measuring touch points, 366–367
  post-test covering, 418
  strategy for creating, 373–374
loyalty programs, 367–368
  social media effect on, 372–373
loyalty score, 347
  determining, 367–369
LPGA Foundation, 64
LPGA Teaching & Club Professionals (T&CP), 64
LPGA Tour, 64
Lucas, Rick, 301
Luntz, Frank (Dr.), 168

M
macroeconomics of golf business
  applying for game to thrive, 57–58
  demand and supply in, 50–57
  financial performance in, 41–44
  multiplier effect of economic impact, 45–46
  number of golf courses, 50–52
  number of golfers, 46–50
  U.S. economic impact study, 44–45
Magnolia course, 288
Mahoney, David, 239
maintenance
  accelerating costs of, 267–270
  calculating cost of, 211–215
management companies, 98
  course conditions under, 99–102
  customer database ownership and, 103–106
  hidden risks of using, 102–103
  largest, 102
  pros and cons of using, 101
Marcus & Millichap, 250, 252
market dynamics, 334–336
marketing
  4 P's of, 286
  coupons, 304–306
  course name and, 286–287
  email, 296–304
  of emotional experience, 288–290
  multi-variant (A/B) testing of message, 299–301
  other forms of, 310–311
  Picket Fence concept of, 370
  priorities for, 286
  shotgun approach to, 286
  social media for, 288, 296–298, 306–310
  Web site use for, 288–295

MarketingGrader, 172
Maslow's Hierarchy of Needs, 27
McAlindon, Harold, 313
McCarley, Mike, 67
McCormack, Mark, 375
McElroy, Scott, 277n
McKee, Howard, 327
media, role of, in growing the game, 393–397
Mendelson's Law, 328
merchandise sales by vendor analysis, 181
Miceli, Alex, 68
Midland Country Club, 145
Miller, Johnny, 69
mission statement, 141–142
Mistry, Pranav, 173
modeling, financial. *See* financial modeling
Moore, Geoffrey, 11, 160
MOSAIC lifestyle database, 116–121
multiplier
  gross income, 251
  net income, 251
multiplier effect of economic impact on golf, 45–46
municipal golf courses
  allocation of resources for, 88–91
  challenges faced by, 92–98
  financial profile of, 91–92
  income statement categories for, 201
  management of, 96–98, 112
  payroll of, 93
  privatization of, 96–98, 99–103
  procurement process of, 94–96
  season pass pricing by, 208

N
Nairn, 380, 383, 386
Nathan, Greg, 48
National Allied Golf Association, 333
National Golf & Resort Properties Group, 247
National Golf Course Owners Association Canada, 188
National Golf Course Owners Associations, 393
  reaction to Colorado tee time model, 83
  role and financial snapshot of, 65
  role of, in financial benchmarking, 186–187
National Golf Foundation, 25, 25n, 26n, 34, 35n, 40, 46, 48, 49, 55, 57, 58, 65, 66, 71, 88n, 91, 91n, 96n, 109n, 119, 127, 165n, 175, 188, 206, 206n, 242, 243, 245, 330n, 331, 332n, 342n, 378n, 401, 402n, 411
  role and financial snapshot of, 65
  role of, in financial benchmarking, 188
National Recreation and Park Association, 65
National Sporting Goods Associations, 47–48

negotiated pricing, 233–236
net income multipliers, 251
Nicklaus, Jack, 264
Nietzsche, Friedrich, 329
Nin, Anaïs, 135
nitrogen (N), 276
Nobilo, Frank, 69
non-equity clubs, 109
Norby, Kevin, 265, 266n, 267, 267n
Norman, Greg, 71
Northstar Technologies, 162

O
OB Sports, 171, 310
Olympic Club, 28
One to One Future, The, 363
Open Site Explorer, 172
operational, defined, 13
operational execution
  cue-routine-reward system, 324–325
  customer-focused, 317–319, 323–327
  enhancing customer experience, 323–327
  post-test covering, 417
  templates for license, 8–9
  touch points, 317–321
O'Reilly, Bill, 22–23
Orender, M. G., 244–245
Osprey Ridge, 288
Outliers, 322

P
Palm course, 288
Palmer, Arnold, 264
Passov, Joe, 262, 384
Path to Success, 15, 37, 58, 85, 113, 135, 148, 174, 197, 220, 237, 256, 282–283, 312, 328, 359, 375, 403–405, 422
Pebble Beach, 146, 260, 403
Pebble Creek Golf Course, 368
Pelican Hills, 382
Pepper, Dottie, 67
Peppers, Don, 363, 370–371
performance indicators
  for golf business, 200, 219
  need to focus on, 200
PerformanceTrak, 72, 127, 128, 188–189, 190, 192, 196, 197, 411, and 415
pesticide, defined, 276
PGA of America, 63
  evolution of, 64
  role and financial snapshot of, 65, 66
  role of, in financial benchmarking, 190–191
  strategic plan of, 72–74
PGA Tour, 64–66

PGA Tournament Players Division, 63
phosphorus (P), 276
Picket Fence concept of marketing, 370
Pine Valley, 260, 302
Pinon Hills, 369
Plateau Effect—Getting from Stuck to Success, 408
Play Golf America, 396, 404
Player, Gary, 71
Player Development Playbook, 74
playing field. *See* golf courses
point of sale (POS) technology, enhancement of, 386
post-test, 409–418
potassium (K), 276
Power of Habit, The, 314, 314n, 323–324, 324n
pre-test, 9
pricing. *See also* yield management
  demand, 222–224
  dynamic, 225–231
  negotiated, 233–237
  season pass, 205–210, 355
private clubs
  financial benchmarking for, 194–195
  governance of, 109–111, 112
  strategic vision of, 29
  strategy for growth of, 393
  supply of, 109
  technology vendors for, 161
  types of, 109
private equity clubs, 109
private non-equity clubs, 109
private resorts, 109
Profitable Food Facilities (PFF), 192
property taxes, 246–248
public golf courses
  financial performance of, 30
  strategic vision of, 29

Q
Queen, Sandy, 77
Quick18, 162, 163, 229
Quintero Golf Club, 236

R
Ratcliffe, Del, 33–34, 213
Ratcliffe Golf Services, Inc., 33–34, 213
Raynor, Seth, 263
Reichheld, Fred, 367
reservations by booking method analysis, 181
reservations by day of week/hour analysis, 181
resorts, 109
  management of, 112
Return Path, 172
revenue benchmarks, 181

revenue by department analysis, 184–185

revenue management, 222–224, 234

revenue per available tee time (RevPATT), 182, 185, 232

revenue per round purchased (RevPUR), 185

rewards programs, 363–364

rhizomes, 272–273

Richie, Kate, 385

Riding, Joe, 382

Ritz-Carlton, 143–144

Robert Trent Jones Trail, 33, 293

Rogers, Martha, PhD, 363, 370–371

Rome, Jim, 312

Roschek, Jim, 156

Rose, John, 307

Ross, Donald, 139

rounds per revenue margin analysis, 183

Royal and Ancient Golf Club of St. Andrews. *See* St. Andrews

Royal Canadian Golf Association, 65, 66

Royal Dornoch, 202, 386

Ruiz, Don Miguel, 10, 10n

rules, bifurcation of, 67–72

Runyon, Damon, 12

Russell, Bertrand, 37

S

Saban, Nick, 197

safety corridors, 265–266

Sand Barrens Golf Club, 34

Sassoon, Vidal, 199

Sassy Golf, 388–391

Satori, Andrew, 41

Scottish Golf Union, 186

role and financial snapshot of, 65

Sea Island Resort, 182

season passes

average cost of, 352

calculating fee for, 205–210

moving away from, 355

segmentation, customer, 366, 368, 369–374

Senderscore.org, 172

service, emphasis on, 384–385

Sharp Park Wetlands, 280–281

Sibelius, Jean, 256

Sinek, Simon, 2–3, 11, 15, 174, 333, 421

skip logic, 340, 348

Smith, Barry C., 222n

Smith, David, 20

Smyth, Rob, 153

Smyth Systems, 153

social media

equipment manufacturer use of, 401

golfer use of, 286

loyalty programs and, 372–373

marketing through, 286, 296–298, 310–314

Society of Golf Course Appraisers, 247, 249, 251–252

Society of St. Andrews Golfers, 61

software. *See* technology

Square wallet, 167

SRI International, 45

St. Andrews, 61, 146, 292, 295

benchmarking at, 186

Stableford, 386

Staples Golf, 271

Start with Why, 3

Staubach, Roger, 15

Sternberg, Stina, 391

stimpmeter, 267

Stranz, Mike, 263

strategic, defined, 13

strategic plan, 14

developing, 140–142

formula for success in, 146–148

of PGA of America, 72–74

vision and mission statements as part of, 142–143

strategic templates for license, 5–6

strategic vision

customer appeal and, 28

defining, 138, 140–143

formula for, 140

illustrated, 18

investment potential and, 140–141

as part of strategic plan, 147–148

of private club, 29

of public facility, 29

strategic vision = brand promise = customer attraction quotient, 140

Strauss, Kris, 310, 311

Streamsong resort, 291–292

Sullivan, Bob, 408

Suny, Armen, 268, 268n

survey

confidence interval, 336

framing, 336–340

margin of error, 336–337

number to send, 339–340

pitfalls of, 339–340

population, 337

questions to ask, 340–358

response rate, 337–339

sample size, 337

Susan G. Komen for the Cure, 64

Swilcan Bridge, 146

Szent-Gyorgyi, Albert, 377

T

tactical
  defined, 13
tactical templates for license, 6–7
Taleb, Nassim Nicholas, 151
Tarde, Jerry, 66
TaylorMade-Adidas Golf
  financial performance of, 66
technology
  benefits of, for golf course management, 154–155
  choosing based on priorities, 155–157
  costs of, 162
  customer relationship management system, 363–365
  for dynamic pricing, 227–230
  evaluating, 157–159
  future evolution of, 167–169
  lack of customization in, 159–160
  leveraging to your advantage, 172
  point of sale, 386–387
  post-test covering, 413–414
  for private clubs, 162
  proper use of, 153–155
  for third-party tee time distribution, 162–163
  tips, tools, and traps, 169–171
  vendor summary, 161–167
  web site and email marketing vendors, 162
Tee It Forward, 32–34, 37, 72, 381, 396, 404
tee time model, third-party, 82–84
tee time vendors, 82–84, 161, 163
  controversy over, 163–166
  customer database ownership and, 105, 106
Teemaster, 162
Tenison Park, 291, 291n
Terrace Hills Golf Course, 382
Textron, 240
thatch, 275–276
Theory of the Leisure Class, The, 378, 378n
third-party management company. *See* management companies
third-party marketing. *See* tee time vendors
third-party tee time model, 82–84
Thompson, Hugh, 408
Titleist (Fila Korea), 66
Tolkien, J.R.R., 149
Tony Butler Municipal Golf Course, 155
tools available for license, 5–9
Torrey Pines, 291
Total Possible Golf Playable Hours, defined, 130
touch points, 8, 28, 145, 151, 313, 317, 319, 320, 364, 366–365, 367, 375, 417
  addressing, 319–321
  measuring, 366–367

TPC Harding Park, 28
TPC River Highlands, 33
trade associations. *See* associations
Treetops, 308
Turner Macpherson, 255
Twain, Mark, 15, 199, 261, 405
Tzu, Lao, 19

U

United States Golf Association (USGA)
  evolution of, 64
  formation of, 61
  research by, 77
  role and financial snapshot of, 65, 66
  role of, in growing the game, 396
US eDirect, 161

V

valuation, golf course
  availability of courses for purchase, 240–241
  building costs, 253–255
  capitalization rates, 249–250
  factors affecting value, 240–243, 248–249
  factors for stabilization, 243–246
  gross income multipliers, 251
  methods of, 249–252
  net income multipliers, 251
  property taxes, 246–248
value = experience – price, 147, 235, 385
value rate, discount vs., 153
Van Cortlandt Golf Course, 88
VCT Corporation, 162
Veblen, Thorstein, 378, 378n
verticut, 275–276
Visa v.Me, 167
vision, strategic. *See* strategic vision

W

Waitkus, Debbie, 390
Walt Disney World, 288
Walters Golf, 171
weather
  impact of, on golf business, 126–129
  management and, 129–131
  post-test covering, 413
  scheduling and, 131–133
Weather Trends International, 125–127, 129, 131, 134, 135, 270
Web site of golf facility, 288–296
Website Grader, 172
Weed, Bobby, 245
weeds, 277–278

Wellshire Golf Course, 139–140

West, Dawn, 275n

Whaley, Suzy, 33, 72

Whan, Michael, 67

What? defined, 5–9

What Americans Really Want...Really: The Truth About Our Hopes, Dreams, and Fears, 168

Why?, 138–140

    defined, 3–4

    marketing that speaks to, 288–294

    post-test covering, 410–412

    translating into effective communication, 321–327

Wild Equity Institute, 281

winter kill, 277

women, increasing golf's appeal for, 388–391

Wood, Andrew, 308

Woodhall Spa, 385–386

World Golf Foundation, 46, 65, 66

World Is Flat 3.0: A Brief History of the Twenty-First Century, 301

Wronowski, Allen, 163

Y

Yelverton, Fred (Dr.), 77

yield management

    demand pricing, 224–226

    discounting, 225–227

    dynamic pricing, 228–234

    matching price to experience, 235–236

    negotiated pricing, 233–235

    pricing compared to other industries, 224–225

    revenue management, 222–224

Young, Michael, 397

Z

Zarrella, Dan, 302, 302n, 303, 303n

Zenji, Dogen, 59

ZIP Code Analysis, 179–181

Zobler, John, 419